Posthumanism and Higher Education

Carol A. Taylor · Annouchka Bayley
Editors

Posthumanism and Higher Education

Reimagining Pedagogy, Practice and Research

Editors
Carol A. Taylor
Department of Education
University of Bath
Bath, UK

Annouchka Bayley
Royal College of Art
London, UK

ISBN 978-3-030-14671-9   ISBN 978-3-030-14672-6 (eBook)
https://doi.org/10.1007/978-3-030-14672-6

Library of Congress Control Number: 2019932954

© The Editor(s) (if applicable) and The Author(s) 2019
This work is subject to copyright. All rights are solely and exclusively licensed by the Publisher, whether the whole or part of the material is concerned, specifically the rights of translation, reprinting, reuse of illustrations, recitation, broadcasting, reproduction on microfilms or in any other physical way, and transmission or information storage and retrieval, electronic adaptation, computer software, or by similar or dissimilar methodology now known or hereafter developed.
The use of general descriptive names, registered names, trademarks, service marks, etc. in this publication does not imply, even in the absence of a specific statement, that such names are exempt from the relevant protective laws and regulations and therefore free for general use.
The publisher, the authors and the editors are safe to assume that the advice and information in this book are believed to be true and accurate at the date of publication. Neither the publisher nor the authors or the editors give a warranty, express or implied, with respect to the material contained herein or for any errors or omissions that may have been made. The publisher remains neutral with regard to jurisdictional claims in published maps and institutional affiliations.

Cover credit: © Alex Linch/shutterstock.com

This Palgrave Macmillan imprint is published by the registered company Springer Nature Switzerland AG
The registered company address is: Gewerbestrasse 11, 6330 Cham, Switzerland

Forward-ing

Doing
    Thinking   together
Undoing and rethinking   collectively   MOVING-ING and
                                                          LOOK-ING forward
                  with an unlimited number of questions
                                        MAYBE-ing
                                          FUTURE-ing
                                          RELATE-ing

It is possible that a posthuman *Forward* to a posthuman book—rather than a Foreword—could be nothing but a human. Maybe a *Forward* of this kind functions as a human-initiated move promoting textual interchanges and shifting related matter while at the same time inviting, acknowledging, and relating to the plants, animals, viruses, and machines surrounding us. After all, it is not that posthumanism rejects the role of human but for many it questions certain independent and autonomous conceptions of the human and humanity.

Forward-ing the posthuman could also draw attention to the complex and relational subjects shaped by the life beyond the self. Braidotti (2013: 66) proposed that posthuman theory 'strikes an alliance with the productive and immanent force of *zoe*, or life in its non-human aspects.' The authors in this book take on the challenging task to engage with life's human and non-human forms and to rethink the status of human while being inspired by the complexity of human and non-human relations, creativity, and imagination. What kind of movement might happen when book, text, dialogue and subject intra-act and relate? What directions might forward-ing take? How might the relations in this book contribute to and stimulate radical transformations, some of which might be multidimensional and moving fast others, while others might be stuttering in their collective mattering and slow singularities. However this happens, these (textual) directions are never independent from other texts, relations, and matter. Maybe some of these transformations and directions take the form of inquiries, prompted by a variety of productive and generative questions including those about the future subjects and becomings of posthuman relations in higher education pedagogy, practice or policy. Such directions may provoke questions of possibility, anticipation, visioning, meeting, becoming, belonging, or perhaps fear, doubt, or worry, and more.

According to Braidotti (2013) critical posthumanist subjects function within eco-philosophies, multiplicities, and differentiation. Inter-connectedness between self and other transposes hybridity. The politics of life itself call for collaborative morality. Human and posthuman practices have co-existed alongside each other as long as humans have populated the earth and now at the time of this newly yet historical posthuman moment scholars need to caution against inhuman(e) ethics which could jeopardize productive inter-connectedness. While human-centered education has dominated the majority of educational discourses and practices one might also argue that relational learning and adaptation across species have existed far before the human cognition, awareness, and knowledges centered by Enlightenment and colonizing educational discourses and technologies. This predominant focus on scholarly and educational practices of the human has been a convenient yet rather selfish choice since humans have always lived in complex ecosystems and relational universes. So, like Braidotti (2013), one might ask how do we know this (and that) humanness in us, how have we come to recognize ourselves as human and who/how is human after all?

Forward-ing vii

How do we constitute and practice our human-ness?

How do we (human and non-human) constitute and practice human-ness?

How do we (human and non-human) constitute and practice non-human-ness?

Posthumanism in higher education forms an interesting paradox to think and do with. Oftentimes higher education functions as a particular spacetime for education: educating longer, deeper, at higher levels, and within particular contexts. Yet, higher education, as any education, is deeply rooted in the practice of educating the student, situated within power-knowledges, shaping representations of human civilization, and systems of life-long learning. Is it possible to divorce human practices from its educative goals? How would posthuman higher education and pedagogies feel like? How could posthuman pedagogies be lived and contextualized?

How might education change when humanism is no longer taken for granted?

Many of us have come to know posthumanism as a rather complex and differentiating scholarly and theoretical orientation, which often cuts across disciplines and phenomena. Connectedness of all kinds, including ecological events, subject-objects, onto-epistemologies, matter-minds, ani-humans, offer alternative ways to think about the presence and/or role of human, human knower, and human activities within complex conditions of humanity at large (see Braidotti and Hjavalova 2018; Braidotti 2013). Connected lives, shifting and eventful worlds, call for different kinds of techniques of practice and inquiry. Singularity and privilege of human experience, experiential logic, and limited systems perspectives can be replaced with inter-species multiplicity, situationality, and continuous (becoming) variation and generative difference. A becoming perspective of inter-relatedness disrupts the dominance, independence, agency, and privilege of 'human' as the only point of significance and mattering in the world.

In this book the authors have taken on the (im)possible task of de/re/unworking humanism in higher education. They use a variety of techniques to undo deeply internalized practices of human-centered learning and education. By doing so the authors illustrate how posthumanism could be lived and assembled within contradictory, paradoxical, damaging and even absurd educational spaces. Minor gestures, affects, senses, and unexpected material connections emerge within different chapters of this book. However, this emergence of minor gestures and particularities call for careful noticing. Tsing (2015) referred to the art of noticing—noticing assemblages, synched and un-synched rhythms, polyphony, and various world-making processes around us (both human and non-human). In this book, the authors are actively noticing and world-making posthumanism and posthuman practices across unpredictable higher education contexts, becomings and uncertain time-spaces. According to Tsing (2015: 20) precarity makes life possible and it 'is the condition of being vulnerable to others. Unpredictable encounters transform us; we are not in control, even of ourselves … we are thrown into shifting assemblages, which remake us as well as our others … everything is in flux, including our ability to survive'. Making worlds collectively sometimes helps humans to look around rather than ahead. Making worlds happens beyond the humans and within the ecological systems where every organism has potential to operate as a change agent—'patterns of unintentional coordination develop in assemblages. To notice such patterns means watching the interplay of temporal rhythms and scale in the divergent lifeways they gather' (Tsing 2015: 23).

Furthermore, the chapters in this book address and work through various troubles. Haraway's (2016) call to stay with the trouble offers intriguing and ecologically oriented positioning: 'Staying with the trouble requires learning to be truly present, not as a vanishing pivot between awful or edenic pasts and apocalyptic or salvific futures but as mortal critters entwined in myriad unfinished configurations of places, times, matters, and meanings' (Haraway 2016: 1). The ubiquitous figure of SF (science fiction, speculative fabulation, string figures and more) functions as a process and practice for Haraway to speak simultaneously to the ongoingness of staying on with the trouble and exercising response-ability. For Haraway (2016: 39), 'it matters what thoughts think thoughts; it matters what stories tell stories'. Narrated partiality connects and unites thoughts, practices, and theories. Moreover, tentacular thinking challenges linearity as it patterns and utilizes attachments and detachments, cuts and knots, and weaved paths. SF, she says, 'is storytelling and fact telling; it is the patterning of possible worlds and possible times' (Haraway 2016: 31). Posthuman response-ability cannot avoid risks when compos(t)ing possible common worlds since it aims to trouble visual clarity as the only sense and affect of thinking.

How could SF be put to work to trace the demise of human centered thinking? According to Braidotti (2013) posthuman theory can be a productive tool to re-think human as a unit of reference. She says: 'The human in Humanism is neither an ideal nor an objective statistical average or middle ground. It rather spells out a systematized standard of recognizability—of Sameness—by which all others can be assessed, regulated and allotted to a designated social location' (Braidotti 2013: 26). Furthermore, the concept and practice of human are normative conventions. For Braidotti, both human and non-human matter are intelligent and self-organizing. When thinking about the role of objects, Wiegman (2012) emphasized the idea that objects do not only matter because of what we want from them or how they constitute our worlds. Rather, Wiegman argued, that objects matter because humans would not know what we would be without them. Matter of all kind is continuous with culture, not opposed to it. For example, machines and viruses are intelligent and self-organizing consistently interacting with human

Forward-ing

and beyond human ecosystems and its parts. Interconnections between human and non-human actors produce new and unexpected subjectivities. 'Eco-philosophy of multiple belongings' (Wiegman 2012: 49) generates hybrid subject multiplicities that work across differences and through differentiations in ways which effect moving and forward-ing from unitary to nomadic and collective subjectivities. Non-human and earth others expand the life and its dimensions.

How do scissors sound? What do they do more than cut?
How might humbling and empowering pedagogy work with animals?
How could weather-bodies of human and non-human engage in collective pedagogical practices?
How and when might diffracted autoethnography leave its cultural traces behind?
Can diffractive readings of oneself include more than human ecologies?
How might dramatic writings concerned with anthropogenic climate change, theatrical performance and spaces of learning activate the traces and processes of becoming-with?

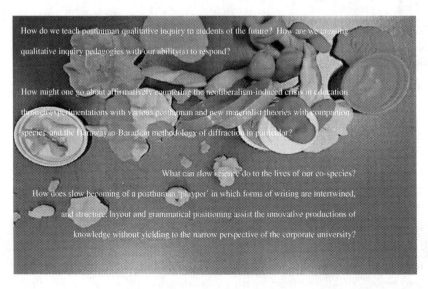

How do we teach posthuman qualitative inquiry to students of the future? How are we creating qualitative inquiry pedagogies with our ability(s) to respond?

How might one go about affirmatively countering the neoliberalism-induced crisis in education through experimentations with various posthuman and new materialist theories with companion species, and the Harrasayan-Baradian methodology of diffraction in particular?

What can slow science do to the lives of our co-species?
How does slow becoming of a posthuman 'playper' in which forms of writing are intertwined, and structure, layout and grammatical positioning assist the innovative productions of knowledge without yielding to the narrow perspective of the corporate university?

What can minor inquiry do to big data science and digitization of both human and non-human experience?
What good comes out of disruption if humans and qualitative scholars are in the middle of ecological mess to begin with?
What are some possibilities of the temporality of emergency when one stays with the trouble?

Too often essentializing human-centered inquiry practices and human desire for answers are treated as verifiable truths exempt from critique (see, for example, Dynarski 2008; Slavin 2004). Posthuman scholars could carefully ponder what might posthumanism and its various assemblages want. What might a posthuman question want? (see also Koro-Ljungberg and Barko 2012). How could collective, ecological, and more-than-human questions facilitate our goal for deeper acknowledgement of non-human and more-than-human forces, energies, and influences? How, then, might posthuman scholars ask different questions and ask questions differently?

How might creative arts help students to develop an awareness of entanglement?
How might teaching journeys, artistic and 'disruptive' pedagogies and rhizomatic emergences, cross-disciplinary approaches to traditional academic teacher education pathways be re-imagined within and through posthumanism?

How might literature help scholars to move from a rejection of humanist abstraction towards a posthuman framing?

How might student, teacher, parent, companion, and animal bodies function as transformers and relay points for the flow of energies?

These questions require a mutation of our (pre-)shaped understanding of what it means to think at all, let alone thing critically. Furthermore, if/when posthuman theory and vital materialism strike 'an alliance with the productive and immanent force of *zoe*, or life in its non-human aspects' (Braidotti 2013: 66), then surely new imaginaries, affective ties, and new vocabulary ensue? And perhaps then de-familiarization might assist to establish 'the open-ended, inter-relational, multi-sexed and trans-species flows of becoming through interaction with multiple others' (Braidotti 2013: 89) that a posthuman higher education reaches for. We may then want to consider how methodological building blocks to promote inter-relationality—such as cartographies and maps, trans-disciplinarity, creative critique, imaginative forms of de-familiarization—help us consider the question: 'what would a geo-centered subject look like?' (Braidotti 2013: 81).

Could we be inspired by playfully reveling in the decentralization of the anthro- within the auto- of autoethnography?
How might we take up language and the power being granted to it in the ways which would address the inter-relatedness between species?
What if the shared and divergent spaces between indigenous and new materialist approaches would challenge (neo-)colonial logics and relationships, as well as enhance commensurate commitments and projects?
What if 'Settler Re-Education' would be taught to all students?

What if the slow and uneasy assemblage, comprising images, media articles and reported responses to scandals, deterritorialize qualitative research practice and allow for an interrogation of how affect mobilizes in the form of gendered violence?
How might vital materialism work?

Posing posthuman questions and questions about posthumanism does not need to exemplify current practices of human organization of knowledge. Instead, these inquiries could be driven by diverging compositions, movement, rest, speed, and slowness including both human and more-than-human forces and matter. Questioning why, how, and what influences posthuman relationalities might serve as one productive way of forward-ing inquiry. Maybe readers of this book could live posthumanism and various forms of posthuman questioning in their higher education becomings while deciding together with multiple companion species what is capable of becoming. Braidotti (2013: 195) says that posthumanism 'is a chance to identity opportunities for resistance and empowerment on a planetary scale'. While living the questions, identifying opportunities, and staying with the confusions, uncertainties and troublings, where might posthuman assemblages and lives move next?

Tempe, USA
December 2018

Mirka Koro-Ljungberg
Mary Lou Fulton Teachers College
Arizona State University

References

Braidotti, R. (2013). *The posthuman*. Malden, MA: Polity Press.

Braidotti, R., & Hjavalova, M. (2018). *Posthuman glossary*. London: Bloomsbury Academic.

Dynarski, M. (2008). Comments on Slavin: Bringing answers to educators: Guiding principles for research syntheses. *Educational Researcher, 37*(1), 27–29.

Haraway, D. J. (2016). *Staying with the trouble: Making kin in the Chthulucene*. Durham, NC: Duke University Press.

Koro-Ljungberg, M., & Barko, T. (2012). "Answers", assemblages, and qualitative research. *Qualitative Inquiry, 18*(3), 256–265.

Slavin, R. (2004). Education research can and must address "what works" questions. *Educational Researcher, 33*(1), 27–28.

Tsing, A. (2015). *The mushroom at the end of the world*. Princeton: Princeton University Press.

Wiegman, R. (2012). *Object lessons*. Durham: Duke University Press.

Mirka Koro-Ljungberg (Ph.D., University of Helsinki) is a Professor of qualitative research at the Arizona State University. Her scholarship operates in the intersection of methodology, philosophy, and socio-cultural critique and her work aims to contribute to methodological knowledge, experimentation, and theoretical development across various traditions associated with qualitative research. She has published in various qualitative and educational journals and she is the author of *Reconceptualizing Qualitative Research: Methodologies Without Methodology* (2016) published by SAGE and co-editor of *Disrupting Data in Qualitative Inquiry: Entanglements with the Post-Critical and Post-Anthropocentric* (2017) by Peter Lang.

Acknowledgements

Our deep and wide thanks go to each contributor for engaging with us so collaboratively and generatively to materialise this book. Your tenaciousness, joy and good humour in craft-ing, draft-ing, making and amending your chapters helped us, as editors, to both pause and attend to what really matters for each of us in our writing and to push on with the book in a timely manner. The care-full attention to detail, and the ethic of response-ability with which you participated in the peer reviewing process, was a keen reminder, too, that writing is never simply about craft or practical skills but is a flesh and blood, mindheartspirit endeavour of time, energy and attention and that we all become more capable through acts of generosity. We appreciate your involvement in the inventive work of connection—in the imaginative work of making trouble—that posthuman endeavours should and must pose to higher education pedagogy, practice and research.

Thank you to our editors Eleanor and Rebecca at Palgrave Macmillan for dealing with our queries promptly and making it easy to navigate the production process. Thanks to our families, friends and furry ones for their love and support during this process. Thanks also to each other for the companionable journey.

January 2019

Carol A. Taylor
Annouchka Bayley

Contents

1   **Unfolding: Co-Conspirators, Contemplations, Complications and More**   1
Carol A. Taylor

Part I   Entangled Pedagogic Provocations

2   **Sounds of Scissors: Eventicising Curriculum in Higher Education**   31
Bente Ulla, Ninni Sandvik, Ann Sofi Larsen, Mette Røe Nyhus and Nina Johannesen

3   **Theatre for a Changing Climate: A Lecturer's Portfolio**   55
Evelyn O'Malley

4   **A Manifesto for Teaching Qualitative Inquiry with/as/for Art, Science, and Philosophy**   73
Candace R. Kuby and David Aguayo

5   Posthuman Encounters in New Zealand Early
    Childhood Teacher Education   85
    Sonja Arndt and Marek Tesar

6   Putting Posthuman Theories to Work in Educational
    Leadership Programmes   103
    Kathryn J. Strom and John Lupinacci

7   Re-vitalizing the American Feminist-Philosophical
    Classroom: Transformative Academic
    Experimentations with Diffractive Pedagogies   123
    Evelien Geerts

8   Undoing and Doing-With: Practices of Diffractive
    Reading and Writing in Higher Education (Viewpoint)   141
    *Sarah Hepler, Susan Cannon, Courtney Hartnett
    and Teri Peitso-Holbrook*

Part II   Inventive Practice Intra-Ventions

9   Staying with the Trouble in Science Education:
    Towards Thinking with Nature—A Manifesto   155
    Marc Higgins, Maria F. G. Wallace and Jesse Bazzul

10 Complex Knowing: Promoting Response-Ability
    Within Music and Science Teacher Education   165
    Carolyn Cooke and Laura Colucci-Gray

11 Dramatizing an Articulation of the (P)Artistic
    Researcher's Posthumanist Pathway to a 'Slow
    Professorship' Within the Corporate University
    Complex   187
    johnmichael rossi

12	A Posthuman Pedagogy for Childhood Studies (Viewpoint) *Amanda Hatton*	211
13	Disruptive Pedagogies for Teacher Education: The Power of *Potentia* in Posthuman Times *Kay Sidebottom*	217
14	Textual Practices as Already-Posthuman: Re-Imagining Text, Authorship and Meaning-Making in Higher Education *Lesley Gourlay*	237
15	Body as Transformer: 'Teaching Without Teaching' in a Teacher Education Course *Karin Murris and Cara Borcherds*	255

Part III   Experimental Research Engagements

16	Playful Pedagogy: Autoethnography in the Anthropocene *Clare Hammoor*	281
17	Refiguring Presences in Kichwa-Lamista Territories: Natural-Cultural (Re)Storying with Indigenous Place *Marc Higgins and Brooke Madden*	293
18	Indigenous Education in Higher Education in Canada: Settler Re-Education Through New Materialist Theory *Jeannie Kerr*	313
19	Posthuman Methodology and Pedagogy: Uneasy Assemblages and Affective Choreographies *Jennifer Charteris and Adele Nye*	329

20 Response-Able (Peer) Reviewing Matters in Higher
 Education: A Manifesto 349
 Vivienne Bozalek, Michalinos Zembylas and Tamara Shefer

21 How Did 'We' Become Human in the First Place?
 Entanglements of Posthumanism and Critical
 Pedagogy for the Twenty-First Century 359
 Annouchka Bayley

Index 367

Notes on Contributors

David Aguayo, M.Ed. is a doctoral candidate in the Educational Leadership and Policy Analysis Department at the University of Missouri. David's research interests encompass community-school-university collaboration, with an emphasis on local educational policy-making and leadership. David is co-founder and Assistant Director in a grassroots movement, Worley Street Roundtable (www.worleystreetroundtable.org) which aims to create educational collaboration across families, schools, communities, and universities for the betterment of underserved children in Columbia, Missouri. David has co-authored *Assessing Spanish-Speaking Immigrant Parents' Perceptions of Climate at a New Language Immersion School: A Critical Analysis Using 'Thinking with Theory'* (2017, with Lisa Dorner) and *Counselors as Leaders Who Advocate for Undocumented Students' Education* (2017, with Emily Crawford and Fernando Valle). Journals in which his scholarship appears include *Education Policy Analysis Archives*, *Journal of Research in Leadership Education*, and *Research in Education*.

Sonja Arndt is a Senior Lecturer in the Faculty of Education at the University of Waikato, New Zealand. Her teaching and research interests intersect early childhood education, intercultural connectedness and cultural Otherness in education and philosophy of education. She has developed a strong interest in Kristevan philosophical conceptions of the subject, has published widely in this area, and her doctoral thesis on this topic has won multiple awards.

Annouchka Bayley (B.A. Hons. SOAS; MRes Warwick; Ph.D. Warwick) is a scholar working in posthumanism, performance studies and higher education. She has published several works, including her new monograph *Posthuman Pedagogies in Practice: Arts-Based Approaches to Developing Participatory Futures* (Palgrave, 2018), commissioned and edited several special issues. Annouchka is programme lead and tutor in creative education at the Royal College of Art (UK). In 2014 she won the Warwick Award for Teaching Excellence. She is also an Emerging Director with the Royal Shakespeare Company.

Jesse Bazzul is Associate Professor of Science and Environmental Education at the University of Regina, Canada. He believes imaginative work in education is needed more than ever to find new collective ways of living together.

Cara Borcherds is a PGCE in Foundation Phase Graduate from the School of Education, University of Cape Town. With a background in the Fine Arts, online marketing and business management (currently Managing Director of a small niche tourism business in Papua New Guinea, Scuba Ventures—Kavieng. www.scubakavieng.com), her teaching practice is grounded in an embodied and aesthetic philosophy. Cara makes extensive use of the arts as a bridge to thinking, expression, social interaction and making meaning in hers and others learning. She plans to embark on a full time career as teacher and to continue exploring and developing the use of the technical image/digital media and augmented reality in her own and others pedagogical documentation.

Vivienne Bozalek is a Professor of Social Work and the Director of Teaching and Learning at the University of the Western Cape. She holds a Ph.D. from Utrecht University. Her research interests and publications include the political ethics of care and social justice, posthumanism and feminist new materialisms, innovative pedagogical practices in higher education, and post-qualitative and participatory methodologies.

Her most recent co-edited books include *Theorising Learning to Teach in Higher Education* with Brenda Leibowitz and Peter Kahn and *Socially Just Pedagogies: Posthumanist, Feminist and Materialist Perspectives in Higher Education* with Rosi Braidotti, Tamara Shefer and Michalinos Zembylas.

Susan Cannon is a Ph.D. candidate in the Department of Middle/Secondary Education at Georgia State University. She works and thinks across the boundaries of mathematics education, qualitative inquiry, and teacher education.

Dr. Jennifer Charteris is Senior Lecturer in Pedagogy in the University of New England. Jennifer's research interests span identity and subject formation, student voice, assessment for learning, and the politics of teacher education and professional learning. She is interested in how theories of affect and materiality can be used to inform education research.

Laura Colucci-Gray is Senior Lecturer in Science and Sustainability Education and Strategic coordination of STEM and STEAM pedagogies in teacher education at the University of Edinburgh. She is an educationalist and science education researcher with experience of interactive and participatory pedagogies for understanding complex, socio-environmental issues. Recent areas of interests include school garden pedagogies, arts-based approaches in outdoor learning and the study of interdisciplinary practices such as STEAM (the addition of the Arts to STEM), within the wider framework of learning for sustainability.

Carolyn Cooke is currently completing a Ph.D. at Edinburgh University exploring music student teachers' experiences of improvisation as a radical apparatus for troubling enlightenment epistemology. Having worked as a music teacher in secondary schools, and more recently as a lecturer both in music and generic education course, she has developed interests in student teacher learning and arts-based pedagogies, as well as writing on musical learning behaviours, music curricula issues, and inclusion.

Evelien Geerts is a Ph.D. candidate in Feminist Studies with a designated emphasis in History of Consciousness at the University of

California, Santa Cruz, and an affiliated researcher at the Institute for Cultural Inquiry at Utrecht University. She previously studied at Utrecht University (research M.A. Gender and Ethnicity Studies) and Antwerp University (M.A. Philosophy) and works on the crossroads of Continental philosophy and contemporary feminist theory. Her research interests include feminist new materialisms, political philosophy, difference philosophies, and critical and diffractive pedagogies. She has published in *Women's Studies International Forum*, *Rhizomes: Cultural Studies in Emerging Knowledge*, and *Angelaki: Journal of Theoretical Humanities*, and is an editor of the Dutch journal *Tijdschrift voor Genderstudies*.

Lesley Gourlay is a Professor of Education at UCL Institute of Education. Her background is in Applied Linguistics, and her current interests include academic literacies, multimodality and digital mediation in higher education, focusing on meaning-making, textual practices, digital literacies. Her recent publications have focused on the relationships between sociomaterial perspectives, posthuman theory and practices in higher education, with an emphasis on the role of textuality and meaning-making. She is a member of the Executive Editorial Board of the journal *Teaching in Higher Education*.

Clare Hammoor is a theatre practitioner obsessed with object-oriented ontologies, clowning, and creating joyful, Absurd theatre with children (and everything else). Equally committed to the possibilities of justice and philosophy, Clare collaborates with men and women who live the realities of the US's system of mass incarceration. Clare holds an Ed.D. from New York University and her work has appeared in international journals and conferences including *Body, Space, Technology* and *Performance Philosophy*.

Courtney Hartnett is a Ph.D. student in the Early Childhood and Elementary Education Department at Georgia State University. Her research interests include new media literacies and posthuman theories.

Dr. Amanda Hatton, Ph.D. is currently a Senior Lecturer in Childhood Studies at Sheffield Hallam University. She previously worked for a local authority for over 25 years in a number of roles with children and young people across primary and secondary settings. Amanda worked as Education Social Worker; case holder for the youth offending service; as project manager for a range of literacy projects providing support for young people excluded from school; young offenders and young people in care and family literacy projects in the early years. Following this she worked as a Senior staff development officer in a safeguarding children's training team, delivering multi-agency training, including early years statutory and voluntary provision. Research for her doctoral thesis was based on the participation of children and young people, using creative arts and methods, from which she developed a model of participative practice.

Sarah Hepler is a Ph.D. student in the Department of Learning Technologies and a Learning Ecologist in the Center for Excellence in Teaching and Learning at Georgia State University, USA. Her course of study has focused on poststructural approaches to higher education.

Marc Higgins is an Assistant Professor in the Department of Secondary Education at the University of Alberta and is affiliated with the Faculty of Education's Aboriginal Teacher Education Program (ATEP). His research labours the methodological space within and between Indigenous, post-structural and post-humanist theories in order to (re)think and practice education which works to ethically respond to contested ways-of-knowing (i.e. epistemology) and ways-of-being (i.e. ontology) such as Indigenous science or ways-of-living-with-Nature.

Nina Johannesen is an Associate Professor of Early Childhood Education at Østfold University College (ØUC), Norway. Johannesen and her colleagues have developed a Master's Program in Early Childhood Studies (0–3 years). Her lectures and research have progressed, with a particular interest in children under the age of three years. Dr. Johannesen is working through ethics as a first philosophy to challenge the understanding of young children and their position in society and pedagogical institutions.

Jeannie Kerr is a researcher and educator concerned with understanding the ways that programs of teacher education can prepare future educators to engage complexity, uncertainty and diversity so as to address local and global inequities that form part of working in education. Her academic work is committed to decolonial theory and practice in education; addressing the material-discursive inequalities in educational settings; and collaboratively repairing and renewing relations in Canadian society. Dr. Kerr engages in her work as a Settler-Scholar on Treaty 1 territory, the traditional territory of the Anishnabeg, Cree, Oji-Cree, Dakota and Dene peoples, and homeland of the Métis nation, at the University of Winnipeg.

Candace R. Kuby, Ph.D. is an Associate Professor of early childhood education at the University of Missouri. Her research interests are twofold: (1) the ethico-onto-epistemologies of literacy desiring(s) when young children work with materials to create multimodal, digital, and hybrid texts; and (2) approaches to qualitative inquiry drawing upon poststructural and posthumanist theories and the teaching of qualitative inquiry. Candace has authored several books including *Go Be a Writer!: Expanding the Curricular Boundaries of Literacy Learning* (2016, Teachers College Press, with Tara Gutshall Rucker) and *Disrupting Qualitative Inquiry: Possibilities and Tensions in Educational Research* (2014, Peter Lang co-edited with Ruth Nicole Brown and Rozana Carducci). Journals in which her scholarship appears include *Qualitative Inquiry*; *International Journal of Qualitative Studies in Education*; *Journal of Early Childhood Literacy*; and *Language Arts*.

Ann Sofi Larsen is an Associate Professor of Early Childhood Education at Østfold University College (ØUC), Norway. Dr. Larsen and her colleagues have developed a Master's Program in Early Childhood Studies (0–3 years). Her lectures and research have progressed, with a particular interest in children under the age of three years. Dr. Larsen is working through continental philosophy in her studies of professions, searching for diverse ways to issue ethics in pedagogical institutions.

John Lupinacci is an Assistant Professor at Washington State University. He conducts research and teaches in the Cultural Studies and Social Thought in Education (CSSTE) program using an approach that advocates for the development of scholar-activist educators. Dr. Lupinacci's research focuses on how educators, educational leaders, and educational researchers learn to both identify and examine destructive habits of Western industrial human culture and how those habits are taught and learned in schools. He is a co-author of *EcoJustice Education: Toward Diverse, Democratic, and Sustainable Communities* (Routledge, 2015), and his experiences as a K-12 classroom teacher, an outdoor environmental educator, and a community activist-artist-scholar all contribute to his research, teaching, and development of projects open to the possibilities of how people can learn to live together in diverse, democratic, and sustainable communities.

Dr. Brooke Madden is an Assistant Professor within the Aboriginal Teacher Education Program and the Department of Educational Policy Studies at the University of Alberta. Brooke's research focuses on the relationship between teacher identity and teacher education on the topics of Indigenous education and truth and reconciliation education. Brooke has also published on whiteness and decolonizing processes, school-based Indigenous education reform, and Indigenous and decolonizing research methodologies. She works to acknowledge both her Indigenous and settler ancestries in complex ways that acknowledge privilege and resist appropriation.

Karin Murris, Ph.D. is Professor of Pedagogy and Philosophy at the School of Education, University of Cape Town. Grounded in philosophy as an academic discipline, her main research interests are in early childhood education, literacies, school ethics, posthumanism, postqualitative research methods, and de/colonising pedagogies such as Philosophy with children and Reggio Emilia. She is Programme Convener of the PGCE Foundation phase, teaches Masters courses and supervises Ph.D. students. Karin is Principal Investigator of the Decolonising Early Childhood Discourses: Critical Posthumanism in Higher Education research project funded by the South African government for three years (2016–2018). Her books include: *Teaching Philosophy with Picture Books* (1992), *The Posthuman Child: Educational Transformation Through Philosophy with Picturebooks* (2016), and (with Joanna Haynes) *Literacies, Literature and Learning: Reading Classrooms*

Differently (2018), *Picturebooks, Pedagogy and Philosophy* (2012) and *Storywise: Thinking Through Stories* (2002). She is also co-editor of the Routledge *International Handbook of Philosophy for Children* (2017).

Dr. Adele Nye is a Senior Lecturer in the School of Education at the University of New England. Her research primarily focuses on Higher Education and the teaching of history. Adele's most recent research output was a co-edited book *Teaching the Discipline of History in an Age of Standards* (2018).

Mette Røe Nyhus is an Associate Professor of Early Childhood Education at Østfold University College (ØUC), Norway. Nyhus and her colleagues have developed a Master's Program in Early Childhood Studies (0–3 years). Nyhus is working through posthumanist theories with pedagogics and didactics concerning the youngest children in kindergarten.

Evelyn O'Malley is a Lecturer in Department of Drama at the University of Exeter. Her monograph *Weathering Shakespeare* is forthcoming with Bloomsbury Academic's Environmental Cultures series.

Teri Peitso-Holbrook is an Associate Professor of literacy and language arts at Georgia State University. Her research—including text creation, analysis, and use—looks at how arts-infused and digital composition alters notions of literacy education, academic and literary writing, and qualitative inquiry.

johnmichael rossi, Ph.D. is a theatre-maker, educator and researcher. He is the current Programme Leader for the B.A. (Hons) Drama at University of Northampton (UK) where he is a Senior Lecturer in Acting and Drama. He is a co-convener for the Performance-as-Research Working Group for the International Federation of Theatre Research. He was the founding artistic director for newFangled theatReR (Brooklyn, NY) which has produced his plays, published in *Play'N AmerikA: a pair of playz* and *gentlefucknation: a beautification*. He is the former Education Director for Women's Project (NYC) and was a member of the Vital Theatre Company's education team that formed and developed Brooklyn Theatre Arts High School.

Ninni Sandvik is a Professor of Early Childhood Education at Østfold University College (ØUC), Norway. Professor Sandvik and her colleagues have developed a Master's Program in Early Childhood Studies (0–3 years). She has a particular interest in children under the age of three years. Professor Sandvik is working through posthumanist theories with pedagogics and didactics concerning the youngest children in kindergarten.

Tamara Shefer is Professor in Women's and Gender Studies, Faculty of Arts, at the University of the Western Cape. Her research is directed towards intersectional gender and sexual justice, including research on young sexual practices, masculinities, memory and apartheid, gender and care, social justice, decolonial and feminist pedagogies and research in higher education. Her most recent edited books are *Engaging Youth in Activist Research and Pedagogical Praxis: Transnational and Intersectional Perspectives on Gender, Sex, and Race* (2018, with Jeff Hearn, Kopano Ratele and Floretta Boonzaier) and *Socially Just Pedagogies in Higher Education: Critical Posthumanist and New Feminist Materialist Perspectives* (2018, Bloomsbury, with Vivienne Bozalek, Rosi Braidotti and Michalinos Zembylas).

Kay Sidebottom is a Lecturer in Education and Childhood at Leeds Beckett University. Recent research projects include the critical examination of decolonising work in U.K. universities; using interdisciplinary approaches (such as art and poetry) in teacher education; and employing philosophical enquiry as a pedagogical method for anti-fascist education. She is currently exploring how teachers and students might enact concepts of nomadism, assemblage, and rhizomatics to develop a 'posthuman curriculum.'

Kathryn J. Strom is an Assistant Professor in the Educational Leadership Department at California State University, East Bay. She teaches courses on critical perspectives on education and qualitative research methods in the Educational Leadership for Social Justice Ed.D. program. Her research focuses on preparing educators to work for social justice in classrooms and school systems and putting posthuman/materialist theories to work in educational research. Dr. Strom received her Ph.D. at Montclair State University in Teacher Education and Teacher Development.

Her recent publications include 'Non-linear negotiations: Hybridity and first-year teaching practice' (*Teacher Education Quarterly*, 2018) and 'Clinging to the edge of chaos: The emergence of novice teacher practice' (*Teachers College Record*, 2018). She is also the co-author of the book *Becoming-Teacher: A Rhizomatic Look at First-Year Teaching* (Sense, 2017). Prior to pursuing her doctorate, Kathryn was a history teacher and school leader in southern California.

Carol A. Taylor is Professor of Higher Education and Gender the University of Bath, UK. She has a longstanding research interest in the intersections of knowledge, space, disciplinary identities and gendered power in further and higher education. Her current research utilises feminist, new-materialist and posthumanist theories and methodologies to explore spatial practices, gendered inequalities, and staff and students' participation in a range of higher educational sites. She has a keen interest in inter-multi-transdisciplinary theoretical and methodological innovation. Carol is co-editor of the journal *Gender and Education*; she is on the Editorial Boards of *Critical Studies in Teaching and Learning*, *Teaching in Higher Education*, and the *Journal of Applied Research in Higher Education*. She co-edited *Posthuman Research Practices in Education* (2016) with Christina Hughes and has published widely in international journals.

Dr. Marek Tesar is an academic and Associate Dean International at the University of Auckland, New Zealand. His research is focused on philosophical methods, childhood studies and early childhood education, with expertise in the philosophy of education and childhood. His research is concerned with the construction of childhoods, notions of place/space, and methodological and philosophical thinking around ontologies and the ethics of researching these notions.

Bente Ulla is an Associate Professor of Early Childhood Education at Østfold University College (ØUC), Norway. Dr. Ulla and her colleagues have developed a Master's Program in Early Childhood Studies (0–3 years). Her lectures and research have progressed, with a particular interest in children under the age of three years. Dr. Ulla is working through continental philosophy in her methodological approaches, searching for diverse ways to problematize bodies, knowledge and power.

Maria F. G. Wallace is an Assistant Professor of Education at Millsaps College in Jackson, Mississippi. Her research interests intersect Science Education, Curriculum Theory, and Women and Gender Studies. Maria's work aims to deterritorialize science teacher subjectivities and practices to re-imagine ways they become known, named, and produced.

Michalinos Zembylas is Professor of Educational Theory and Curriculum Studies at the Open University of Cyprus. He is also Honorary Professor at Nelson Mandela University in the Chair for Critical Studies in Higher Education Transformation. He has written extensively on emotion and affect in relation to social justice pedagogies, intercultural and peace education, human rights education and citizenship education. His recent books include: *Psychologized Language in Education: Denaturalizing a Regime of Truth* (with Z. Bekerman), and *Socially Just Pedagogies in Higher Education* (co-edited with V. Bozalek, R. Braidotti and T. Shefer). In 2016, he received the Distinguished Researcher Award in 'Social Sciences and Humanities' from the Cyprus Research Promotion Foundation.

List of Figures

Fig. 2.1	Body	34
Fig. 2.2	Cutting	36
Fig. 2.3	Body parts	37
Fig. 2.4	Circle-dot	47
Fig. 2.5	Leftovers	49
Fig. 7.1	Copyright ©Subversive Philosophy Memes (2018)	134
Fig. 8.1	Posthuman feasting	146
Fig. 8.2	Destabilized but never detabalized	148
Fig. 8.3	Hairline fractures (Latysheva 2018; Villain 2018)	149
Fig. 10.1	Music student teachers' response to exploratory listening	174
Fig. 10.2	Music student teachers' response to exploratory listening	175
Fig. 10.3	Sensory map trailing the path	178
Fig. 10.4	Microphone as a 'doing'	181
Fig. 11.1	'Dottore JoMiRo' and JuJu the Pig in *The S'kool of Edumacation* (July 2015)	196
Fig. 11.2	'D-Spair' participates in re-staging of 'Battle of Iwo Jima' (June 2016)	199
Fig. 11.3	Union Square 'Post-It' Protest (December 2016)	201
Fig. 13.1	David Ball. Collective	222
Fig. 13.2	Kay Sidebottom. Becoming teacher	224
Fig. 13.3	Kay Sidebottom. Study companion-rabbit	227

Fig. 14.1	Agents entangled in this text	242
Fig. 14.2	Student bed and devices	247
Fig. 14.3	Student representation of essay-writing practices	248
Fig. 14.4	Student iPad, for academic reading in the bath	249
Fig. 14.5	Student papers and external hard drive	250
Fig. 14.6	Student depiction of his digital engagement	252
Fig. 15.1	Cara and other students' responses to the first Childhood Studies reading: *The Posthuman Child* (2016)	258
Fig. 15.2	In the left Cara's first school day. On the right her body mindmap as made in the university classroom	264
Fig. 15.3	Bodymind maps hung up on a washing line in our university classroom	269
Fig. 15.4	The humanist child subject (left image) and the posthuman (child) subject (right image)	272
Fig. 15.5	Ontologically re-moving the boundary of the human subject	273
Fig. 19.1	Powerpoint slide: Responses to the article from the public (Our researcher notes are in italics)	335
Fig. 19.2	Powerpoint slide: A further response to the article (Our researcher notes are in italics)	336
Fig. 19.3	Remaking the space	336
Fig. 19.4	Cornered by the technology	338

List of Tables

Table 15.1 A map of figurations of child that presuppose
the Nature/Culture dichotomy   261
Table 17.1 Reconfiguring presences + nature/culture
and Indigenous storywork   300

1

Unfolding: Co-Conspirators, Contemplations, Complications and More

Carol A. Taylor

Unfolding/Enfolding/Folding

What is an introduction? A beginning, a preliminary part, a preamble which leads to the main part. Perhaps. If so, then I want to resist the act of 'introducing'. I don't wish to lead you 'in' and I certainly don't want to lead you in a straight line either up or down that fabled hill. I am not the Grand Old Duke of York and would like to eschew any kind of 'Introduction' that works to frame and condition your reading. Perhaps then, instead of an introduction, it would be better to invoke an unfolding. Deleuze (2006: 6) says that 'unfolding is … not the contrary of folding, but follows the fold up to the following fold.' This suggests a re-conception of the inside and outside, the intensive and extensive, linearity and circularity, the up and down, light, colour and texture, the immaterial and material, individuation and differentiation—seeing them not as separate or contrasting aspects of an entity but as produced

---

C. A. Taylor (✉)
Department of Education, University of Bath, Bath, UK
e-mail: C.A.Taylor@bath.ac.uk

© The Author(s) 2019
C. A. Taylor and A. Bayley (eds.), *Posthumanism and Higher Education*,
https://doi.org/10.1007/978-3-030-14672-6_1

in continually differentiating relation through their continual movements, mixings and morphings. The fold is *'entre-deux'*—something produced in-between as a difference being differentiated—never something preformed (Deleuze 2006: 11). Although this Unfolding is situated where an Introduction would otherwise go (at the beginning!) and it is likely you will read it (or at least skim it) first, it is un/en/folded together with its various 21 chapters and 3 parts, all of which during this book un/en/fold as deviations, creases and pleats riffing on posthumanism and higher education. It and they aim to make a small gesture toward an alternative ontology—an ontology of differentiation and becoming—which, in de Freitas and Sinclair's (2012: 143) words, can give rise to possibilities which 'resist the closure of the enveloping eye.' The closure, in this case, being the marketized performatives, the accountability metrics, the outcomes reckonings, and the bare, pared down measurement technologies which characterise the 'accelerated academy' (Carrigan 2016) of contemporary higher education.

Plung(e)ing-In

So, I invite you, reader, to open the book where you may, dive in where you wish, take the plunge when and as you like. Perhaps you may even want to try un/en/folding yourself with/in this book in a spirit of dancing-with, so that your dancing moves—be they basic step or back spin, chugging or lindy circle, oversway, floating, reverse wave, gliding or sliding—work to choreograph your feet, body, hands, mind, brain with the chapters as they un/en/fold in the way that works best for you. There is no right way to read this book but, however you read it, I hope you find enjoyment, provocation, ideas and imaginings that give you scope for push-back against the panoply of neoliberal measurement technologies that constitute the 'enveloping eye' of contemporary Higher Education. If/how/when/whether you take the plunge I wonder how the book's un/en/foldings—of becomings which are 'folded within a fold' (Deleuze 2006: 6) and whose 'unfold[s are] the continuation or extension of [the fold], the condition of its manifestation'

(Deleuze 2006: 40)—work for you, perhaps in some barely perceptible but nevertheless important ways, to make new modes of thinking and unthinking, doing and undoing, possible. Perhaps you will let me know.

In the meantime, my feet find the breadcrumb path of clues laid down by Clare Hammoor in Chapter 16 who tells of how three chairs and a bottle of water shape the aesthetics of her teaching practices and how, inspired by educational philosopher Maxine Greene's (1977) notion of 'wide awakefulness,' she aims to enact a performative pedagogy of 'playful instability' to help promote a cross-culturally responsive understanding of what she calls the 'fantastic now', so that we might better attend to the entangled ecologies we ourselves are deeply intertwined within. In Chapter 10, Carolyn Cooke and Laura Colucci-Gray entice my feet with more breadcrumbs, telling of how, in their performative sensory experiments with 18 music student teachers and 30 primary science education students, learning bodies are oriented to their expressive, corporeal and mobile capacities as a means of conjuring up virtual ('as-if') worlds. Such pedagogic practice/ings trouble dominant modes of undergraduate and Initial Teacher Education replacing a pedagogy of controlled plans and known outcomes with a pedagogy of feeling-sensing-tasting as pedagogy is un/en/folded with particles of wind, air, water and fire, practices are un/en/folded with organic and inorganic matter(ing)s, and research is un/en/folded with events, occurrences, happenings.

Co-Conspirators, Without Whom

Breadcrumbs. Mmm. Tasty. A different yet equally nourishing metaphor comes from Manning and Massumi (2014: 13) who refer to the 'commotional complexity of the moment in gyration' and the relational potential such gyrations release. These gyrations have touched me affectively as I've been assembling this book, producing a sort of pleasurable 'lightness'—an onto-ethico-epistemological joy—that has made the labour of working on/with the book energising, both methodologically and theoretically. Like its predecessor (Taylor and Hughes 2016), materializing this book with authors–co-editor–collaborators has been a joy, a flight, a highline, a refuge, a release, a finding, and a co-e-motional coming-to-treasure. Treasure, that is, as a little something or other you take home, hoard up as a source of succour, or self-protection even, and share with those you trust. Such a notion of 'treasure' speaks to the chapters' blending of serendipities, commitments, passions and knowledges; of their authors' sharings, findings, tellings and provokings; of the affects, inspire-ations, aerations, bodyings-forth, and human-nonhuman confederations, that can unfurl from posthuman higher education doings. Treasure in this sense offers an antidote to higher education as national trophy (as x-percent of GDP), or public showpiece (those universities named and taking pride in being in the global 100 'best' universities), or royal crown jewels (that unhospitable discourse of social division which equates elite with 'best'). The authors in this book try hard to work against such performative reductiveness which sees treasure as capital—as pieces of eight, gold coin, swag, plunder or loot. Their attempts at reconfiguring pedagogy, practice and research in posthuman vein make them co-conspirators of difference, without whom … Thanks to each and all.

Measurement

In fortuitous happenstance a few weeks ago I came across Sword's (2017: ix) words:

> We long for 'air and light and time and space,' an architecture of possibilities and pleasure; instead, we find ourselves crushed under the weight of expectations and the rubble of our fractured workdays.

and wonder if the longing for 'lightness' (and a bit of air and space and time) that this book may offer could work as a sort of inoculation against the 'grubby scramble' that Ingold (2011: xiii) characterises as the contemporary competitive marketised academy. Ingold's comment appears in Chapter 19 (written by Jennifer Charteris and Adele Nye), along with his view that:

> The prostitution of scholarship before the twin idols of innovation and competitiveness has reduced once fine traditions of learning to market brands, the pursuit of excellence to a grubby scramble for funding and prestige, and books such as this to outputs whose value is measured by rating and impact rather that by what they might have to contribute to human understanding. (Ingold 2011: xiii)

Such sentiments are echoed by Watermeyer (2019: 6) who speaks of the 'brutal and discomfiting' decline of criticality, activism and 'agency theft' in the accelerated academy, of how the 'cognate seductions of neoliberalism' have eroded academics' political capital by banishing them to the margins of their institutions, and how entrepreneurial and performance management regimes have instituted a culture of 'competitive accountability' which has diminished, even corrupted, academics' ability to be, act and work as public intellectuals. These sad tales of decline and fall are linked to a sense of how, in Watermeyer's (2019: 14–17) words, the 'erosion, depurification or disappearance of the intellectual as a public figure' consigns academics to perform the role of 'minor celebrity' through competitive acts of 'intellectual exhibitionism' both on social media and via national accountability regimes such as the UK Research Excellence Framework. Indeed, this refrain has become the major literature of contemporary higher education (Alveson 2013; Brown and Carasso 2013; Cantwell and Kauppinen 2014; Collini 2017; Giroux 2014; Naidoo 2016).

> I recognise all of this.
> I imagine you do too.
> And yet.
> I wonder.

I wonder if such a lamentable situation is less a description of a general condition and more a partial perspective capturing a certain sort of melancholia—a euro/western, leftist, white, masculinist melancholia? Perhaps the nostalgia for a better state of being in HE is less about loss and more about a complicated entanglement in which those who were formerly central to shaping a certain sort of (neo-colonialist) discourse about the role of intellectuals in public life now find themselves uncomfortably placed and jostling for position with those 'others' who have (always) been peripheralized within the humanist (masculinist) university run on Enlightenment goals of rationality, progress and civilisation. I suggest this because: higher education, historically and contemporaneously, remains riven by exclusivity and exclusion as many black, brown, Indigenous, dis/abled, trans, and older people know (Gabriel and Tate 2017; Smith 2012); because universities are far from being safe spaces for women as those who are on the receiving end of lad culture and strategies which misreport and hide sexual harassment know (Jackson et al. 2015; Phipps 2018); and because even robust critiques of universities as machines for the reproduction of human capital (Marginson 2017) offer an account of the potential social justice aims of higher education entirely in terms of the long-standing humanist narrative which takes human exceptionalism for granted as a *sine qua non* of higher education. Such an account elides the fact that nonhuman bodies of all kinds (rats, mice, dogs, rabbits amongst others)—along with the agencies of life (microbes, genes, stem cells)—have been routinely destroyed and experimented upon as subjects or simply 'stuff' in servitude to the relentless push for progress via knowledges which are hamstrung and in hock to capitalism's imperious spread.

Higher Education

So, the 'and yet' matters as a gesture to other ways of doing, being, becoming, sensing, feeling, relating and knowing within the capacious venture which is higher education. While any posthuman moves towards that 'architecture of possibilities and pleasures' Sword refers to above are enmeshed within the marketisation, hierarchization and competition that neoliberalism has undoubtedly ushered in, it is, surely, a false premise to think that *all* of learning, teaching and research is conditioned and contained by these imperatives. Something escapes, as Kathleen Stewart (2007) would say, something always escapes. Posthuman pedagogy, practice and research is about seeking out those 'and yets', those escapes, being open to them when they arise, riding on them and with them, co-creating them, giving them space to happen, attending to them, and embedding them in curricula, materials, methods, and intra-actions, so that, as teachers, researchers and learners, we can attend in more nuanced ways to what matters (and how and why and to whom and when). Tending towards the 'and yet' as a mode of joyful life-affirming 'doing otherwise' in higher education can, then, help support us to 'think beyond and outside dominant representations of higher education as a contemporary time-space damaged beyond repair by neoliberalism, and of HE learning and teaching as [already] irremediably deformed' (Taylor 2018).

Zoe

A number of chapters locate these tendencies in relation-with Braidotti's (2013: 194) notion of '*zoe*', with the view that 'becoming posthuman is regulated by an ethics of joy and affirmation that functions through the transformation of negative into positive passions.' Thus, in Chapter 13, Kay Sidebottom conjoins Hlavajova's (2015) injunction that 'art [i]s a thing that does' with Braidotti's 'potentia' in an ethically-affirmative pedagogic move which introduces artistic approaches into curricula designed to develop teacher trainees as 'reflective practitioners.' In Chapter 4, Candace Kuby and David Aguayo present a manifesto for disrupting traditional approaches to qualitative research in which they note how pedagogy-with-philosophy orients us—as students and teachers—to the world's becoming, so that we may know, feel, relate and become in ways that foregrounded the tensions and politics of qualitative inquiry. Their manifesto is an ethical invitation to a pedagogy of messiness, difference and productive unsettle-ment. And Katie Strom and John Lupinacci, in Chapter 6, inflect Braidotti's notion of affirmative ethics with Barad's (2007) ethico-onto-epistemology, to show how the development of posthuman frameworks for leadership education can work as an ethical imperative in an era of the anthropocene. They argue that the depredations wrought by runaway capitalism, the damage caused by climate change to habitat, and the suffering arising from impoverishment puts many humans and nonhumans in peril. Their pedagogic interventions show how relational ethics can be put to work to forge connection, solidarity and collaboration through entangled thinking-becoming-knowing.

Ethico-Onto-Epistemology

Who, when watching the BBC1 television documentary, *Drowning in Plastic* (BBC 2018) and seeing the 260 individual pieces of plastic found in just one flesh-footed shearwater dead chick's stomach can fail to be sickened by what we have put into the ocean? Who, going to http://www.atlas.d-waste.com, a scientific open source map that visualizes solid waste management data from all over the world, and clicking on 'sanitary landfills' and 'dumpsites' can fail to be horrified at the global extent and location of rubbish and trash, and the many millions (estimates vary between 15 and 45 million) of people who live on, near or survive in relation to such dumps? And who, reading about Cuvier, White, Lyell and Darwin and the establishment in the nineteenth century of evolutionary-based explanations (aka racist justifications) of racial extermination—one of which entailed the violent, systematic, government-funded and organised killing of every last indigenous inhabitant of Tasmania by 1876 (Lindqvist 1997)—can fail to be (… please add your own word here because words failed me at this point …) at the euro-western annihilations carried out under the banner of progress and civilisation? Looking at this, and other abundant evidence, who would demur that a new ethico-onto-epistemological contract is needed?

Zoe-philia, which posits optimistic, non-anthropocentric, ecologically oriented modes of nonhuman-human being and becoming, seems to offer that new onto-epistemological-ethical contract. *Zoe*-philia's grounding in a-personal life energies and vitalities suggests new ethical modes of connectivity, responsibility and accountability, and sounds a sorely needed note of ontological hope beyond the shrivelled scope of capitalist-patriarchal-racist-colonial means and ends which have wrought such devastating damage on the planet's infrastructure and lifeforms. Such hope is needed right now in higher education. Posthuman approaches aim to place higher education with-in-relation-to worldly concerns, positioning it, in Barad's terms, not in the world or part of the world but *of* the world. As Barad (2007: 184) says, 'we are not outside observers of the world. Neither are we simply located at particular places in the world; rather, we are part of the world in its ongoing intra-activity'. The revaluation of value offered by *zoe*-philia is undergirded by a more capacious sense of human-nonhuman onto-ethical flourishing and is generative of more profoundly hopeful modes of knowing—including affect, sensuousness, relationality, intuition, hap-hazard, experiment and love—which seem to offer better epistemological alternatives to the self-centred arrogance of human exceptionalism and the forms of knowing—cognitive, individualised, objectivising, specular—it requires and promotes. One practical instance of how such an ethico-onto-epistemology can be put to work via posthuman pedagogy, practice and research can be found in Chapter 20, written by Vivienne Bozalek, Michalinos Zembylas and Tamara Shefer. Their manifesto for response-able (peer) reviewing shows how to reshape an often destructive, critical, competitive and anonymous process of judgement, via expansive modes of ethical response-ability, into one that is care-full, attentive and affirmative. Another is provided by johnmichael rossi in Chapter 11 whose resistance to the pressures of the Corporate University Complex utilizes Slowness as a mode of Practical Artistic Research and whose emergent Playper offers a diffractive, multi-linear narrative for collaborative learning.

Im/Patience

If you are impatient to proceed—especially if you are keen to urge others to take their fracking foot off the fracking gas/plastic/meat/commodity producing pedal so that humans and other species may thrive together in more wholesome ways—you may be im/patient with the injunction to hang on or, rather, hang about. To stay awhile. To slow down. Donna Haraway (2010: 177) talks about the '*specific* work to be done if we are to strike up a coherent form of life' and that 'refiguring conversations with those who are not "us" must be part of the project'. Such heterogeneous conversations are not easy and are certainly not quick. As Haraway later (2016: 10–11) notes, multispecies recuperation is likely to be 'partial' and 'modest', requiring attention to 'complex histories that are as full of dying as living', but however partial and flawed it is, such recuperation is, she thinks, 'still possible' in conditions where 'response-ability [can] be cobbled together.'

Haraway's phrase for such work is 'staying with the trouble' which, as Strom and Lupinacci in Chapter 6 point out, is humble and hard work. Such work asks us to stop, dwell, contemplate deeply, inhale, focus, face the problem fully in its difficulties *and* to (try to) attend to what's going on meanwhile in the spaces where small and large injustices occur when no-one is apparently looking, or are deliberately looking the other way. If such work is part of the work that needs to be done to craft an ethical posthuman mode of being-and-becoming-with, then it is a sort of relentless work of ongoing risk in which the joys and pleasures will be hard won—and it needs to be if it can at least begin to address (again and again) the brutal legacies of the Enlightenment fantasies and humanist follies which continue to shape everyday lives. Haraway (2016) finds the term 'posthumanism' inadequate to the task of staying with the trouble. Posthumanism, for her, is allied to Anthropocentric narratives as a History of Progress, Development and Civilisation; a history which centres on Species Man and his Deeds and Sciences; and whose history is intimately linked to the Future as a Coming Chaos, an Apocalypse of Scarcity and Death, in which only those possessing Technological or Biogenetic means to extract or engineer new resources will Survive, unless we develop the Scientific Tools to take us to new planets to Colonise.

All of those capitals are deliberate: a way of mocking the grand narrative of human exceptionalism that anthropocentrism entails because I agree with Haraway (2016: 49) that 'bad actors need a story, but not the whole story … Species Man does not make history.' If posthumanism is to be worth anything as a scholarly and political project, then, it has to make do and mend in and with stories oriented to ongoingness; with knowledges which work with and towards 'webbed, braided, and tentacular' worldings (Haraway 2016: 49); and with multiply twisted, linked and enmeshed historical lineages. From these, it has to co-compose practice/ings which are relational, sympoietic and ethically sustainable for all participants. Such un/en/foldings would make posthumanism worthy of the disruptive and affirmative power it is often said to have and, if positioned as central to the aims, purposes, hopes and aspirations of higher education pedagogy, curricula, practice and research, might ('might' rather than 'can' is appropriate to the contingent, unfinished and problematic nature of this positioning) increase possibilities for liveable and flourishing lives. The slowing down, hanging around, the work of the now and the meantime I alluded to above, is necessary in order to begin to re-think and re-imagine ways in which higher education, when based in a commitment to the ethical-political project of de-acceleration, might be engaged as a critically posthuman endeavour able to 'contribute to the collective construction of social horizons of hope' (Braidotti 2018: 11).

One possible response to this challenge is outlined in Chapter 9, *Staying with the Trouble in Science Education: Towards Thinking with Nature*. Marc Higgins, Maria F. G. Wallace and Jesse Bazzul's manifesto explores the multiple ways in which science education continues to uphold problematic enactments of power, and calls for a slower critical science education based on two principles: (1) science education needs to think, but not like that; and (2) science education must think otherwise, but not like that. Such care-full work of thinking, they suggest, is about facing the urgent work of building and sustaining social and ecological relations while not being waylaid by the temporality of emergency.

Decolonization

A long time ago when I was a student at Leeds University I walked home past a giant billboard. While I cannot remember the product being advertised (it was either a car, or tyres, or petrol) I remember the image: A huge American car in the foreground zooming along a deserted white road, immediately behind it a sign with three words naming the product, its brand and its quality, behind that a dusty, parched landscape with cactus trees, distant hills, a small wooden building, and an overbearingly blue sky with radiating sun. In the foreground a dirty looking child with big black eyes. The tagline across the top: 'these are the only three words of English he knows.' Some athletic graffiti artist had scaled the advertisement's huge structure to spray paint out the three advertiser's words and add their own in their place: Yankee Go Home. Those words made me smile every time I walked past.

Many years later, I encounter Tuck and Yang's (2012: 1) work. They say: 'decolonization brings about the repatriation of Indigenous land and life; it is not a metaphor for other things we want to do to improve our societies and schools.' This statement throws into sharp relief recent moves in the UK to 'decolonize the higher education curriculum' and raises worries about the ease with which the language of decolonization might be appropriated as a means to produce superficial changes which serve to enclose decolonization within White theory and practice. Approaches such as 'add some Indigenous or Black authors to your course reading list' can, therefore, only be a useful start; such moves do not close down the need for the much more difficult—and profoundly unsettling—work of decolonization. In Tuck and Yang's words: 'The too-easy adoption of decolonizing discourse (making decolonization a metaphor) … problematically attempt[s] to reconcile settler guilt and complicity, and rescue settler futurity.'

Tuck and Yang's work also brings to mind recent protests about racism, white supremacism and decolonization arising from the #RhodesMustFall movement at the University of Cape Town in South Africa, then at Oriel College in Oxford University, UK. In Cape Town, the statue of Cecil Rhodes—racist coloniser and architect of apartheid—has been removed. In Oxford, it remains in place, subject to equivocation about adding a plaque to provide more historical contextualization, and generating debates in high-end newspapers about how Rhodes was not worse than any other coloniser. In other places, imperialist statues of Great White Men have begun to be quietly removed. In the USA, for example, up to 30 Confederate monuments have been removed, but the statue of Robert E. Lee in Charlottesville, protests against which resulted in the death of Heather Heyer, remains in place currently protected by Virginia state law. In Budapest, Memento Park is an open air museum housing Soviet statues removed from the city after the fall of communism. In Delhi, Coronation Park corrals statues of the British Raj that previously littered the city. Such instances of dis-placement matter in memorialising a certain line of history and in enabling that particular line to be positioned by, and put in relation with, other histories, histories which tell of desires for a future free of colonial rule.

So, statues matter. Statues are material monuments to a particular version of the past told by those who seized, wielded and abused power, who used their privilege to legitimize their rule, establish their 'civilising' schools and universities, and institute their laws, culture and norms—all of which cast long shadows. As Gray van Heerden (2018) notes, universities in South Africa remain largely eurocentric spaces, they are severely underfunded with the burden of fee increases falling most heavily on African and coloured (mixed-race) students, and, as yet, no university or college has seriously addressed decolonization. Her proposal, to enact higher education pedagogies which politicize ontology, so that personal and situated knowledges can be woven into a posthuman assemblage which undoes authorized knowledge production, is one mode of effectuating socially just pedagogies, and one which chimes with many authors' approaches in this book.

However, the point remains: Statues matter but statues are not land. The removal of a statue is, perhaps, little more than a symbolic peccadillo in decolonization terms and one quite easily oriented as a 'move to innocence [which] relieve[s] the settler of feelings of guilt or responsibility without giving up land or power or privilege, without having to change much at all' (Tuck and Yang 2012: 10). Here, 'settler' is not coterminous with 'coloniser.' As Tuck and Yang (2012: 5) explain: 'Settler colonialism is different from other forms of colonialism in that settlers come with the intention of making a new home on the land, a homemaking that insists on settler sovereignty over all things in their new domain.' This insistence necessarily (in order to establish their dominion) entails the material, ontological and epistemological destruction and disappearance of the Indigenous peoples who live there. Settlers may themselves be racialized and minoritized colonial subjects, themselves victims of colonial displacement, which 'exponentially complicates what is meant by decolonization, and by solidarity, against settler colonial forces' (Tuck and Yang 2012: 7).

Geopolitics of Knowledg(e)ing(s)

It is, perhaps, not surprising, then, that scholars who work within decolonization practices and Indigenous studies—and for whom the term 'anthropocene' is likely to be 'a term most easily meaningful and usable by intellectuals in wealthy classes and regions' (Haraway 2016: 49)—put forward the most piercing critiques of posthumanism. Hinton et al. (2014: 2) point out that posthumanism and new materialisms 'still miss a strong link with post- and de-colonial theories as well as with critical race and migration studies' studies. Hinton et al. (2014) cite Panelli's (2010) work which suggests that posthuman geographies remain largely located within eurocentric scholarship, and Sundberg's (2014) view that posthumanism largely reproduces colonial ways of knowing and being because, in taking the nature/culture dualisms as a point of departure, it continues to work within western epistemological frameworks. Such critiques add heft to the view that posthumanism and new materialism's 'white episteme' and its constitution as a white academic field is bound up with the geopolitical materialization of racialized modes of knowledge production, points which are extended and amplified by Rosiek and Snyder (2018) whose incisive insights highlight the problematic elisions and erasures that posthuman scholarship has to address if it is to engage meaningfully with Indigenous concerns.

One such concern is the presumption of ontological agency of nonhuman entities such as objects, animals and nature which is often seen as a novel and central principle of various brands of posthumanism and new materialism, including Actor Network Theory, agential realism, thing theory, and object-oriented ontology (although it is fair to say that the differences between these theories is as important as their similarities). Rosiek and Snyder (2018: 2) point out that the idea of other-than-human agency is 'not new' but has 'received sustained development and application in Indigenous studies literature and Indigenous traditions of thought and practice.' Indeed, they say:

Many Indigenous studies' scholars have taken nonhuman agency as a given in their social and philosophical analysis and, thus, have more experience working out its practical and performative implications (e.g., through protocols for working with places and land, protocols for acknowledging the stakes of nonhuman entities in deliberative processes, ceremonies that acknowledge reciprocal ethical relations with nonhuman agents, a vocabulary that frames nonhuman entities as agential and ethically significant).

A second concern regards the role played by reading and citation practices in communicating, reproducing and potentially changing dominant knowledge-making practices. Feminists—see Sara Ahmed (2017: 16) on citation as 'feminist bricks … the materials through which, from which, we create our dwellings,' and Feminist Educators Against Sexism's cite club at https://feministeducatorsagainstsexism.com/cite-club/—have long discussed how citation practices do powerful work in reconfirming the eminence of white male theorists. Rosiek and Snyder (2018: 3) make an equally powerful point about indigenous scholarship:

> Unfortunately, Indigenous studies' scholarship is frequently overlooked in the current discussions about agent ontology among settler colonial social scientists. If read, it is rarely cited or substantively engaged. The politics and economies of citation are no doubt complex, but one must assume that the dearth of engagement reflects the influence of settler colonialist ideologies (Rosiek, Snyder, & Pratt, in press). Such ideologies frame Indigenous studies' literature as an expression of simplistic identity politics. It frames this literature as lacking the theoretical rigor of methodology scholarship grounded in continental philosophy. Such views are simply false and indefensible and can only be sustained by failing to read this literature.

Surely it behoves those (of us) who are allied with posthumanisms and (new) materialisms to do something to contend with these critiques? Perhaps that 'something' might at least begin with extending our own reading and our citations so that we take up Haraway's (2016) call for 'response-ability' which refuses to put the onus on people of colour to 'tell [us] what to do' because 'you're the experts here' (Mawhinney, cited in Tuck and Yang 2012: 10).

Such work requires thoughtfulness, humility and dedication, engendering as it should difficult encounters and conversations. It demands that we be 'more impatient with each other' (Tuck and Yang 2012: 10) so that we are less likely to accept false smoothnesses, platitudinous inclusions or easy reconciliations. Thinking *and doing* 'decolonization as material, not metaphor', according to Tuck and Yang (2012: 28), might be best considered, and effectuated, as 'an ethic of incommensurability', as always only ever possible via 'strategic and contingent collaborations [because] lasting solidarities may be elusive, even undesirable.' That, they think, is the sort of 'unsettling' that is required. Such an unsettling, they contend, is preferable to the 'dangerous understanding of uncommonality that un-coalesces coalition politics' (ibid.: 35) but it will, no doubt, 'feel very unfriendly' because unsettling means, to return to the point, that decolonization is 'accountable to Indigenous sovereignty and futurity' and that means repatriating land.

Two chapters in this collection speak into these debates, suggesting ways in which posthuman higher education practices might, with the necessary im/patience, attend to these concerns. In Chapter 17, Marc Higgins and Brooke Madden pursue the question posed by Ahenakew (2017: 81), 'how can we (re)learn to listen to and be taught by the land, in the context of ongoing efforts to objectify, to commodify, to silence, or to speak for the land?' Their chapter, 'Refiguring Presences in Kichwa-Lamista Territories: Natural-cultural (Re)storying with Indigenous Place', engages with the (never innocent) task of acknowledging, accounting for, and being ethically accountable to Indigenous place (as more than 'nature'). Using 'decolonial ethics of unsettling presences and absences' (Nxumalo and Cedillo 2017: 104) to orient their work, Marc and Brooke attend to absent presences (e.g. curriculum of Land as settler property and economic resource) and present absences (e.g. Indigenous resurgence) and discuss how Indigenous relational ontologies—with deep roots in living places and spiritual practices—enhanced their understanding of their role in reimagining pedagogy, practice and research in higher education. Jeannie Kerr, in Chapter 18, tells of her work engaging teacher education candidates of predominantly Settler and newer immigrant backgrounds with Indigenous knowledges, pedagogies and perspectives to inform their developing K-12 classroom praxis. Situated in the context of the Truth and Reconciliation Commission of Canada which seeks to acknowledge the dispossession and displacement of Indigenous peoples in relation to their territories, she uses Barad's (2014) concept of *re-turning* to suggest four ways in which new materialist theorizing has potential to disrupt the problematic epistemic certainties that arise from euro-western thought and practice and which condition, and serve to preclude, Settler students from forming an ethical relationship with Indigenous peoples, knowledges and territories.

We

All of this rightly calls attention to, and radically complicates, any easy assumptions about who 'we' are, who 'we' can be and become, who 'we' can/should/might want to speak for, and who 'we' include/are including when we use the word 'we.' As Annouchka Bayley notes in Chapter 21, 'we' need to proceed with care and caution with this particular word, particularly when making statements about how 'we' have 'cut the world into pieces.' Posthumanist engagements happily draw their theoretical scope wide, using inter-trans-multi-and post-disciplinary approaches to break down malestream forms of knowledge that work to discipline knowing within pre-determined tram tracks and guide ropes. That posthumanist and new materialist thinking can put theory to work in such ways to ask different questions, produce hybrid and innovative methodologies, and provoke different answers is a good thing because, as I mention elsewhere, this vastly expands the range and variety of conceptual resources available in educational pedagogy, practice and research and opens novel, multiple and heterogeneous knowledge pathways (Taylor 2016a). But, it is worth re-membering—and I mean re-member as in putting bodies (of knowledge) (back) together to generate non-dominant ways of knowing, being and doing— that Indigenous, Black, feminist, decolonial scholarship is not to be deployed by White scholars as means to 'support' or 'scaffold' posthumanist/new materialist accounts. As Todd (2016: 18), citing Indigenous scholar Dwayne Donald, says, 'The systems through which thought is produced in the Euro-Western academy would do well to incorporate the reciprocity Donald (2009: 6) references in his work on 'ethical relationality':

> Ethical relationality is an ecological understanding of human relationality that does not deny difference, but rather seeks to more deeply understand how our different histories and experiences position us in relation to each other. This form of relationality is ethical because it does not overlook or invisibilize the particular historical, cultural, and social contexts from which a particular person understands and experiences living in the world. It puts these considerations at the forefront of engagements across frontiers of difference.'

Such engagements across 'frontiers of difference' are, precisely what constituting any posthuman 'we' needs to entail: 'we is not a foundation but what we are working towards. By working out what we are for, we are working out that *we*' (Ahmed 2017: 2). Any posthuman 'we' worth being part of is an ongoing and questioning struggle animated by practices of hope and difficulty. Only in such differentiating un/en/foldings might posthumanism and new materialism present the means to think through the 'possibility of possibility' (Hinton and van der Tuin 2014: 6).

However, realizing the possibility of possibility is not easy. Indeed, if we pursue Barad's (2007) point that every intra-action matters with seriousness, then every pedagogic, practice or research instance could conceivably be reconceptualized as an ongoing, delicate and necessary engagement with a 'we' made anew moment by moment. There are glimmers of how this might be done in Chapter 15, for example, where Karin Murris and Cara Borcherds discuss a painful *and* affirmative pedagogic process emanating from a bodymind mapping provocation which shifted a Childhood Studies course into a mode of 'teaching without teaching' and effected new ideas about child and childhood. And Evelien Geerts in Chapter 7 talks us through a journey she went on with her students while teaching a course on feminist philosophy and new materialisms and how a series of daily acts of resistance against the neoliberal corporatization of the university helped to contest the monologic, dialectical nature of the Western philosophical canon in intersecting and energizing ways. Working-with/working-through a posthuman imaginary for a more inclusive higher education means forging a 'we' in ways which mobilize desires and affects in contentious and collaborative ways.

Authorship

At the end of Chapter 7 Evelien Geerts included a list of acknowledgements as follows:

> The author would like to thank the editors of this book volume, Carol Taylor and Annouchka Bayley, together with Clare Hammoor, for their affirmative, constructive feedback. Special thanks go out to my undergraduate students at the University of California, Santa Cruz for their generosity; to Donna Haraway for our wonderful pedagogical lunch conversation in Santa Cruz in 2016; to Bettina Aptheker for teaching me all about feminist pedagogies; to Maija Butters, Delphi Carstens, Lou Mycroft and Kay Sidebottom – my posthumanist companions – and to Iris van der Tuin for her mentorship, and for inviting me to participate in a panel on diffractive pedagogies during the ACLA in Utrecht in 2017.

Evelien's homage (femage?) gives me a helpful handhold to elaborate a particular point about authorship in posthuman mode in higher education: Authorship is always a collaborative process even when there is only one name at the 'top' of the page. So often, one name—that of a bounded human individual—subsumes all the nonhuman, thingly and human others which/who have influenced what materializes on the page, a page which is attended by ghostly presences who hover lovingly at its edge. Acknowledging posthuman authorship as a confederate mattering matters to me because I have a lead role in my university department for the REF—the UK Research Excellence Framework which requires all academics on teaching and research contracts to submit up to five 'outputs' which are then rated on a 1–4 star rating scale in a national rating exercise conducted every six or seven years. The REF intensifies the competitive and individualistic (and divisive and structurally unequal) machine of contemporary higher education, and its lauding of 4 star papers segues all too easily into the lauding of 4 star academics—those heroic individuals of single-authored publications with high citations in the best/top journals—as a better breed of personage, deserving of better pay, perks and pension.

Instead, let's consider authorship as copoiesis (Haraway 2016), as transindividual subjectivity (Spinoza 2002), as close encounters in embodied diffractive musing (Taylor 2016b). Considered thus, the gang who inform my writing help me travel wider and deeper and further; their comings and goings are often *unheimlich*, unbidden, fortuitous, happenstance; and they bring me things I didn't know I needed until they appear. I welcome them because they push, shove, goad, cheer and encourage me on; they are my familiars, my secret-sharers, my friends and sometimes my unfriends, helping me in subtle, tendentious, imaginative, energising, maddening, critical, provoking, kind, care-full, and ingenious ways with the hard and joyful work of reading-writing-thinking. Authorship as confederation. Authoring as spinning, yarning, circling, hands-bodies-minds engaged in affective-affirmative-intellectual-sensory comings-to-knowing-and-being. Authoring as material polyphony in which there is 'no "I" separate from the intra-active becoming of the world' (Barad 2007: 394).

One implication of this: It matters what concepts we think with, how we un/en/fold ourselves with concepts, and where and how we travel with them. Lesley Gourlay in Chapter 14 uses Barad's concept of 'apparatus' to consider the nature of texts, devices, the writer and the notion of authorship in the digital university setting, and draws attention to how textual practices are material practices *are already* posthuman meaning-making practices which are socially, politically, temporally and physically situated. In Chapter 5, Sonja Arndt and Marek Tesar re-examine Julia Kristeva's theory on the subject in process to effect a philosophical-pragmatic bridge which affirms the humanity in conceptions of posthumanism and elevates the complications of the 'human I' in posthuman becomings. They situate the complicated-ness of how this endeavour affects their pedagogies in relation to multiple cultural obligations arising from the Treaty of Waitangi in Aotearoa New Zealand. Sarah Hepler, Susan Cannon, Courtney Hartnett and Teri

Peitso-Holbrook in Chapter 8 use Haraway's concept of diffraction to focus on work emerging from their experiencing/being/thinking posthumanist reading group in which readings-writings are entangled in novel texturizings that bring new texts into being, texts which refuse to get straightened out by the linearities of usual academic writing practices, prompting them to ask the crucial question: What other stories can we write? Using concepts in the 'unrestrained' ways evident in these chapters is, in the manner of Deleuze and Guattari, a useful way of focusing 'a set of circumstances, at a volatile juncture' (Massumi 1988: xiii).

Another implication of this: It matters that educational experience can be conceived as an ethic of joy, in which learning is related to material conditions of possibility for action, transformation and resistance. Here, I am drawing on Tamboukou (2018) who, following Spinoza, proposes that education considered as 'a joyful agonistic process brings in imagination, active affects, reason, the gradual formation of adequate ideas and ultimately intuitive understanding, as the highest level of knowledge'. This prompts knowing in/as-becoming. This suggests knowledge as adventure. This opens learning to and, and, and—knowledge as rhizome, assemblage, map—in which what matters, also in the manner of Deleuze and Guattari, is not 'is it true. But does it work? What new thoughts does it make it possible to think?' (Massumi 1988: xv).

Ruptures-Reconfigurings-Refusings

The concept-practice of student engagement has done a great deal of hard work in the international terrain of higher education over the last 20 years, bringing into its orbit multiple aspects of students' learning, knowing and experiencing in and beyond the classroom and making them available to measurement. The USA and Canada have the National Survey of Student Engagement (NSSE), established in 1998 and first administered in 2000 which is the oldest of the international SE measurement systems. The UK has the National Student Survey (NSS) which began in 2005 and was quickly absorbed into national government policy frameworks. The Australasian Survey of Student Engagement (AUSSE) was first run in 2007 in Australian and

New Zealand HE institutions. In the Netherlands, there is the NSE; in China, there is the China College Student Survey (CCSS) and the National College Student Survey (NCSS); and in India, the Indian Student Survey (ISS)—inspired by the UK's NSS—was launched as a pilot in 2017. Before long, the student whose 'satisfaction' is not available for measurement will be a rare beast.

While such measurements can guide lecturers' reflection on teaching and learning and help enhance students' learning (Taylor 2012), they are also often co-opted into authoritarian and bureaucratic managerial regimes of surveillance and control which produce stress and damage staff morale. Under conditions of tighter fiscal restraint, results from student surveys can be used to justify cuts to courses and effect staff redundancies. The economic instrumentalism that now shapes global higher education and which has intensified competition for students also means that institutions willingly press student surveys into service to highlight the 'quality' and 'excellence' of their learning, teaching and research in national, international and global league tables. Student surveys, harnessed as evidence-machines in shaping higher education as measurable input-output, fall far short of the posthuman pedagogic passions of those who wish to shape learning as an experimental adventure aimed at enhancing students' engagement in the love and joy of learning. This book contains a good dose of such experimental learning adventures, crafted by educators who themselves are learning by doing pedagogy, practice and research otherwise—by trying things out, by having a go, by seeing what happens if…?

Evelyn O'Malley, in Chapter 3, presents a diffractive autoethnography—a writing-learning-teaching eco-dramaturgical experimental practice with undergraduate students on a BA (Hons) Drama programme which entangles students in plays, theory, weather, spirits, spaces, objects, grass, jokes, mud, statistics, phlegm, air, stage directions, paper, crayons, breath, rain, and and and. These ands help rupture higher education pedagogy-as-usual; they help reconceptualise assessment by altering what a 'portfolio' can be and become; and they help to recast the ego-centric 'I' of competitive individualism by mobilising pedagogic possibilities for, in Evelyn's words, thinking of ourselves as less than exceptional. In Chapter 12, Amanda Hatton discusses the use of a multisensory activity using objects which aimed to support Childhood Studies undergraduates in developing both a new sense of research and a more affective understanding of childrens' experiences. In Chapter 2, Bente Ulla, Ninni Sandvik, Ann Sofi Larsen, Mette Røe Nyhus, Nina Johannesen work with the co-operative forces unleashed by the sound of scissors in a Masters programme in Norway, showing how the joyful and critical fuss produced by four speculative 'flashtags' wove personal, professional and political dimensions together to produce new creations and re-imaginings.

For Higher Education

And so, as an un/conclusion to this un/en/folding, I want to say thank you (if you are still here/there) for staying with me through these rhizomic musings regarding the pleasures, possibilities and pains that attend posthuman, new materialist endeavours to do higher education differently. Doing higher education pedagogy, practice and research otherwise than business-as-usual unleashes both vulnerability and response-ability and requires passionate powers and daredevil thoughts (to borrow the words of Bente-Ninni-Ann Sofi-Mette-Nina-students) because the work of refusing the usual and creating spaces for play-full ruptures and generative reconfigurings is full of risk, mess and difficulty. Those inspired by the possibilities of a more experimental, more capacious, higher education—a higher education brought into being in the 'scrumpled geography [of] disadjustment, destabilization, and disjointure' (Doel 1996)—can take heart from recent Indigenous, decolonizing, feminist, post-qualitative, new materialist, posthuman research, such as Benozzo et al. 2016; Bozalek et al. 2018; Cajete 1994; Koro-Ljungberg 2016; Manning and Massumi 2014; Taylor and Hughes 2016; Van der Tuin 2015 (and see reference lists throughout this book!). My hope, reader, is that you will be lured by curiosity and that your own byways, highways, detours and joyrides help generate a more capacious higher education, an education of 'adding to' which, as Stengers (2018: 128) notes, is about 'accepting that what we add makes a difference to the world' and it is our responsibility to 'answer for the manner of this difference.'

References

Ahenakew, C. (2017). Mapping and complicating conversations about indigenous education. *Diaspora, Indigenous, and Minority Education, 11*(2), 80–91.

Ahmed, S. (2017). *Living a feminist life*. London: Duke University Press.

Alveson, M. (2013). *The triumph of emptiness. Consumption, higher education and work organization*. Oxford: Oxford University Press.

Barad, K. (2007). *Meeting the universe halfway: Quantum physics and the entanglement of matter and meaning*. Durham: Duke University Press.

Barad, K. (2014). Diffracting diffraction: Cutting together-apart. *Parallax, 20*(3), 168–187.

BBC. (2018). *A year on from Blue Planet II, BBC one film reveals the devastating consequences of the plastic pollution crisis in our oceans*. Retrieved from https://www.bbc.co.uk/mediacentre/latestnews/2018/drowning-in-plastic.

Benozzo, A., Koro-Ljungberg, M., & Carey, N. (2016). Five or more IKEA customers in search of an author. *Qualitative Inquiry, 22*, 568–580.

Bozalek, V., Braidotti, R., Shefer, T., & Zembylas, M. (Eds.). (2018). *Socially just pedagogies: Posthumanist, feminist and materialist perspectives in higher education*. London: Bloomsbury.

Braidotti, R. (2013). *The posthuman*. Cambridge: Polity Press.

Braidotti, R. (2018). A theoretical framework for the critical posthumanities. *Theory, Culture & Society*. https://doi.org/10.1177/0263276418771486.

Brown, R., & Carasso, H. (2013). *Everything for sale: The marketization of UK higher education*. London: Routledge/Society for Research into Higher Education.

Cajete, G. (1994). *Look to the mountain: An ecology of indigenous education*. Skyland, NC: Kivaki Press.

Cantwell, B., & Kauppinen, I. (2014). *Academic capitalism in the age of globalization*. Baltimore, MD: John Hopkins University Press.

Carrigan, M. (2016). *The accelerated academy*. Retrieved from http://sociologicalimagination.org/archives/18743. Accessed 18 December 2018.

Collini, S. (2017). *Speaking of universities*. London: Verso.

de Freitas, E., & Sinclair, N. (2012). Diagram, gesture, agency: Theorizing embodiment in the mathematics classroom. *Educational Studies in Mathematics, 80*(1/2), 133–152.

Deleuze, G. (2006). *The fold*. London: Continuum.

Doel, M. A. (1996). A hundred thousand lines of flight: A machinic introduction to the nomad thought and scrumpled geography of Gilles Deleuze and Felix Guattari. *Environment and Planning D: Society and Space, 14*(4), 421–439.

Donald, D. (2009). Forts, curriculum, and indigenous metissage: Imagining decolonization of aboriginal-canadian relations in educational contexts. *First Nations Perspectives, 2*(1), 1–24.

Gabriel, D., & Tate, S. A. (Eds.). (2017). *Inside the ivory tower: Narratives of women of colour surviving and thriving in British academia*. London: Trentham Books.

Giroux, H. (2014). *Neoliberalism's war on higher education*. Chicago: Haymarket Books.

Gray van Heerden, C. (2018). #Itmustallfall, or, pedagogy for a people to come. In V. Bozalek, R. Braidotti, T. Shefer, & M. Zembylas (Eds.), *Socially just pedagogies: Posthumanist, feminist and materialist perspectives in higher education*. London: Bloomsbury.

Greene, M. (1977). Toward wide-awakeness: An argument for the arts and humanities in education. *Issues in Focus, 79*(1), 119–125.

Haraway, D. (2010). Otherworldly conversations, terran topics, local terms. In S. Alaimo & S. Hekman (Eds.), *Material feminisms* (pp. 157–187). Bloomington: Indiana University Press.

Haraway, D. (2016). *Staying with the trouble*. Durham: Duke University Press.

Hinton, P., & van der Tuin, I. (2014). Preface. *Women: A Cultural Review, 25*(1), 1–8.

Hinton, P., Mehrabi, T., & Barla, J. (2014). *New materialisms/new colonialisms*. Position paper for New Materialisms: How Matter Comes to Matter. COST. ISI3017. Retrieved from http://newmaterialism.eu/wp-content/uploads/2015/12/Subgroup-Position-Paper-_-New-materialisms_New-Colonialisms.pdf.

Hlavajova, M. (2015, August 26). *Critique-as-proposition: Thinking about, with, and through art in our time*. Utrecht: University of Utrecht.

Ingold, T. (2011). *Being alive. Essays on movement, knowledge and description*. New York, NY: Routledge.

Jackson, C., Dempster, S., & Pollard, L. (2015). 'They just don't seem to really care, they just think it's cool to sit there and talk': Laddism in university teaching-learning contexts. *Educational Review, 67*(3), 300–314.

Koro-Ljungberg, M. (2016). *Reconceptualizing qualitative research. Methodologies without methodology*. London: Sage.

Lindqvist, S. (1997). *Exterminate all the brutes*. London: Granta Publications.

Manning, E., & Massumi, B. (2014). *Thought in the act: Passages of ecology of experience*. Minneapolis: Minnesota University Press.

Marginson, S. (2017). Limitations of human capital theory. *Studies in Higher Education*. https://doi.org/10.1080/03075079.2017.1359823.

Massumi, B. (1988). Translator's foreword. Pleasure of philosophy. In G. Deleuze & F. Guattari (Eds.), *A thousand plateaus: Capitalism and schizophrenia*. London: Continuum.

Naidoo, R. (2016). The competition fetish in higher education: Varieties, animators and consequences. *British Journal of Sociology of Education, 37*(1), 1–10.

Nxumalo, F., & Cedillo, S. (2017). Decolonizing place in early childhood studies: Thinking with indigenous onto-epistemologies and Black feminist geographies. *Global Studies of Childhood, 7*(2), 99–112.

Panelli, R. (2010). More-than-human social geographies: Posthuman and other possibilities. *Progress in Human Geography, 34*(3), 79–87.

Phipps, A. (2018). Reckoning up: Sexual harassment and violence in the neoliberal university. *Gender and Education*. https://doi.org/10.1080/09540253.2018.1482413.

Rosiek, J., & Snyder, J. (2018). Narrative inquiry and new materialism: Stories as (not necessarily benign) agents. *Qualitative Inquiry*, 1–12. https://doi.org/10.1778/1007471808074814837286326.

Smith, L. T. (2012). *Decolonizing methodologies: Research and indigenous peoples*. London: Zed Books.

Spinoza, B. (2002). *Ethics*. London: Everyman.

Stengers, I. (2018). *Another science is possible: A manifesto for slow science*. Cambridge: Polity Press.

Stewart, K. (2007). *Ordinary affects*. Durham, NC: Duke University Press.

Sundberg, J. (2014). Decolonizing posthumanist geographies. *Cultural Geographies, 21*(1), 33–47.

Sword, H. (2017). *Air and light and time and space: How successful academics write*. Cambridge, MA: Harvard University Press.

Tamboukou, M. (2018). The joy of learning: Feminist materialist pedagogies and the freedom of education. *Educational Philosophy and Theory, 50*(9), 868–877.

Taylor, C. A. (2012). Student engagement, practice architectures and *phronesis* in the student transitions and experiences project. *Journal of Applied Research in Higher Education, 4*(2), 109–125.

Taylor, C. A. (2016a). Edu-crafting a cacophonous ecology: Posthuman research practices for education. In C. A. Taylor & C. Hughes (Eds.), *Posthuman research practices in education* (pp. 7–36). London: Palgrave Macmillan.

Taylor, C. A. (2016b). Close encounters of a critical kind: A diffractive musing in/between new material feminism and object-oriented ontology. *Cultural Studies—Critical Methodologies, 16*(2), 201–212.

Taylor, C. A. (2018). Edu-crafting posthumanist adventures in/for higher education: A speculative musing. *Parallax, 24*(3), 371–381.

Taylor, C. A., & Hughes, C. (Eds.). (2016). *Posthuman research practices in education*. London: Palgrave Macmillan.

Todd, Z. (2016). An indigenous feminist's take on the ontological turn: 'Ontology' is just another word for colonialism. *Journal of Historical Sociology, 29*(1), 4–22.

Tuck, E., & Yang, K. W. (2012). Decolonization is not a metaphor. *Decolonization: Indigeneity, Education & Society, 1*(1), 1–40.

Van der Tuin, I. (2015). *Generational feminism: New materialist introduction to a generative approach*. Lanham, MD: Lexington Books.

Watermeyer, R. (2019). *Competitive accountability in academic life: The struggle for social impact and public legitimacy*. Author's pre-publication copy.

Part I

Entangled Pedagogic Provocations

Chance May 2017. Photo: Carol A. Taylor

2

Sounds of Scissors: Eventicising Curriculum in Higher Education

Bente Ulla, Ninni Sandvik, Ann Sofi Larsen, Mette Røe Nyhus and Nina Johannesen

Plaiting Poetry, Politics and Pedagogy in Higher Education

```
Scrutinizing eyes
Fingers going over the skin as a fine-tooth
comb
Carefully becoming scanned by a child on
the lap.
Lines in my face becoming invaded by little
fingers
detecting details
```

B. Ulla (✉) · N. Sandvik · A. S. Larsen · M. R. Nyhus · N. Johannesen
Østfold University College (ØUC), Halden, Norway
e-mail: bente.ulla@hiof.no

N. Sandvik
e-mail: ninni.sandvik@hiof.no

© The Author(s) 2019
C. A. Taylor and A. Bayley (eds.), *Posthumanism and Higher Education*,
https://doi.org/10.1007/978-3-030-14672-6_2

```
Glazing back
How to discover?

The   imminent   danger   of   becoming   scanned
right through
Inside/outside/inbetween.
Soul, skin, spirits. Errors

Fingernails, scratching, scrutinizing…

Skinscan-station. Skinscan-sensation.
```

This chapter suggests an eventicising of curriculum in higher education with an ongoing project—'Pedagogy in the Anthropocene: Eventicising Curriculum in Higher Education'—as a point of departure. The project title paraphrases an article written by Olsson (2012). Based on cooperative explorations between lecturers and students in an event called 'Sounds of Scissors' from a Norwegian master's program entitled *Early Childhood Studies (0–3 years)*, we seek to rework epistemology and ontology in academic practice and research. The participating students were fully trained preschool teachers, most of whom work in early childhood education with children aged zero to three.

The issues raised are not exclusive to the Norwegian context. As globalised neoliberal discourses have changed educational research and practice worldwide (Bayley 2016), we especially search for countermeasures to three problematics within the neoliberal educational canon: (1) anthropocentric approaches which ignore the interwovenness of the human and the more-than-human (Nyhus 2016); (2) the individual and cognitive focus on learning/teaching (Sandvik 2016); and (3) the belief in 'evidence-based', stable and verbally articulated knowledge.

A. S. Larsen
e-mail: ann.s.larsen@hiof.no

M. R. Nyhus
e-mail: mette.r.nyhus@hiof.no

N. Johannesen
e-mail: nina.johannesen@hiof.no

2 Sounds of Scissors: Eventicising Curriculum in Higher Education

We argue that these three problematics diminish educational potentialities, leaving academia in a coagulated condition relying on knowledge as stable and innocent.

Fortunately, higher education is not doomed to remain the humble servant of neoliberalism. Deleuze and Guattari's (1994) work exposing the invented nature of philosophical concepts encourages us to claim that higher education likewise does not wait for us 'ready-made, like heavenly bodies' (Deleuze and Guattari 1994: 5). Rather, we take Taylor (2017) by the hand and 'push the already working interdisciplinary trends further, reorienting learning beyond anthropocentrism and speciesism, making postdisciplinarity a curriculum resource' (Taylor 2017: 431). Thus, the time has come to 'create a radical shift in the way knowledge-making is perceived *within* academia… and explore how performative pedagogies may become centrifugal forces in the development of necessary thinking-strategies for (un)imaginable futures' (Bayley 2016: 45).

Driven by the previously mentioned need for counteractions and encouraged by Bayley, the event 'Sounds of Scissors' drew on cooperative forces within a group of lecturers, part-time students and various more-than human elements. Senses, affects and thoughts unfolded into interesting/confusing/frustrating connections and expansions in the event. Ruptures were laid open. Questions were not necessarily answered. As in Olsson's (2012, 2013) research with young children, we argue for processual and creative orientations, rather than aiming for results, ending points and closures, and hope to encounter 'flashes of understanding' (Deleuze in Hurley 1988: iii). We regard understanding as bodily/corporeal, affective/passionate and cognitive, seeing body and mind as two intertwined and correlated domains, in line with our opposition to the neoliberal privileging of cognition. Approaching understanding in such a manner implies seeing the flashes of understanding as volatile moments in which we experience connections and flows. To further expand thoughts and knowledges and discuss our experimentations, we suggest some key Spinozan and Deleuzian ideas—passionate powers, daredevil thoughts and a-personal energies—as the theoretical tools of our speculative propositions. These ideas will be elaborated after a brief description of the event.

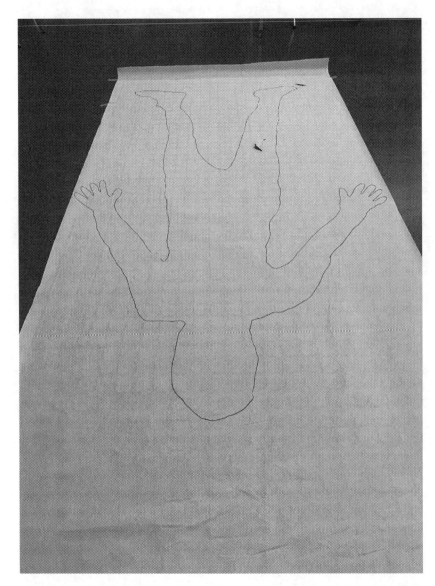

Fig. 2.1 Body

Sounds of Scissors: A Brief Description

Inspired by children's chalk drawings on asphalt, one of the teachers laid a large sheet of paper on the floor of the campus classroom. Another teacher volunteered to lay down on the paper, and the first teacher drew a curved line from her feet all the way up to her head/hair before returning to the feet and forming a full-sized figure. As the lying teacher arose, the outline of 'a body' became visible, created by the black line boldly contrasting with the white paper. Thereby, associations with a crime scene surfaced, followed by laughter and smiles (Fig. 2.1).

After the first joyful and critical fuss about bodies and crime scenes, the students formed groups and were asked to start cutting out a chosen body part. One group cut out a knee, others chose fingers, the nose, the navel or the heart (Figs. 2.2 and 2.3).

Connections between the personal, professional and political were established and articulated. We will return to some of these speculative propositions through four 'flashtags' after brief comments on our ontological and epistemological premises.

Premises: Passionate Powers, Daredevil Thoughts and A-Personal Energies

We build our arguments on three interconnected elements, all three inspired by the philosophers Baruch de Spinoza and Gilles Deleuze, who go beyond anthropocentric cognitivism, by focussing on powers, creations and energies. Thus, they lead us toward posthumanist landscapes. Our three elements derived from their philosophies are 'passionate powers', 'daredevil thoughts' and 'a-personal energies'. The premises are analytic tools facilitating our speculative propositions (Manning 2016) and are not to be taken literally.

As we see it, the concept of 'passionate powers' is a dual one. First, it relates to Spinoza's analyses of human passions: joy, sadness and desire.

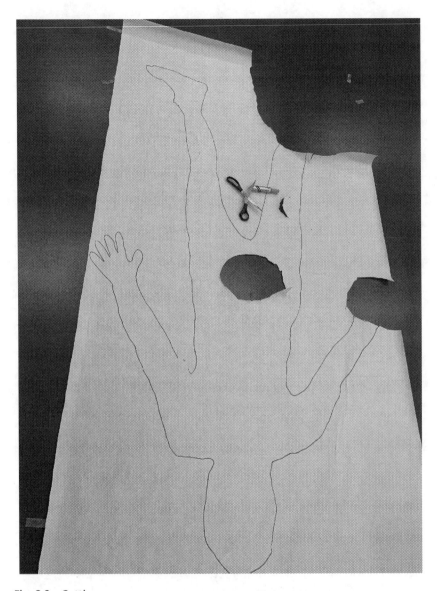

Fig. 2.2 Cutting

2 Sounds of Scissors: Eventicising Curriculum in Higher Education

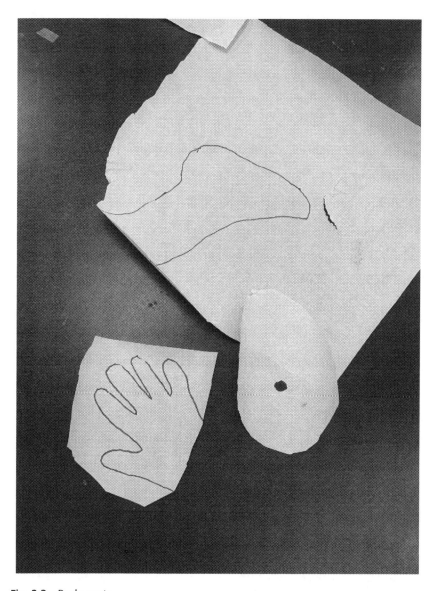

Fig. 2.3 Body parts

'Human passions are for Spinoza changes, that is, increases or decreases, in the power with which we, or parts of us, strive. Active affects are all increases in the power with which we strive' (LeBuffe 2015: Section 2.1). As we will see later, they are also related to Spinoza's denial of the freedom of the will, albeit in a more implicit way. Consequently, we suggest that higher education might be regarded as a collection of temporal and spatial incidents in which passions operate in mysterious ways, enabling both a decrease and an increase in productive and creative powers.

The second aspect of our premise is based on Deleuze's image of thought, and another aspect of the Spinozan rejection of the freedom of the will unfolds here. Deleuze conceptualises thought as a vertiginous meetings of chaotic and rending forces (Deleuze 2004b). Thought, then, is only interesting as long as it possesses enough chaotic force and intensity to be sufficiently traversable and ductile to produce new ideas. Consequently, to think is to create. This is creation beyond the freedom of will, with no obligation whatsoever to reveal an overarching or underlying principle. Accordingly, we accept and invite the readers to accept the Deleuzian invitation (referred to in Hurley 1988: iii) to approach the event as if reading poetry, however intricate and multifaceted it may seem:

> What if one accepted the invitation – come as you are – and read with a different attitude, which might be more like the way one attends to poetry? Then difficulty would not prevent the flashes of understanding that we anticipate in the poets we love, difficult though they might be. (Deleuze in Hurley 1988: iii)

Finally, we follow Deleuze's (2001, 2004a) immanent philosophy and try to read the event with attention to a-personal energies, rather than focussing on subjects as isolated and fixed entities. On this note, Spindler (2007) speaks of a dissolved subject. Such a dissolution is not a loss, but a multiplication—a perpetual ongoing creation of new becomings that transgress the borders of each subject. Deleuzian immanent philosophy points out the lack of distinct borders between humans and between humans and the more-than human, which is also applicable to time/place. May (2005: 70) echoes this in his book on Deleuze: 'The present always holds more than it seems. It is pregnant with its past, which is also is future.' This does not mean, May continues, 'that there *is* only what is present to us. There is more than meets the eye. Being folds itself, unfolds itself, refolds itself into the specific forms that constitute the world of our experience' (May 2005: 69). Despite our focus on the a-personal, this text refers to specific subjects when describing the event to enable the reader to follow the event's various actions.

The three premises serve as interlocutors as we move into a discussion of the event and the paradoxes that emerged as it evolved. In the next section, we move into further problematisations when marking off 'I' and 'you'.

Sounds of Scissors: Four Interwoven 'Flashtags'

In the introduction of this chapter, we briefly described the 'Sounds of Scissors' event. In this section, we offer further elaboration in four interwoven 'flashtags': a line, a cut, a dot, a lab and crumbled leftovers. The term 'flashtag' was constructed by merging the idea of 'flashes of understanding/thinking/sensing' and the term 'hashtag'. The flashtags arise from an urge to counteract the dominance of neoliberalism in academia by considering the cooperative bodily and affective aspects of teaching and learning, including our counteractions to the previously mentioned habitual anthropocentric focus and the coagulated idea of knowledge as stable and innocent. Each flashtag is elaborated with elements from the premises presented earlier: passionate powers, daredevil thoughts and a-personal energies. Hopefully, this will guide the reader into our struggles with creations and new or re-imaginings.

Throughout the planning process, the lecturers reminded each other to remain open to possibilities and hook onto what arose. Even when feeling that we had arrived at what appeared to be an ending, we urged each other to slow down, try to recharge the students' curiosity and search once again for any micro-element in the creative research laboratory that offered further possibilities to create, fabulate and construct.

As described earlier, the event began by rolling out a sheet of paper on the classroom floor. Before we entered the classroom, the lecturers prepared some statements for verbal sharing. The scissors, sheet and pencils were brought into the classroom before the students arrived. The choreography of the performance was planned: One of the teachers was to lay down, another to sketch. The collaborative work of cutting, suggesting ideas and sharing associations proceeded slowly, offering possibilities for hesitation. However, the cooperative production of speculations intermittently accelerated the tempo as astonishing questions and unknown practices of body modelling filled the air. To quote Deleuze and Guattari (1983: 57), it is possible to 'be fast, even by standing still', which is not to be confused with stagnation. Here, it seemed, being fast emerged from within the hesitative tempo.

In addition, we sometimes dwelled upon intriguing quotes as poetry. In particular, we collectively worked with a poetic approach related to the aforementioned Deleuzian invitation to 'come as you are'. As we considered the quote, striving to grasp the invitation, an association flashed into the discussion:

```
            Come as you are
                  [...]
            Take your time
               Hurry up
```

Kurt Cobain/Nirvana, 1992

The band Nirvana and their song 'Come as You Are' echo Deleuze's invitation. The lyrics operate beyond temporal linearity, beyond consistency, making it possible to combine slowing down and speeding up in ways that smoothly connect with the temporal experiences mentioned above. In some ways, the lyrics seemed to ridicule the prevailing neoliberal educational discourses that promote linearity, control and consistency—for example, by suggesting that one can be both a 'friend' and an 'enemy' at the same time. The paradoxes are always breathing down our necks. Thinking in this way makes us realise that the 'I' and 'you' are not fixed and separate entities but fluid becomings: if you come as you are, and simultaneously as I want you to be, then the subjects melt into each other. In the amalgamation of 'I' and 'you', becomings of new singularities (together with other elements of the world) are created. As we strove to challenge the idea of the subject as an isolated and fixed essence, we also searched for ways to follow the immanent energies of the various assemblages of human and more-than-human elements existing in the past, present and future.

During the 'Sounds of Scissors' event, though we do not claim to have fully engaged with thought in the Deleuzian sense, seemingly irrelevant connections to elements outside the event forced themselves into the process like minor 'jolts of thought' (Deleuze 1995: 8–9). Cobain's lyrics sent us into unknown territory far away from what is usually involved in educational work with young children. Simultaneously, various connections to toddler practices were created. The opening sequence involved the teacher laying down on the floor in the classroom. In the next section, we follow the marks of the pencil as it outlined the body on the floor. This may have seemed the most obvious and visible element in the event, so let us start by moving into the first flashtag: a line.

Flashtag I: A Line

We drew the contour of the body and started discussing how we could explore the figure. The black outline seemed like a paradox. We had concentrated on drawing a curved line all the way around the arranged body (Fig. 2.1), but simultaneously, this line was not seen as a skin imprint, nor was it necessarily a fixed and isolated border between a body's inside and outside. Even so, its stable and integrated image was soon to end, with the scissors waiting in ambush. Following Manning (2009: 34), we drew the body contour as a possibility of creating loci of leakiness within the black outline and raising issues regarding a leaky sense of self:

What if the skin were not a container? What if the skin were not a limit at which self begins and ends? What if the skin were a porous, topological surfacing of myriad potential strata that field the relation between different milieus, each of them a multiplicity of insides and outsides? (Manning 2009: 34)

The contour was intended to establish a myriad of questions. It had a shape recognisable as a body, but as a Foucauldian comment (Foucault 1983), we started by optimistically suggesting: 'This is not a body.' The following conversation took place:

```
:…even though the line was created around
my body, it may look like me, or be recog-
nised as me…
:…hi hi…your leg is very crooked and nar-
row; it looks like it is broken…
:…hi hi…yes, actually I fell down the
stairs yesterday…maybe it is broken, and I
have not noticed…ha ha…but then again…it is
not me. I am here (slapping herself on the
belly).
:…the figure on the floor…is it just an
image, a symbol, maybe a text..?
```

But wait a minute: Weren't we suggesting question marks? How is continuous talk of 'someone's body' possible when the desire to move in a-personal directions operated so intensively? We suggest that the pencil mark had hooked onto anthropocentric forces operating as windbreakers to our desire to turbulently begin the event, concretising the seducing forces of human privileges.

Together, we managed to rework the focus by not approaching the marked body contour as representative of a fixed and isolated human subject. Instead, we moved in a-personal directions, reframing the body beyond the categories of the human and the more-than-human (Ulla 2017). Questions starting with 'What if…'—paraphrasing questions set out by Manning (2009: 33): 'What if the skin were not a limit at which self begins and ends?'—encouraged creations beyond habitual anthropocentric ideas. This also engendered the poetic passages from the opening lines: 'What if my face became invaded by little fingers detecting details? Fingernails, scratching, scrutinising…What if the skin becomes skinscan-stations?' The poetry made visible the porous aspects of the pencil marks/skin. In glimpses, the questions and poetic passages constructed the potentiality of crisscrossing multiple layers of the subject: 'from interiority to exteriority and everything in between' (Braidotti 2016: 113).

In the flashtags that follow, we dwell on how we tried to emphasise the micro-politics of relations as we search for the potential leakage-productions of such politics. As Braidotti (2016) underlines, this follows 'the Spinozist switch to a monistic political ontology (Braidotti 2016: 115)'. By stressing such ontology, we worked to escape from the tendency to separate inside/outside, me/you, human/more-than human.

Flashtag II: A Cut

Before the scissors started slicing, one of the teachers gave a prompt: 'Cut any part of the papered body and start storytelling'. In saying this, we trusted the stories, believing that they could create flashes of understanding/thinking/sensing beyond discourses, passions, lights, shadows, smells, sounds etc. After splitting into groups, the students selected and cut off a body part, sometimes adding details to it. The sounds of scissors slicing through paper blended with the students' mumbling, and as the paper body became parcelled out piece by piece, becomings of discomfort related to body amputation became sensible. For a second or two, the room vibrated with fear and tender excitement.

If we read this part of the event in the light of Spinoza's conception of passions, our attention shifts to 'the power with which we strive' (LeBuffe 2015: Section 2.1) and to the passions that increase or decrease this power. The evolving atmosphere included both fear and joy, activating the potential to both increase and decrease the a-personal action forces in the room. The cuts seemed to affect all the present bodies beyond the level of cognition, as smiles, laughter and expressions of disgust became visible and audible. Thus, we argue that flashes of understanding/thinking/sensing evolved without being able to prove their implications. The poems in this chapter materialise some verbal unfoldings that occurred during the event, and the poems remain as traces of these speculations. The cuts create ruptures in the order of things—that is, in the idea of the body as a whole, delimited and private. Laughter accompanied the following:

```
Oh,
I can feel
the cold temperature
from the floor
on your thigh
standing close to you

my thigh next to yours

…seconds later

is it my chill?
yours?
the floors?

Temperatures-becoming-skin-sensation
```

The mere fluctuation of temperature opens possibilities of recognising a-personal connectedness and entanglements, even when it comes to physical body parts. Just like that, speculations were laid open: 'Is there such thing as a frontier guard of skin temperatures? What if… and…and…what if not…is it possible to claim territorial ownership of temperature?' We sensed glimpses of the immanent interwovenness of the human and the more-than human as a certain temperature/skin machinery was caught in a becoming. Together, we speculated through interwovenness: Temperatures-becoming-skin-sensation.

Earlier, we pointed at the term 'flashes of understanding/thinking/sensing' as a vital aspect of our work and argued for the value of understanding bits and fragments without striving to understand the whole.

2 Sounds of Scissors: Eventicising Curriculum in Higher Education

In cutting the paper body, we experienced a cornucopia of virtual variations alongside cognition: memories, expectations, dreams and desires. These virtual variations do not belong to anyone in particular; they emerge from within the event.

Flashtag III: A Lab

The event turned into a research laboratory in which every element participated in explorative elaborations on what was previously unknown (Deleuze 1995). The unpredictable and chaotic forces seemed to intensify a-personal affective energies.

As four students cut out a foot and started to dwell upon what a foot might be, or become, in their professional lives, questions arose: 'What does the foot tell us? How do we deal with feet?' Through shared stories, the foot started to travel across cultures, climates and landscapes and became connected to the temperature outside the window and the cold floor on which the students were standing. The foot was connected to the freezing Norwegian December air, which called for it to be placed in woollen stockings and closed shoes. Again, the in(side) and out(side), between humans and more-than humans, seemed fluently immanent (Deleuze 2001, 2004b).

```
cold feet wrapped in socks

socks taken off
whos going sock-hunting?
high and low
dancing barefoot, heading for a spin...
motion-emotion
     (switching to Cobain)...take your time -
     hurry up

flirty feet - under the table
separated - entangled...
slowing down and speeding up
what happens to the feet under/over/on/
beside the table?
```

Here, the foot stepped into interdisciplinary terrain, and the cooperative focus moved to globalisation and world travellers. Subsequently, age surged into the experimentation: 'mmmm... the smell and softness of baby feet. Young feet, teenage feet, adult feet...yuck...get a pedicure!' In a flash, the beauty industry entered the room.

Another group had cut out the figure's eyebrows and linked Botox to fading facial expressions. Moral standards regarding capitalism and feminism added to the discussion. Voices got louder and new questions emerged: 'What is ignored? What constitutes a human being? Age, gender, ethnicity...looks, movement, a body? Where are the lines drawn: Human, less-than-human, more-than-human? How can we reimagine...when, or where, do we start starting, become becomings?'

Flashtag IV: A Dot

Passionate powers transitioned into questions concerning the origins of life and piqued interest in the separations of bodies when children are born. The scissors had cut out a circle with a dot in the middle from the belly region of the figure (Figs. 2.2 and 2.4).

The dot led to reimaginations and hooked onto stories of cicatrices from umbilical cords.

```
Cutting and connecting
Life, tissue, life
Umbilical cord
Body inside body: voices and music
Inside the inside: heartbeats
```

The question of whether we ever start starting or become becomings arose and extended an invitation to establish nuances: being 'in'/'of' the world. Barad (2007) and her groundings intermingled with the speculations given by both students and teachers. How is it possible

2 Sounds of Scissors: Eventicising Curriculum in Higher Education

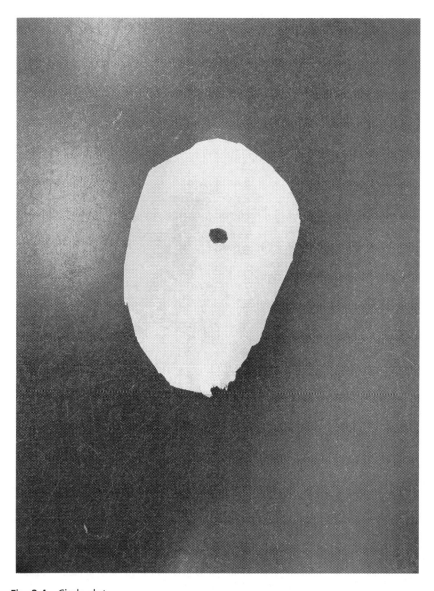

Fig. 2.4 Circle-dot

to reimagine becoming worldly? A narrative of a finger searching for a belly button made its entrance.

```
Child on lap
Fingers - searching for the belly button
Belly button - searching for the finger
Skinscan-station. Skinscan-sensation
```

The story of a fingertip energised the classroom: child on lap, resting, listening, talking…and fingers searching for its belly. A whole hierarchy of organs emerged, giving the finger a privileged position. Its movements and radius of action placed it on a throne, while the belly seemed a passive, flat stretch of skin. In switching the agencies of the finger and the belly button, a nuance of equality might come to the fore.

```
Sensations coming into existence, as skin
touches skin
Belly button meets fingertips
Movements bring desire into the moment
```

The dot and the belly button may augment our ability to reimagine how bodies entangle—in Deleuzian terms, how they create a belly button/lap/fingertip machine (Deleuze and Guattari 2004)—and thereby point at the fragility of knowledge.

Flashtag V: Crumbled Leftovers

At the end of the session, the crumbled leftovers (Fig. 2.5), a pile of unexplored components, remained in the classroom and offered an opportunity to explore 'parts' and 'wholes'.

Leaning on Hansson (2012), we accept that isolated studies of parts never can ensure a whole picture. We cannot understand something like a whole body, nor do we strive to create a cohesive puzzle of knowledge.

Fig. 2.5 Leftovers

There is always a supplement, some leftovers and something more (Larsen 2017). Here, 'something more' does not point at a modernist hunger for a logical chain of arguments. The leftovers do not tell stories of incompleteness. Rather, they remind us of the additive forces of the stuttering—and, and, and—opening us to impulses, connections, body/thought associations disallowing any primacy of the one over the other, leading us on 'strange adventures, far afield from ourselves,' to quote May (2005: 86). The stuttering is welcomed in this classroom, leading to an explosion of imaginable utterances as we (re)search. Research becomes study, becomes lecture, becomes leftovers, and, and, and…as poetry accumulates through the events. The leftovers help us continue looking and continue trying. Something unexpected occurs every time we gather. Unexpected energies emerge in discussion. Trouble and turbulence occur but do not impede the flashes of understanding; we keep trying, trusting in the connections, associations and disruptions.

Closing the Chapter: An Invitation for Others

This chapter provides a glimpse into shared stories within the event 'Sounds of Scissors,' offering a path towards reworking epistemology and ontology in line with an eventicising of curriculum in higher education. We have explored some key aspects from the work of Spinoza and Deleuze: passionate powers, daredevil thoughts and a-personal energies. We have given examples of how higher education might change by embracing immanence and instability to counteract the previously mentioned anthropocentric approaches—a focus on the individual and the idea of stable knowledge—when working in line with the chosen premises. The ways in which the event dissolved boundaries have been elaborated under five flashtags. While we are aware of the organisational limitations of academia, we underline the need to rearrange work schedules to work more cooperatively. In addition, we suggest twisting the classroom into a creative research laboratory to make time and space for events. Such strategies 'equip students [and lecturers] with the kind of entangled participatory and transdiciplinary thinking-strategies required by a complex and increasingly post-human world' (Bayley 2016: 49).

Referring to Braidotti, Siddiqui (2016: 64) writes: 'The neoliberal university is here, she says, and we best be getting on our way of working within this framework'. This chapter presents our suggestions of how this getting on may be possible.

```
                the scissors cut
      politics
passions
      pedagogy interweave
                passionate powers increase,
                come to climax, and fade away
```

References

Barad, K. (2007). *Meeting the universe halfway: Quantum physics and the entanglement of matter and meeting.* Durham: Duke University Press.

Bayley, A. (2016). Trans-forming higher education: Towards posthumanist strategies of teaching and learning. *Performance Research, 21*(6), 44–49. https://doi.org/10.1080/13528165.2016.1240930.

Braidotti, R. (2016). The posthuman as becoming-machine. In S. Arrhenius (Ed.), *Insomnia: Sleeplessness as a cultural symptom.* Stockholm: Bonniers Konsthall.

Deleuze, G. (1995). *Negotiations 1972–1990* (M. Joughin, Trans.). New York: Columbia University Press.

Deleuze, G. (2001). *Pure immanence. Essays of a life* (A. Boyman, Trans.). New York: Zone Books.

Deleuze, G. (2004a). *Difference and repetition* (P. Patton, Trans.). London, NY: Continuum.

Deleuze, G. (2004b). *The logic of sense* (M. Lester, Trans.). London, NY: Continuum.

Deleuze, G., & Guattari, F. (1983). *On the line* (J. Johnston, Trans.). New York: Semiotext(e).

Deleuze, G., & Guattari, F. (1994). *What is philosophy?* (H. Tomlinson & G. Burchell, Trans.). New York: Columbia University Press.

Deleuze, G., & Guattari, F. (2004). *A thousand plateaus* (B. Massumi, Trans.). London, NY: Continuum.

Foucault, M. (1983). *This is not a pipe* (J. Harkness, Trans. and ed.). Berkeley: University of California Press.

Hansson, D. (2012). Unpacking Spinoza: Sustainability education outside the Cartesian box. *Journal of Sustainability Education, 3,* 1–17.

Hurley, R. (1988). Preface. In G. Deleuze (Ed.), *Spinoza: Practical philosophy.* San Francisco: City Light Books.

Larsen, A. S. (2017). Når vanskeligheter vernes om og ønskes velkommen [When difficulties are appreciated and welcomed]. *Kognition & Pædagogik. Tidsskrift om Gode Læringsmiljøer, 27*(106), 32–45.

LeBuffe, M. (2015). Spinoza's psychological theory. In E. N. Zalta (Ed.), *The Stanford encyclopedia of philosophy* (Spring). Retrieved from https://plato.stanford.edu/archives/spr2015/entries/spinoza-psychological/. Accessed 25 January 2018.

Manning, E. (2009). What if it didn't all begin and end with containment? Toward a leaky sense of self. *Body & Society, 15*(3), 33–45. https://doi.org/10.1177/1357034X09337785.

Manning, E. (2016). *The minor gesture.* Durham and London: Duke University Press.

May, T. (2005). *Gilles Deleuze. An introduction.* New York: Cambridge University Press.

Nyhus, M. R. (2016). Læring sett som flyt [Learning as flux]. In N. Sandvik (Ed.), *Småbarnspedagogikkens komplekse komposisjoner* [Complex compositions in toddler pedagogy]. Bergen: Fagbokforlaget.

Olsson, L. M. (2012). Eventicizing curriculum. Learning to read and write through becoming a citizen of the world. *Journal of Curriculum Theorizing, 28*(1), 88–107.

Olsson, L. M. (2013). Taking children's questions seriously: The need for creative thought. *Global Studies of Childhood, 3*(3), 230–253. https://doi.org/10.2304/gsch.2013.3.3.230.

Sandvik, N. (Ed.). (2016). *Småbarnspedagogikkens komplekse komposisjoner* [Complex compositions in toddler pedagogy]. Bergen: Fagbokforlaget.

Siddiqui, J. R. (2016). Restyling the humanities curriculum of higher education for posthuman times. *Curriculum Inquiry, 46*(1), 62–78. https://doi.org/10.1080/03626784.2015.1133220.

Spindler, F. (2007). Att tappa ansiktet. Om subjekt, individ och vänskap hos Gilles Deleuze [Losing face. Subjects, individuals and friendship in the work of Gilles Deleuze]. *Aiolos, 29,* 47–51.

Taylor, C. A. (2017). Is a posthumanist *bildung* possible? Reclaiming the promise of *bildung* for contemporary higher education. *Higher Education, 74*(3), 419–435. https://doi.org/10.1007/s10734-016-9994-y.

Ulla, B. (2017). Reconceptualising sleep: Relational principles inside and outside the pram. *Contemporary Issues in Early Childhood, 18*(4), 400–408. https://doi.org/10.1177/1463949117742781.

3

Theatre for a Changing Climate: A Lecturer's Portfolio

Evelyn O'Malley

Introduction

This chapter proceeds by presenting diffracted extracts of autoethnographic writing, undertaken alongside my teaching on two theatre modules at the University of Exeter in 2017, one seminar and one studio-based module. Grasping at a diffracted form of autoethnography, it aims to disclose and expose my attempts to craft a curriculum that eschews human exceptionalism in attendance to more-than-human matters and materials in dramatic writing concerned with anthropogenic climate change, theatrical performance and spaces of learning. My proposition-in-the-making is for a posthuman pedagogy that notices its own intra-active 'becomings-with' (Haraway 2016: 4) 'entangled phenomena' (Barad 2007: 333), aspiring to reach toward 'ethico-onto-epistemological' possibilities of creative learning in a becoming-world.

E. O'Malley (✉)
Department of Drama, University of Exeter, Exeter, UK
e-mail: E.OMalley@exeter.ac.uk

For a long time—although without referring to their work as new materialist—scholars and practitioners working in the field of drama, theatre and performance studies have been concerned with materiality in a wide range of practices that foreground ecology, scenography, costume, puppetry, site-specificity, immersion, aurality and animals, to name a few. Erika Munk's introduction to a special issue of *Theater* (1994) on 'Theatre and Ecology', which features Una Chaudhuri's influential article 'There Must Be a Lot of Fish in that Lake' (1994), is often cited as the first call to scholarly interest in this area, and work in this field has proliferated especially within the last decade. As theatre and performance that either decentre the human or that do not feature human performers at all becomes increasingly common, the incorporation of new materialist ideas and concepts into thinking around the practices has become likewise prevalent. A couple of recent and compelling examples include David Shearing's immersive multimedia installation *The Weather Machine* (2015), which invites audience members into an embodied encounter with the weather without the presence of live human performers, and Sheila Ghelani and Sue Palmer's *Common Salt* (2018), where the performers present and interact with objects on a 'nature table,' telling a story of connected environmentalisms, colonialism and cultures. The American Society for Theatre Research (ASTR)'s 2014 Conference in Baltimore, USA took 'What performs?' as a theme and asked delegates to respond to the following questions:

> What might our discipline gain from decentering the human as theatre's actor, author, and agent? What else performs? How does placing non-humans center stage expand our historiographic imagination, putting new pressure on familiar methods, and breathing new life into objects/subjects long dismissed as the inert material from which performance, and performance history, is fashioned? (ASTR 2018, landing page)

Although less overtly new materialist in its theoretical attachments, the 2016 Performance Studies International Conference (PSi) on 'Performing Climates' in Melbourne, Australia also demonstrated growing commitments to acknowledging humans as part of a more than human world. The conference landing page sought to 'reflect [...] on the climactic conditions within which societies function, and under which life can best flourish,' and aspired to identify 'ways of re-thinking this radically inter-connected world across many scales of human and non-human activity' (PSi 2016: 2).

The influence of these new directions in scholarship has begun to reach the teaching of theatre in higher education where, as I mentioned above, it often transpires they have been lurking all along. Specifically, the 'Performance Climates' conference yielded an issue of the online journal *Global Performance Studies* (GPS), including a range of curated 'Syllabi for the Future' (GPS 2018). Of these imaginative syllabi, Augusto Corrieri's proposal for an undergraduate course on 'Performance Without Human Exceptionalism' engages with posthuman approaches materials-on, beginning with a video clip of a girl cartwheeling for dolphins in an aquarium (Corrieri 2018). In the UK, a Theatre and Performance Research Association (TaPRA) symposium for postgraduates in February 2018, themed around 'Materials and Materiality: How do they matter?' (TaPRA 2017), suggests that new materialist thinking in the discipline is driven by postgraduate students as much as by more established researchers.

Teaching Posthumanism and Performance

My intra-vention described in this chapter seeks less to present itself as a shining example of how posthumanism might be applied in pedagogy for teaching theatre and performance, than to offer diffractive readings of my own—often clumsy—attempts to bring posthuman ideas into the seminar room and studio. In the edited book by Hall et al. (2017), *Teaching Climate Change in the Humanities*, Cheryl Glotfelty (2017: 177), a founding figure for literary ecocriticism, reflects upon her choice to teach ecological 'restoration', in light of what she refers to as 'crisis fatigue' accumulated through years of teaching climate change. Mindful of Glotfelty's experience, I chose Donna Haraway's (2016) *Staying with the Trouble* as a core text for an elective third year undergraduate module I teach to third year students on the BA (Hons) Drama programme at the University of Exeter: *Theatre for a Changing*

Climate (2017). The University of Exeter is a research-intensive UK institution and research-led teaching is one of the offers made to students on this programme. The work on *Theatre for a Changing Climate* is underpinned by a desire to respond to Haraway's (2016: 1) cry to 'stay with trouble' that anthropogenic climate change presents to all life forms on the planet rather than fixating paralyzed upon 'awful or edenic pasts and apocalyptic or salvific futures.' The module is an invitation not to succumb to apathy or despair—although we nevertheless bump into these feelings along the way—but to stay attentive to the mess and the muck of the present. *Theatre for a Changing Climate* looks specifically at plays that engage with anthropogenic climate change— some directly and others more obliquely—written in the last decade, bringing a range of theatre criticism, theoretical frameworks and perspectives from the environmental humanities to bear on analysis. The plays for 2017 included Chantal Bilodeau's *Sila* (2015), Frances Ya Chu Cowhig's *Snow in Midsummer* (2017), Shonni Enelow's *Carla and Lewis* (2014), Ella Hickson's *Oil* (2016), and Lucy Kirkwood's *The Children* (2016). The theoretical approaches included readings from Stacy Alaimo's *Bodily Natures* (2011), Jane Bennett's *Vibrant Matter* (2010), and Haraway's aforementioned *Staying with the Trouble* (2016) but were not entirely limited to new materialist and posthumanist works. Each week students undertook a short writing task in response to either a critical writing prompt or a creative writing task. These related to the plays, critical texts, student-led staging explorations presented during seminars, presentations and tiny plays that they wrote themselves.

In tandem with *Theatre for a Changing Climate*, I also taught as part of a team on *Acting and Not Acting*, a practical studio-based module with a group of twenty first year students. *Acting and Not Acting* was originally designed as an introduction to devising for newly arrived undergraduates at the University of Exeter, and the teaching involves initial explorations of 'play' via children's games and theatre games by a range of twentieth and twenty-first century practitioners to enable the creation of their own devised 'plays'. Toward the second half of *Acting and Not Acting*, students encounter lecturers with different specialist foci to give them initial entry points, tools and stimuli to support them to create their own performances. To complement and counterpoint the work with third year students on *Theatre for a Changing Climate*, I focussed on 'ecodramaturgial' practices with the first years for the three weeks of focussed studio-work. Ecodramaturgy is Theresa J. May's term for 'theater and performance making that puts ecological reciprocity and community at the center of its theatrical and thematic intent' (Arons and May 2012: 4), for forms that seek 'to emphasize the ways [ecodramaturgy] might imaginatively intervene to forward environmental justice, sustainability and democracy' (May 2017: 1). Ecodramaturgy brings together various existing and emerging approaches to performance-making under its capacious umbrella, rather than outlining a new and particular way of working that leads to a certain style of performance. Ecodramaturgy lends itself to posthumanist approaches although it is of course possible to think about ecological reciprocity from the vantage of the human and with only human interests at heart. Likewise, ecological community in May's open definition may refer to human gatherings with shared ecological interests as much as to multispecies collectives. It was not my particular intention to think with or of posthumanism in choosing exercises that might enable ecodramaturgical work for *Acting and Not Acting*, then, but I became aware of shared concerns, of practices that were always already entangled with the place of the human in a more than human world, as the months of teaching unfolded. These shared concerns and differences presented themselves diffractively over the weeks of teaching, as—intentionally or not—the modules bounced off in different directions, demonstrating what Barad (2007: 333) refers to as 'phenomena [that] are ontological entanglements', entanglements that only become-with and become apparent through the doing.

Diffractive Autoethnography

What follows is a diffractive autoethnography, which shares patches of my own creative and critical portfolio from the term, presented as short pieces of writing undertaken weekly alongside the two modules, attending to the affects, accidents, discoveries and limits of posthuman pedagogy in these theatre teaching contexts. Methodologically, it aligns itself both with affective and non-representational approaches to ethnography (Vannini 2015) and approaches to autoethnographic performance and writing practices, attempting an 'emotional texturing of theory [and] reliance upon poetic structure to suggest a live participative embodied researcher' (Spry 2001: 709). The mode of non-representational autoethnographic writing that I employ diffractively (rather than reflectively or reflexively) seeks to illustrate 'patterns of difference that make a difference' (Barad 2007: 72) across both modules. As Barad argues:

> Diffraction apparatuses [...] highlight, exhibit, and make evident the entangled structure of the changing and contingent ontology of the world, including the ontology of knowing. In fact, diffraction not only brings the reality of entanglements to light, it is itself an entangled phenomenon. (Barad 2007: 73)

Following Barad (2007: 89), the extracts are attempts at 'marking differences from within and as part of an entangled state,' shifting between the two modules, teaching plays, performances and perspectives, in studio and seminar spaces, and across different student levels of learning. Diffraction disrupts the 'auto' of the autoethnographic approach, queering the sense of myself as a stable subject narrator objectively positioned outside of the narrative. As Barad (2014: 181) puts it, 'There is no 'I' that exists outside of the diffraction pattern, observing it, telling its story'. Rather, the extracts of writing presented below are attempts to show the pedagogy '(re) (con) figuring' the lecturer in processes of 'ongoing (re) patterning'. Concordant with Barad's proposition, the autoethnographic 'I' is 'neither outside nor inside' but rather '*of* the diffraction pattern'.

Seminar: Weather and Climate

It's October and still warm, bright outside. Twenty-four third year students and I are upstairs in our Tuesday morning seminar room where old cast iron radiators pump out heat and cannot be turned down.

All windows are wide open to let the last of the summer into the room. We look out at the arrival of autumn colours on the hills to our left. This week we are thinking about representations of weather and climate in Frances Ya Chu Cowhig's play *Snow in Midsummer* (2017). The first task is to get a sense of how they differ in the play. 'Climate may be the big slow-moving backdrop', as Richard Mabey (2013: 3) puts it, 'but weather is what happens here and now, to our settlements and landscapes, to us'. Students have read Cowhig's play alongside Astrida Neimanis and Rachael Loewen-Walker's (2014) article on 'Weathering: Climate Change and the Thick Time of Transcorporeality'. Neimanis and Loewen-Walker (2014: 558) build on Barad's (2007) 'intra-action' and Stacy Alaimo's (2010) 'transcorporeality' work to propose that humans are neither 'masters of the climate, nor are we just spatially "in" it. As weather-bodies, we are thick with climatic intra-actions'. In *Snow in Midsummer* the wrongful execution of the young widow Dou Yi, prompts changes in the local weather. Before her death, Dou Yi prophesises that aberrant snow will fall and be followed by three years of drought until her name is cleared. The audience meets the play toward the end of the three-years, when the prophesised weather has transformed the local climate to the point that the parched town of New Harmony is almost uninhabitable.

In preparation for the seminar, a group of students has staged the scene of their choice from *Snow in Midsummer* using Brechtian Epic Theatre techniques, involving 'making-strange' the story by distancing the audience from the characters and encouraging critical modes of spectatorship. The group has chosen the scene that ends Act 1, where, from the spirit world, Dou Yi's ghost laments the harvesting and dispersal of her organs, sold illegally for transplants. In today's seminar staging, we are seated in rows evocative of an ordered auction room where Dou Yi's organs are to be sold. At the front of the room, an inflatable globe is attached to a stool, as though the globe is a head on top of a human body. Plastic body parts are affixed with string: severed hands, a giant inflatable heart, oversized papier-mâché eyes. As the ghost speaks of the new climates encountered by her redistributed hands, heart and eyes, confusing their recipients, student performers fly tiny airplanes around the globe, placing the body parts in their new homes. Watching the objects flying around the globe, we are encouraged to think of the residents of New Harmony as global *and* 'planetary' (Chakrabarty 2014; Heise 2008) subjects, who experience climates locally as weather over sustained time periods. It is prolonged unfamiliar weather in New Harmony that indicates a change in the local climate. Instead of allowing us to be consumed by the play's narrative, the material presence of objects in the scene encourage us to attend to the 'the spatial overlap of human bodies and weathery nature' (Neimanis and Loewen-Walker 2014: 560).

Conversations with the students after the performance suggest that the current weather and our own sense of climate complements our reading of the play. Is it warm for October? Or are these the kinds of October days we think we remember from childhood? How is October different for those of us not from the UK? How important are the reassuring autumnal oranges, yellows and reds on the hills outside to our sense of a stable climate? What has walking up two flights of stairs done to our bodies in the hot seminar room? How do our multiple bodies change the weather in the room, increasing the heat? Where and in what ways might our bodies remember this weather if the local climate changes significantly?

The play and the theoretical reading bring us to questions that will be familiar territory for those who study or teach climate change and representation. How might climate—and not just weather—be (re)presented on stage? Is it ever really possible to convey a sense of climate in theatrical time? Cowhig's play succeeds in evoking a changed climate, by showing humans living in altered weather conditions in conjunction with their spoken references to past weather, and past events that have caused the changes in the weather. The play shows human bodies struggling, unable to adapt to drought conditions and eventually forced to abandon their home. In staging the scene without utilizing human characterisations but instead relying on objects, props and distancing techniques, students offer one way of encouraging an audience to think critically about how bodies experience and remember weather as climate. We care less about the human (and ghostly) subjects than we might if we were to see them performed sympathetically, but we become more attuned to the materiality of human/nonhuman intra-actions. Every now and again a breeze makes it way in through the window. It's a relief to descend the stairs and to venture out into the relative cool of the world outside.

Studio: Elemental Bodies

Storm Ophelia has picked up Saharan sand from North Africa and Iberian forest fires, colouring the sky eerily pink outside the studios where we are working this morning. It feels unseasonably warm for October and is still dark at 9.30 a.m. First year students joke uncomfortably about the end of the world. We start the session by going outside and standing on the grass. It would have been nice to stand under the tree where there's usually a bit of quiet, contained space, but the wind is so vicious it doesn't feel safe today. Volunteers read aloud poems and epigraphs from *Elemental: An Arts and Ecology Reader* (Brady 2016) and we talk through the four classical elements as materials present in the landscape and in our bodies—earth, water, air, fire. Whilst recognising the contingency of these tenuous categorisations that have been refined and amended by contemporary scientists and across cultures, today's exploration is about how they continue to be utilised in theatre and performance practices. What uses might they have in creating ecodramaturgical works?

The question we begin with is where are the elements materially in the world around us? Where can we identify them in the substances of the world we can see and touch here and at this moment, and where do we recognise them in our bodies? The earth is beneath our feet. Soles of shoes are muddy from the walk uphill to the studio. We crouch down and touch the moist brown mud on shoes and in the grass. We rub it between fingers and it crumbles, melts. What's solid in human bodies? The weighty parts. The bits of us that crumble, melt, end up as soil. Muscle mass, bones, flesh, eyeballs, teeth, hair? It's water that's in the ground, on the ground, moistening the mud we've just been touching and sticking it to our shoes. Dew droplets cling to blades of grass. The water is the life inside the grass too, inside the giant oak we aren't standing under. A stream is running through the bottom of the Taddiford Valley that the studio slopes toward—across a road—and water approaches in the form of dark rainclouds beyond the valley. What percentage of the human body is water, someone prompts? We fumble for half-remembered statistics: 'two thirds of a human body,' 'we start out watery and dry up a bit as we get older'? The water in our human bodies is tears and sweat and blood and pee. So is Freshers' flu: it's early in the term and many of us are streaming noses and phlegmy coughs, leaking into the world. Fire is the pink sun heating the earth, keeping us alive, and colouring the atmosphere ominously luminous this morning. Our own fire is in our nervous systems. It's the heat we create when we rub our hands together fast. It's the hairs that stand on end: goosebumps. It's passion, so prized by drama students. The air is the wind blowing all around, whipping long hair in front of faces, making leaves and branches audible, visible, entering and leaving our lungs as breath and hacking.

The flavour of these conversations demonstrates a development of an exercise I first encountered in workshops with Glynn MacDonald, movement director at the reconstructed Shakespeare's Globe Theatre in London (2011). MacDonald draws inspiration from the elemental references in Shakespeare's plays and early modern understandings of the body and Renaissance cosmology, hence her alighting on earth, water, fire and air. She has devised a physical position to accompany each element and asks performers to hold these postures for a number of minutes at a time, encouraging them to connect with the elemental parts of their own bodies, shared with the planet, before sharing them with other human bodies. In extending MacDonald's exercise, my intention is to encourage students to identify in a tangible way—however scientifically dubious—the shared, entangled materiality of human bodies and nonhuman materials. This might move us toward the kind of knowing Stacy Alaimo (2016: 7) seeks to bring to the world with her notion of trans-corporeality: one that 'originates with a recognition of the self as solidly located and denies the splitting of subject and object: the subject, the knower, is never separate from the world that she seeks to know.' Although the intention with this week's learning is to begin to create weather and elements in the studio and less to think across bodies, these exercises nevertheless cultivate a sense of shared materiality, of humility, of the performer's body as made of and entangled and becoming-with the world.

Back inside, we observe traces of the elements in the room, blurring inside/outside distinctions, even as we acknowledge what shelter and exposure mean for human creativity. Draughts enter at the cracks of doors and windows, moisture feels sticky as we run around, the sun comes through the window—although it's still uncannily dark out—and gravity drops us to the solid, earthy materiality of the space. Having learnt MacDonald's four positions, students draw on the British theatre-company Complicité's elemental exercises, adapted from Jacques Lecoq's work for devising physical theatre: they are moving like a river, embodying the air currents in the room even as they change them, moulding one another like clay, and dancing like fire (Alexander 2001: 14–15). So many theatre practices are always already elemental—even where they have never identified themselves as ecodramaturgical—forgoing human exceptionalism to find forms of bodily knowing that indicate we have *always* been entangled with the rest of the stuff from which the world is continually made: recognising what is already posthuman within our human bodies.

Seminar: Changing the Weather

It's November. I'm with the third year students again and we're finally grateful for the overheated learning space. We have read *Carla and Lewis* (2014), a play by Shonni Enelow, alongside the introduction to Jane Bennett's *Vibrant Matter* (2010) for this week's seminar. Enelow's play was performed in New York as part of The Ecocide Project, undertaken with Una Chaudhuri. My engagement with this play from the UK has therefore always been as a text, enabling its reader to imagine performance possibilities. One stage direction has always fascinated me. A well-intentioned art curator has commissioned 'punk butterflies' named Carla and Lewis to make a piece of art concerning anthropogenic climate change. She invites a scientist in to speak to the artists. The scientist's measured explanation of her research escalates to a rant about the plight of the freshwater crustacean *Daphnia pulicaria*, which is going extinct. Her tirade ends with what the extinction of the *D. pulicaria* means for humankind: the end of the world as we know it. After the scientist finishes speaking, '*The weather changes*' (Enelow 2014: 105). Carla and Lewis respond provocatively, playfully undermining her earnest apocalyptic forecast:

> *Lewis*: [...] We're not scared of the polar ice caps melting!
> *Carla*: We ARE the fucking polar ice caps melting!
> *Lewis*: We are the hurricanes and the tsunamis and the flash floods and the fires. And we are the dead animals. The dead animals falling dead from the dead trees to the dead forest floor covered with other dead animals! So don't screech to us about science, GRANDMA! Take your fucking medication and leave us alone! (Enelow 2014: 105)

Again, '*The weather changes*' (105), as the stage directions indicate dramaturgical shifts that are both material and metaphorical. Is the changing weather caused by the emotive responses and spent exhaustion at the end of the scientist's rant, followed by Carla and Lewis's retort? And how does an audience encounter the weather changing? Materially on stage? In the imagination? Would 'real' weather be visible through a window? Or presented inside the New York apartment? After all, mud is already seeping through the walls. And what kind of weather is changing anyway? Wind to heavy rain to gentle rain to the sun coming out to hail? Or does an audience sense the changing weather from the dialogue's tonal shifts, in beats that denote the nonlinear structure of the play? Students are invited to consider: when was the last time something nonhuman—muddy, mouldy or otherwise—interfered in your life or burst its way into your day-to day activities?

Tasked with presenting Enelow's stage directions for changing weather, the students arrive for their seminar with large sheet of flipchart paper, pastel crayons and a cardboard 'wheel of weather' that spins on a broom handle. They begin the scene from *Carla and Lewis*. When the changing weather is called for, a student performer announces himself the host of a participatory game show, calling for volunteers to spin the wheel. Its pointer lands on 'hurricane.' Those of us seated at tables are given thirty seconds to draw that weather with coloured pastels while recorded hurricane sounds play over speakers. The images are discarded onto the floor and the exercise is repeated. The next time wheel spin gives 'rain.' Then 'heatwave.' The performance ends as our host thanks the group for "helping to change the weather." It dawns on us that choices as well as chances bear some responsibility for altering the climate. After the exercise, wiping coloured chalky residue from hands and smudged faces, picking up the crackly sheets of flip-chart paper, we discuss Bennett's (2010: 4) central provocation that 'things, too, are vital players in the world' and marvel at how what we do is entangled with these things: weather, pastels, paper, games, agency and power.

Studio: Weatherlapse

Elsewhere I have mentioned the shared credentials of drama students and environmentalists as negative stereotypes: drama students stand around pretending to be trees and environmentalists hug trees (Morgan et al. 2017: 351). Typically, such stereotyping serves to denigrate both theatre students and green political advocates as those that pretend to be trees and those that hug them, labelling both as ineffectual, disengaged with the 'real' world and just a little too committed to unnecessary and eccentric occupations to be taken seriously. As with trees, so with the weather. Although Sarah Ruhl (2014: 98) jokes that 'I thought that once you got your Equity card, you refused on principle to ever make the sound of wind again,' in the elemental studio exercises outlined above students present themselves 'as' the weather, using their bodies to change it with alterations of tempo, rhythm, dynamics, spatial patterns and breath. Their bodies are the resources and they become the weather.

In preparation for creating their own devised performances, the first years undertake self-directed tasks, returning with a short performance-in-progress to share. Having explored bodies *as* weather earlier in the term, they are tasked with going out to observe bodies *in* weather. The invitation is to draw on observations of people in everyday situations and create a "weatherlapse" in response to the following pedagogic invitation:

Weather-lapse

Richard Mabey worries that faced with the need to adapt to a changing climate '…we will doubtless continue with our tragicomic street theatre of daily coping.' (Mabey 2013: 90)

Show us a **street theatre of daily coping** by creating a weather-lapse.

As a group, find somewhere to observe people in weather. Note movements as precisely as possible. Think about what people do to adjust to different temperatures and weather conditions?

Back in the studio, choose three further contrasting weathers and re-enact your scene in these weathers. What changes? Try to push beyond 'rainy' and 'sunny'. What kind of rain? What temperature? How can you show an audience that you're all in the same weather at the same time.

Transitions between weather conditions may be gradual or abrupt.

Although this is an anthropocentric task, where students replicate human behaviours observed elsewhere, the objective is also to encourage an understanding of how their behaviours are made intra-actively *with* that world. Students return to the studio with physicalized images of people smoking in coats in car-parks, shielding smartphone screens from the sun on a cold day, sharing space under bus shelters in the rain and picking up dog-poo on icy pavements. Watching them perform their weatherlapses, I wonder whether the exercise's focus on the human *in* weather gives us a better sense of what it means to be human whilst acknowledging ourselves as always intra-acting with the weather, perhaps more so than the exercises that turn us *into* weather. In which case, perhaps pedagogy that embraces posthumanism is less about losing a sense of the human altogether but finding a better sense of the human entangled with the rest of world. And, thinking of Haraway (2016: 4), whose words I've been reading in other spaces with other students on *Theatre for a Changing Climate,* maybe the learning in this exercise is about rehearsing 'staying with the trouble', about developing the awareness that bodies 'become-with each other or not at all', attentive to how differentiated these becomings-with may be.

How Practices Matter

The 'iterative (re) configuring of patterns of differentiating-entangling' (Barad 2014: 168) that I present above includes some practical provocations for pedagogy in theatre and performance. In practical terms, it gestures to how portfolio assessment might accommodate diffraction patterns which work 'outside' that which is purely reflective or reflexive and which work in relation to critically-engaged prompts that incorporate creative practices of doing, writing and being. In such a diffractive auto-ethnographic practice—as, indeed, with Barad's own writing—the queered 'I' of the writing disappears and returns in the selection and presentation of any extracts of writing. Such writing is itself co-emergent with the learning and opens to an understanding that 'identity is not essence, fixity or givenness, but a contingent iterative performativity' (Barad 2014: 173–174).

Rob Nixon (2011: 30) asks what kind of future is possible for the humanities in a less specialised environment? A changing climate means that humanities teaching in higher education has to engage with disciplines beyond its comfortable edges, even where that teaching is not wholly inter-disciplinary. A posthuman pedagogy may therefore cultivate an awareness that we can't answer certain questions without collaborating-with, becoming-with others—human and nonhuman. The pedagogic challenge is to enable students to stretch out tentacles of their own—to borrow another of Haraway's (2016: 30) metaphors—to reach toward possibilities and find the courage to address global challenges as future scholars, theatre-makers, collaborators, advocates and activists. The work students that engage with on these two modules holds open pedagogic possibilities for thinking of ourselves as less than exceptional and becoming-with(in) shifting assemblages. There appears to be something worthwhile in *being* the weather for a while too. For Barad (2007: 391), '[l]earning how to intra-act responsibly as part of the world means that "we" are not the only active beings—though this is never justification for deflecting our responsibility onto others'. In provisional ways, a posthuman pedagogy might begin to move away human exceptionalism in a way that is simultaneously humbling *and* empowering, performing the rediscovery of ourselves as weather-bodies, stuck with others in the trouble (whether we "think" we're entangled with it or not).

References

Acting and Not Acting. (n.d.). https://humanities.exeter.ac.uk/drama/modules/DRA1004/. Accessed 27 February 2018.

Alaimo, S. (2010). *Bodily natures: Science, environment, and the material self*. Bloomington: Indiana University Press.

Alaimo, S. (2016). *Exposed: Environmental politics and pleasures in posthuman times*. Minneapolis and London: University of Minnesota Press.

Alexander, C. (2001). *Complicité teachers notes—Devising*. London: Complicité. http://www.complicite.org/media/1439372000Complicite_Teachers_pack.pdf. Accessed 27 February 2018.

Arons, W., & May, T. J. (Eds.). (2012). *Readings in performance and ecology*. Basingstoke and New York: Palgrave Macmillan.

ASTR/TLA Conference 2014: What Performs? (2018). http://www.astr.org/events/EventDetails.aspx?id=484678&group=. Accessed 25 February 2018.

Barad, K. (2007). *Meeting the universe halfway: Quantum physics and the entanglement of matter and meaning*. Durham and London: Duke University Press.

Barad, K. (2014). Diffracting diffraction: Cutting together-apart. *Parallax, 20*(3), 168–187.

Bennett, J. (2010). *Vibrant matter*. Durham and London: Duke University Press.

Bilodeau, C. (2015). *Sila*. Vancouver: Talon Books.

Brady, J. (Ed.). (2016). *Elemental: An arts and ecology reader*. Manchester: Gaia Project Press.

Chakrabarty, D. (2014). Climate and capital: On conjoined histories. *Critical Inquiry, 41*(3), 1–23.

Chaudhuri, U. (1994). There must be a lot of fish in that lake: Toward an ecological theater. *Theater, 25*(1), 23–31.

Corrieri, A. (2018). *Performance without human exceptionalism*. http://gps.psi-web.org/issue-1-2/syllabi-future-playlist/. Accessed 27 February 2018.

Cowhig, F. (2017). *Snow in midsummer*. London: Methuen.

Enelow, S. (2014). Carla and Lewis. In U. Chaudhuri & S. Enelow (Eds.), *Research theatre, climate change, and the ecocide project* (pp. 87–116). Basingstoke and New York: Palgrave Pivot.

Ghelani, S., & Palmer, S. (2018). *Common salt*. http://www.sheilaghelani.co.uk/commonsalt/. Accessed 21 August 2018.

Global Performance Studies. (2018). *Syllabi for the future: A playlist*. http://gps.psi-web.org/issue-1-2/syllabi-future-playlist-6/. Accessed 15 October 2018.

Glotfelty, C. (2017). Teaching ecological restoration in the climate change century. In S. Hall, S. LeMenager, & S. Siperstein (Eds.), *Teaching climate change in the humanities* (pp. 177–182). London and New York: Routledge.

Hall, S., LeMenager, S., & Siperstein, S. (Eds.). (2017). *Teaching climate change in the humanities*. London and New York: Routledge.

Haraway, D. (2016). *Staying with the trouble: Making kin in the Chthulucene*. Durham and London: Duke University Press.

Heise, U. K. (2008). *Sense of place and sense of planet: The environmental imagination of the global*. Oxford: Oxford University Press.

Hickson, E. (2016). *Oil*. London: Methuen.

Kirkwood, L. (2016). *The children*. London: Nick Hern Books.

Mabey, R. (2013). *Turned out nice again*. London: Profile Books.

MacDonald, G. (2011, February 2–11). *Movement Director*, movement classes at the Globe theatre. The Globe Theatre.

May, T. J. (2017). Tú eres mi otro yo—Staying with the trouble: Ecodramaturgy & the anthropoScene. *The Journal of American Drama and Theatre, 29*(2), 1–18.

Morgan, I., O'Malley, E., Clarke, C., & Ang, G. P. (2017). Answer the question: How does nature nurture your training? *Theatre, Dance and Performance Training, 8*(3), 350–355.

Munk, E. (1994). A beginning and an end: Green thoughts. *Theater, 25*(1), 5–6.

Neimanis, A., & Loewen-Walker, R. (2014). *Weathering*: Climate change and the "thick time" of transcorporeality. *Hypatia, 29*(3), 558–575.

Nixon, R. (2011). *Slow violence and the environmentalism of the poor*. Cambridge, MA: Harvard University Press.

PSi 22 Conference Melbourne: Performance Climates. (2016). *Conference programme*. Melbourne: Performance Studies international.

Ruhl, S. (2014). *100 essays I don't have time to write: On umbrellas and sword fights, parades and dogs, fire alarms, children, and theater*. New York: Farrar, Straus and Giroux.

Shearing, D. (2015). *The weather machine*. http://davidshearing.com/works/the-weather-machine/. Accessed 27 February 2018.

Spry, T. (2001). Performing autoethnography: An embodied methodological praxis. *Qualitative Inquiry, 7*(6), 706–732.

TaPRA. (2017). *Postgraduate symposium: Materials and materiality: How do they matter?* http://tapra.org/postgraduate-symposium/. Accessed 27 February 2018.

Theatre for a Changing Climate. (2017). http://humanities.exeter.ac.uk/drama/modules/DRA3092/. Accessed 27 February 2018.

Vannini, P. (2015). Non-representational ethnography: New ways of animating lifeworlds. *Cultural Geographies, 22*(2), 317–327.

4

A Manifesto for Teaching Qualitative Inquiry with/as/for Art, Science, and Philosophy

Candace R. Kuby and David Aguayo

Introduction

Feminist-physicist-philosopher, Karen Barad writes, "we inherit the future" (2013: 23). This phrase sounds impossible. How can we inherit the future when it hasn't happened yet? However, this phrase causes us to pause and consider why it matters that we think about the pedagogies of qualitative inquiry (QI) courses. How we teach QI to students is the future we will inherit in the academy and the communities we work with as researchers. Our manifesto is an invitation for instructors of QI to consider how Deleuze and Guattari's (1991/1994) writing on art, science, and philosophy might be a catalyst and an orientation for pedagogy. Philosophical concepts should not be 'applied' but rather seen as useful in 'reorienting thought and in inspiring and sustaining the long

C. R. Kuby (✉) · D. Aguayo
University of Missouri, Columbia, MO, USA
e-mail: kubyc@missouri.edu

D. Aguayo
e-mail: da79c@mail.missouri.edu

© The Author(s) 2019
C. A. Taylor and A. Bayley (eds.), *Posthumanism and Higher Education*,
https://doi.org/10.1007/978-3-030-14672-6_4

preparation of reading and studying' philosophy (St. Pierre 2017: 695). Our hope is that in reading-with-and-thinking-with art, science, and philosophy as concepts, we are reoriented in how we think of pedagogy. Therefore, we write our manifesto for a pedagogy(ies) of QI inspired by Deleuze and Guattari's writings on art, science, and philosophy to help us foster pedagogical spaces for students to become qualitative inquirers who create newness and difference. We use the term 'qualitative inquiry' to shift our conceptualizations of *doing research as inquiry,* an uncertain process of thinking, rather than a pre-set method that 'qualitative research methods' connotes.

Deleuze and Guattari were interested in creation and difference, not representation and sameness. They discussed three powers of thinking: art as a plane of composition, science as a plane of reference, and philosophy as a plane of immanence (see Colebrook 2002; Deleuze and Guattari 1994 [1991]; Smith 2012). We wondered: what if we teach QI with/as/for art, philosophy, and science? What *and* where might it get us as instructors, students, the academy? If we thought of QI as a knowing/being/doing/thinking of art, science, and philosophy, could these powers of thinking transform the language we use to talk about (and do) QI pedagogy? We think so.

We invite readers to imagine how QI and the teaching of it becomes arting, sciencing, and philosophizing to/with/and by students (and teachers, art materials, books, theories, languages, histories, politics, digital tools, and…and…and…). Our manifesto about teaching/learning QI is always, already entangled with our experiences with students, textbooks, assignments, and…and…and… Thus our manifesto, our public declaration, troubles both the genres of a manifesto *and* what might be termed a 'teacher's reflection'. Below we share our manifesto as/with a few comments from students in an introductory QI course intentionally designed to disrupt a methods first approach to QI. A methods first approach focuses on teaching students 'methods' of data production and analysis rather than perhaps digging deep into philosophical and theoretical readings as a way into thinking/analysis. As instructors of QI courses, we feel pressures to teach QI as an exact science (see Foucault 2005 [1966]) or what has become a normal science (see Kuhn 2012 [1962]), when students inquire about the 'right' way to do research. Students are seeking a recipe, a scripted method, a how-to, a checklist (Schulte 2018; St. Pierre 2016).

Deleuze and Guattari describe science as "fix[ing] the world into observable 'states of affairs,'" art as that which "creates affects and percepts," and "philosophy creates concepts." Philosophical concepts 'do not label or represent the world so much as produce a new way of thinking and responding to problems' (Colebrook 2002: 27). In other words, a philosophical concept doesn't just add another word to a language; it transforms the language (Deleuze and Guattari 1994 [1991]). In our practice as educators, we thought-with these powers of thinking and (re)oriented them to become a pedagogy of QI. For example, we see science in the pedagogy of QI as institutionalized methods (that often students seek); art as the affectual or forces of perception during class engagements (and when students work-with communities as researchers); and philosophy as the art of forming, inventing, fabricating concepts, specifically concepts that we think-with to *do* inquiry. Thus, we verb these three concepts to indicate the lively, mobilization of these concepts in practice. Art*ing*, scienc*ing*, and philosophiz*ing* produce new ways of thinking and are the possibilities of how QI (and higher education pedagogy) could be otherwise—other than a normalized recipe. With these powers of thinking, QI can be inventive, art-full, force-full with/in/against the neoliberal, positivist, and normalized ways of doing qualitative research method/ologies.

Arting, Sciencing, and Philosophizing

This manifesto emerges from a larger study which examines the pedagogy of two introductory QI courses for graduate students (both had masters and doctoral level students) which disrupted traditional approaches and assumptions to qualitative research. Inspired by posthumanist and feminist 'new' materialist theories (Barad 2007; Bennett 2010; Braidotti 2013), we (Candace instructor, David teaching/researching intern) intentionally created learning engagements that fostered spaces for students to create and think with theory, data, art supplies, digital tools, and others (humans, nonhumans, more-than-humans) as a way to produce new ways of thinking/knowing/be(com)ing/doing QI.

Candace conceptualized this pedagogy as intra-active or as an ethico-onto-epistemological pedagogy (Lenz Taguchi 2010). In other words, it wasn't about creating an arts-based pedagogy or simply adding materials to a course. Rather, it was a philosophically inspired orientation to how the world comes to be and how we come to know (i.e., epistemology) in our relationships (i.e., being and doing or ontology and axiology) or through material-discursive intra-actions (Barad 2007). A quote by St. Pierre at the top of the syllabus, informed students to our beliefs on qualitative research becoming 'a low-level description of process, procedure, design, and method and so, not surprisingly, too often produced and continues to produce as 'findings' inconsequential themes, untheorized stories' (St. Pierre 2011a: 2–3). We provided our students with our rationale on *why* traditional qualitative research needs to be disrupted. Our objective was to have students understand the politics of inquiry and structures that enable (and constrain) certain analytical approaches.

With this in mind, we chose textbooks to create tensions between conventional humanist qualitative methodologies (St. Pierre 2011b), research ideas, and thinking-with theories (for example, two of the books we chose were Brown et al. 2014 and Savin-Baden and Howell Major 2013). We also started the term with discussions on theory instead of a methods first approach. We had students read theory and examples of more disruptive approaches to qualitative research alongside more traditional, normalized examples so we could 'stay with the trouble' as Haraway (2016) writes, work the tensions, and imagine otherwise. The assignments, such as a 'thinking with theory' paper inspired by Jackson and Mazzei's (2012) scholarship, created spaces for students to wrestle with how theory becomes analytic, thinking tools. Candace often used the phrase 'it depends' to answer questions students asked as she hoped this would help them consider how paradigmatic views enable research questions and practices. We also created spaces for students to physically think-and-create-with art and digital materials as a way to learn differently about QI (see Kuby and Christ 2018a, 2018b).

For example, students worked-with their thinking with theory assignment papers, articles on/about theories, paint, coloured paper, iPhones, and…and…and… to become-with and make news ways of knowing/be(com)ing/doing the theories they were reading. However even with these attempts, students wrestled between needing procedural guidelines and embracing an ability to be creative. One of our students, Pam (all student names are pseudonyms) stated, 'in my mind I needed a box [a chart about] paradigm[s] – the books [e.g., Savin-Baden & Howell Major] tried, I wanted that…but don't think you can ever really get that [boxes in QI].'

Scientific Performances

In the beginning of the course, our students saw the many possibilities for QI as threatening to their socialized, scientized idea of research, yet they also questioned their preconceived notions. Omie, a student, said in previous qualitative research courses she felt there was a right or wrong way to do research. However, in our course Omie was given permission to do otherwise, she stated 'maybe there isn't a way to make everything fit … no way to wrap them [paradigms and research approaches] up nicely.' The course enabled students to question ingrained conceptions of traditional qualitative research. Andrew commented:

> I thought that qual [qualitative research] was more like a clean slate [not seeking a hypothesis]. You could just sit down and look for things and pick people's brains and find new concepts. I really like qual for that. But [I] had no idea that it was deeper than that and that there were theories, paradigms, and all that stuff.

Over the semester, we noticed a shift of perspectives from students: a shift from solely a scientized idea of QI to embracing an arting and philosophizing perspective of QI that has depth and infinite possibilities.

Students began to welcome the complex, uncertain, variations in doing research, which permitted to them a different way to approach

QI. A third book we used in the course, *Reconceptualizing Qualitative Research: Methodologies without Methodology* (Koro-Ljungberg 2016), enabled students to challenge normative, science thinking. Omie said the book 'pushed my thinking. That is the book that I find myself going back to…it was a challenge, [it] made me uncomfortable … maybe there is no [right] answer [in how to do QI].' The uncomfortable space of not having *an* answer or *the* way to do QI was a (welcomed) challenge for our students. However, several mentioned going back to this book and yearning for the thinking it provoked for them. The course challenged their ideas of scientific ways to do QI, ways they thought they were to perform social science researcher. The uncomfortableness experienced by students is an a/effect which perhaps was a catalyst to engage in arting, opening a possibility into philosophizing the creation of new concepts and ways of inquiring (hence, sciencing, arting, and philosophizing are mutually constitutive of each other).

Secretive Identities

Students spoke of their identities as taking a significant shift from a place of secrecy (i.e., not following paths of inquiry that they thought the academy and/or advisors would not approve of) to unravelling and peeling off layers of fear and shame. From the beginning of the course we provided an invitation to do QI by engaging in arting, philosophizing, and sciencing. For example, they took their thinking with theory paper assignment and worked-with paint, tissue paper, discarded books, and yarn as a way to create newness through playing/thinking. When we asked the students to talk about these experiences, Julia Ann stated,

> I thought it was really interesting to have an opportunity to play with materials … I was more excited to go back and look at some of my work because I think I got some sort of liberation because [in this class], oh you're not doing something strange…when I did this [artistic mapping of paradigms and theories] I thought this is actually really empowering in that there's value [a teacher values my way of thinking through/with materials].

Julia Ann was able to think *through* mapping (sciencing, arting, and philosophizing), which was validated, enabling her to feel liberated, instead of stifled by the academy's rigidity.

Another student saw his identity as removed from his research based on previous experiences with advisors. Andrew stated:

> I feel like it would be dangerous in a way, to do it [a personal narrative inquiry on his aromantic identity, an aromantic is a person who experiences little or no romantic attraction to others]. I feel like it's that thing that I'm doing on the side. I haven't even told my advisor that I've been working on this, it feels like it's, I feel like, not that it's personal and I shouldn't talk about it, but it feels like it doesn't belong to the research I should be doing here [in the academy].

Here, Andrew had learned that his official grounded theory thesis on international students in higher education was an acceptable topic and approach for research in the academy, but his nagging passion to study aromanticism through a personal narrative inquiry was not. The rigidity of the academy in conducting effective, rigorous 'science' stifles students like Andrew and Julia Ann from engaging in inquiries that are affectual (arting) and that produce depth and newness of concepts (philosophizing). Andrew was trying to suppress himself as part of his research in order to survive (and thrive) in higher education. As we heard and witnessed students' shifts in thinking through the course, we noticed them working through what they believed were acceptable (scientific) research strategies and topics in relation to more art-full approaches to inquiry. Students described being afraid to be creative or keeping their artful ways a secret in relation to research they thought their advisors and disciplines would allow.

Craving-Resisting the Messiness of Becoming Qualitative Inquirers

As the course progressed, students began to welcome the (inherently) messy aspects of QI. The course provided a space where students were able to challenge their beliefs, while at the same time it gave them permission to explore otherwise. Some students noted that many of their graduate courses did not challenge their philosophical thinking. Entering this course, students not only wrestled with new concepts, but they were asked to embrace being uncomfortable. For many, this space was welcomed, yet difficult. Omie shared:

> Most of my life I felt different; this way of doing [creative QI] allowed me to be different. [After] reading Foucault [and] creating [with materials, it] symbolized to be okay to not know or to be unsure. That my work didn't have to look like writing, like academic pieces of paper. It could look creative, messy.

This arting, sciencing, and philosophizing that Omie describes helped us to see the need to 'give permission' (a phrase Candace often said) to students to imagine inquiry as otherwise. The students, like Omie, called this pedagogical space 'an allowing'—allowings of doing QI otherwise.

Aware of the politics of inquiry and power dynamics of teacher/student, we tried to create spaces of becoming-with (Haraway 2016) or thinking/learning/teaching in relation-with students. We wanted students to engage in arting, sciencing, and philosophizing without fear and we tried to be transparent about our own struggles as inquirers. Thomas noted the course was attempting to shift 'academic culture' and that the course exposed them 'to new academic culture'. This 'new academic culture', if it is such, would be one that enables students to think and to think differently. Perhaps a new way of conceptualizing sciencing. Andrew stated the course 'felt like a philosophy class. It wasn't like a 'step one, step two' class. It taught me this is your thinking process, but it is up to you [me] ultimately, that there are no guidelines [recipes].' Pam described the intensity of the course and the readings, for example: 'The Koro-Ljungberg book was all over the place, I liked the white spaces [to write in the book], but the thinking was all over and too much for my brain.' Overall, we heard this mixture about how the course was one of the hardest students had taken, how the readings challenged them and caused them to think, yet at the same time students expressed a yearning, craving for thinking about the messiness of *doing* inquiry.

An Ethical Invitation

This manifesto is an invitation for instructors to consider how arting, sciencing, and philosophizing as powers of thinking could be (inspiration for) pedagogy *and* therefore the QI practices our students engage in/with. Concepts need conceptual personae or, as Massumi translates it, 'rhythmic characters' (Deleuze and Guattari 1994 [1991]: 2). How might these three powers of thinking create rhythmic characters that produce difference—of QI pedagogy *and* research practices? How might doing QI be the discipline of creating/thinking? How do these powers of thinking a/effect *what* curriculum we teach and *how* we teach it pedagogically?

For us, this (re)orientation to arting, sciencing, and philosophizing is an ethical call and response-ability (Barad 2007; Haraway 2016). As instructors, we plan our courses but also make in the moment decisions that a/effects who (and how) our students become as qualitative inquirers. We have the ability to respond in the pedagogies of QI and this matters. How we teach QI to students is the future we will inherit in the academy and the communities we (and they) work with as researchers. How are you creating QI pedagogies with your ability(ies) to respond? We think it is our ethical response-ability to art, to science, to philosophize QI pedagogy *with* our students.

References

Barad, K. (2007). *Meeting the universe halfway: Quantum physics and the entanglement of matter and meaning*. Durham, NC: Duke University Press.

Barad, K. (2013). Ma(r)king time: Material entanglements and re-memberings: Cutting together-apart. In P. R. Carlile, D. Nicolini, A. Langley, & H. Tsoukas (Eds.), *How matter matters: Objects, artifacts, and materiality in organization studies* (pp. 16–31). Oxford, UK: Oxford University Press.

Bennett, J. (2010). *Vibrant matter: A political ecology of things*. Durham, NC: Duke University Press.

Braidotti, R. (2013). *The posthuman*. Cambridge: Polity Press.

Brown, R. N., Carducci, R., & Kuby, C. R. (Eds.). (2014). *Disrupting qualitative inquiry: Possibilities and tensions in educational research*. New York: Peter Lang.

Colebrook, C. (2002). *Gilles Deleuze*. New York: Routledge.

Deleuze, G. and Guattari, F. (1994 [1991]). *What is philosophy?* New York: Columbia University Press.

Foucault, M. (2005 [1966]). *The order of things: An archaeology of the human sciences*. New York: Routledge.

Haraway, D. (2016). *Staying with the trouble: Making kin in the Chthulucene*. Durham, NC: Duke University Press.

Jackson, A., & Mazzei, L. (2012). *Thinking with theory in qualitative research: Viewing data across multiple perspectives*. New York: Routledge.

Koro-Ljungberg, M. (2016). *Reconceptualizing qualitative research: Methodologies without methodology*. Thousand Oaks, CA: Sage.

Kuby, C. R., & Christ, R. C. (2018a). An ethico-onto-epistemological pedagogy of qualitative research: Knowing/being/doing in the neoliberal academy. In V. Bozalek, R. Braidotti, M. Zembylas, & T. Shefer (Eds.), *Socially just pedagogies: Posthumanist, feminist and materialist perspectives in higher education* (pp. 131–147). London: Bloomsbury Academic.

Kuby, C. R., & Christ, R. C. (2018b). Productive aporias and inten(t/s)ionalities of paradigming: Spacetimematterings in an introductory qualitative research course. *Qualitative Inquiry, 24*(4), 293–304.

Kuhn, T. (2012 [1962]). *The structure of scientific revolutions*. Chicago and London: University of Chicago Press.

Lenz Taguchi, L. (2010). *Going beyond the theory/practice divide in early childhood education: Introducing an intra-active pedagogy*. New York: Routledge.

Savin-Baden, M., & Howell Major, C. (2013). *Qualitative research: The essential guide to theory and practice*. New York: Routledge.

Schulte, C. (2018). Deleuze, concept formation, and the habit of shorthand inquiry. *Qualitative Inquiry, 24*(3), 194–202.

Smith, D. (2012). *Essays on Deleuze*. Edinburgh, UK: Edinburgh University Press.

St. Pierre, E. A. (2011a). *Philosophically informed research*. Paper presented at the Annual Meeting of the American Educational Research Association, New Orleans, LA.

St. Pierre, E. A. (2011b). Post qualitative research: The critique and the coming after. In N. K. Denzin & Y. S. Lincoln (Eds.), *The Sage handbook of qualitative research* (pp. 611–625). Thousand Oaks, CA: Sage.

St. Pierre, E. A. (2016). The long reach of logical positivism/logical empiricism. In N. Denzin & M. Giardina (Eds.), *Qualitative inquiry through a critical lens* (pp. 19–30). New York, NY: Routledge.

St. Pierre, E. A. (2017). Haecceity: Laying out a plan for post qualitative inquiry. *Qualitative Inquiry, 23*(9), 686–698.

5

Posthuman Encounters in New Zealand Early Childhood Teacher Education

Sonja Arndt and Marek Tesar

Introduction

> Life … is neither a metaphysical notion, nor a semiotic system of meaning; it expresses itself in a multiplicity of empirical acts: there is nothing to say, but everything to do. Life, simply by being life, expresses itself by actualizing flows of energies, through codes of vital information across complex somatic, cultural and technologically networked systems. (Braidotti 2013: 189–190)

The posthuman turn has intensified the argument for rethinking the human in its sheer relationality. In higher education and university settings, it unleashes potentialities for vibrant and creative transformations of conceptualizing teacher education pedagogies, to see early childhood student teachers as enmeshed in diverse actualisations of

S. Arndt (✉)
University of Waikato, Hamilton, New Zealand
e-mail: sonja.arndt@waikato.ac.nz

M. Tesar
University of Auckland, Auckland, New Zealand

'flows of energies', as the opening quote suggests. However, what does this thought mean for teacher educators' posthuman pedagogies, and for undergraduate students, entangled in codes of information and knowledges that are somatic, cultural and technological, as Braidotti suggests? Must we forgo, forget, or dissolve our human-centric existence, life, loves and ways of being and knowing, to follow a posthuman argument in teacher education? Braidotti's work acts as a powerful provocation for thinking with the intricacies of the known and the unknown in our university spaces and practices. It places early childhood teacher education at a crossroads of conceptions of social, political, educational and cultural imperatives—and of the possibility of a certain 'undoing' of these conceptions, and of how we might 'imagine, invent and do the doing differently' as Taylor (2016: 6) challenges us, if we apply a posthuman lens to our traditional human theorisations. This chapter focuses on potentialities of a posthuman orientation in teacher education, and in the higher education sector more generally, provoked and bridged through a re-examination of Julia Kristeva's theory on the subject in process.

The emphasis in this bridging affirms the humanity in conceptions of posthumanism. It elevates the complications and nuances of the 'human I' in posthuman becomings. Braidotti's (2013: 190) notion of the posthuman neither involves negating the human, nor being 'indifferent to the humans', nor dehumanizing our thinking or being. Our examination might then be called a 're-humanising' effort, in that it involves (re)sensitising ourselves to the deeply ethical, relational values, senses and embodiments of human and more-than-human subjects and objects. It uses Kristeva's theory in a re-cognition of what is relationally present in all our/their entangled, messy interconnectednesses. As such, posthuman theory, as Braidotti (2013) argues, is a positive and affirmative approach to our shared, collective life project. Adopting this orientation, we argue that a posthuman lens offers an important escape from the risk of stagnation, or stasis, lack of imagination, creativity or divergent feeling, thinking or acting in higher education.

Our experiences as teacher educators in Aotearoa New Zealand undergraduate early childhood programmes are central to our negotiations between the human 'I' and posthuman orientations. These negotiations re-envigorate, re-enliven, re-activate thought, feeling, meaning, and ethical imperatives in the spaces that we share with our students. As Braidotti (2013) suggests, life itself reveals the relational complexities of the posthuman subject, object, or other manifestation of 'life', which we may not even know. As we attempt to illustrate this idea, we insert posthuman potentialities into what we perceive as cracks opened up by theorising higher education student teacher subjectivities through Kristeva's ostensibly human-centric poststructural, feminist philosophies.

Our argument for rethinking higher education pedagogies is not necessarily a bursting out into a new, never thought of way of thinking. Rather it is an attempt to reinsert, re-articulate, rethink, what is already there, already occurring, already felt. The posthuman subject, Braidotti (2013: 188) claims, 'is materialist and vitalist, embodied and embedded … firmly located … multifaceted and relational.' Thinking with Braidotti (2013: 188) helps us to see ourselves, our colleagues and our students in our university settings, then, as 'actualized by the relational vitality and elemental complexity that mark posthuman thought itself.' This chapter resets the fundamental grounding of our pedagogies in thinking of us as unequivocally, already, relationally dependent and influentially involved with the active and vital forces and energies emanating from other beings, things, and interactions throughout our teaching/learning spaces and places. Furthermore, and following on from the intricacies involved in such thinking, its sedimentation, directions, movement and speed shape us all as nomadic and 'non-unitary, posthuman subjects' (Braidotti 2013: 189). This lens exposes cracks in what now appears to be an unrealistic simplicity of a human-centric perspective on teacher education.

Exposing the Cracks

Nomadic and non-unitary, the human and non-human subjects implicated in our pedagogies demand our constant attention. They demand what Haraway (2016) calls in her book with the same title 'staying with the trouble.' Staying with the trouble, Haraway (2016: 1) says, implicates all of us in 'unfinished configurations of places, times, matters, meanings.' Rethinking the provision of early childhood teacher education pedagogies therefore calls for us to perpetually rethink our pedagogies, to 'stay with the trouble', amongst other things, by troubling the 'human I' and de-elevating the human subject. If we are to take Haraway's notion of our collective implicatedness seriously, we should ground ourselves in the human and non-human experiences affected in, by and through our own inseparable lives and relationships, within the entanglement of teachers-students-histories-worlds-things. These conceptualizations help us to recognise cracks, tensions and sparks in the posthuman encounters with/in early childhood teacher education.

Rethinking higher education pedagogies through such cracks requires us to destabilise the certainty, comfort and knowability of dominant human-centric theorisations and practices. We see in this exposure a critical and urgent intervention in the damaging, narrowing anaesthesia of increasingly dominant neoliberal demands for expediency in teaching practices, outputs at all costs, quick-fix solutions that emerge from the neoliberal higher education mindset (Peters and Tesar 2017). Instead of the complexity of life of which Braidotti reminds us, we see espoused in universities a reduction in complexity, an oversimplification and universalisation of pedagogies, and a dangerous lack of attention to the co-dependencies in which we and our students are, wittingly or unwittingly, enmeshed. Exposing cracks in human-centric theories that inform our pedagogies creates both spaces and bridges for the insertion of non-human beings and things, into configurations of the 'places, times, matters, meanings' in our pedagogies. Our undergraduate teacher education classes are heterogeneous and embedded in the already-existing interrelationships and unknowabilities entangled in our student teacher-lecturer practices and realities.

Contextual Underpinnings: Dangerous, Insidious and Ruinous

Two university contexts in urban settings in Aotearoa New Zealand—a bicultural country with a multicultural society and a large proportion of international students—are the sites from which this examination of posthuman pedagogies opens up. Here the realities of higher education are embroiled in the strong influence of a neoliberal ideology and its unrelenting, free market, competition focus on being engaged, connected, and generating 'high-quality' outputs (Ball 2016; Peters and Tesar 2018). This neoliberal ideology has been argued as dangerous, insidious and ultimately ruinous of individuals, their interdependence, collective responsibilities and the planet's environment, and points to a need for 'new regimes of truth beyond [its] suffocating strictures' (Springer 2016: 2). The pressures of this environment is often evident in surface-level, risk-averse pedagogies that attempt to achieve certainty of outcomes and productivity, and assume an elevated status and control by humans and humanity, of processes, student success and material rewards. At the same time, they de-elevate, rather than seek out, the complexities of wider relationalities in educational and pedagogical relationships and knowledges with wider contexts. Such an ideology as we experience it has the effect of stifling creativity, imagination and 'risky' endeavours in our pedagogies, by an enforced busy-ness, surface level foci, aimed at seeking instead to extend comfortable, known practices and popular courses, towards increasingly economic levels.

In addition, the higher education context of Aotearoa New Zealand carries with it a conflicting comfortableness with diverse cultural responsibilities. By 'conflicting comfortableness' we refer to the pronounced way in which multiple cultural obligations arising from the Treaty of Waitangi affect our pedagogies. The Treaty was signed between the British settlers and most Māori indigenous tribes in 1840, promising equal rights to participate in Aotearoa New Zealand life and society, and to the protection of properties and of cultural treasures (Orange 1989). These obligations have been translated into teaching qualities and aspirations and are, for example, strongly affirmed and intertwined throughout the early childhood curriculum framework, *Te Whāriki* (Ministry of Education 1996, 2017). Even though there remains scepticism and pressure as the sector is seen as failing in its delivery of a bicultural curriculum, interpretations of indigenous conceptions permeate our teaching and pedagogies in ways that stretch our own ways of knowing and being (Ritchie 2015) and open the context to critiques of neocolonialism (Tesar 2015). Much work remains to be done to meet Treaty obligations as fully as possible, and we acknowledge both the risks and dangers of an ongoing colonisation of beliefs and language (Mika 2012). We recognize that our own Euro-centric, Western backgrounds and knowledges prohibit, in certain ways, our ever *really* understanding or knowing them (Arndt and Tesar 2018). In another sense, our human-orientedness does too.

The weaving of such divergent realms of knowing and being of the indigenous Māori in educational settings are grounded in the educational history and regulatory frameworks of Aotearoa New Zealand (Ritchie and Skerrett 2014; Tesar and Arndt 2017). The intricacies and nuances of both neoliberal and bicultural confluences have led to a relative—but often contested—sense of comfort in an educational system in which humans are unquestioningly elevated. This alone complicates our human-ness and cultural, meaning-oriented approach to our teaching. Our complication of our own pedagogies in this chapter is further impacted by a convergence of multiple cultures in a country that is not new to social, cultural and religious diversity (Ministry of Social Development 2016). We ourselves both grew up in different countries and contexts, as did many of the students in our teacher education programmes. The wider cultural and indigenous ways of knowing with which we are surrounded underlie metaphysical, more-than-human, more-than-articulable, ways of thinking and being. From a bicultural perspective, there never *was* a human/non-human distinction (Jones and Hoskins 2016: 79), and Māori 'never truly differentiated "culture" and "nature".' Conceptualising ourselves and our students as not merely a 'human I', then, but as already entangled in nature/culture relationships, and as nomadic and posthuman subjects, as Braidotti (2013) sees it, forces us to stay with the trouble (Haraway 2016). In the next section we attempt to articulate and shift our orientations beyond the human-non-human binary. We explore the cracks exposed, and bridges offered, by troubling elements of Kristeva's (1998) theory on the subject in process. We focus particularly on her notion of the semiotic, and its potentialities for posthuman student/lecturer pedagogical entanglements.

Unfinished Configurations: Subjects Always in Process

According to Kristeva (2008), all of us are always subjects in process. That is, we all are 'infinitely in construction, de-constructible, open and evolving' (Kristeva 2008: 2), and, even when we culturally belong to a team, culture, milieu, or university faculty, 'we are never completely the subjects of our own experience' (Oliver 1998). The intrinsic heterogeneity that complicates teacher education classes, whether they include new immigrant students, well-settled students, or others from diverse backgrounds, is revealed as infinite and unknowable, and as the foundation for examining and acknowledging the student teacher, and ourselves, as already unsettled, beyond known human-non-human margins. This inherent heterogeneity in early childhood teacher education, unmasking all students and lecturers as in-process, opens up to wider mutually affecting, affected and crucial connectivities, the 'actualizing flows of energies' to which Braidotti alerted us in the opening quote.

Accordingly, the notion of the subject in process opposes ideals that favour ontological or epistemological sameness or simplicity. It offers no easy answers or solutions to the problem of identifying nature/culture binaries, but rather it offers potential bridges that open up new spaces for theorising and thinking in which to conceptualise nature/culture as inseparable, non-binary, human-non-human-thing-object-forces. The notion of the subject in process offers a theoretical point of entry to complicate and rethink static, stagnant or surface level human-focused orientations and practices. This examination takes literally the translation of Kristeva's title of her theory from the French. '*Sujet en procès*', means both the subject on 'trial' and the subject in 'process'. Kristeva plays on both meanings (Ffrench and Lack 1998), raising possible tensions and concerns in constructions of student teacher subject formations as human-centric and beyond human relationalities. The theory of the subject in process emerges from Kristeva's psychoanalytic influences through Freud and Lacan, at the same time as it represents a shift away from psychoanalytic theory. In this philosophical engagement we utilise her theory as a productive and destabilising investigation of the human subject. Kristeva's theory informs and provokes details and nuances in subjectivities, that lead not only to critical insights but to what we might call 'un'sights, that which we cannot, do not, and will never, see. In what follows, we stay with the trouble, through the subject in process.

Kristeva's Theory of the Subject in Process

Stone (2004) refers to Kristeva's subject in process as a mystery. Subjects are never completely products only of their own experiences, but instead, she says, are always 'split subjects', and as such 'we must call ourselves (continually) into question' (Stone 2004: 124). For Kristeva, the ongoing construction of the self, of identity, subjectivity, as subjects in process, connects our evolution as subjects with the evolution of language as a signifying practice, as such signifiers appear in discourse, literature, and art, for example. It counters any positivist theoretical neutrality by highlighting the motility and ongoing formation of the subject (Kristeva 1998). Since the subject is in process, its motility differentiates it (and the body) from linguistic structures: The structures of language, or text, represent an element of stasis according to Kristeva, whereas the subject in process opens up to the complexity of the subject's drives which move it beyond any structural stasis (Prud'homme and Légaré 2006). The concept of the subject in process moves beyond the structures by which subjects are constituted. For Kristeva, it challenges the linguistic structures in subject formations, emerging through Saussure's structural linguistics, and also through Lacan's psychoanalytic work. For us, it shifts conceptions of humanness into the unknown, beyond fixed structures, beyond the discursive, into, and potentially beyond, the human.

Our teacher education pedagogies are governed by a broad structural milieu, as outlined earlier. This milieu is made up of governing structures at a national, local and university level, including government policy (such as teacher education and immigration policy), local laws and regulations, and university policies, as well as the structures of wider societal and local community attitudes and understandings.

These structures might be seen as what Kristeva calls the symbolic. The symbolic structures represent the environment in which the subject in process develops and makes meaning as semiotic occurances. Kristeva's (1984) semiotic is a key element of the subject in process and is useful to us as a concept in questioning the intricacies of student teacher and lecturer subject formations as and beyond the human.

The Semiotic

The semiotic makes a significant contribution to more complex articulations of human formation. It is what creates meaning in the signifying process of the construction of the self, and what opens up to more complex, unsignified unknowabilities. In conceptualising the subject as in constant process, meaningful signification depends on the connectedness of the subject. It always 'requires both the semiotic and symbolic modalities' (McCance 1996: 147). The semiotic, then, must be seen alongside and within the symbolic milieu. The symbolic co-exists with the semiotic and, following Kristeva (1984), gives the process of signification its structure, through the governing laws, rules and attitudes as referred to above. For Kristeva the symbolic creates a structural framework, and the semiotic exists alongside, or within, the symbolic. The semiotic adds 'the heterogeneity of meaning' (Prud'homme and Légaré 2006: 4). It alerts us to multiple interpretations and implications of and within the symbolic milieu, and it creates the opening for potential heterogeneous meanings that move beyond human understandings, meanings, relationships or correlations.

For Kristeva the semiotic exists in the chora, an inner space that cannot be represented. This means that the semiotic acts in unknowable ways, as '[d]iscrete … energy' or drives, that occur in the not yet formed and the continually forming subject, as a result of 'constraints imposed … by family and social structures. In this way the drives', are '"energy" charges'. The chora is 'a nonexpressive totality formed by the drives and their stasis in a motility that is as full of movement as it is regulated' (Kristeva 1984: 25). The semiotic chora, then, ties the symbolic influence to the semiotic meaning-making. It 'designates a heterogeneousness beyond representation, an unconscious supplementarity that belongs inescapably to the process of significance' (McCance 1996: 147). It represents, perhaps, what we, or our student teachers, may feel but be unable to articulate, that is nevertheless meaningful in relation to our/their sense of belonging or alienation, elation and despair, or other sensations, throughout their studies.

Through this chora the semiotic performs multiple roles in the subject in process (Kristeva 1998). It entangles the subject in process with its context, landscape, wider milieu of space, place, relationality; it counters the homogeneity of the symbolic structures; and it represents that which pre-exists the subject. The semiotic energises the subject in its process, by heterogenising it through the nuances through which it communicates, adding to and moving beyond the sign systems, or symbolic environment (Prud'homme and Légaré 2006). We now examine the nuances of the semiotic as pre-existing subject formations in our pedagogies.

Pre-existing the Subject

From a Kristevan perspective, the semiotic arises in the realm of the maternal body, suggesting that the semiotic already exists before the subject itself. This also suggests that its elements and drives arise from a pre-existing environment in which the subject comes about and is formed (Kristeva 1998). So, conceptualising ours or our student teachers' subjectivities through the semiotic reaffirms that the subject in process is irreducible to a particular theoretical model or conceptual framework, but rather it is a 'non-verbal semiotic articulation of the process'. It further opens up the idea of the subject to the pre-symbolic that again transgresses our knowing, identification or articulation. The semiotic is, then, a 'space of mobility' (Prud'homme and Légaré 2006: 2), that introduces and provokes movement in the subject away from a belief in the static unitary subject, to one of uncertainty, of being in process. Kristeva (1991: 8) illustrates this process with her conception of the foreigner:

> Not belonging to any place, any time, any love. A lost origin, the impossibility to take root, a rummaging memory, the present in abeyance. The space of the foreigner is a moving train, a plane in flight, the very transition that precludes stopping. As to landmarks, there are none.

The uncertainty arising in the swings when the present is 'in abeyance' between, for example, our student teachers' highs and lows, stability and instability, or what Kristeva (1991: 10) also describes as the foreigners' sensation of being 'always elsewhere, … belong[ing] nowhere,' underlines the notion that meaning, through the semiotic, already pre-exists the subject. It shifts the subject beyond the ego, stasis, and homogeneity, into a space and a history that is both uncertain and already existing, in a similar way to the posthuman connectedness and 'unity of all living matter' and its already existing relationships with 'contemporary subjectivity' (Braidotti 2013: 57). It actualizes the flows of energies, to which Braidotti points us, as an unsettling of the comfort and certainty of a present that is known and knowable, to invoke complex histories and realities in posthuman subjectivities.

Posited as arising within the maternal body also implicates the semiotic in the materiality of the body which, like subjectivity itself, is always in process via bodily drives, rhythms, tones and movements (Oliver 1998). Importantly, inserting Kristeva's semiotic shifts body and gender from an historical association 'with the feminine, the female, or woman, that is often "denigrated as weak, immoral, unclean, or decaying"' (Oliver 1998), and towards the:

> connection between mind and body, culture and nature, psyche and soma, matter and representation, by insisting both that bodily drives are discharged in representation, and that the logic of signification is already operating in the material body. (Oliver 1998)

For us, Kristeva's inclusion of materialities of and beyond bodies offers theoretical access points to forces that exist beyond the human. It provides opportunities to transform our pedagogies beyond the 'logic of signification' by incorporating the unknowable interdependencies of the semiotic and the symbolic, from an environmentally connected perspective. Implicating us in the worldly concerns of sustainability and the Anthropocene, it is through such unpredictable and unknowable notions, that the semiotic can further be seen to energise our students and ourselves as subjects.

Nomadic Posthuman Subjects

If early childhood student teachers, and we ourselves, are 'infinitely in construction, de-constructible, open and evolving', as Kristeva (2008: 2) claims, and nomadic, complex and relational, as Braidotti (2013) claims, then our pedagogies in early childhood teacher education programmes too remain open, always in flux and evolving. Braidotti's (2013: 198) nomadic subject orientation suggests a positive view of potentialities that becomes further connected through the idea that desire is a positive and transformative notion, a 'plenitude' of a 'posthuman ethics.' It contrasts with desire being seen as a lack to be satisfied, as it is commonly conceptualised in the psychoanalytic field. Embedded as we are within the Aotearoa New Zealand global and uniquely local higher education landscape, Kristeva's thinking alerts us to the ways in which neither our students nor we ourselves can ever think that we know ourselves fully, and that we can also never know others in any complete or total way. Kristeva's (1991) thinking on the foreigner encourages us to suggest that we are all foreigners within, constantly constructing ourselves through our lived, felt and examined and also our unexamined unknowable experiences, immersions, inter- and intra-relationships and energies. Building on this attack on certainty, if we add Braidotti's notion of desires as forward moving, affirmative, nomadic and transformative, we perceive an element of pedagogical hope, direction and opportunity for forward thinking in our teaching.

Conceptualising the Kristevan subject in light of Braidotti's transformational desires produces a hopeful surge towards new ways of thinking and being, that from both perspectives depend on and are driven by their surrounding context—local and global, natural, technological, anthropocentric, anthropomorphic, and beyond, as Wallin (2017) and Latour (2011) insist. In other words, our own and our student teachers' teaching subjectivities are always shaped in ways that we may or may not be aware of, affected in ways that we might notice, or not notice, implicated by and working always within the complications of our cultural, political and historical milieu of beliefs, systems, histories and desires. This loose outline of influences helps to explain the inexplicable in our teaching encounters. On one occasion we might sense an unexpected bodily reaction in response to comments from our students, or our line managers, while, on another day, in another affective state or circumstance—of which we may or may not be conscious—our reaction to a similar comment may be completely different, even though, on the surface, the situation might appear the same.

Kristeva's notion of the subject in process, and particularly the element of the semiotic, help to bridge the nomadic nature of the subjects in our teacher education programmes: from, between and beyond human-posthuman, nature-culture binaries. Bridging and blurring these boundaries sets us up to perceive and enact our pedagogies differently. Reorienting ourselves through and beyond Kristeva's humanist theory, enables us to entangle the human with that which is more than human, unknown, pre-existing each of us as open and evolving subjects. It enables us to conceive of potentialities to move beyond the human, not as a literal act in ourselves or our students, but in our conceptions. Orientations matter, and orientations constrain, so if we are oriented towards the possibility of non-meanings, non-knowing and uncertainty, we can present to our students a very different stance, than if we are fundamentally oriented towards clarity and understanding, towards performative outputs delivered in neoliberal frames.

Rethinking the human subject in this way leads to new orientations but does not leave the subject behind. We do not propose that the subject be eliminated. However we do suggest that the subject be de-elevated and de-glorified. Ahmed (2010) reminds us of the need to open up to unexpected, on the surface invisible, histories and depths of particular things, knowledges and beings. Re-theorising the subject in Kristeva's subject in process through a posthuman lens affirms Jones and Hoskins' (2016) suggestion of the already present invisible histories and diverse knowledges. It leads us to conceive of the unknown in Kristeva's subject in process as what Wallin (2017) sees as the 'unfathomable'—that is, to a mode of thinking beyond the Anthropocene, beyond representation, where we may not expect, for example, to fully 'understand', see as 'true', or expect 'representation' in our student teachers' essays or assignments. And further, it may energise us to desist from reterritorializing, re-naming, or re-appropriating into some kind of normality, those uncertainties and unfathomabilities with which we are *too* uncomfortable. These shifts in our orientations away from a human-centric cognition and knowing may also relax us, in a sense of instilling a form of posthuman trust. In other words, if we de-elevate the human as unitary and glorious, we are enabling also a view that life exists and goes on, with or without us. Together with our students, we might be nomadic subjects in a tightly interwoven and connected world, which unfathomably both affects us and our pedagogies, but which also, unfathomably, pre-and post-exists us.

In our view, Kristeva and Braidotti's work opens up serious possibilities for seeing early childhood teacher education through a less human-centric lens, as involving 'complex and relational subject[s] framed by embodiment, sexuality, affectivity, empathy and desire as core qualities' (Braidotti 2013: 26). It allows the human 'I' to be encompassing of and recognized as within a vast range of different relationships—seen and the unseen, humans and non-humans, 'real' and the 'unreal'—and in relation to a deliberate openness, to diverse beliefs, practices, ways of being and relating to pasts, presents and futures. It allows us to consider more intentionally that it is not only fine, but important, for us not to understand students' orientations, or all situations. This means doing the doing differently, as Taylor (2016) urges.

But recognising that we ourselves are foreigners within ourselves, in and beyond the human realm, can be frightening—experienced as a loss of control. We argue that this can be seen in a different light. Given that even the notion of what is human is a contested space, there is a certain liberation in the realisation that opens us up further and more comfortably, to the discomfort of unknowability, not just of us, but of our nomadic existence, physically, emotionally and conceptually (Braidotti 2013). In this realisation, our nomadic posthuman*ness* becomes, overall, a more affirmative, positive orientation towards divergences in our teaching, in our orientations towards humans—ourselves and our students—as well as towards our/their relationships with metaphysical, wider worldly connections, invisible pasts, and framings of the present and their and all of our future.

Concluding Comments

In Kristeva's (2008: 2) work, subjects are always in a process of ongoing formation 'open and evolving.' This chapter has considered how being 'open and evolving' thrusts the subject of the human 'I' into a realm of unknown-ness. At the same time, it has aligned all 'human subjects'—that is ourselves, our student teachers, and other humans involved in the teaching milieu—with Braidotti's (2013) notion of subjects as nomadic. It is these two notions, of the open and evolving human subject, and the transformation of the nomadic human subject through the potential of desire, that leads to re-thinking our pedagogies as posthuman possibilities.

This repositioning of Kristeva's human-centric philosophical perspective demonstrates the potential of destabilising the focus in conventional, dominant higher education pedagogies, towards foregrounding more-than-human things, beings and matters. Such a re-theorisation for teacher education programmes is complex and urgent, arising from the vibrant forces of new materialisms, the revelation of further kinds of voices, alternative meanings and matter (Barad 2015), and inter-relationships with other beings and species (Haraway 2007). It questions not only our own, but future teachers' pedagogies and abilities to respond to the ecological concerns that Latour (2011) situates in contemporary anthropocentric challenges, but also alerts us to thinking beyond an environmental conceptualisation. Nuanced intricacies throughout this chapter reveal an already tangled inter- and intra-dependent web with and beyond human actors in our two university settings, as we attempt to (re)imagine thing/energy/nature/culture connections in their messy, multidirectional, unpredictable performances of our early childhood student teachers' and our own histories, politics and realities. These philosophical analyses expose unexpected onto-epistemological connections of human and posthuman relationships with multiple wider worlds and promise possible new 'regimes of truth' (Springer 2016) which help us escape the 'suffocating strictures' not only of neoliberalist performative pressures, but of strictly humanist views on the subject, which we have only begun to examine. Exposing these cracks through posthuman encounters in New Zealand early childhood teacher education is not a comfort then, of sameness, smoothness or familiarity, but an enlivening elevation into further possible student teacher-lecturer explorations, realities and uncertainties.

References

Ahmed, S. (2010). Orientations matter. In D. Coole & S. Frost (Eds.), *New materialisms: Ontology, agency and politics* (pp. 234–257). Durham, UK: Duke University Press.

Arndt, S., & Tesar, M. (2018). Narrative methodologies: Challenging and elevating cross-cultural complexities. In S. M. Akpovo, M. J. Moran, & R. Brookshire (Eds.), *Collaborative cross-cultural research methodologies in early care and education contexts*. New York, NY: Routledge.

Ball, S. J. (2016). Neoliberal education? Confronting the slouching beast. *Policy Futures in Education, 14*(8), 1046–1059. https://doi.org/10.1177/1478210316664259.

Barad, K. (2015). Transmaterialities: Trans*/matter/realities and queer political imaginings. *GLQ: A Journal of Lesbian and Gay Studies, 21*(2–3), 387–422. https://doi.org/10.1215/10642684-2843239.

Braidotti, R. (2013). *The posthuman*. Cambridge, UK: Polity Press.

Ffrench, P., & Lack, R.-F. (Eds.). (1998). *The Tel Quel reader*. London, UK: Routledge.

Haraway, D. (2007). *When species meet*. Minneapolis, MN: University of Minnesota Press.

Haraway, D. (2016). *Staying with the trouble: Making kin in the Chthulucene*. Durham, UK: Duke University Press.

Jones, A., & Hoskins, T. K. (2016). A mark on paper: The matter of indigenous-settler history. In C. A. Taylor & C. Hughes (Eds.), *Posthuman research practices in education* (pp. 75–92). London, UK: Palgrave Macmillan.

Kristeva, J. (1984). *Revolution in poetic language* (M. Waller, Trans.). New York, NY: Columbia University Press.

Kristeva, J. (1991). *Strangers to ourselves*. New York, NY: Columbia University Press.
Kristeva, J. (1998). The subject in process. In P. Ffrench (Ed.), *The Tel Quel reader* (pp. 133–178). London, UK: Routledge.
Kristeva, J. (2008). *Does European culture exist?* Paper presented at the Dagmar and Václav Havel Foundation VIZE 97 prize, Prague Crossroads. Retrieved from http://www.vize.cz/download/laureat-Julia-Kristeva-en-speech.pdf.
Latour, B. (2011). Politics of nature: East and West perspectives. *Ethics & Global Politics, 4*(1), 71–80.
McCance, D. (1996). L'écriture limite: Kristeva's postmodern feminist ethics. *Hypatia, 11*(2), 141–160.
Mika, C. (2012). Overcoming 'being' in favour of knowledge: The fixing effect of 'mātauranga'. *Educational Philosophy and Theory, 44*(10), 1080–1092. https://doi.org/10.1111/j.1469-5812.2011.00771.x.
Ministry of Education. (1996). *Te Whāriki - he whāriki mātauranga mō ngā mokopuna o aotearoa: Early childhood curriculum*. Wellington, New Zealand: Learning Media.
Ministry of Education. (2017). *Te Whāriki he whāriki mātauranga mō ngā mokopuna o aotearoa: Early childhood curriculum—Draft for consultation*. Wellington: New Zealand Government.
Ministry of Social Development. (2016). *The changing face of New Zealand*. Retrieved from https://www.msd.govt.nz/about-msd-and-our-work/work-programmes/initiatives/connecting-diverse-communities/why-was-this-work-started.html.
Oliver, K. (1998). Summary of major themes: Kristeva and feminism. *Julia Kristeva*. Retrieved from http://www.cddc.vt.edu/feminism/kristeva.html.
Orange, C. (1989). *The Treaty of Waitangi*. Wellington, New Zealand: Bridget Williams Books.
Peters, M. A., & Tesar, M. (2017). Bad research, bad education: The contested evidence for evidence-based research, policy and practice in education. In J. Lynch, J. Rowlands, T. Gale, & A. Skourdoumbis (Eds.), *Practice theory: Diffractive readings in professional practice and education* (pp. 231–246). London, UK: Routledge.
Peters, M. A., & Tesar, M. (2018). Philosophy and performance of neoliberal ideologies: History, politics and human subjects. In M. A. Peters & M. Tesar (Eds.), *Contesting governing ideologies: An educational philosophy and theory reader on neoliberalism* (pp. 2–18). New York, NY: Routledge.

Prud'homme, J., & Légaré, L. (2006). The subject in process. *Signo [online], Rimouski (Quebec)*. Retrieved from http://www.signosemio.com/Kristeva/semanalysis.asp.

Ritchie, J. (2015). Social, cultural, and ecological justice in the age of the anthropocene: A New Zealand early childhood care and education perspective. *Journal of Pedagogy, 6*(2), 41–56.

Ritchie, J., & Skerrett, M. (2014). *Early childhood education in Aotearoa New Zealand: History, pedagogy and liberation*. New York, NY: Palgrave Macmillan.

Springer, S. (2016). *The discourse of neoliberalism: An anatomy of a powerful idea*. London, UK: Rowman & Littlefield International.

Stone, L. (2004). Julia Kristeva's 'mystery' of the subject in process. In J. D. Marshall (Ed.), *Poststructuralism, philosophy, pedagogy* (pp. 119–139). Dordrecht, The Netherlands: Kluwer Academic.

Taylor, C. A. (2016). Edu-crafting a cacophonous ecology: Posthumanist research practices for education. In C. A. Taylor & C. Hughes (Eds.), *Posthuman research practice in education* (pp. 5–24). London, UK: Palgrave Macmillan.

Tesar, M. (2015). *Te Whāriki* in Aotearoa New Zealand: Witnessing and resisting neoliberal and neo-colonial discourses in early childhood education [invited chapter]. In V. Pacini-Ketchabaw & A. Taylor (Eds.), *Unsettling the colonial places and spaces of early childhood education* (pp. 145–170). New York, NY: Routledge.

Tesar, M., & Arndt, S. (2017). Cross cultural complexities of educational policies. *Policy Futures in Education, 15*(6), 665–669. https://doi.org/10.1177/1478210317736181.

Wallin, J. J. (2017). Pedagogy at the brink of the post-anthropocene. *Educational Philosophy and Theory, 49*(11), 1099–1111.

6

Putting Posthuman Theories to Work in Educational Leadership Programmes

Kathryn J. Strom and John Lupinacci

Introduction

Educators are socialized into 'commonsense' ways of seeing the world that support rational, humanistic, anthropocentric thinking. The U.S. schooling system further reinforces this reductionist logic by defining education in quantitative terms, turning teachers, students, and learning processes into numerical data points. These perspectives tend to shape educational leaders' (i.e. those occupying a range of leadership positions in educational settings) understandings of leadership and research. As they enter professional doctorate, or three year Ed.D. programmes, many educational leaders bring with them entrenched

K. J. Strom (✉)
Educational Leadership Department,
California State University, East Bay, Hayward, CA, USA
e-mail: kathryn.strom2@csueastbay.edu

J. Lupinacci
Washington State University, Pullman, WA, USA
e-mail: john.lupinacci@wsu.edu

© The Author(s) 2019
C. A. Taylor and A. Bayley (eds.), *Posthumanism and Higher Education*,
https://doi.org/10.1007/978-3-030-14672-6_6

views of objectivity and and linearity, as well as a view of leadership as enacted by individual human actors. This chapter discusses ways to disrupt commonsense thinking reinforcing individualistic, representational, and anthropocentric worldviews by drawing on pedagogies informed by posthuman thinkers (including Braidotti 2013; Code 2006; Deleuze and Guattari 1987; Plumwood 2002) to reframe practice and educational research in more affirmative, connected, multiplistic terms that emphasise productive difference and relations with the more-than-human world. We begin by locating ourselves in our geographical contexts and theoretical genealogies, followed by a description of the ways that we put theory to work (Strom and Martin 2013) in our practices in two social-justice focused graduate education programmes in the United States.

Locating Ourselves in Contextual and Theoretical Assemblages

We begin by acknowledging that our 'selves' are not bounded individual subjects, but rather, are collective enunciations of the assemblages of *zoe-techno-geo* (human-nonhuman, technology, and earth-bound elements) (Braidotti 2017) and that we are produced with and by in an ongoing process. Simultaneously, we affirm our commitment to a feminist politics of location (Rich 1984), that is, an understanding that we are embodied and materially embedded in particular areas of the world and in particular communities, which afford us particular privileges and ways of being in the world, as well as shape our worldviews and our work (Braidotti 2013). Locating oneself politically vis-a-vis one's knowledge construction activities—which includes teaching—promotes accountability and transparency and resists what Haraway (1988: 584) terms 'the god trick' of being the voice 'from nowhere and everywhere.' Instead, we must speak from where we are to emphasise that no knowledge exists free from context or creator, but rather is produced from a particular location and is thus partial (though no less real for that partiality). We are also shaped by the theories and ideas that we bring to the classroom, which contribute to our practices. While we both position ourselves under a theoretical umbrella that encompasses similar ontological shifts, we enter into the posthuman conversation through slightly different emphases and bodies of scholarship, which in turn materialise in our pedagogies in different ways. We each locate ourselves next.

Katie

I grew up in a working class family in Montgomery, Alabama, and throughout my early years and adolescence was confronted constantly with issues of social justice, namely around race and poverty. These experiences drew me into teaching high-poverty students of color near the border of San Diego, California and Mexico, and later to a social-justice focused doctoral programme in teacher education. I now teach at one of the 23 California State University campuses, a system that, due to its commitment to social justice, has earned the nickname 'the People's University.' My colleagues and departmental/college leadership are supportive of my agenda to explore critical posthuman perspectives in my research and my teaching in the Educational Leadership for Social Justice Ed.D. programme, a three-year professional doctorate that serves mainly students of color in a variety of educational leadership positions (for example, teachers, principals, school district administrators, non-profit leaders, and higher education administrators). This supportive environment for different ways of thinking creates a 'smooth space' (Deleuze and Guattari 1987) that allows freedom to experiment.

My instruction and research is further produced within and by a theoretical assemblage of sociocultural theory (Vygotsky 1978), rhizomatics (Deleuze and Guattari 1987), and feminist nomadic theory/critical posthumanism (Braidotti 1994, 2011, 2013). Sociocultural theory was an initial influence in my work regarding pedagogy and teacher learning/development (the focus of my research). Sociocultural theory (Vygotsky 1978) views learning as a social, relational and collaborative activity where learners create increasingly complex understandings by engaging with others who can help scaffold, or provide contextual and responsive supports, to aid in the ongoing construction of knowledge.

These understandings inform my planning of activities with appropriate supports to help students grapple with difficult ideas. While sociocultural theory might be viewed as an entrypoint into a more complex framework that acknowledges a multiplicity of factors, both human and non-human, that play a role in the learning process, sociocultural theory does not entail an explicitly political analysis that helps to explain why we cannot seem to change the overall patterns of teaching, nor how individual teachers navigate the multiple shaping factors in their own settings. I moved to Deleuze and Guattari (1987) whose process ontology and concepts like 'assemblage' were fruitful for conceptualizing the vital multiplicity of shifting human, material, and discursive elements that work together in particular ways to co-produce teaching and other activities. However, searching for a more explicit theory of decentered subjectivity, I took up Braidotti's (1994, 2011) nomadic theory and Spinoza-through-Deleuze-inspired brand of critical posthumanism (2013).

Johnny

I grew up in an Italian working class family in Detroit, Michigan. Given the socio-political climate of Detroit, my early experiences were close to the tensions and activism of civil rights work in combination with intense labor organizing surrounding the increasing outsourcing and collapsing economy of the automotive industry. Forged in the fires of these experiences, I was drawn to a career as a teacher in schools working with youth to connect place-based mathematics and science learning with activism aimed at addressing local issues of social justice and environmental degradation. Later, I turned toward critically-oriented doctoral programmes and theories to help think, and teach, differently about education and the possibilities for very different futures. I currently research and teach at Washington State University (WSU) in the College of Education as faculty in the Cultural Studies and Social Thought in Education (CSSTE) Ph.D. programme and a statewide Educational Leadership Ed.D. programme. Unique to both of these programmes is a strong identification with and a deep commitment to diversity, social justice, and sustainability. With support from current and past students and colleagues, the College of Education at WSU fosters critical perspectives in education, including posthumanist philosophy, as part of a larger commitment to my work with teachers, researchers, and educational leaders to engage in (re)imagining education (Lupinacci and Lupinacci Ward 2017). This rare kind of institutional support for students to learn to recognize and rethink who and what we consider and value as teachers in our learning communities has undoubtedly made it possible to experiment with radical pedagogies and to teach with/for the more-than-human world.

My work focuses on interrupting human supremacy through such scholarship as ecocritical pedagogy (Lupinacci and Happel-Parkins 2015, 2017), which includes critical animal studies (Best 2009; Nocella II et al. 2015; Twine 2010), anarchism (Amster et al. 2009; Nocella II et al. 2015), and ecofeminism (Code 2006; Plumwood 1993, 2002; Warren 1990, 2000). For many scholars and teachers there is a tremendous amount of privilege associated with Western industrial culture, and I often teach students who also are deeply influenced by Western culture. Therefore, I focus intensely on what Foucault (2010) referred to as an ontology of ourselves and practices, turning a critical and ethical lens inward while recognizing that the position of teacher educator and educational researcher is often one of a privileged member of Western industrial culture. Thus, my approach involves engaging in how 'we' can, together, critically (re)imagine education in ways that critically interrogates how that notion of 'we' is often a humancentered, and Eurocentrically, constructed idea. Furthermore, I am interested in how critical posthumanist pedagogies are a political act of ceasing to do such harm as social injustice and environmental degradation and learning to do better for one another and the more-than-human world.

We both recognize that there are also centuries of wisdom in indigenous epistemologies not explicitly included in this chapter. However, the work in this chapter is aimed not at those whose narratives and knowledges embody an ecological worldview but, rather, at the majority of educators and educational leaders who go about business-as-usual without critically examining their—and our—implicit and explicit roles in reproducing injustice in the world. With this in mind, in the following section, we each share an example of a pedagogical experiment.

Katie describes a series of activities meant to help students develop a relational and political perspective of themselves in relation to their research, and Johnny illustrates a unit of instruction that challenges the anthropocentrism of who is recognized as a 'teacher.' These examples are intended to disrupt commonsense thinking reinforcing the dangerous myth of the separated, objective researcher, and instead reframe research in more situated, fluid, relational, and complex terms. They aim to help educators recognize the way a humanist/humancentric worldview is implicated in maintaining both human and White heteropatriarchal supremacy, and to begin considering as part of imaginative projects ecological, multiplistic alternatives that are socially just and encompass all living systems.

Katie: Developing Critical and Complex Orientations to Research

To problematize the deeply internalized humanist ideals of objectivity, researcher transcendence, reduction of complex phenomena, and one-to-one correspondences, I begin all my research classes with a jigsaw activity entitled 'The Parable of the Three Scholar Practitioners,' the main text of which encompasses a set of three fictional narratives, written by me, about Ed.D. students from different contexts in the U.S. The general premise is that all three were interested in the same problem—disparities in academic achievement between dominant and marginalised groups of students, as demonstrated by standardised testing scores—but each created very different studies that promised a very different material impact. These narratives are provided below in shortened form.

Narrative 1

Bob, a White man in his late forties, grew up on the eastern coast of the United States in a wealthy and exclusively White community. He went on to coach various high school sports and eventually became a high school principal. After his first year, Bob and his staff examined their testing data and discovered that the Black and Latino students at his school lagged far behind their White peers. Bob was told by his district superintendent that he needed to address this issue. Bob was frustrated—all the students in his school got the same opportunities, so he didn't understand why the superintendent seemed to be blaming him for these students' underachievement. While he was dealing with this situation, Bob was also getting ready to plan his dissertation study in his Ed.D. programme, which had a programme focus on 'accountability' and 'ensuring all students can achieve at high levels.' For his project, Bob decided to interview teachers to find out what was going on with the students of colour who were bringing his scores down. He titled the study 'Solving the Problem of the Achievement Gap among At-Risk Students.' He scheduled time with ten different teachers at his school and, using the achievement data to frame the conversation, elicited his teachers' thoughts about why the Black and Latino students in their classes were doing so poorly.

Narrative 2

Gloria was in her final year in an Ed.D. programme that emphasized critical, participatory pedagogy and social-justice focused professional development as a way to disrupt oppressive patterns of schooling. A Latina whose family had immigrated to California when she was seven, Gloria grew up attending high-poverty schools with other mainly black and brown children. From the time she entered elementary school, she was classified as 'Limited English Proficient,' a label that made her feel inferior. Luckily, she was able to transfer to a school with a strong bilingual programme, and she eventually graduated and became a bilingual middle school teacher, teaching students ages 10–12, and later the Bilingual Coordinator for her district. There, she prided herself on her advocacy for English learner students and families, whose knowledge and experiences were often disregarded. Despite her work, the test scores in her district continued to show that English learners, as a group, performed at a rate much lower than that of their native-English speaking peers. Knowing that English learners were often not provided the pedagogical supports needed for them to simultaneously learn the language and content, she decided to turn a critical pedagogy lens on teacher knowledge and instruction for her dissertation. She conducted case studies with three teachers at three different schools, each with significant numbers of English learners in their classes, and took off two weeks from work to observe lessons for a full unit of instruction for each teacher.

Narrative 3

A Black woman in her fifties, Assata grew up in Oakland, California in the 1970s. She attended public school, where the teachers often told her to 'speak proper English' and where she was constantly in trouble for talking or being loud. Despite many negative experiences, Assata graduated with top honors and pursued her teaching degree at Howard University, a historic Black university in Maryland. After fifteen years in the classroom in Baltimore, Assata became a vice principal at a middle school, where she saw that White teachers often over-disciplined Black students because they didn't meet their teachers' expectations for white behavioral norms and language. She decided to go back to school for her Ed.D. to study the impact of these cultural chasms and find solutions to mediate them. Her Ed.D. programme focused on culturally and linguistically responsive leadership, and she learned to put a theoretical term to her experiences in school and what she was seeing as a vice principal: 'Cultural Mismatch.' As Assata entered her third year, the district conversation was once again on the 'achievement gap.' For her project, she chose to look into the issue of disparities, but decided to focus on the tests themselves and the ways students interacted with them. She designed a qualitative study with two main parts. First, she conducted interviews with a sample of equal numbers of Black and Latino eighth grade students in her district regarding how they perceived the test and how it impacted their self-esteem and attitude toward school. Then, she conducted a content analysis of the test, using a frame of cultural mismatch.

Participants begin in homogenous groups, reading and discussing one of the narratives. As a group, they identify the factors and conditions that influenced the ways the ways the Ed.D. student-researcher identified a research problem and designed a study to investigate that issue. The cases each show that a specific, situated combination of elements—including, but not limited to, the student-researcher's background/experiences and current professional position, the emphasis of the Ed.D. programme they were attending, and their district's focus on accountability/testing—shaped their approach to the problem and the methodological decisions they made in designing and carrying out their study, which in turn shaped the findings that were produced. In these homogenous groups, students consider, from the findings that were generated, what knowledge might have been constructed from the findings and whether, for instance, this knowledge might play into dominant narratives of deficit about students, or whether it might be utilized for disrupting inequitable status quos. Students also imagine what the possible material impact of that knowledge might be—for example, how it might be used to inform a school district initiative, impact policy, and so on.

Students then move into heterogeneous groups, where they discuss their ideas with peers who read the other two stories. From this discussion, they work together to draw out some of the dimensions of an assemblage of elements that might shape a research study and affect what that study might do in terms of impact. Typically, students identify that the researcher brings a multiplicity of background factors which works together with specific contextual factors, methodological decisions, theoretical influences, and political power flows to shape the projects and subsequent knowledge constructed from them. Students then take part in a whole-class conversation where I introduce the idea of 'assemblage' (Deleuze and Guattari 1987) as substantive multiplicity of human and non-human, material and discursive elements that work together to produce something. Together, we discuss the implications of this decentered perspective and problematize traditional ideas of researcher objectivity and distance in research. Using the ideas we have just distilled from the 'three researchers' activity, we then reframe our understanding around the notion that human actors do not autonomously carry out their research and make decisions in a vacuum. Rather, agency is distributed across these assemblages of human and nonhuman elements and forces (Bennett 2009).

However, we cannot totally disregard the human in research, either—to do so would merely construct another kind of transcendence (Braidotti 2013). Therefore, in later classes we build on the activities described above by applying the feminist notion of a politics of location (Rich 1984; Haraway 1988) to research to begin to develop a grounded and accountable practice. As part of this learning we call out the 'god trick' of research that claims to be objective, and we connect the notion of the 'vision from everywhere and nowhere' (Haraway 1988: 584) to the long history of harm and exploitation of marginalized 'others' in research studies. Drawing on these understandings, as well as their previous learning, students begin to create cartographies that map out their own geo-political locations (Braidotti 2013) and explore other material-discursive flows that could possibly shape their future research projects and the evental impact that might have.

Through these activities, students begin to develop a more complex, decentered understanding of the process of inquiry and the ways we construct knowledge. These activities also set the stage for a qualitative research sequence that promote situated forms of research of which the researcher has an agential, yet partial, role, and help students learn to conduct research consistent with goals of social justice and local change-making. After three years of piloting these activities (in continuously evolving forms), I have found that they help students develop a more multiplistic understanding of the self, as well as a commitment to critical reflexive processes of interrogating the agency of the researcher and probing other influences that shape the knowledge produced by research inquiry.

In addition, students have also been willing to consider the complexity of the 'human-and' in research: the idea that, while we can recognise that multiple elements on the material-discursive continuum contribute to the process of inquiry and knowledge production, that we must remain accountable to the organizing structures we, as the researcher, impose (such as coding and categorizing processes and choices made in the representation of findings). While students have reported, in informal course feedback, that they are eager to disrupt positivist ideas around objectivity and neutrality and firmly ground themselves in relation to their research, encouraging them to take on a post-anthropocentric lens has proved more challenging.

However, students I am able to work with in a longer term capacity, such as those I have continued to support through their dissertations, have developed projects in which they demonstrate that they view the research process, and their own phenomena, as entailing multiplicities of human and more-than-human factors, and have even approached research conventions like the literature review from a perspective that accounts for a complex constellation of quasi-causes contributing to the central issue guiding the study. It takes time to practice these more complex and decentered ways of thinking, and more than a single course or set of activities may be required to help students begin to think differently about themselves, their research, and the world.

The activities described above both decentre humanism and anthropocentrism in efforts to work toward a 'human-*and*' paradigm. Posthumanism has multiple entry points, as it is not a unified philosophy, but rather composed of a proliferation of many fields and lines of thinking: anti-humanism, new materialism, indigenous epistemologies, anti-anthropocentrism, science and technology studies (STS), and more (Braidotti 2017; Taylor 2016). Some of these fields are related, while others come from very different intellectual genealogies. These genealogies, and how they inform the intentions and practices from that type of posthumanism, matter. As Braidotti (2013) notes, some forms of posthumanism merely work to reinforce humanist and anthropocentric cores, such as those that focus on the exploitative power of technology and possibilities of human perfectability. Others, such as speculative posthumanism and object ontology (Latour 2005), move the focus entirely away from the (human) subject, which raises the possibility of reinforcing the same physical and cultural/epistemic violence that has come from failing to practice the politics of location. The above activities represent a pedagogical experimentation that attempts to keep the human researcher in the conversation as part of a decentered posthuman assemblage, keeping the researcher both grounded and accountable, while also connected outward and entangled with exteriorities (Braidotti 2018).

Johnny: Learning from More-Than-Human Teachers to Disrupt Human Supremacy

In my practice, I have found it powerful to share accounts of animal intelligence and care. In this example, I share one of the small stories about elephants that I include in classes to illuminate the ways teachers exist not only in diverse human cultures, but also among our animal kin. In Africa poaching and massive habitat loss devastate elephant communities, and as a result, they additionally suffer from a loss of elder elephant knowledge. Over the past 100 years, the elephant population on the continent of Africa has dropped dramatically. The World Wildlife Fund for Nature (WWF) report that 3–5 million elephants were roaming Africa in the 1930s and 1940s, but due to hunting for trophies and tusks in the 1950s, elephant populations plummeted. The WWF further state (2017): 'In the 1980s…an estimated 100,000 elephants were being killed per year and up to 80% of herds were lost in some regions. In Kenya, the population plummeted by 85% between 1973 and 1989.'

While recent efforts to protect the population have seen some success, an increase in hyperaggression, depression, and unpredictable behaviors amongst elephants has also been observed. Sadly, but also fascinatingly, scientists are reporting that changes in communication among this non-human species is due to a loss of elder elephants in the elephant communities. In an essay titled 'Elephant Breakdown,' Bradshaw et al. (2005) explain that elephants are renowned for their close social relationships. Further, Bradshaw et al. (2005: 807) report that 'male socialization begins during infancy with the mother and a tight constellation of all mothers. But in adolescence, males leave the natal family to participate in older all-male groups.' They explain that the elder males in elephant societies play a critical role in the socialization of adolescent male elephants to quell aggression and learn to be adult elephants, as do female elephants—as this work shows, younger female elephants separated from their elder counterparts are not socialised regarding to how to raise young elephants. Bradshaw et al. (2005: 807) explain: 'Young elephants are reared in a matriarchal society, embedded in complex layers of extended family. Culls and illegal poaching have fragmented these patterns of social attachment by eliminating the supportive stratum of the matriarch and older female caretakers.'

What this highlights is that without elders to teach young elephants how to live and become contributing members of strong, healthy elephant communities, future generations of elephants are susceptible to dangerous behaviors. This situation perpetuates a cycle in which the elephants are further separated from one another and from the habitat in which they would mostly likely thrive together as social beings. This example also teaches us that humans are not the only species teaching our young through a complex communicative system of language that passes on important knowledge for collective survival. It not only reminds us of the importance of elder knowledge, but also poses a fundamental disruption of human exceptionalism: *we are not the only species with teachers.* After sharing the story about the loss of elder elephants, I ask the educational leaders in class to consider the more-than-human teachers in their diverse communities. I ask them to also to consider who in their communities are doing the kind of teaching modeled by the elder elephants in the story. This story and the dialogue among students writing, and sharing, about the kind of teaching and leadership modeled by the elder elephants becomes a strong catalyst for discussing intelligence, knowledge, and language as something that extends beyond the humanist and Eurocentric constructions of thought and communication.

Extending this idea, in most of the courses I teach, I often assign Quinn's (1995) novel *Ishmael* in which a wonderfully rich and complex learning relationship unfolds when an eager human being responds to an ad placed by what he quickly learns was a gorilla. The ad in the story reads: 'TEACHER seeks pupil. Must have an earnest desire to save the world. Apply in person' (Quinn 1995: 3). Accompanied by some laughter and confusion when the human character in the book finds out that his potential teacher is not human, a vibrant class dialogue ensues after the educational leaders complete the reading, and they talk through this fiction in very real, material ways. I end the discussion by introducing an assignment: over the course of the semester we will all be writing reflectively about a learning relationship in which we seek out a more-than-human teacher. Then, I invite students, as part of the coursework, to identify one such more-than-human teacher for the semester and to write this teacher a letter expressing their interest in learning from what this teacher is willing to offer.

After writing this letter, I ask the students to keep a weekly diary where they journal what they learn from this *different* sort of teacher-student relationship. Often students begin by writing about how different and challenging the assignment may be, but after a few weeks, the discussions deepen and, as we are addressing how to teach for social justice and sustainability, students share about what they are learning from their more-than-human relationships. The stories shared are rich and provide an excellent context for discussing how we are learning to teach from participating in a different sort of teaching and learning relationship. Simultaneously, we are practicing listening to the more-than-human world and learning together how to respect diverse species and their intrinsic worth and value in our living, local ecologies—our community. Students write about sitting in silence and what they hear, smell, and feel. I ask students to consider what they are learning and how that learning process is in relationship to social justice and sustainability. In efforts to build their abilities to share such often-shamed relationships, the students provide feedback to each other and report out to each other regarding their learning. The results are exciting conversations.

Although students' often begin by anthropomorphizing non-human others, I use this as teaching moment to reframe and acknowledge that this act is not so much a problem as it is a step toward recognizing how deeply entrenched in human supremacy we are. Such conversations provide an opportunity to challenge students to learn open to communication with another species that is not bound entirely in humanness. As an example of how this plays out, students often journal about learning from stacks of trees, or a particular tree. They frequently start the journaling by referring to the trees as having a gender (often female), and then refer to the ways she speaks to them. It is not until a few journal entries later, perhaps even after a few weeks, that things settle and students begin journaling about being with trees (or a tree). They notice more around the trees, pointing out the birds, insects, moss, and signs of other life co-existing within this system. In this way, their journaling moves from a high anthropomorphic fiction (which is not problematic as an initial step) to an often very attuned perception of multiple species in communication. These journal entries produce learning-in-relation-with the more-than-human world and provokes deep questions about what constitutes a teacher and who/what can influence, and ought to be influencing, our learning.

Learning from more-than-human teachers is a theme that runs throughout my classes. Whether we discuss stories about crows that teach each other to fabricate and use tools (Kenward et al. 2006), explore the adventures of the escape-artist orangutan Ken Allen, or discover the fungal wonders of mycelial networks, we make connections from these stories to our everyday lives and ask ourselves a fundamental question: how is it we continue to treat one another and the more-than-human world with such disregard, disrespect, and cruelty? While it is easy to say, 'Let us learn from our more-than-human teachers,' it is much more difficult to confront our human-supremacist illusions of superiority and autonomy. And so, we (try to) learn together to listen to the many wise voices we often do not hear, and certainly do not consider as our teachers, while sharing stories and engaging in critically examining our assumptions and the lessons we are learning. This project illustrates that a critical, relational animal pedagogy has many things to teach us if we humble ourselves and learn to listen to the river, the wind, the maple tree, the osprey, the wolves, the worms… and the list goes on.

Extending Beyond the Humanist Conclusion(s): Posthuman Possibilities and Pedagogical Departures

This chapter has outlined pedagogic practices which are oriented within a posthuman paradigm and do important critical work—work which disrupts oppressive systems of power harmful to humans and more-than-human others as well. This is explicitly political work, and requires continual location in in a hybrid, 'and, and, and' paradigm that is non-dialectical (Braidotti 2013). Such work seeks to resist binaries even as they are continually constructed by systems that segment and separate us (Deleuze and Guattari 1987), while simultaneously recognizing that we (as teachers and students) are inextricably part of those systems and connected up to their normalizing power flows. We also have to be alert to resist the creation of new binaries in posthumanism between those who are posthuman and those who are not; the posthuman is an assemblage, and so must be our practice and our scholarship. If our aim is to change the way people think and relate to each other, we must actively disrupt exclusionary boundaries traditionally drawn around philosophy that dictate who is able to engage with these ideas (Strom 2018). We must also be able to articulate convincingly why these ideas matter—both in terms of their value but also in material terms of what they *do*, or what might be possible in thinking with them, to work toward goals of social, economic, environmental, species, and cosmic justice. This chapter has how this critical posthumanist work might be done through accessible pedagogical interventions in higher education.

We contend that the use of posthuman frameworks is an ethical imperative in an era of the anthropcene (Braidotti 2017)—an era where runaway capitalism has put the Earth and its many human and nonhuman others in peril, where extreme poverty and violence worldwide is resulting in massive suffering, and where rising neofascist, ethnonationalist movements are doubling down on fear of difference (Strom and Martin 2017). It is imperative that we develop a relational ethics, a worldview that, while starting from the embedded and embodied subject, entails a deliberate connection to multiple human/more-than-human others, forces, and affects. This humble approach decenters the myth of human exceptionalism and instead desires the solidarity and collaboration of all *zoe* (Braidotti 2013; Haraway 2016). Our pedagogic interventions show how we, in our contexts, are trying to do this. In our view, higher education has a responsibility not to evade this ethical imperative. Although it is true that the neoliberal university is an increasingly marketised entity with many rigid macropolitical structures to be navigated, there still exists some smooth space to pursue different types of thinking, such as that afforded by our two respective universities. We urge readers to seek out these smooth spaces in your own practices and institutions in order to proliferate the type thinking that can help create affirmative alternatives to our current oppressive status quo.

References

Amster, R., DeLeon, A., Fernandez, L., Nocella, A. J., II, & Shannon, D. (Eds.). (2009). *Contemporary anarchist studies: An introductory anthology of anarchy in the academy.* New York, NY: Routledge.

Bennett, J. (2009). *Vibrant matter: A political ecology of things.* Durham: Duke University Press.

Best, S. (2009). The rise of critical animal studies: Putting theory into action and animal liberation into higher education. *Journal for Critical Animal Studies, 7*(1), 9–52.

Bradshaw, G. A., Schore, A. N., Brown, J. L., Poole, J. H., & Moss, C. J. (2005). Elephant breakdown: Social trauma: Early disruption of attachment can affect the physiology, behaviour and culture of animals and humans over generations. *Nature, 433,* 807.

Braidotti, R. (1994). *Nomadic subjects: Embodiment and sexual difference in contemporary feminist theory.* New York, NY: Columbia University Press.

Braidotti, R. (2011). *Nomadic theory: The portable Rosi Braidotti.* New York, NY: Columbia University Press.

Braidotti, R. (2013). *The posthuman.* Cambridge, MA: Polity Press.

Braidotti, R. (2017, August). *The posthuman condition.* Presentation at the University of Utrecht, The Netherlands.

Braidotti, R. (2018). Affirmative ethics, posthuman subjectivity, and intimate scholarship: A conversation with Rosi Braidotti. In K. Strom, T. Mills, & A. Ovens (Eds.), *Decentering the researcher in intimate scholarship: Critical posthuman methodological perspectives.* Dordrecht: Springer.

Code, L. (2006). *Ecological thinking: The politics of epistemic location.* New York, NY: Oxford University Press.

Deleuze, G., & Guattari, F. (1987). *A thousand plateaus: Capitalism and schizophrenia* (B. Massumi, Trans.). Minneapolis: University of Minnesota Press.

Foucault, M. (2010). What is enlightenment? (C. Porter, Trans.). In P. Rabinow (Ed.), *The Foucault reader* (pp. 32–50). New York, NY: Vintage Books.

Haraway, D. J. (1988). Situated knowledges: The science question in feminism and the privilege of partial perspective. *Feminist Studies, 14*(3), 575–599.

Haraway, D. J. (2016). *Staying with the trouble: Making kin in the Chthulucene.* Durham, NC: Duke University Press.

Kenward, B., Rutz, C., Weir, A., & Kacelnik, A. (2006). Development of tool use in new Caledonian crows: Inherited action patterns and social influence. *Animal Behaviour, 72,* 1329–1343.

Latour, B. (2005). *Reassembling the social: An introduction to actor-network-theory*. Oxford, UK: Oxford University Press.

Lupinacci, J., & Happel-Parkins, A. (2015). Recognize, resist, and reconstitute: An ecocritical framework in teacher education. *The SoJo Journal: Educational Foundations and Social Justice Education, 1*(1), 45–61.

Lupinacci, J., & Happel-Parkins, A. (2017). Ecocritically (re)considering STEM: Integrated ecological inquiry in teacher education. *Issues in Teacher Education, 26*(3), 52–64.

Lupinacci J., & Lupinacci Ward, M. (2017). (Re)imaginings of "community": Perceptions of (dis)ability, the environment, and inclusion. In A. J. Nocella II, A. George, J. L. Schatz, & S. Taylor (Eds.), *Weaving nature, animals and disability for social justice: From theory to experience in eco-ability* (pp. 63–78). Lanham, MD: Lexington Books.

Nocella, A. J., II, White, R. J., & Cudworth, E. (2015). *Anarchism and animal liberation: Essays on complementary elements of total liberation*. Jefferson, NC: McFarland.

Plumwood, V. (1993). *Feminism and the mastery of nature*. London, UK: Routledge.

Plumwood, V. (2002). *Environmental culture: The ecological crisis of reason*. New York, NY: Routledge.

Quinn, D. (1995). *Ishmael*. New York, NY: Bantam.

Rich, A. (1984). Notes towards a politics of location. In R. Lewis & S. Mills (Eds.), *Feminist postcolonial theory: A reader* (pp. 29–42). New York, NY: Routledge.

Strom, K. J. (2018). "That's not very Deleuzian": Thoughts on interrupting the exclusionary nature of "high theory". *Educational Philosophy and Theory, 50*(1), 104–113.

Strom, K. J., & Martin, A. D. (2013). Putting philosophy to work in the classroom: Using rhizomatics to deterritorialize neoliberal thought and practice. *Studying Teacher Education, 9*(3), 219–235.

Strom, K. J., & Martin, A. D. (2017). Thinking with theory in an era of trump. *Issues in Teacher Education, 26*(3), 3–22.

Taylor, C. (2016). Edu-crafting a cacophonous ecology: Posthumanist research practices for education. In C. Taylor & C. Hughes (Eds.), *Posthuman research practices in education* (pp. 5–14). London, UK: Palgrave Macmillan.

Twine, R. (2010). *Animals as biotechnology: Ethics, sustainability and critical animal studies*. New York, NY: Routledge.

Vygotsky, L. S. (1978). *Mind in society: The development of higher psychological processes*. Cambridge, MA: Harvard University Press.

Warren, K. (1990). The power and the promise of ecological feminism. *Environmental Ethics, 12*(2), 125–146.

Warren, K. (2000). *Ecofeminist philosophy: A Western perspective on what it is and why it matters*. Lanham, MD: Rowman & Littlefield.

World Wildlife Fund for Nature (WWF). (2017). Threats to African elephants. *WWF Global*. Retrieved from http://wwf.panda.org/knowledge_hub/endangered_species/elephants/african_elephants/afelephants_threats/.

7

Re-vitalizing the American Feminist-Philosophical Classroom: Transformative Academic Experimentations with Diffractive Pedagogies

Evelien Geerts

Introduction: The Need to Re-vitalize Higher Education Pedagogy in Contemporary Neoliberal Times

Present-day higher education is in dire straits. Even though global youth literacy and education participation rates have been on the rise (UNESCOstat 2017; UNdata 2018), and the democratization of education has become a top priority for human rights-driven agencies such as UNESCO (2016), it is at the same time obvious that higher education institutions and pedagogical praxes should be pushed into more radical directions. For example, UNESCO's (2018) discourse on education still is drenched in the exclusivist human rights vocabulary of the Enlightenment: Given that such discourses neglect societies' marginalized Others as rights-deserving subjects, often ignore the impact of structural power imbalances, and disregard how human

---

E. Geerts (✉)
University of California Santa Cruz, Santa Cruz, CA, USA
e-mail: egeerts@ucsc.edu

© The Author(s) 2019
C. A. Taylor and A. Bayley (eds.), *Posthumanism and Higher Education*, https://doi.org/10.1007/978-3-030-14672-6_7

actors relationally co-exist with(in) human and non-human subjects and worlds, as many posthuman and new materialist scholars have noted (Barad 2007; Braidotti 2013; van der Tuin 2015; Alaimo 2016; Haraway 2016), these discourses seem to be in an urgent need of an update. Higher education is, additionally, increasingly conceptualized in a development-based language, as UNESCO's example illustrates, which frames education not as a telos of its own but as an instrumental means to eradicate poverty or stimulate economic development. But it is the now worldwide-spread ideology of neoliberalism that is really damaging education as a formational praxis, as neoliberalism has materialized itself into what philosopher Wendy Brown in *Undoing the Demos* has called 'a peculiar form of reason that configures all aspects of existence' (2015: 17) (also see Foucault 2008; Peck 2010; Dardot and Laval 2013 for similar analyses). Now a mode of governmental rationality, neoliberal reason has reduced citizen-subjects to mere *homines oeconomici*, and turned self-investment, hyper-individualism, and an enforced attitude of resilience into today's dominant modes of living.

All of this is particularly problematic because escaping the instrumentalizing claws of neoliberal reason seems impossible, since, to put it in a Braidottian way, every little piece of living matter—human and non-human—has been transformed into something sellable, profitable and potentially disposable (Braidotti 2013). We all have become self-responsibilizing market actors disciplined into calculating and promoting our worth. This has damaged our collective psychological well-being: as various psychiatrists indicate, hyper-individualism and de-rootedness engendered by neoliberal reason mean we are all living in 'borderline times' (De Wachter 2012) in which meaning itself has been brutally economized, which makes fruitfully engaging in existentialist meaning-making praxes much harder. It has impacted on higher education as well. In such a context, contemporary posthuman and new materialist philosophies, for example Braidotti's human-decentring '[z]oe-centred egalitarianism' (2013: 60) that emphasizes

7 Re-vitalizing the American Feminist-Philosophical Classroom

how life in all of its different and differing materialized forms is relationally connected because of a shared vital materiality, are in my view, more needed than ever before. Such philosophies, I suggest, are not only to help us make sense of the neoliberal world today but also offer a philosophical-political alternative, one that is suspicious of over-economization and states that everything of matter matters, and that there are productive ways out of the multitude of crises we are currently experiencing.

I take these concerns up from my situated viewpoint of an international instructor at a large public research university in the United States. My experience in the USA thus far has made it clear that institutions of higher education, its teachers, its programmes and disciplines—and even the material space of the classroom—are caught up in the same profit-focused and hyper-consumerist logics I outlined earlier, and are in dire need of re-vitalization. In this chapter I will take the reader on a journey of re-imaginings by sharing some of my personal intra-active experiences of co-learning with college undergraduates in an American classroom, while addressing how this neoliberalism-induced educational crisis can be affirmatively counteracted by experimentations with (feminist) new materialist theories and the methodology of diffraction (Haraway 1997, 2004; Barad 2007). I focus on the joint journey I went on with my students in the Winter of 2017 while teaching a course on feminist philosophy and new materialisms. I outline how the pedagogic experiments I undertook contested the monologic, dialectical nature of the Western philosophical canon, and how we actualized in our classroom various intersecting and energizing daily acts of resistance against the neoliberal corporatization of the university. Along the way, I include a variety of feminist new materialist pedagogical principles and tools. These experimentations will be examined in this chapter's final part to underline how feminist new materialist philosophies are actualized in the intra-actions between theory and praxis in the classroom, and how these philosophies could re-vitalize the American college classroom.

An Affirmative Critique of the Negative Impact of Neoliberal Profit-Based Thought on the American College Classroom Today

Starting from the claim that higher educational institutions around the world, and the Humanities in particular, are caught up in the earlier-described neoliberal logics (Groenke and Hatch 2009; Nussbaum 2010; Giroux 2014), instructors and pedagogues are confronted with a corporatized educational model that does not centre on students' holistic formation. As indicated above, my concern in this chapter is how higher education pedagogy is being negatively affected by such a profit-focused logics. Writing myself into the traditions of critical, feminist and now also posthumanist and new materialist pedagogy (see Freire 2001, 2006; Giroux 1988, 2014 [critical pedagogy]; see Aptheker 1989; hooks 1994, 2003 [feminist pedagogy]; and see van der Tuin 2015; Snaza et al. 2016; Hickey-Moody and Page 2016; Braidotti et al. 2018 [new materialist-inspired pedagogy]), it seems that higher education in the United States is less and less about making students understand their place as engaged citizens in today's world and that of the future. Leaving the issue of declining social mobility aside (Leatherby 2016), the core problem seen from a more micro, classroom-based standpoint is that we, as teachers, are being confronted with a pedagogical praxis in which students are to be spoon-fed easily-digestible materials in short sessions, demarcated by neoliberal academic clock-time.

Many in higher education fear that this is about promoting societal conformism, and what critical theorists Theodor Adorno and Max Horkheimer have called 'blindly pragmatized thought' (1997 [1944]: xiii), rooted in an educational banking system that reproduces socio-economic inequalities, keeps the already-marginalized silenced, and into which teachers have to 'make deposits which the students patiently receive, memorize, and repeat' (Freire 2006: 72). My questions then are: Where in this disembodied form of instrumentalist instruction, and one-directional teaching and learning, is the scope for celebrating what black feminist thinker bell hooks calls '[e]ros [...] as a motivating force' (1994: 194)? How can we, as teachers, pedagogues and philosophers make a valuable pedagogical intervention in these neoliberal borderline times? And how can we create possibilities for such interventions that transcend the level of negative critique? I address these questions below in my discussion of some of the diffractive pedagogical strategies used during my 2017 class. I draw on the philosophies of Braidotti and Barad, in which 'critique and creation work hand-in-hand' (Braidotti 2016) and critique is 'a practice of reading for the constitutive exclusions of those ideas we can not do without' (Barad in Dolphijn and van der Tuin 2012: 49), to emphasize the entanglements between the ontological, epistemological, and the ethico-political. But first the genealogy of diffraction is briefly outlined (see Geerts and van der Tuin 2016 for a fuller discussion).

The Feminist-Philosophical Classroom Re-examined: The Complex Conceptual Genealogy of Diffraction

Diffraction—next to being a physical phenomenon—has its roots in feminist science studies scholar Donna Haraway's oeuvre. Haraway's first engagement with diffraction appears in "The Promises of Monsters", an essay in which she refers to literary theorist Trinh Minh-ha's notion of inappropriate/d others—which expresses how subjects are 'in a diffracting rather than reflecting (ratio)nality', as Haraway also puts it (2004 [1992]: 69). Framed by Haraway's life-long project of 'epistemological electroshock therapy' (1988: 578), diffraction is a 'more subtle vision' (2004 [1992]: 70) than the traditional reflective scientific forms of optics and thought that is capable of revealing 'where the effects of difference appear' (70). Haraway in *Modest_Witness@Second_Millenium* later on expands on this by labelling diffraction as 'an optical metaphor' that stands in contrast with '[r]eflexivity' (Haraway 1997: 16). The latter is a representationalist, distancing practice that 'displaces the same elsewhere' (16) and creates oppositional distinctions between the real and the figural, whereas diffraction is about making 'a difference in the world' (16) by paying attention to 'the interference patterns on the recording films of our lives and bodies' (16). Thinking and seeing diffractively for Haraway is thus a critical, situated, non-innocent way of thinking about the world that provides us with the opportunity to be more attuned to how differences—together with micro and macro webs of power—become materialized.

Philosopher-physicist Karen Barad's new materialist understanding of diffraction (Barad 2007), which she integrates within agential literacy (Barad 2000, 2001), builds on this Harawayan metaphor. Barad's take suggests that we, because of our agential being-with(in)-the-world, are ethically responsible for our intra-actions—or intense, always entangled, co-constituting interactions—with(in) the world and each other. For Barad, the hermeneutics of diffraction expresses what a self-accountable feminist type of critique, and textual and pedagogical engagement, should consist of: Rather than employing a hierarchic methodology, diffractively approaching texts and theories means that they are dialogically read 'through one another' (2007: 93) to engender creative, unexpected outcomes. Diffraction is thus a valuable resource for higher education because it promotes a relational model of pedagogy and learning able to contest the now nostalgic, outdated Humanities-based educational models as well as the hyper-instrumentalized neoliberal ones. Diffractive thinking—in combination with an affirmative feminist politics—is inspirational, in my opinion, because it enables us to counter the many crises induced by a still dominant Eurocentric humanism, climate change, and present-day's neoliberal reason-fuelled increase in socio-economic inequalities, to name a few. Diffraction offers a prototype for pedagogy that is centred on critique and creativity, situatedness, geopolitical (self-)awareness, accountability, and an immanent ethical attitude that takes current-day political constellations and complications into account. The remainder of this chapter puts diffraction into practice and takes the reader on my own feminist new materialist-inspired pedagogical journey of re-imaginings.

The Feminist-Philosophical Classroom Re-vitalized: Diffractive Pedagogical Approaches and Tools

Pedagogic Context

At the start of the eleven weeks Winter term, I was excited to work with my students on various challenging topics—such as feminist science studies; queer, disability and critical race studies; critiques of which bodies come to matter in society and in new materialist thought; the contested validity of academic critique in today's post-truth climate—using different transdisciplinary frameworks and authors. My feelings of excitement however quickly turned into concern upon realizing that many of the registered undergraduates not only came from different disciplines (feminist theory, literature, history of consciousness, politics, chemistry, and Latin American and Latino studies) but also had never taken any philosophy courses before. This forced me to carefully and continuously reflect upon my own teaching pedagogy and usage of— often rather alienating—philosophical jargon. Furthermore, time pressures—there were only eleven weeks of class that had to be taught in two ninety-minute sessions per week—and life pressures—many of my students had jobs, were dealing with complex personal issues, and felt financially pressured to graduate as fast as possible—meant that we frequently all showed up to class with drained bodies and brain fatigue. The pedagogic context, then, was one in which we were constantly being pressured by neoliberal reason and academic clock-time, which made it hard for the students to be as intellectually invested as they would have liked to be, and made it at times equally difficult for me to teach in a truly dialogical, communal manner.

I had initially planned to experiment with dialogical pedagogy and a radically-altered idea of collaboration to foster more knowledge production from the ground up, thereby following in the footsteps of anthropologists Anna Tsing and Miyako Inoue (Choy et al. 2009), who use the notion of "'strong collaboration'" (Tsing in Choy et al. 2009: 381) to describe their situated, collective research praxis as a means of fore-fronting more creative, open-ended, and in a way *diffracting and diffractive* research, thereby going against academia's neoliberalization in which individualism and unhealthy competition are now core principles. I however soon found out that both teachers and students are constantly restricted by certain systems and their limits—whether it be the academic educational system itself (grade letter evaluations were for instance required), the classroom's limited physical space, or the educational-cultural capital we have grown up with. These phenomena at times forced me to step back into a more instructional-based didactic pedagogy. But amidst trying to find the balance between didactics, dialogue, and said idea of strong collaboration, there were surprisingly also a couple of non-traditional, diffractive pedagogical strategies and tools that were engendered through our collective acts of resistance against the further neoliberalization of our institution and class environment. And these strategies were informed by several pedagogic principles as well, while at the same time reciprocally intra-acting with the latter, and slowly but surely transforming them into principles that could be interpreted as feminist new materialist. I discuss both types of intra-ventions in what follows.

Diffractive Intra-ventions and Feminist New Materialist-Inspired Principles

The Jointly-Designed Syllabus

At the start of our intense period of co-learning, I knew that I wanted to disrupt the educational banking system as much as I could, and my students had likewise expressed their interest in experimenting with a less didactics-based pedagogy. After having some introductory conversations, in which I also explicitly opened up about my own situated position—i.e. that of a white, Western European queer woman from a working-class neighbourhood—and how those elements affect my teaching praxis, we decided that we wanted to try and break through the traditional power hierarchies-based gap between instructor and instructed, a gap that is central to both more classic and nostalgic

Humanities-based pedagogies and the neoliberal instrumentalist ones. We wanted to become co-learners, and one way to do so was by experimenting with the traditional academic syllabus. This re-imaging of the syllabus felt particularly necessary, as several students with Native American heritage at the start of class had shared their negative experiences with the field of science studies, and how they felt like Western scientific knowledge production processes had for centuries delegitimized their onto-epistemological relational understanding of the world. Limited by the traditional evaluative framework of the university, however, we did start out with a collection of various texts regarding feminist philosophy and new materialisms, as one must hand in a sample syllabus before getting a course approved. But wanting to consider all of our situated lived experiences and knowledges, we quickly decided to experiment with a syllabus that would remain re-designable throughout the course, as to incorporate even more articles and essays that resonated with the students' experiences and interests. The jointly-designed syllabus thus intra-actively came into being, and was meant to be ever-evolving. And even though that made everyone anxious at first, being confronted with a lot more academic freedom than usual, we had many productive discussions about the limitations of the Western canons of philosophy and feminist theory with regards to the (de)legitimization, marginalization and exploitation of certain subjugated knowledges; especially in relation to particular local Indigenous knowledges and relational onto-epistemologies. This jointly-designed syllabus could be regarded as a diffractive pedagogical strategy-in-action, as it not only materialized some of the negative affects students had about the university and the classroom as (de)legitimizers of certain knowledges and world orientations, and morphed these feelings into something more affirmative, but it also demonstrated some of the critical creativity that is so central to the Harawayan-Baradian idea of diffraction. This experiment was also a concrete materialization of our shared wish to subvert the dichotomized ways of binary-thinking and the onto-epistemological cuts (see Barad 2007) between the so-called knowledge-producing subject/examined object/knowledge produced that are central to more traditional learning systems: We were now at least partially co-learners, intra-actively encountering one another in dialogue, and the joint syllabus was an expression of attempting to treat one another as situated agential actors with valuable lived experiences. And in this more strong collaboration-based context, the ideal of purported neutral and one-directional knowledge production and transference was deconstructed in a feminist, accountable manner (Haraway 1988) by making space for everyone's perspectives and opinions in class while taking a step back as the instructor when needed.

The Collaborative Google Documents-Based Midterm

Wanting to step out of the traditional evaluative framework, we also collectively thought about redesigning the midterm exam during the first two weeks of class and decided that a collaborative Google Documents-based writing project would be ideal: All of the students were asked to write about a material-discursive phenomenon that they themselves were allowed to pick, such as gold, UCSC's geographical location, the components of a laptop, …, while trying to trace this specific phenomenon's ethico-political entanglements; an exercise that was philosophically inspired by Barad's agential realist philosophy of entanglements and philosopher of science Bruno Latour's *Dingpolitik* (Latour 2005). Because of the focus on entanglements, the exercise was already transcending mere description and reflection—as the students were explicitly asked to think about how certain phenomena like resource-based neoliberal capitalism, the production of laptop components, Hewlett-Packard, and the American military industrial complex are all connected to one another. Instead of having to fill out some midterm questions on a couple of sheets of paper, students now had to collaborate with one another on an online platform. They were asked to write creative essays together by using a Google Document that was shared with the whole class so that we could all be part of the writing-process-in-action. This project worked out really well: While it started out as another tiny act of resistance against the hyper-individualization and self-responsibilization that is now so central to American academia, the experiment quickly transformed into a pedagogical strategy worthy of the label of diffraction. The Baradian idea of dynamic intra-actions even came to the foreground, as all students ended up digitally commenting on the pieces, therefore breaking out of their solipsistic learning bubbles. Plus, the end-result also showed us the multiple intra-active re-visions that had been made during the rewriting processes—which reminded me of Barad's agential realist queering of temporalities and the idea of re-configurations (Barad 2007, 2010). Everyone really felt part of and responsible for this intra-active writing assemblage, which was a great event to witness!

Classroom-Based Memes

The final potentially diffractive pedagogy that came into being during our time together as co-learners in this class, has to do with memes. Memes are (non-)textual photo-based images that are digitally circulated amongst Internet-users because they are expressing—and often also are giving a twist on—a certain socio-cultural idea or practice. Memes are said to go viral once a huge amount of people belonging to the same online community start employing them as a means of socio-political commentary.

The memes that I came up with during our eleven weeks of class, some of which ended up on my *Subversive Philosophy Memes*-Tumblr, were a mix of socio-political and pedagogical commentary. I will briefly discuss a couple of memes that were engendered during our intense class intra-actions and that were later on pedagogically re-used in the classroom.

Although the idea to add customized memes to our class materials came directly from me (as coming up with philosophy-related memes is one of my secret geeky hobbies), something else was going on as well here. The following four memes, of which one is depicted above (Fig. 7.1), only came into being after thinking through the course materials with the students. When addressing Western idealist philosophies, for instance, the topic of Hegelian dialectics came up, which turned into a variety of Hegel memes that tackled not only the density but also the problematic difference-erasing qualities of Hegelian thought. The confrontation with Irigaray's obscure feminist psychoanalytical language

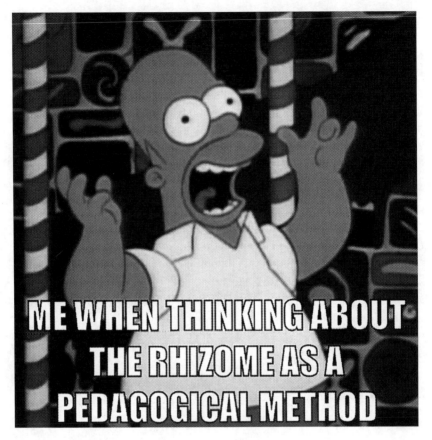

Fig. 7.1 Copyright ©Subversive Philosophy Memes (2018)

in class engendered a meme with Irigaray's smiling face on it, and the text 'Irigaray: making her readers go bonkers since '74'. One of the students was also convinced that Latour was 'one of those dead white male philosophers', and the meme with Latour's image and the imprint 'Latour is alive!' made us chuckle throughout our time together, while also helping us focus on why some of Latour's work could be regarded as problematic seen through several Indigenous perspectives. And last but not least, the meme illustrated above (Fig. 7.1) can be regarded as a somewhat cathartic expression of my own after having read Deleuze and Guattari while preparing to teach a session on pedagogies. Although I do not wish to overstate these memes' subversive power, they clearly came into being in response to several types of affect, such as confusion, joy and wonder, expressed by my undergraduates and myself when being confronted with several canonical and marginalized philosophical oeuvres. Bringing together different titbits of memories in unexpected new combinations and becoming some sort of cultural-pedagogical capital of their own after having been shared online, these memes possess diffractive pedagogic potential upon being re-used in the classroom. These memes not only relationally linked the students to innovative modes of digital image production and circulation, but they also clearly disrupted the image's representationalist function as such, while bringing all the co-learners in this course together via a shared humorous taunting and re-configurations of the Western philosophical canon. This affirmative yet critical engagement with the canon again underlined our dialogical and hierarchy-destabilizing encounters in the classroom.

These three diffraction examples demonstrate how theory and praxis may go hand in hand in feminist theory and philosophy, and how the presumed gaps between (feminist) new materialisms and the world may be blurred when these diffractive pedagogical strategies are engendered in—and bring new energy to—the classroom. Or as feminist new materialist pedagogues Anna Hickey-Moody and Tara Page have put it so nicely in *Arts, Pedagogy, and Cultural Resistance*: 'Practices, teaching and art production practices are modes of thought already in the act' (2016: 1). Matter has 'transformative capacities' (1), and '[n]ot only are we always with/in bodies, but we are always with matter' (4). Explicit feminist new materialist pedagogies, such as the aforementioned diffractive pedagogical strategies and principles, rise up from within the classroom, and materialize themselves in entanglement with the physicality of the classroom, the socio-cultural capital that is (re-)produced and/or disrupted, and the co-learners (students-and-teacher) participating in the course. The syllabus and midterm project are, in my view, particularly important diffractive pedagogical approaches. They both pull the teacher and students out of their self-reflexive minds and neoliberal-propelled hyper-individualized learning attitudes and, instead, accentuate the flows, passions, affects and intensities between them as co-learners. Furthermore, they express the new materialist idea that the teacher and the student, plus the teaching apparatuses and environment, are all interconnectedly involved (and transformed) when intra-actively collaborating with one another in the classroom.

Afterthoughts: Diffraction 'Versus' Reflection?

I end this chapter with some thoughts about diffraction and reflection and connect these to my earlier philosophical musings about the now-firmly established presence of neoliberal reason in higher education, and how feminist new materialist pedagogies have the power to subvert the latter. The potential complementarity of both diffractive and reflective pedagogical strategies has been touched upon before (see Bozalek and Zembylas 2017) but it does not hurt to underline their co-existence again. Critical reflective methodologies can first of all not be that easily avoided, as we have all been disciplined by neoliberal reason that lauds the hyper-individualism and solipsism attached to reflection and (self-)reflexivity. Reflective pedagogical approaches and tools additionally still have their use in the classroom, because we, as co-learners, are operating within institutional frameworks and power relations that restrict us in our experiments with diffractive approaches. I am personally still a supporter of learning analysis assignments which, as self-reflexive pedagogical tools, ask the student to engage in an introspective moment, and are based upon a more representational, self-referential learning model. And, interestingly enough, these moments of pure introspection, although self-reflexive, can oppose neoliberal reason, as they promote slow thinking. And, last but not least, it is not unimaginable that a reflection-based pedagogical tool ends up morphing into a diffractive one. To give an example: During my course, we all prepared for our classes by scribbling down notes and comments in the margins of assigned articles. These remarks and markings, often accompanied by colourful Post-its, were first introspective in nature but, when shared with one another in class by projecting them onto a screen, they became something more: They not only had the potential to become diffractive re-workings of the text in question—and the canonical knowledges that are represented by the textual—but also provided us with several moments of material encounters between a group of eventual co-learners. And this, to conclude, is exactly what diffraction does: It affectively provokes, makes us re-think what is traditional and canonical, and produces unexpected, creative outcomes.

Acknowledgements The author would like to thank the editors of this book volume, Carol Taylor and Annouchka Bayley, together with Clare Hammoor, for their affirmative, constructive feedback. Special thanks go out to my undergraduate students at the University of California, Santa Cruz for their generosity; to Donna Haraway for our wonderful pedagogical lunch conversation in Santa Cruz in 2016; to Bettina Aptheker for teaching me all about feminist pedagogies; to Maija Butters, Delphi Carstens, Lou Mycroft and Kay Sidebottom—my posthumanist companions—and to Iris van der Tuin for her mentorship.

References

Adorno, T. W., & Horkheimer, M. (1997 [1944]). *Dialectic of enlightenment* (J. Cumming, Trans.). London and New York: VERSO.
Alaimo, S. (2016). *Exposed: Environmental politics and pleasures in posthuman times*. Minneapolis: University of Minnesota Press.
Aptheker, B. (1989). How to do meaningful work in women's studies. *Women's Studies, 17*(1–2), 5–16.
Barad, K. (2000). Reconceiving scientific literacy as agential literacy. In R. Reid & S. Traweek (Eds.), *Doing science + culture*. New York: Routledge.
Barad, K. (2001). Scientific literacy → agential literacy = (learning + doing) science responsibly. In M. Mayberry, B. Subramaniam, & L. H. Weasel (Eds.), *Feminist science studies: A new generation*. New York and London: Routledge.
Barad, K. (2007). *Meeting the universe halfway: Quantum physics and the entanglement of matter and meaning*. Durham and London: Duke University Press.

Barad, K. (2010). Quantum entanglements and hauntological relations of inheritance: Dis/continuities, spacetime enfoldings, and justice-to-come. *Derrida Today, 3*(2), 240–268.

Bozalek, V., & Zembylas, M. (2017). Diffraction or reflection? Sketching the contours of two methodologies in educational research. *International Journal of Qualitative Studies in Education, 30*(2), 111–127.

Braidotti, R. (2013). *The posthuman.* Cambridge: Polity Press.

Braidotti, R. (2016). Don't agonize, organize! *e-flux.* https://conversations.e-flux.com/t/rosi-braidotti-don-t-agonize-organize/5294. Accessed 10 March 2018.

Braidotti, R., Bozalek, V., Shefer, T., & Zembylas, M. (Eds.). (2018). *Socially just pedagogies: Posthumanist, feminist and materialist perspectives in higher education.* London and New York: Bloomsbury Academic.

Brown, W. (2015). *Undoing the demos: Neoliberalism's stealth revolution.* Brooklyn, NY: Zone Books.

Choy, T. K., Faier, L., Hathaway, M. J., Inoue, M., Satsuka, S., & Tsing, A. (2009). A new form of collaboration in cultural anthropology: Matsutake worlds. *American Ethnologist, 36*(2), 380–403.

Dardot, P., & Laval, C. (2013). *The new way of the world: On neoliberal society* (G. Elliott, Trans.). London and New York: VERSO.

De Wachter, D. (2012). *Borderline times: Het einde van de normaliteit.* Leuven: LannooCampus.

Dolphijn, R., & van der Tuin, I. (2012). *New materialism: Interviews & cartographies.* Ann Arbor: Open Humanities Press.

Foucault, M. (2008). *The birth of biopolitics: Lectures at the Collège de France, 1978–79* (M. Senellart, Ed. and Graham Burchell, Trans.). New York: Picador.

Freire, P. (2001). *Pedagogy of freedom: Ethics, democracy, and civic courage* (P. Clarke, Trans.). Lanham and Boulder: Rowman & Littlefield.

Freire, P. (2006). *Pedagogy of the oppressed* (M. B. Ramos, Trans.). New York and London: Continuum.

Geerts, E., & van der Tuin, I. (2016). Diffraction & reading diffractively. *New materialism almanac.* http://newmaterialism.eu/almanac/d/diffraction. Accessed 10 March 2018.

Giroux, H. A. (1988). *Teaching as intellectuals: Toward a critical pedagogy of learning.* Westport and London: Bergin and Garvey.

Giroux, H. A. (2014). *Neoliberalism's war on higher education.* Chicago: Haymarket Books.

Groenke, S. L., & Amos Hatch, J. (Eds.). (2009). *Critical pedagogy and teacher education in the neoliberal era: Small openings.* Dordrecht: Springer.

Haraway, D. J. (1988). Situated knowledges: The science question in feminism and the privilege of partial perspective. *Feminist Studies, 14*(3), 575–599.

Haraway, D. J. (1997). *Modest_witness@second_millennium. FemaleMan©_meets_oncoMouse^{TM}: Feminism and technoscience.* New York: Routledge.

Haraway, D. J. (2004). The promises of monsters: A regenerative politics for inappropriate/d others. In *The Haraway reader.* New York and London: Routledge.

Haraway, D. J. (2016). *Staying with the trouble: Making kin in the Chthulucene.* Durham and London: Duke University Press.

Hickey-Moody, A., & Page, T. (Eds.). (2016). *Arts, pedagogy and cultural resistance: New materialisms.* London and New York: Rowman & Littlefield.

hooks, b. (1994). *Teaching to transgress: Education as the practice of freedom.* New York and London: Routledge.

hooks, b. (2003). *Teaching community: A pedagogy of hope.* New York and London: Routledge.

Latour, B. (2005). From realpolitik to dingpolitik or how to make things public. In B. Latour & W. Peter (Eds.), *Making things public: Atmospheres of democracy.* Cambridge: MIT Press.

Leatherby, L. (2016). US social mobility gap continues to widen. *The Financial Times.* https://www.ft.com/content/7de9165e-c3d2-11e6-9bca-2b93a6856354. Accessed 10 March 2018.

Nussbaum, M. C. (2010). *Not for profit: Why democracy needs the humanities.* Princeton and Oxford: Princeton University Press.

Peck, J. (2010). *Constructions of neoliberal reason.* Oxford and New York: Oxford University Press.

Snaza, N., Sonu, D., Truman, S. E., & Zaliwska, Z. (Eds.). (2016). *Pedagogical Matters: New materialisms and curriculum studies.* New York: Peter Lang.

Subversive Philosophy Memes. (2018). https://estarthewicked.tumblr.com/. Accessed 1 March 2018.

UNdata. (2018). *Social indicators.* http://data.un.org/en/reg/g1.html. Accessed 3 March 2018.

UNESCO. (2016). *Education 2030: Incheon declaration and framework for action for the implementation of sustainable development goal 4.* http://unesdoc.unesco.org/images/0024/002456/245656E.pdf. Accessed 5 March 2018.

UNESCO. (2018). *Education transforms lives.* https://en.unesco.org/themes/education. Accessed 5 March 2018.

UNESCOstat. (2017). Fact Sheet No. 45. September 2017. FS/2017/LIT/45 Literacy Rates Continue to Rise from One Generation to the Next. http://uis.unesco.org/sites/default/files/documents/fs45-literacy-rates-continue-rise-generation-to-next-en-2017_0.pdf. Accessed 5 March 2018.

van der Tuin, I. (2015). *Generational feminism: New materialist introduction to a generative approach.* Lanham and Boulder: Lexington Books.

8

Undoing and Doing-With: Practices of Diffractive Reading and Writing in Higher Education (Viewpoint)

Sarah Hepler, Susan Cannon, Courtney Hartnett and Teri Peitso-Holbrook

Becoming with Bernard: An SF Welcome

Possessed with the desire to write, I'm wrenched awake at 4:05 AM on a Saturday. Rain patters the darkness. I reach for the nearest touch-screen. 'Bernard reads Le Guin's <u>Left Hand</u> with me, widd—.' iPhone autosuggests, its cyborg authors feverishly helpful in the integrated circuit: widespread? widget? wider show? I ignore them. '…widdershins.' Counter-clockwise. Anti-sunwise. From the German widersinnig: against common sense….

S. Hepler (✉)
Center for Excellence in Teaching and Learning,
Georgia State University, Atlanta, GA, USA
e-mail: shepler2@gsu.edu

S. Cannon
Department of Middle and Secondary Education,
Georgia State University, Atlanta, GA, USA
e-mail: scannon5@student.gsu.edu

© The Author(s) 2019
C. A. Taylor and A. Bayley (eds.), *Posthumanism and Higher Education*,
https://doi.org/10.1007/978-3-030-14672-6_8

I thumb-tap on: Bernard reads Le Guin's Left Hand with me, widdershins. Common sensibly, I would read Bernard, decoding his fictional character from Virginia Woolf's typed words. But he is no more or less real to me than the authors whose work I can cite. I think I think with him just as much as I think I think with many Haraways, Deleuzes, Barads. 'Truth is a matter of the imagination,' writes Le Guin (1969: 1). Oh, good. I can cite her, too.

Outside, the rain is hard pearls. It clatters the sunrise. In a matter of hours, I'll make my way to the drinking hall where my colleagues and I will talk about our readings and wonder a bit uncomfortably if the thinking we think we are thinking is 'academic' enough. Bernard's chair pulls up beside me. '"But when we sit together, close," said Bernard, "we melt into each other with phrases. We are edged with mist. We make an unsubstantial territory."' iPhone's cyborg literati desperately aid me: unsure terrible? unsuccessful terror? unsubscribed terrific? I cite Woolf (1931: 11, 2010: 13) and sink/synch under the quilt. We are reading companions in an unsubstantial territory. We are academics becoming with Bernard.

(Wool) Gathering

We (PhD students, Kindles, bifocals, professor, desk, iPhones, thrift store novels…) are a doctoral reading group engaged in diffractive reading/writing (Dolphijn and van der Tuin 2012). Diffractive

---

C. Hartnett
Early Childhood and Elementary Education,
Georgia State University, Atlanta, GA, USA
e-mail: cbertrand1@gsu.edu

T. Peitso-Holbrook
Literacy and Language Arts,
Georgia State University, Atlanta, GA, USA
e-mail: tholbrook@gsu.edu

reading/writing happens when we lean into the accidental and unaccounted for—in this case, the gut yearning to take together Woolf's (1931, 2010) *The Waves* and Donna Haraway's (2016b, c) *Staying with the Trouble*. As we read these texts together, we uncovered a surprising serendipity of tentacles and threads in the reachings between Haraway and Woolf. They frayed and knitted us. As posthuman multiplicities, we recognized that we were simultaneously radically separate from and impossibly intertwined with each other and our shifting perceptions of these (and other) unstable works. We recognize that fibers might not resonate with thoughts of diffraction, which Barad (2014: 168) described as a 'an optical phenomenon that might seem lifeless,' but we point to the snarled life of fibers, the teeming earthiness of them before they are domesticated, stitched and hemmed, and want to think with the metaphors they give us.

That's what I said, thinks Bernard. "We melt into each other with phrases. We are edged with mist" (Woolf 1931: 16, 2010: 8). Our readings and writings are always already intertwined, and then we straighten and sort (prose, citations, data, language) for academic purposes. We write as we are expected to write in neat paragraphs with clearly defined pronouns. What other stories can we write? In our experiencing/being/thinking posthumanist reading group we become in a mist, texts atomize, we melt into each other.

Below we share some of this diffractive thinking/writing/reading/texturizing. We think diffraction with Haraway and Barad as an intra-action between texts that brings new texts into being. In our reading/writing, we 'read various insights through one another to produce something new, new patterns of thinking-being' (Barad, cited in Dolphijn and van der Tuin 2012: 58). We made space for and followed an ontology of immanence as we were 'less interested in what is and more interested in what might be and what is coming into being' (St. Pierre 2018: 2). In diffracting humanist notions of reading group and posthumanist notions of reading/writing/thinking, we plied the anatomy and practices of the binary to think difference and how those differences come to matter.

In this viewpoint we break with the flow of the academic text and then break with making sense and ease in and out of the sensational. What we offer here are renditions of those breakings. As we worked with written, spoken, unwritten, unspoken, thought, unthought, words, images, concepts—'all we can muster' (St. Pierre 2011: 622)—we also worked with conventions of paper, ink, gutters, spines, glue, staples and their virtual descendents in Google Docs cyberspace. We worked with sentences, paragraphs, arrows, lines, boxes, and, as will be evident, tables. We clashed and made kin with these forms/concepts/materials to create a textualized space. Does it help if you have read Woolf and Haraway? We don't know how to answer. Instead, we ask you to come along with quiet expectations into the woven scraps of our writings/readings in intra-action. Tentatively/tentacularly, we ask that you let them melt into you.

Edging with Mist: Tentacular Writings

A person enters. Another one leaves. Is the paper in the middle or are we in the middle of the paper? 'The tentacular are not disembodied figures; they are cnidarians, spiders, fingery beings like humans and raccoons... matted and felted microbial and fungal tangles, [How do we mat and felt flesh without destroying it?]' (Haraway 2016b: 3, 2016c: loc. 835–848). Le Guin, Haraway, and Woolf clashing and then making kin. Reading groups angered/anchored in time and space and focus—meet here, bring this—*can* be matted, *can* be felted in all the interdependent yearning of things snarled and lively. (I am enmeshed in humanism. It is inescapable—one cannot get outside of it). Instead, reading groups come to feel pre-combed: Their coats have had a wool weaver's carder taken to them. *Read pages xx–yy:* brush out the fibers. *Discuss metaphor z:* clack out the dirt. All the potentials in their muds dessicate into dusty motes. I read with dirt under my fingernails from planting seeds. Text met my dirt and my desire '[a]s I sit here under the cut flowers' (Woolf 1931: 174, 2010: 179), continuing in my humanist ways of futuristic, goal-oriented productivity. 'We have all been colonized by those origin myths with their longing for fulfillment in apocalypse' (Haraway 2016a: 55). How do we work ourselves, write ourselves, read ourselves into not-yet difference—different spaces, different ways of being with/in texts that cannot be yet, but somehow must look as if they are? 'All the characters explore the limits of language; the dream of communicating experience; and the necessity of limitation, partiality, and intimacy even in this world of protean transformation and connection' (Haraway 2016a: 64). The answers regurgitated from theorists live on pages and slowly seep through, bubbling, a node here, a node there, almost unrecognizable when surrounded by taken-for-granted presence.

Serging an Unsubstantial Territory: Tablings

> "Bubbles form on the floor of the saucepan," said Jinny. "Then they rise, quicker and quicker, in a silver chain to the top". (Woolf 1931: 11, 2010: 3)

> 'I am going to nestle into the comfort of the humanist embrace' (one of us, some time, some place).

> Staying stratified – organized, signified, subjected – is not the worst that can happen; the worst that can happen is if you throw the strata into demented or suicidal collapse, which brings them back down on us heavier than ever. (Deleuze and Guattari 1987: 161)

Throughout our time together the four of us—Sarah, Susan, Courtney, Teri—gathered around many tables: Teri's office table topped with a motley-colored, candy-filled bowl worked from clay; Susan's twin tables (most times pushed together to make one continuous space, but when we were there, children at one, adults at the other); a variety of restaurants, coffee shops, and bars. These surfaces of wood, smudged glass, and plastic, peopled with papers, human bodies, technological partners, flashing cursors, and food both shared and coveted

Fig. 8.1 Posthuman feasting

provided us with mediums for our mappings of a posthuman academic reading group. It seems appropriate—and playful—that we share our tables as we commence personal and collective posthuman feasting (Fig. 8.1).

We feasted greedily, taking up texts and ideas and concepts and materials, going out of bounds and over lines. Wine glass rings became atols and words coursed around grease stains. There was/is joy in this unboundedness, in this freedom to go beyond. Yet we also grappled with the push and pull constraints of chapter requirements, work, child-rearing, health complications, and living. It all seemed so mattedly, feltedly, fungally *boundless*. Guiltily, we sought a humanist guide to organize our bookish wanderings: a schematic table with three headings: traditional/humanist reading group, posthuman reading group, what else? We hoped the confining boxes could nudge us towards the unthought, and yet we felt abashed. What *would* Haraway say?!?

With our heads swimming in and beyond readings, thoughts woven through doctoral lives, the table tacked us. Read vertically, the traditional/humanist column echoed the confines of space and time into a material presence: in such a reading group, you are in attendance in a particular room at a particular time to meet with particular people with a particular text prepared, ready to co-confirm what is knowable. But our reading group was not that. It became dispersed, timed-less, asynchronous. It bloomed on walks, in cars, together, separate. It clustered around Sarah, Susan, Courtney, and Teri, but also Bernard, Jinny, Donna, Ursula. It threaded out into scholarly thought fictions—imaginary conversations and textual weavings of ideas and notions both thick and tendrilly that happened regardless of who else was around. As readers/writers, we were destabilized, but, never de*tabalized*. In our schematic tables, we sketched in lines so that we could cross them (Fig. 8.2).

If we had tabled our table, resisted bringing forth table as 'grid of intelligibility' (Foucault 1970: 93), as dusty humanist tool; if we had delegitimized our all-too-humanist thinking as backwards, as inferior, as 'before,' we would have slipped into the black holes of radical destratifying death that Deleuze and Guattari (1987) warned us about. In hope, we continued to map the diagonal lines of flights, the momentary planar possibilities, the promise of columnar rupture, and the interstitial perversions and pleasures. The comforts of our tables (our schematic tables and our other gathering tables), gave us something to lean our elbows on as we questioned how the posthuman moves we embrace work ourselves, write ourselves, read ourselves into difference—different spaces, different ways of being within text in conjoined response-ability (Barad 2014) to each other. The far-right column, *What Else?*, is left blank because as MacLure acknowledges, 'what comes next must always be in some fundamental way unknowable' (Denzin et al. 2017: 490), and we don't know what else is to come. There is fear in such unknowing, Derrida's 'fear of the unpredictable not yet' (St. Pierre 2018: 2). This active fear is both awareness and invitation, it pushes the boundaries, making hairline fractures in taken-for-granted practices (Fig. 8.3).

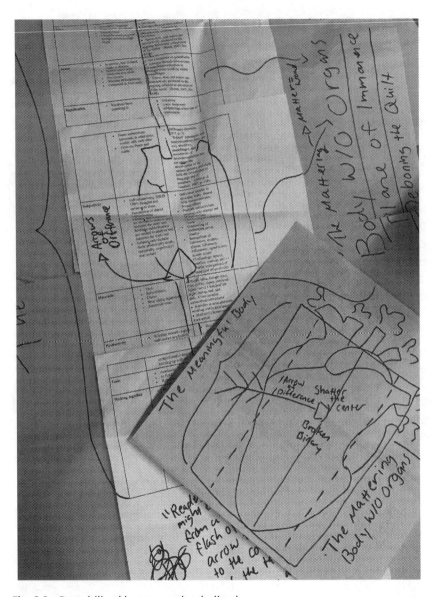

Fig. 8.2 Destabilized but never detabalized

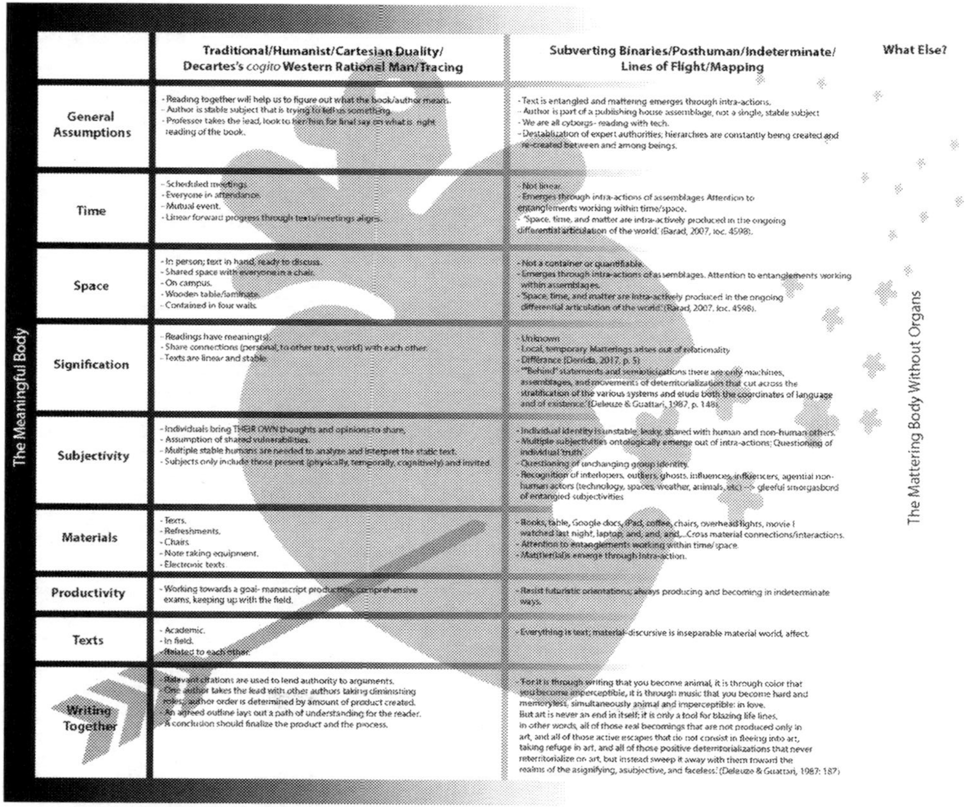

8 Undoing and Doing-With: Practices of Diffractive …

	Traditional/Humanist/Cartesian Duality/ Descartes's *cogito* Western Rational Man/Tracing	Subverting Binaries/Posthuman/Indeterminate/ Lines of Flight/Mapping	What Else?
General Assumptions	- Reading together will help us to figure out what the book/author means. - Author is stable subject that is trying to tell us something. - Professor takes the lead, looks to her/him for final say on what is right reading of the book.	- Text is entangled and mattering; emerges through intra-actions. - Author is part of a publishing house assemblage, not a single, stable subject. - We are all cyborgs– reading with tech. - Destabilisation of expert authorities; hierarchies are constantly being created and re-created between and among beings.	
Time	- Scheduled meetings. - Everyone in attendance. - Mutual event. - Linear forward progress through text/meetings aligns.	Not linear. Emerges through intra-actions of assemblages. Attention to organs/moments working within time/space. "Space, time, and matter are intra-actively produced in the ongoing differential articulation of the world." (Barad, 2007, loc. 4598).	
Space	- In person; text in hand; ready to discuss. - Shared space with everyone in a chair. - On campus. - Wooden table/furniture. - Contained in four walls.	- Not a container or quantifiable. - Emerges through intra-actions of as-semblages. Attention to entanglements working within assemblages. "Space, time, and matter are intra-actively produced in the ongoing differential articulation of the world."(Barad 2007, loc. 4598).	
Signification	- Readings have meaning(s). - Share connections (personal, to other texts, world) with each other. - Texts are linear and stable.	Unknown Local, temporary. Meanings arise out of relationality. Difference (Deleuze, 2017, p. 5) "Refrain" statements and semiotic-izations that cut across the stratification of the various systems and strata (with the coordinates of language and of existence)." (Deleuze & Guattari, 1987, p. 146).	
Subjectivity	- Individuals bring THEIR OWN thoughts and opinions to share. - Assumption of shared vulnerabilities. - Multiple stable humans are invited to analyse and interpret the static text. - Subjects only include those present (physically, temporally, cognitively) and material.	- Individual identity is unstable; leaky; shared with human and non-human others. - Multiple subjectivities ontologically emerge out of intra-actions; Questioning of individual 'truth.' - Questioning of unchanging stable identities. - Recognition of intellopers, outliers, ghosts, influencers, agencies, agential non-human actors (technology, spaces, weather, animals, etc.) —> gleeful smorgasbord of entangled subjectivities.	
Materials	- Texts. - Refreshments. - Chairs. - Note-taking equipment. - Electronic texts.	- Books, table, Google docs, iPad, coffee, chairs, overhead lights, movie ! -weird-last night, laptop, and, and, and... Cross material connections/interactions. - Attention to smellthearhearbreathe-seeing within time/space. - Materiality emergy through Intra-action.	
Productivity	- Working towards a goal: manuscript production, comprehensive exams, keeping up with the field.	- Resist futuristic orientations; always producing and becoming in indeterminate ways.	
Texts	- Academic. - In field. - Related to each other.	- Everything is text; material-discursive is inseparable material world, affect.	
Writing Together	- Reviews and lit reviews are used to lend authority to arguments. - One author takes the lead with other authors taking diminishing authority and/or order is determined by amount of product created. - An agreed outline lays out a path of understanding for the reader. - A conclusion should finalise the product and the process.	Text is through writing that you become animal, it is through color that you become imperceptible, it is through music that you become hard and memoryless, simultaneously animal and imperceptible in love. "But art is never an end in itself; it is only a tool for blazing life lines, in other words, all of those real becomings that are not produced only in art, and all of those active escapes that do not consist in fleeing into art, taking refuge in art, and all of those positive deterritorializations that never reterritorialize on art, but instead sweep it away with them toward the realms of the asignifying, asubjective, and faceless. (Deleuze & Guattari, 1987: 187)."	

(left margin, vertical) The Meaningful Body

(right margin, vertical) The Mattering Body Without Organs

Fig. 8.3 Hairline fractures (Latysheva 2018; Villain 2018)

Fulling: Posthumus Wanderings/Wonderings

Still—always—the humanist guilt of not-enough hangs in the air. But by pushing up against and dematerializing boundaries, we can rearticulate what reading and writing can look like in the academy. Occupying a single position in space at a shared moment in time, working within hierarchies, differentiating and corralling fictive pieces that complicate our thinking—as are assumed in traditional reading groups—are neither precursor nor prerequisite to communion. When we question our constraining ideas of reading and writing together, we step into the *What Else?*; what else becomes visible, possible, that at first we couldn't see?

The acts of reading and writing were our companions on long walks, while sitting in meetings, watching YouTube, visiting museums, and innumerable other places that diffractively entangled with Haraway, Woolf, countless texts, theory, things, and each other. Attending to these thoughts brought awareness to the loose and wandering threads that flirted at the edges and became entangled. In ending, we offer a beginning. During this project, Google Docs has been a technological co-conspirator in our work, a small plot of land, a Room of [Our] Own, a body without organs, a humus-rich compost heap of insight, anxiety, quotes, jokes, comments, and conversations. We invite you to meddle/muss/muck about with each other, always already in the middle and with joyous abandon, creating 'connection[s] of desires, conjunction(s) of flows, continuum(s) of intensities… your own little machine, ready when needed to be plugged into other collective machines' (Deleuze and Guattari 1987: 161). You can leap into the heap at bit.ly/compostheap.

References

Barad, K. (2014). Diffracting diffraction: Cutting together-apart. *Parallax*, *20*(3), 168–187.

Deleuze, G., & Guattari, F. (1987). *A thousand plateaus: Capitalism and schizophrenia*. Minneapolis: University of Minnesota Press.

Denzin, N. K., Lincoln, Y. S., MacLure, M., Otterstad, A. M., Torrance, H., Cannella, G. S., et al. (2017). Critical qualitative methodologies: Reconceptualizations and emergent construction. *International Review of Qualitative Research, 10*(4), 482–498.

Dolphijn, R., & van der Tuin, I. (2012). Interview with Karen Barad. In *New materialism: Interviews & cartographies* (pp. 48–70). Ann Arbor, MI: Open Humanities Press.

Foucault, M. (1970). *The history of sexuality. Vol. 1: The will to knowledge*. New York, NY: Pantheon Books.

Haraway, D. (2016a). *Manifestly Haraway*. Durham, NC: Duke University Press.

Haraway, D. (2016b). *Staying with the trouble: Making kin in the Chthulucene*. Durham, NC: Duke University Press.

Haraway, D. (2016c). *Staying with the trouble: Making kin in the Chthulucene* [kindle]. Durham, NC: Duke University Press.

Latysheva, O. (2018). *Arrow*, icon. https://thenounproject.com/latyshevaoksana/. CC BY 2.0. Accessed June 2018.

Le Guin, U. K. (1969). *The left hand of darkness*. New York, NY: Ace Books.

St. Pierre, E. (2011). Post qualitative research: The critique and the coming after. In N. Denzin & Y. S. Lincoln (Eds.), *The SAGE handbook of qualitative research* (pp. 611–625). Los Angeles, CA: Sage.

St. Pierre, E. (2018). Post qualitative inquiry in an ontology of immanence. *Qualitative Inquiry*. https://doi.org/10.1177/1077800418772634.

Villain, C. (2018). *Heart organ*, icon. https://thenounproject.com/search/?q=human%20heart&i=644079/. CC BY 2.0. Accessed June 2018.

Woolf, V. (1931). *The waves*. Orlando, FL: Harcourt Press.

Woolf, V. (2010). *The waves*. Garsington, UK: Benediction Classics.

Part II

Inventive Practice Intra-Ventions

Something August 2017. Photo: Carol A. Taylor

9

Staying with the Trouble in Science Education: Towards Thinking with Nature—A Manifesto

Marc Higgins, Maria F. G. Wallace and Jesse Bazzul

Initial Premise

We begin from the premise that Nature (which, following posthumanist convention, we capitalize to signal the *totality* of nature: the ways in which space, time, and matter are always already co-constitutive) always already has a role in the construction of scientific knowledge (i.e., 'nature') and that our ability to 'tune-in' matters: epistemologically, ontologically, *and* ethically. With the advent of the ontological turn in education, the role

---

M. Higgins (✉)
University of Alberta, Edmonton, AB, Canada
e-mail: marc1@ualberta.ca

M. F. G. Wallace
Millsaps College, Jackson, MS, USA
e-mail: wallamg@millsaps.edu

J. Bazzul
University of Regina, Regina, SK, Canada
e-mail: Jesse.Bazzul@uregina.ca

© The Author(s) 2019
C. A. Taylor and A. Bayley (eds.), *Posthumanism and Higher Education*,
https://doi.org/10.1007/978-3-030-14672-6_9

of Nature in the construction of 'nature' is increasingly being considered (as well as the role of Nature in constructing Culture). Under the banner of posthumanist and new materialist approaches to education and educational research, there is increasing awareness that the (re)production of 'nature' is only *in part* a human meaning-making practice and to take seriously the notion that it may not only be co-constructed with other humans, but also with other-than-humans, and more-than-humans as well.

Nature, 'Nature' and Science Education

However, science education has yet to take this on fully. But it is a rich site of possibility: describing and defining 'nature' is at the heart of science education, for example in school science and science teacher education. Yet, at the moment, there is a telling and troubling paucity in the way science education is taking up questions generated by the ontological turn. We see this as being inseparable from the ways in which science education is premised on Othering Nature. The two predominant methods of teaching and learning science entail either coming-to-know what scientists know (i.e. cognitivism, intra-personal learning, scientific knowledge as representation of nature) or enculturation into how scientists come-to-know (i.e. socio-constructivism, interpersonal learning, scientific knowledge as representation of culture). In both, Nature remains in danger of being posited as 'nature'. That is, as no more than an anthropocentric representation culturally mediated by the culture of science and school science to be pedagogically conveyed (as scientific knowledge) or co-constructed (through thinking like a scientist). Nature remains a passive backdrop against which 'nature' is constructed and remains separate and separable from its co-constitutive realm of Culture and its plural questions of politics, economics, discourse, and life.

In this manifesto for an other science education, therefore, we echo Isabelle Stengers' (2018: 106) *Manifesto for Slow Science* and argue that 'another science [education] is possible!' However, the path to even *an* other science educations is fraught: science education has an over-reliance on practice divorced from theory and on hiding theoretical commitments in plain sight. Firmly, we repeat Haraway's (2016: 47) mantra for *Staying with the Trouble:* 'think we must; we must think.' We must engage in the critical task of identifying, examining, and addressing the multiple ways in which science education continues to uphold problematic enactments of power. We call for a slower critical science education: a science education which does not dismiss the urgent work of building and sustaining social and ecological relations through the temporality of emergency. We do not just call for a strict slowing down for more time to think, but also to think about *how* we think: 'it matters what thoughts think thoughts' (Haraway 2016: 35). Call it staying with the trouble in science education.

There are two principles at the core of our manifesto. The first principle, *Science education needs to think, but not like that*, outlines three onto-epistemological moves that often occur within science education and (fore)close possibility: (a) commonplace thoughtlessness; (b) stupidity; and (c), circular reasoning. The second principle, *Science education must think otherwise, but not like that*, offers three orientations for *troubling* thought which do not engage in the hubris of waving away the *trouble*. They are thinking as: (a) slow science; (b) minor inquiry; and (c) disruption.

First Principle: Science Education Needs to Think, *But Not Like That*

Thinking Against Commonplace Thoughtlessness

Thought is both the possibility of thinking *anew* and thinking *again*. So 'it matters what thoughts think thoughts' (Haraway 2016: 35). If we are to engage Nature from a position that is 'not *in* the world; but *of* the world' (Haraway 2016: 14), we must think, but not *like that:* thought in science education is far too often circular, stratified, dogmatic, and foreclosed. Haraway (2016) refers to thought which *thinks again*, that is thought that reproduces sameness rather than difference in its repetition, as 'commonplace thoughtlessness.' We must take heed of thoughtlessness in science education which, Haraway (2016: 36) explains, derives from Man, the Subject of Western modernity, who enacts it:

Unable to make present to himself what was absent, what was not himself, what the world in its sheer not-one-selfness is and what claims-to-be inherent in not-oneself... someone could not be a wayfarer, could not entangle, could not track the lines of living and dying, could not cultivate response-ability, could not make present to itself what it is doing, could not live in consequences or with consequence, could not compost.

We must reject commonplace thoughtlessness which, as Haraway makes clear, is not a *lack* of or *lapse* in thought. It is thought-full-ness of another kind shaped by 'a deeper surrender to ... immateriality, inconsequentiality' (Haraway 2016: 36) which reinforces dominant ways-of-knowing-in-being. But what we know from the posthuman, ontological turn is that entire parts of the world do not come to matter in commonplace thoughtlessness as the world is already (fore)closed by what we already (think we) know of the world. Our reading, being, and learning must yield fresh ideas, not reproduce and reaffirm the things that we already know and the systems of power through which they come to be.

Thinking Against Stupidity

Similarly, Stengers (2015: 119) states that the ways in which we too-readily and -quickly reify taken-for-granted notions in science education, could be referred to as 'stupidity.' Stupidity does not here refer to stupor, to paralysis, or to impotence. Stupidity is active, it feeds on its effects, on the manner in which it dismembers a concrete situation, in which it destroys the capacity for thinking and imagining of those who envisaged ways of doing things differently, leaving them stunned. Stupidity works towards being unable to respond to that which truly necessitates it. Yet, 'It will not be said that 'people are stupid' as if it was a matter of some personal defect. Stupidity is something ... *that it seizes hold of certain people*' (Stengers 2015: 117). It is deeply entangled within the forces and flows of power which shape how we become and manufacture science educators.

Science education's identity and 'epistemic privilege' is premised on refusing, repudiating, and defining itself against its multiple Others, rendering their contributions inadmissible and at times unimaginable. For example, for a scientist to be agentic in constructing 'nature,' its other must be agency-less; science's ability to define and describe Nature is contingent on Nature being mute or treating it as such. The inability to see or respond across the binary separation of Nature and Culture is in the interests of power and by design:

> The bifurcation of nature could not, however, have acquired this 'all-terrain' power of disqualification had it not been accompanied by an activity of the devaluation of thought—that I have referred to as stupidity—in its capacity to define what is important at any given moment. (Deblaise 2018: 27)

Thinking Against Circular Reasoning

We must, therefore, refuse the ways in thoughtlessness and stupidity circuitously operate through binary thinking, but also recognize that these logics operate circularly. Connecting the dots between concepts of 'what counts' and 'what works' in science education reveals a circle, a relation of closure to that which is non-science (e.g., Indigenous, feminist, spiritual, and many other ways-of-knowing-in-being-with-Nature). These circular articulations (re)produce systems of power through which they are producible. Objectivity rearticulates validity, which reaffirms reliability, which reinforces repeatability, ad nauseam. They are so circular that Lars Bang (2018) recently referred to them as Ouroboros-like, the figure of the snake who eats its own tail. Science education is an Ouroboros who has been self-consuming for so long that it has either become so-bloated or atrophied that it has lost all appetite for all thought outside itself.

This is why 'our task is to make trouble' (Haraway 2016: 1), not wave it away. We must (attempt to) break away from these problematic systems of thought but also non-innocently consider how we participate in the very thing we work against. As Haraway (2016: 38) states, 'this is not a longing for salvation or some other sort of optimistic politics;

neither is it a cynical quietism in the face of the depth of the trouble.' Making trouble need not be audible, especially if it involves rethinking the Ouroboros-like circularity that governs our thoughts and desires in the sciences. Instead, it is to follow Patti Lather's (2007) critical and complicit question: How do we think about how we think without using the thing with which we think (when the thing with which we think is part of the problem)?

Second Principle: Science Education Must Think Otherwise, *But Not Like That*

Thinking with Slow Science

This manifesto proposes the need to pedagogically make science stutter, slow, or stop with regard to taken-for-granted and received meanings and matters, and not by rejecting meaning, but through scepticism towards the authority that meanings already hold. For Stengers (2018: 100):

> Slow science is not about scientists taking full account of the messy complications of the world, it is about them facing up to the challenge of developing a collective awareness of the particularly selective character of their own thought-style.

This is a way of *getting lost* (Lather 2007). Not only is this a means of losing *the* way, particularly of importance in science education where *the* way comes to stand as a monolithic singularity which makes unimaginable the possibility that another science and science education is possible! It is also a process of losing *the* destination (e.g., the economic/scientific subject and/or fixed images of 'progress'), which often re-territorialize creative and critical efforts. Making science stutter, slow, or come to a stop requires creating interruptions which place us in new relations with what we already 'know' or, more importantly, that which we do not yet and we cannot yet know. Yet, this is never as simple as engaging in self-reflexivity and the optics it enacts: pedagogical conditions matter in making thought stutter in how we think about our selves, science, and science education. We must re(con)figure pedagogy so that it perpetually produces moments of hesitation that enable us to think/enact ethics and politics in our construction of Nature.

Thinking with Minor Thought

Working towards the production of such moments of hesitation requires a recognition that the thoughts we think are often inherently caught up in geographies of majority. Majority is territorial—reproducing a 'constant and homogeneous system' (Deleuze and Guattari 1987: 105). Science education, as we *think it*, 'implies a constant, of expression or content' (Deleuze and Guattari 1987: 105). Because of the homogeneity we consent to in science education, geographies of majority ground what is thought, what is thinkable, and the ways that major power structures are maintained. Majority thinking in science education values (only) dominant discourses, epistemologies, and views of reality (what students 'ought' to think), while minor thinking follows (ethical) lines of thought away from what rigid majorities would have us think and embody. In other words the minor follows, the 'mights' of science education. Thus, becoming-minor in science education is an ethical imperative; a refusal to think *like that* without vacating the territory of thought.

Becoming-minor is a refusal to move to directly to the centre of circular thought and draw from those at the periphery, along its contour; becoming-minor is 'very complex, with musical, literary, linguistic, as well as juridical, and political, references' (Deleuze and Guattari 1987: 105). These characteristics of minority are implicit within scientific inquiry but they often become overcoded by the major characteristics of science education. For example, the orthodoxy of *Nature of Science* (NOS) is often articulated as the only 'proper scientific inquiry', without specifying under what conditions a particular 'NOS' becomes proper. Without contextualizations, becoming-major in science education is therefore laden with forces and flows of anthropocentrism, capitalism, racism, sexism, and other vectors of power. Rather than reterritorializing NOS as it has become known *and* knowable, thinking minor thoughts demands science education question ontological and epistemological assumptions of 'Nature': Nature according to whom? Nature under what conditions? Nature for what purposes? Similarly, the same questions of "Science" could be asked: Science according to whom? Science under what conditions? Science for what purposes? We urgently need to engage these minor thoughts in science education.

Thinking with Disruption

We need minor thinking which thinks with (not against or away from) the diverse beings, critters, and potential kin who live life-in-the-detritus of the Anthropocene. In these strange times, staying with the trouble in science education necessitates finding ways to commune together: spiritually, politically, and ecologically. This is not only to disrupt science education, but also acknowledge that disruption happens. These ruptures are at once plural, diverse, yet interconnected. They are ecological, social, cultural, and psychic. Yet, we must learn from the ways more-than-human, other-than-human, and human entities responsively organize their lives in kinship and around commons. Following Anna Tsing (2015), this is a necessary aspect of all life and livability in capitalist ruins. Disruption matters. As Haraway (2016: 31) states, 'nobody lives everywhere; everybody lives somewhere. Nothing is connected to everything; everything is connected to something.' Disruption is complex and complicated force that provides necessary conditions for the emergence of different beings, ethics, and ways of living. Science education must learn to understand disruption on an a more intimate level. Not only so that it can responsibly learn of its complicities, but also because we must learn to learn from those tangled up in the trouble so that their details, stories, histories, science facts, and speculative fictions will have mattered and will come to matter.

What questions might we ask in a science education which thinks otherwise (but not like that)? For example, in the context of North America, a question might include: how does sustainability science seriously contend with the genocides of large Indigenous populations (as a marker of the Anthropocene) and our more-than-kin (such as the disappearance of Buffalo herds and grass species)? How are practices of forgetting these disruptions, intentional or not, part of genocides-in-the-making? What does staying with the trouble in science education invite you to ask?

Conclusion

Thought, but not like that, can only provoke us to know otherwise from outside that which we already know. Staying with the trouble in science education means working towards thinking *with* Nature (not 'about' Nature). We must work to disrupt and displace the very logics through which we become science educators without succumbing to the fantasy of transcending them.

> It matters what matters we use to think matters with; it matters what stories we tell to tell other stories with; it matters what knots knot knots, what thoughts think thoughts, what descriptions describe descriptions, what ties tie ties. It matters what stories make worlds, what worlds make stories. (Haraway 2016: 12)

References

Bang, L. (2018). In the maw of the Ouroboros: An analysis of scientific literacy and democracy. *Cultural Studies of Science Education, 13*(3), 807–822.

Debaise, D. (2018). The minoritarian powers of thought: Thinking beyond stupidity with Isabelle Stengers. *SubStance, 47*(1), 17–28.

Deleuze, G., & Guattari, F. (1987). *A thousand plateaus: Capitalism and schizophrenia*. Minneapolis: University of Minnesota Press.

Haraway, D. J. (2016). *Staying with the trouble: Making kin in the Chthulucene*. Durham, NC: Duke University Press.

Lather, P. (2007). *Getting lost: Feminist practices toward a double (d) science*. Albany: SUNY.

Stengers, I. (2015). *In catastrophic times: Resisting the coming barbarism.* Chicago, IL: Open Humanities Press and Meson Press.

Stengers, I. (2018). *Another science is possible: A manifesto for slow science.* Cambridge: Polity Press.

Tsing, A. (2015). *The mushroom at the end of the world.* Princeton, NJ: Princeton University Press.

10

Complex Knowing: Promoting Response-Ability Within Music and Science Teacher Education

Carolyn Cooke and Laura Colucci-Gray

Introduction

We invite the reader to join us for a walk along the small, cobbled streets of old Aberdeen University campus: standing at the traffic lights on one of the busiest roads in the city, large trucks are carrying fish, pigs, and oil ropes; rain is hitting the roofs, the metal guttering, stone work and concrete; Dylan's music comes to mind, 'it's a hard, it's a hard rain's a-gonna fall … and nobody listenin?' (Dylan 1962).

Dylan's lyrics, layered with issues of social justice, ask us to listen to, not just to hear the world, to let ourselves be touched by it as an embroilment in our relational, material, and interpersonal affairs. Yet such an involvement may be 'troublesome' in Haraway's terms (2016: 1) as 'All of us on Terra live in disturbing times, mixed up times, troubling

C. Cooke (✉) · L. Colucci-Gray
The University of Edinburgh, Edinburgh, Scotland, UK
e-mail: carolyn.cooke2@abdn.ac.uk

L. Colucci-Gray
e-mail: Laura.Colucci-Gray@ed.ac.uk

and turbid times.' The word 'trouble' from the original French, is used here to capture emotional, social and material dimensions of our being in the world. Etymologically, to trouble means to 'stir up', 'make cloudy' as it happens when the apparent order and stillness of things is being disrupted. To 'stay with this trouble' however, is also to challenge learnt ways of behaving and perceiving, in order to become response-able to the complex, unplanned and emergent (Haraway 2016).

Inviting Trouble into Teacher Education at the University

As educational researchers working within the same University department, in Initial Teacher Education (ITE), we have become increasingly concerned with the purpose of preparing future teachers for the world of practice. In line with many scholars who have commented on the impact of neo-liberal economy at all levels in education (see Taylor and Bovill 2018), we both share a preoccupation for the ever growing 'gap' between the abstract knowledge to be transferred, acquired and increasingly measured, and the practical, performative knowledge which students are expected to use.

Most troublesome for us, is the nature of teacher preparation. Often conceived of as a seemingly linear process, involving stateable intentions or outcomes, the preoccupation with the 'production' of teachers is anchored to an approach seeking standardisation, largely unconcerned with difference and diversity of both teachers and children's needs. Far from the simple 'delivery' of skilled professionals, teacher education is fundamentally a socio-political endeavour, intermingled with difficult questions about the purpose of the educational process and the meaning of being 'educated', in an increasingly unequal, and changing world (see Biesta 2015 for an extended discussion).

Drawing away from this linear and simplified picture, this chapter aims to provide a richer and livelier account of the learning and teaching process that incorporates a sense of the unforeseen and the possible. We take the lead from Donna Haraway's text (2016) *Staying with the*

Trouble to re-position teacher preparation within the wider context of human and non-human relations, whereby greater attention is paid to the performative and sensorial aspects in the production of knowledge. We draw upon the insights of two areas of the curriculum, music and science, to uncover assumptions about what 'may be perceived' to be worth knowing, and to uncover the opportunities that arise when these assumptions are destabilized, inviting complementarity between apparently different modes of being in the world. The effect is a more textured view of the learning and teaching process in teacher education, as a dynamic response to the current context of socio-environmental transformation.

Sketching the Posthuman View Across Different Disciplines

Staying with the Trouble collates Haraway's extensive reflections on the mismatch between knowledge and action in response to the environmental crisis. With the word 'trouble', Haraway aimed to deconstruct the dominant 'humanist' view of the world, which has served Western socio-environmental discourse with a view of humans as either victims or heroes, within a linear future of destruction or miraculous solution; a caricature of human figures as fleetingly touching the surface of the Earth (Colucci-Gray 2018).

Tracing back to the metaphysics of A. N. Whitehead (1929: 191), the problem with 'humanism' may be identified with the idea of 'simple location' at the basis of Newtonian physics, for which matter is just 'there', without relations or reference to other regions of space-time. By extension, the human body is designed to 'detect' material signals that are recorded as abstract impressions on the human mind. The world is perceived as a mirror image, in reflection, as a representation of a reality 'out there'. By extension, all forms of knowledge can be traced back to a set of objectified and measurable quantities within the bi-dimensional frame of Newtonian science. However, as Whitehead (1929) explains, this idea of knowledge is fallacious because Newtonian's ideas of matter are an abstraction, only accountable for a certain realm of reality, and levels of generalisation, that are explicitly defined.

This insight has become central to an understanding of 'abstraction' and 'reflection' in the philosophy of scientific knowledge, with important applications across many fields, from anthropology to the arts, and increasingly, in educational research. Seeking to overcome the dualisms of the Newtonian's view, Haraway (2016) puts forward a relational and posthuman view of knowing and being, taking the spider's web as a non-hierarchical interspecies metaphor: all lives are interwoven, sustaining kinship, mutuality and life in the making. Yet Haraway's position (2016) is far from offering a romanticised account. She describes interspecies relations with the powerful and performative analogy of the 'critters', which 'interpenetrate one another, loop around and through one another; [the critters] eat each another [sic], get indigestion, and partially digest and partially assimilate one another' (Haraway 2016: 58). Biologically, this imagery resumes the array of multiple inter-relations, spatial, social, behavioural, and physical which enable life on Earth, thus swapping the linear with a systemic view. Physically, it foregrounds fundamental ecological processes of material recycling and energy flows across living and non-living forms, which may be distributed but also unequally appropriated by different species. In this cosmology, there is no room for anthropocentric accounts of human agency as external to worldly phenomena. Rather, what is being proposed is an ontology according to which humans are not seen as separate from 'nature' but within 'nexuses' of entangled material practices, protruding forward in productive and destructive tensions, as 'generative unfolding' (Haraway 2016: 61).

The Posthuman in Education

Central to Haraway's cosmology is a different view of the organism; not as a bounded object cut out of a background, but as a distributed system of information, materials, and energy across and through its internal and external environs. Moving to education, it was John Dewey (1929: 232) who first argued for an understanding of the human organism as the 'body-mind', to designate 'the continued and the conserved, the registered and cumulative operation of factors continuous with the rest of nature, inanimate as well as animate.' Dewey's account foregrounds the *sensorium*, that is, the extended set of bodily operations which enable the ongoing tuning of oneself in space; the sensorium is at the heart of one's sense of 'being' and so perception is at the heart of all action. Such theoretical insights have led to important post-representational, enactivist and material accounts of the nature of knowledge both in the sciences and the arts (Obrador-Pons 2009). As Brown (2004: 50) indicates, knowledge frameworks in science largely involve spatial and action-orientated notions, such as verticality, distance, front-back and in-out, with 'extension of the senses in the form of scientific instruments.' This idea resonates with Hermansson's (2014: 28–32) argument that 'music can only be understood through metaphors which are gathered from our material world' but notes caution that such metaphors are insufficient to define the 'musical experience, which is grounded in the body.'

This leads to two important points. First, that scientific and musical knowledge are largely conceived not only of 'factual elements', but in terms of metaphorical understandings based on 'embodied, unconscious reasoning' (Brown 2004: 51); and second, that the nature of the inquiry will be effectively 'led' by the intelligence of the body, thus breaking away from exactness to embrace the acute sense of place of 'nomadic', multi-sensorial and affective perception. Such understanding directly challenges the notion of fixed, reified, universal and cognitively received knowledge by inviting instead a greater sensitivity towards the different ways in which we can be 'response-able' (Haraway 2016)—that is, in ongoing knowing relation—and sensorial attunement—with the more than human world. We will see how these considerations about bodily and material practices can be fundamental to a critique of teachers' learning.

More-Than-Human-Inquiries in Teacher Education

Within a humanist epistemology, teacher education institutions are measured on the basis of the quality of the teachers they can 'produce', where the actions and impacts of teachers are 'evidenced' by measurable outputs (Biesta 2015). Similar criticisms can be found in the realms of the arts, with authors pointing to the reification of knowledge, neglecting texture, affect or frictional sensations as subordinate to what may be packaged, sold, and dispatched (Krueger 2015).

The abstraction of knowledge from contexts, as seen (and critiqued) in the reification of 'arts' as an object and in the notion of universality of knowledge in 'science', permits the assumption that (a) a teacher's job is to 'fill' children's 'empty' singular minds with products of knowledge (Freire 1990), and (b) that learners are first and foremost *receivers* of declarative, transferable and assessable knowledge products (Osberg et al. 2008). For those choosing to become teachers, these behaviours also seep into personal and professional responses, such as the concern for 'what to expect' which chimes with the notion that there must be a 'correct' or 'natural' way of responding to tasks and situations. Taking the posthuman critique into music and science teacher education, 'troubling' would thus begin from a review of the so conceived 'objective knowledge' (and its oculocentric semantics) as a prime site for ontological reversal; the idea of separation which highlights either the input (the teacher) or the output (the learning outcome) is confronted by the possibility of experiencing the non-hierarchical, interwoven relationships and entangled bodily practices, between students and teachers, knower and known in a world that is more than human.

Barad's (2007) socio-material account offers the first pointers for this analysis, by inviting us to think differently about 'visibility.' Drawing on quantum physics, she proposes 'diffraction' instead of 'reflection' as metaphors for knowing. Considering the dual nature of light rays as both waves and particles, and their material effects when they come into contact, diffraction—Barad explains—is evidence of 'superposition' rather than mixture. While in a *mixture* the value of each particle can be known in relation to their contribution to the effect (e.g. via statistical analysis), superposition 'represent ontologically indeterminate states' (Barad 2007: 265), allowing for interference effects, in a way that mixtures do not. In practice, this means that diffraction recognises the possibility of multiple, ontological statuses of being and knowing that need not to be reduced to a quantifiable variable. Secondly, such fluidity allows for multi-modal ways of thinking and working in empirically-oriented research, which destabilize the focus on factual knowledge to favour the creative interweaving of the material and metaphorical in language (Colucci-Gray 2018).

Following Barad (2007), we discuss our experience with music and science to illustrate the multiple, diffractive effects on the relationship between knower and reality. In our case, the students' own body, encapsulating their embodied memories and past, physical experiences, constituted the apparatus 'diffracting' their perceptions across the realm of the auditory, tactile, postural and/or visual. The sense of 'playfulness' in these cases is foregrounded in a similar way in which it is common in music to 'play' with an instrument; however, 'playfulness' is not intended to superficialise scientific observation or careful listening in favour of a more entertaining account, but to legitimise the capacity of the body-mind to expose the multifarious process of making sense of phenomena in the world, thereby pointing to the creative process of knowing as 'integral with the course of experience itself, not imported from the external source of a reality beyond' (Dewey 1929: 139).

The remainder of this chapter offers an account of our experimental activities, focussing on the methodological dilemmas and opportunities that this approach may offer.

A Note on Methodology

The experiences recounted in this chapter were conducted separately, with two different groups of students; 18 music student teachers on an ITE course preparing them for teaching music in secondary schools and 30 primary science education students who had elected the module *Science, Education and Society*. While the experiences were separate, they were conceived of in parallel, as they were both designed as explorations of sensory aspects of our subject areas (listening in music and observing in science). Following Obrador-Pons (2009), the intention here was not to 'replace' and 'subsume' one sense (e.g. hearing in music) with the other (e.g. seeing in science), for we wished not to reiterate the dualism between 'liberation/ fun' and 'factual inscription'. On the contrary, more akin to 'play', the process was to resemble a 'performative experiment', building on the expressive capacity of the body to conjure up virtual ('as-if') worlds in ongoing continuity with physical perception (Brown 2004). Specifically, we adopted walking as a research methodology to enable us to engage with the rhythmic, affective, multi-sensorial and temporal dimensions of movement and the body and develop 'attentionality' to one's surrounding and oneself (Springgay and Truman 2017). Walking with the students and being led by them, sharing the corporeality of each other's body and feelings, and being affectively open to one another, troubles acquired learning behaviours in systems whereby teachers plan for intended knowledge outcomes, the learning environment is controlled, and students are expected to receive and reproduce the intended 'answer'. Instead, being attentive to the emergent qualities of the experiences, and developing what Van Boeckel (2015: 114) calls 'aesthetic sensibilities' in which 'we allow one's prejudices of how things 'should' look to fall away and we experience a 'cleansing' of our very process of seeing', troubles notions of intention. An array of methods, from drawing to dialogical inquiries and written reflections on the discussion board were adopted not simply as a means to 'record' but of 'seeing more and seeing differently' (Van Boeckel 2015); by opening up to different space-time zones (Bozalek and Zembylas 2017), and thus 'draw out' different aspects of the students' experience.

Thinking with Barad (2007), diffraction afforded us the opportunity to read the artefacts created by the students, the literature we have jointly engaged with and our own research positions, through each other, exploring their intra-actions and allowing us 'to engage aspects of each other in dynamic relationality' (Barad 2007: 93). Hence the examples offered here are not drawn from data collected 'about the students', but they 'materialised' as offerings 'from' the students, in response to our call for sharing experiences. Ethical permission to report on the experiences was granted by the students upon submission of their drawings and their agreement to include elements which generated discussion and dialogue during the course. 'Data' in this case may be more aptly defined in the language of St. Pierre (1997: 407) as 'figurations' that 'prod and poke at positivities and foundations'; to enable one to think in a multidirectional manner. In contrast to the process of reflection, which as Haraway states 'only displaces the same elsewhere' (Haraway 2016: 16), the purpose was to make visible the unexpected and to highlight the process of 'becoming', in which 'trouble' had emerged.

Going for a Walk on a Rainy Day

The Listening Walk

In music education, the term 'listening' has significant connotations with aesthetic listening, involving the identification of abstracted musical concepts and sounds (e.g. triple time or a bassoon), in which the listener's role is 'simply to contemplate the work, to try to understand it and to respond to it, but that she or he has nothing to contribute to its meaning' (Small, cited in Spruce 2016: 147). This was evident in music student teachers' discussions of being pupils in school, relating such listening activities to feelings of pressure waiting for the music from the CD or computer to be amplified through less-than-ideal speakers, trying to make sure that they heard the right musical concepts to answer the predefined questions. The nature of listening, they felt, was an individual cognitive processing, individually perceived and individually responded to. In the music session, the invitation was thus to go for a walk and explore connections between the music student teachers' bodies and senses, with the behaviours of listening. The body and particularly the ears in our walk became the 'apparatus' (Barad 2007: 148), the entangled juxtaposition of the listener and the sound world, the entanglement between us as a group, and the spaces and materials that we encountered.

Fig. 10.1 Music student teachers' response to exploratory listening

Our walk was a meandering, led by different members of the group at different times. The route was not pre-planned, the sonic encounters were impossible to predict. The music student teachers were free to respond to the sensorial stimulations using words, images and mark-making as they wished. Pictorial responses (Figs. 10.1 and 10.2) were completed as a response to the experiences, with these two being selected as illustrating many of the elements which were common across the whole classes responses, showing clear associations between sound, sound production, material and musical understandings.

Fig. 10.2 Music student teachers' response to exploratory listening

The Observational Walk

The science education session focused on 'observation' and 'mapping' as key dimensions of canonical scientific method. Mapping epitomises the Newtonian idea of objective tracing of an impression of the world using a tool (i.e. the hand) that is exterior to the mind. Yet, mapping is a profoundly culturally-laden practice embodying the specific concerns as well as physical characteristics of the 'mapper'. As Wainwright and Bryan (2009) note, old maps reveal colonial concerns for the tracing of borders, abstraction and labelling which conferred the power to rule to some people over others. Besides, maps are often used in literature to better understand how a geography has influenced an author or 'how the narrative is 'locked' to a particular geography or landscape' (Caquart and Cartwright 2014: 101). The making of a map powerfully conveys the entangled material apparatuses of 'colonial conquest, democracy, trains, clocks' (Barad 2007: 55), as mapping as practical activity is at once 'material economic necessity *and* cultural imaginary' (Galison 2000: 367). The activity, therefore, aimed to engage students with an embodied, tactile, and auditory understanding of place through map-making. Students were asked to go for a walk across campus; collect artefacts, take pictures and then, in small groups, produce a 'sensory map' to bring together their experiences and stimulate discussion.

Water Diffraction Across Musical and Scientific Apparatuses

When discussing the detail in the sonic pictures and the maps, interesting considerations emerged about energy and temperature. Science education students commented on the moisture in the air diffusing on their skin and behaving differently from the cold, hard splashes of the big trucks. Their comments appear to resonate with the qualities of the sound patterns, the rhythms and intensity 'picked up and traced' on paper by the music teachers, from the repetitive patterns to the particular qualities of the water sounds in relation with the environment as represented by the metaphorical jug and tap. The Science students further reflected on how the city itself had changed over time, through new materials configurations mirroring new choices and new, (and growing) energy needs:

> It created such a lot of dialogue and enthusiasm; […] This led us to wondering how the landscape used to look…how the town had grown and developed through time… [and] how things might continue to change in the future. (Science education students' discussion board)

It would have been interesting at this point to reflect further on what it means for water to flow dramatically from collection to usage; the politics of water trade, consumption, and disposal, as pictorially illuminated by the responses of the music teachers. The jug and the tap as tools for intra-acting with water are also tools for intra-acting with other beings. The dripping of the tap sets agency along the trajectory of large-scale consumption whereby water is carried through a long distance which precludes 'our perception of how things may flow and be related' (Barad 2007: 135). Conversely the jug recounts the story of manual harvesting of water that being from a well or even form a tap. Carrying the jug and feeling its weight makes us response-able (Haraway 2016) as we make decisions about how much can be carried, for what purpose and for whom. It is in sensorial awareness that we can disclose the links between educating the way we see and the social and ecological (in)-justice advocated by Freire (1990).

Troubling Relationships with Knowledge

Working with student teachers who have likely lived (in their schooling and degree) an Enlightenment epistemology of knowledge involves moving from a focus on knowledge, which is intrinsically tied to humans, to meaning and the body, which as Snaza et al. (2014) note, relates to everything, human and non-human alike. The process of drawing brought the students into embodied and affective relationality with place, not only to question the singularity of knowledge or perception but most importantly to disclose what Haraway (2016) describes as the 'energetic' work of holding open the possibility that there might be surprises about to happen. However, this only happens if one 'cultivates' the 'virtue of letting those visits intra-actively shape what occurs' (Haraway 2016: 127). For the science education students, this process was recounted by a nomadic and highly affective tracing on paper (see Fig. 10.3).

What often appear as separate sets of concerns, with sharp edges and no relation (i.e. the University campus depicted as separate from the Botanic gardens) is diffracted by the students as an ability to move—affectively—from one set of experiences to another. The coloured account chimes with Braidotti (1994: 5) 'empathic proximity, intensive interconnectedness that allows one to think through and move

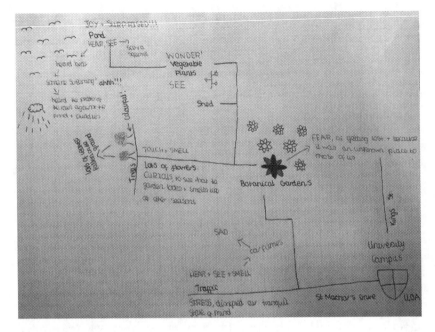

Fig. 10.3 Sensory map trailing the path

across established patterns and levels of experience.' This point was an important aspect of the process of sharing their learning through the experience:

> We had all gone on the same walk in the same conditions and yet our maps were all slightly different, with different areas of focus. Allowing us to widen and construct our knowledge even further. (Science education students' discussion board)

Likewise, the music students were intrigued by how meaning can be 'missed' if not allowed to surface through 'listen-as-usual' practices (Murris 2016: 136). Drawing on Rinaldi, Murris argues for disrupting our tendencies to hear what we expect and instead to develop an emergent listening in which we suspend our prejudices (Rinaldi in Murris 2016: 137).

This was clear in the diversity of responses, both physical (one student 'played' a grate with a pencil, another played with a door to 'feel' the sound), to their pictorial responses:

> In the picture responses there was a mix of recurring themes (water depicted as wavy lines, images of birds and leaves, the use of taps, jugs) and stark differences (two images were urban, whereas the majority were focused on nature). (Music student teachers' discussions)

Here, meaning is regarded as a 'doing' with others (human and non-human), promoting the need for response-ability to the unforeseen, emergent properties of what is created in the 'in-between' (Haraway 2016). This promotes a performative, rather than representative view of learning, in which the collaborative efforts of meaning-making are given high value and spaces to emerge.

Troubling Relationships with Matter

Despite the materialist nature of science and music (the use of instruments, the development of the subjects through technological advances, the materially rich learning environments often involved), the increase in socio-materialist literature has exposed how materiality has become 'subordinate to human cognition' in classrooms (Taylor 2013). This has significant implications for the way relationships with materiality in music and science are enacted. Pederson's (2010: 241–242) argument that schools not only 'continually re-inscribe and 'close' categories of 'human' and 'animal' but also tends to sustain and reinforce…particular forms of species performativity' applies equally to universities. This was experienced during the listening walk which meandered through the music department, education corridors and communal areas, with a sense of dissonance when activities and 'ways of being' in spaces were at odds with expectations, as noted in the comment below.

> (Music student teacher response on listening walk): There is singing in the café – so wrong! – they are making up the words.

Thinking about knowledge as a mode in which matter is intra-active in meaning-making, denotes a movement from a view of learning as contained within a person to a view of learning as occurring 'in the space 'between'… [people]… and the material world (Murris 2016: 6). This view shifts humanist notions of matter as 'tools', towards a flattened relationality, a response-ability:

> One member of the group described how, on hearing a van's engine, he'd identified it as a diesel (due to the pitch and timbre), had noted the length of time it was idling, and the rhythm of the pitch changes. Another group member was surprised, adding that it had just made them turn to check they weren't going to be run over! (Music student teachers' conversations)

These comments are akin to Mamlok's (2017) distinction between hearing and listening. There was a clear distinction between students who had just identified the engine's sound (hearing) and the student who had actively responded to it in order to create an affective meaning (listening). The music student teachers' conversations made connections between the difference of being asked to identify a musical feature as separated from the rest of the musical meaning (as in aesthetic listening activities within music classrooms) and the processes of listening as a performer where there is an active response to what is heard. This aligns with Murris's (2016) work which recognises the importance of the microphone, as depicted by a music student teacher (Fig. 10.4), not as a tool for transmission, but as a 'doing.'

Similarly, for the science students, the sound patterns of road traffic were given pictorial relevance by one of the groups, with showed cars neatly lined up in a queue at the traffic lights, and produced these comments:

> The conversation raised an observation about the sense of hearing and the anatomical structure of the ear channel… the vibrations of water beyond a certain threshold impair our aural perception…cars in the head… making us less able to respond.

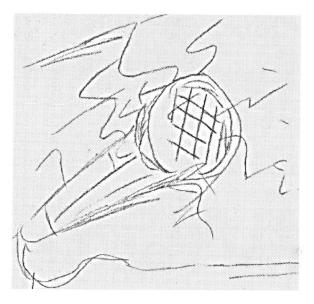

Fig. 10.4 Microphone as a 'doing'

In troubling learning behaviours we aimed to develop material awareness of how such sensorial manipulations occur and what they do for the 'organism-environment' nexus. 'Material conditions matter' (Barad 2007: 244) and by attending to it differently our students might be enabled to connect to the geo-political, economic, social and cultural landscape of their being:

> How different it was to be on the side of the road and be unable to hear anything, and how it all went quiet when we reached the botanic gardens. (Discussions with science education students)

Listening to one's surrounding as a means of recognising one's responses and one's role as part of a context, resonated further with the music student teachers when operating indoors, in a space where relationships tend to be 'set' according to particular patterns and social norms.

There was recognition that, in an otherwise empty stairwell, our not talking (as we were listening) changed the nature of the space as we walked through it. The laughter of someone else entering the stairwell was suddenly subdued in response to our quietness. (Music student teachers' discussions)

This leads us to contend that becoming conscious of one's mode of observation or listening to the world equates to becoming conscious of one's positioning in the world as argued by Østergaard (2017), and which may include social, gender, linguistic, biological, or economic factors. Such understanding equates to Bateson's ideas of deutero-learning, that is, the reflexive arch which allows for the perception of oneself in relation to others as well as to the un-learning of patterns of behaviours in relation to their manifestations (Bateson 1972). However, this is also an important aspect of becoming *response-able* as individuals who are capable to respond, that is *to attend to*, changing and changeable conditions by means of heightened embodied awareness, improvisational creativity, affect and community (Haraway 2016: 68).

Staying with the Trouble

On those rainy days, standing by the traffic lights and exploring the contrasting, adjoining spaces of the university campus resonated strongly with us as lecturers. The level of unpredictability was high, the route wasn't fixed, the encounters were unplanned, we didn't know the students' response-ability to these experiences, or what meaning they would make. Turning our back to the classroom space opened up opportunities for the group as a whole to view learning as a collective action, situated on the 'rough ground' of life and thought as advanced by Dunne (1997), where the unexpected and the unexplored were invited in.

In the opening of this chapter we put forward a socio-political view of teacher education (Biesta 2015), to support our work with student teachers. As we have attempted to recount in this chapter, the experience has generated new relationships and configurations which existed via bodily intra-actions in the space-time moments of those intra-actions (Barad 2007). Hence shifting the performative into Higher Education can trouble inherent power dichotomies, between theory and practice, knowledge and skills, and between types and spaces for learning:

> The student forewarned me that what she was going to say might come across as offensive. Encouraging her to continue, she explained that the sessions were all very well but that in 'real life' they, as student teachers, were told how to teach by the school and she just wanted to pass the course. (Conversation with a Music student teacher)

Therein lies the most inherent trouble of all. We continue to wonder if Biesta is right and posthumanism is ineffective in introducing system change. Nevertheless, the experience we offer here is aimed to encourage teacher educators to indeed 'go on a walk' with the students, share corporeality and attentiveness to each other. The greater provocation of posthumanism lies in relationality, how we pursue response-ability in ITE in an ethical, attentive, and sustainable way.

Acknowledgements Pictures courtesy of Cairi MacIntosh, Scott Coutts, Claire Cameron, Chloe Stephen, Erin MacGregor and Lynn Erskine.

References

Barad, K. (2007). *Meeting the universe halfway: Quantum physics and the entanglement of matter and meaning.* New York: Duke University Press.

Bateson, G. (1972). *Steps to an ecology of the mind.* New York: Ballantine Books.

Biesta, G. J. J. (2015). What is education for? On good education, teacher judgement, and educational professionalism. *European Journal of Education, 50*(1), 75–87.

Bozalek, V., & Zembylas, M. (2017). Diffraction or reflection? Sketching the contours of two methodologies in educational research. *International Journal of Qualitative Studies in Education, 30*(2), 111–127.

Braidotti, R. (1994). *Nomadic subjects: Embodiment and sexual difference in contemporary feminist theory.* Toronto: Columbia University Press.

Brown, T. L. (2004). *Making truth: Metaphor in science*. Chicago: University of Illinois Press.
Caquard, S., & Cartwright, W. (2014). Narrative cartography: From mapping stories to the narrative of maps and mapping. *The Cartographic Journal, 51*(2), 101–106.
Colucci-Gray, L. (2018). Undertaking research at the interface between disciplines: Questions of purpose, method, and possibilities. *Granite: Aberdeen University Postgraduate Interdisciplinary Journal, 2*(1), 4–15.
Dewey, J. (1929). *The quest for certainty: A study of the relation of knowledge and action*. New York: Putnam.
Dunne, S. (1997). *Back to the rough ground: Practical judgement and the lure of technique*. Paris: University of Notre Dame Press.
Dylan, B. (1962). *A hard rain's a-gonna fall*. Columbia Records.
Freire, P. (1990). *Pedagogy of the oppressed*. New York: Continuum.
Galison, P. L. (2000). Einstein's clocks: The place of time. *Critical Inquiry, 26*(2), 355–389.
Haraway, D. (2016). *Staying with the trouble: Making kin in the Chthulucene*. New York: Duke University Press.
Hermansson, E. (2014). *A posthumanist aesthetics of physicality in music: An understanding of the mind-body problem with music by Marie Samuelsson*. Stockholm: Stockholm University Press.
Krueger, J. (2015). Musicing, materiality, and the emotional niche. *Action, Criticism & Theory for Music Education, 14*(3), 1–19.
Mamlok, D. (2017). Active listening, music education, and society. In *Oxford Research Encyclopedia of Education*. Oxford: Oxford University Press.
Murris, K. (2016). *The posthuman child: Educational transformation through philosophy with picture books*. Oxon: Routledge.
Obrador-Pons, P. (2009). Building castles on the sand: Repositioning touch on the beach. *The Senses and Society, 4*(2), 95–210.
Osberg, D., Biesta, G., & Cilliers, P. (2008). From representation to emergence: Complexity's challenge to the epistemology of schooling. *Educational Philosophy and Theory, 40*(1), 213–227.
Østergaard, E. (2017). Earth at rest. Aesthetic experience and students' grounding in science education. *Science & Education, 26*(5), 557–582.
Pedersen, H. (2010). Is "the posthuman" educable? On the convergence of educational philosophy, animal studies, and posthumanist theory. *Discourse, 31*(2), 237–250.

Snaza, N., Appelbaum, P., Bayne, S., Carlson, D., Morris, M., Rotas, N., et al. (2014). Toward a posthumanist education. *Journal of Curriculum Theorizing, 30*(2).

Springgay, S., & Truman, S. (2017). A transmaterial approach to walking methodologies: Embodiment, affect, and a sonic art performance. *Body and Society, 23*(4), 27–58.

Spruce, G. (2016). The ideology of aesthetic listening. In C. Cooke, C. Philpott, K. Evans, & G. Spruce (Eds.), *Learning to teach music in the secondary school*. London: Routledge.

St. Pierre, E. (1997). Circling the text: Nomadic writing practices. *Qualitative Inquiry, 3*(4), 403–417.

Taylor, C. (2013). Objects, bodies and space: Gender and embodied practices of mattering in the classroom. *Gender and Education, 25*(January), 688–703.

Taylor, C., & Bovill, C. (2018). Towards an ecology of participation: Process philosophy and co-creation of higher education curricula. *European Educational Research Journal, 17*(1), 112–128.

Van Boeckel, J. (2015). Angels talking back and new organs of perception: Art-making and intentionality in nature experience. *Visual Inquiry: Learning and Teaching Art, 4*(2), 111–122.

Wainwright, J., & Bryan, J. (2009). Cartography, territory, property: Postcolonial reflections on indigenous counter-mapping in Nicaragua and Belize. *Cultural Geographies, 16*(2), 153–178.

Whitehead, A. N. (1929). *Process and reality*. Cambridge: Cambridge University Press.

11

Dramatizing an Articulation of the (P)Artistic Researcher's Posthumanist Pathway to a 'Slow Professorship' Within the Corporate University Complex

johnmichael rossi

Prologue

Today's steadfast and hyperlinked neo-liberal tendencies have enabled an advanced neo-imperialist, globalized capitalism that de-humanizes the purpose of education, emphasizing 'schooling' the masses to stay within the borders of prescribed functionality, becoming gravely ill-equipped to solve worldly problems that we do not yet have the answers to. These new norms further enable systemic racism and sexism, as is evident in current social discourses on the stages of both world politics and popular culture. Posthumanism counters this, forcing us to wonder at how narrow our entire conception of politics is, while 'recognizing that a wide variety of seemingly disparate critical approaches (feminism, anticolonial and antiracist thought, technology studies, ecology, etc.) have a common ground in directly challenging the ways humanism has restricted politics and education' (Snaza et al. 2014: 41, 49).

---

j. rossi (✉)
University of Northampton, Northampton, UK

© The Author(s) 2019
C. A. Taylor and A. Bayley (eds.), *Posthumanism and Higher Education*,
https://doi.org/10.1007/978-3-030-14672-6_11

Adopting a posthumanist perspective within Higher Education offers educators a renewed ethos of learning that forges new pedagogical approaches where problematizing the human can (paradoxically) re-humanize the field.

To resist the pressures of the Corporate University Complex, Berg and Seeber (2016: 57) provide a pathway to Slowness, 'asserting the importance of contemplation, connectedness, fruition, and complexity... letting research take the time it needs to ripen'. My training as a theatre-maker, more specifically as a playwright and director, forges my methodological approach, which is framed by craft, tradition and intuition, in which writing and reading plays are embodied acts. I crawl through perspectives, characters, and imagined spaces expressed through theatre production. Drawing from my craft as a playwright, and my own ongoing development in pedagogical practice, in addition to the cybernetic triangle of human → animal → machine which sets the stage for a posthumanist discourse as it relates to pedagogy, I consider two further triangulations: playtext → reader → playwright and curriculum → learner → educator. These two triangulations overlap in the space of higher education learning, which becomes a site of resistance within the Corporate University Complex where the marketeers advocate their own triangle: degree → customer → salesperson. Brecht perhaps forecast this when he said: 'knowledge is just a commodity. It is acquired in order to be resold' (Willett 1964: 72). Current systems of education being implemented by the Corporate University Complex continually disconnect the two key players, educator and learner.

Within Academia, the theatre practitioner endures an unstable status owing, in part, to the dispersed and diverse research methodologies that are gathered underneath the umbrellas of Practice-[led/based/as/for]-Research. Any research methodology that involves arts practice maintains a problematic existence within Academia, and perhaps it is the range of suffixes to 'practice,' that initially keeps the researchers of this ilk on shaky ground. In this chapter, I will use the term '(P)Artistic Research' as shorthand for 'Practical Artistic Research,' inclusive of the various iterations of practical research in the arts. (P)Artistic Research is difficult to define, no less validate, in a result-oriented, data-driven, 'performance'-measuring culture. The (P)Artistic Researcher, by nature, stands in opposition to the prevailing Corporate University Culture with its individualistic and competitive ethos, as the nature of most artistic research is process-oriented, collaborative and solution-finding.

Haraway's seminal work, *A Cyborg Manifesto* (1991) examines the world as 'radically hybridized, contaminated, integrated' (Snaza et al. 2014: 43), while Patrice Pavis discusses the 'contamination of practice by theory,' specific to postmodern theatre, explaining that 'theory overflows into practice; it becomes difficult to separate or distinguish the apparatus of production/reception from the spectator's hermeneutic activity… Theory is no longer nourished by an uncontested a priori practice; rather theory generates that practice' (Pavis 1992: 71). This chapter is 'contaminated' by aspects of my playwrighting practice. As a becoming-'playper', the chapter draws from and intermingles aspects of my playwrighting practice, in order to compose a poly-vocal analysis of my current practical arts research as it relates to my posthumanist pedagogical approaches and my theatre-making craft. As the chapter takes on the structure and form of a dramatic play, this 'playper' will reveal four semi-autobiographical characters: THE CRACKADEMIC, FIRE IN DA BELLY, THE HAIR and THE PRIVILEGED ALLY. Here, my playwrighting practice is entangled with Barad's (2014: 168) notion of 'diffraction,' as 'an iterative (re)configuring of patterns of differentiating-entangling [where] there is no moving beyond, no leaving the "old" behind'. These characters (a workaholic, a flame, a hair and an id) are 'diffractions' of my (P)Artistic Researcher-self.

The four diffractive characters form a dialogue crafted through a multi-linear narrative. This models an approach to academic writing that evokes the embodied nature of (P)Artistic Research, and embraces Gertrude Stein's (1935) notion of the 'landscape play' to deny Aristotle's traditional 'centre.' In his *Poetics*, Aristotle (1970: 32) establishes 'six constituent elements' of drama where he emphasizes the necessity for a plot that 'ought to be both unified and complete, and the component of events ought to be so firmly compacted that if any one of them is shifted to another place, or removed, the whole is loosened up and dislocated'. But Barad's (2014: 176) entanglements 'are not unities. They do not erase differences; on the contrary, entanglings entail differentiatings, differentiatings entail entanglings. One move – cutting together-apart.' The processes of playwrighting and play reading continue to be governed by Aristotelian aesthetics in the twenty first century. However, Stein's 1935 essay, *Plays*, expands the possibility of what a play could be. For Stein, the play is centre-less, and the experience of the play is created around the reader's own unique perspective, which inevitably loosens Aristotle's concrete structure. Stein was a student of psychologist William James, and her larger body of written work is anchored within James' notion of the 'continuous present,' which can be described as the reader's experience of time as fluid with many events occurring simultaneously in his/her mind (Miller 1949: 19). In Stein's 'spatial conception of dramaturgy… the activity of thought itself creates an experience' (Marranca 1977: x). I see Stein's 'landscape play' as providing a foundation for a posthuman approach to not only playwrighting, but also the curating of an experience, albeit in the space of a theatre, a classroom or rehearsal laboratory. The dramatic structure of the 'playper' will attempt to make visible my own developing posthuman understandings of the world in order to inspire new curricula for twenty first century learners. As you experience this 'landscape,' I invite you to let the diffractions richocet between the two triangulations introduced (playtext → reader → playwright and curriculum → learner → educator).

I hope to meet you on the other side, as a collaborator in this journey.

Act 1

The theatre artist turned academic has left Academia. He wonders whether or not he should re-enter this displaced community in its current state. His passion for education pulls him in that direction, but his stubbornness and arrogance require him to find a pathway back on his own terms. Perhaps this is his tragic flaw, from which a series of crises will emerge?

In a 2013 *Guardian* article titled, *Open-plan offices were devised by Satan in the deepest caverns of hell*, Burkeman affirms that this 'cheap way of cramming more people into less space' is 'associated with less persistence at challenging tasks, lower motivation, higher stress and blood pressure.' Coincidentally, it was that same year, when my former employing institution crammed the Performing Arts and English departments into a makeshift open-plan office, just prior to my being hired as a full-time permanent lecturer.

>THE CRACKADEMIC
>I am walking away. In the rain.
>I am walking away from my empty desk
>in that open-plan office in that badly-shaped building
>on that poorly constructed campus that
>part of me, hopes
>to never step into again.
>I suspect and expect that, in time, I might…

>FIRE IN DA BELLY
>Back in NYC, 'Reichman,' a close friend and long-time collaborator,
>reveals that he is hungry to form a new theatre group
>to engage in a long process without the pressure of a production.
>He asks me if I was aware that Aeschylus' *Prometheus Bound*
>was part of a trilogy of plays; Of the other two parts, he explains,
>only fragments remain. I am not aware of this. **Sparks.**

>THE CRACKADEMIC
>Today was a 'swan song' sort of a day;
>dramatic pomp and circumstance:
>The commencement of my first graduating class:
>A 'motley crew' who, I met when everything felt promising and new.
>Now, we get to leave that place together.

>FIRE IN DA BELLY
>Reichman is a Shakespeare-lover, whereas I prefer the Greeks.
>He **strikes the match:**
>Would I be interested in writing an adaptation of the Prometheus trilogy?

THE CRACKADEMIC
I sat on stage, looking into the sea of shining faces about to enter the 'real world;' Tarnished, I saw myself reflected in them.
I sat next to Professore Poetry, my mentor.
In those in-between moments, we made jokes and snapped 'selfies.'

THE HAIR
People keep asking me about his facial hair:
A long beard adorned with an over-sized handle-bar moustache, accented by the white hairs that were once auburn traces of his mother. His face has become its own spectacle:
A display of madness, and a mask…He has gone mad!
I have been plucked, by him, a trichotillomaniac.

THE PRIVILEGED ALLY
i have been procrastinating with the writing of this play, *d;vine*, which has been shelved in my mind for quite some time.
i am afraid of this piece.
i am afraid of its relevance.
i am afraid that i am too naïve to do it justice. But,
i trust that i will tend to it soon. It is unavoidable.

Everything I know deeply, I know through having worked on a play. The process of producing a theatrical work is a learning event that continues beyond the performance itself. I am still reflecting on and learning from works that I produced as an undergraduate, almost twenty years ago. I often discuss the nature of plays with my students, as riddles, or onions, with many layers to be unpeeled by the various makers and readers involved. Plays are peculiar puzzles that must be solved, yet have no concrete solution or fixed final picture. Plays can be simultaneously direct and covert. They can agitate, educate, provoke and yes, entertain. A play implies critical thinking, and for makers and readers alike, a play invites collective and creative problem-solving.

For me, playwrighting is an embodied process; I write on a hunch, from my gut. Here is the dilemma for playwrights (and most artists) who become (P)Artistic Researchers: as playwright, I layer, I veil and I soak the work in symbolism. I flirt with subtext. I create a work that requires analysis from a multitude of perspectives that, in order to curate an aesthetic and dramatic experience, are preferably not explained directly. But, as (P)Artistic Researcher, I must critically unpick and unpack these guttural, embodied intentions. Stein's radical positioning of the play as an open field to experience a 'continuous present' doubles over in the classroom, where '*the play's the thing*' to be studied (Shakespeare 2018: 60). Bennett's (2004: 348) notion of 'thing-power,' which suggests 'the possibility that attentiveness to (non-human) things and their powers can have a laudable effect on humans,' both problematizes, and is problematized by, the play: the play has a life which is both material, as literature, and ephemeral as live performance. The 'thing-ness' of a play is questionable, and ricochets between Stein and Aristotle.

THE PRIVILEGED ALLY
i can only recently begin to articulate this play: *d;vine*. It stems back to my fascination and intrigue with Dante's *Divine Comedy*.
i first encountered *The Inferno* when i was in high school.
i studied *Paradiso* in a university class called *The Philosophy of Love*.

During the first two years in my first permanent position at an academic institution in the UK, there was a spiked increase in the awareness of police shootings of African Americans, usually unarmed, in the US. I say 'awareness' because it is the advent of technology, the ability to document and 'live-stream' these horrific events that has forced (some) white Americans to confront the realities of what it means to be black in America. Hill (2017: xi) states that in a 'surveillance society' where 'everything we do is being watched, we can actually watch the things we do, and see them for what they are.' This optimism for society's capacity to be critically reflective, ebbs and flows in my heart.

THE PRIVILEGED ALLY

i must come to terms with the reality that despite my education, my liberal upbringing and all of the friends, lovers, colleagues and students who have familiarized me with, and included me in aspects of Black culture; that i know very little of the Black experience.
And for all that i think i know, i must admit that this knowledge is not **embodied**. i too, am part of a tradition of naiveté and ignorance within White culture.

The 'Black Lives Matter' movement emerged during this period. The terms 'White Guilt' and 'White Privilege' were increasingly becoming part of public discourse. I felt compelled to acknowledge my own experiences of guilt and privilege, but had no tools for doing so. I decided to confront these terms with the tools I did have: theatre-making and research. I aimed to use playwrighting to become 'woke;' to position myself as an ally in the fight for social justice. I suspected that the play developing in my mind could have the potential to awaken others: 'Differences are within; differences are formed through intra-activity, in the making of "this" and "that" within the phenomenon that is constituted in their inseparability (entanglement)' (Barad 2014: 175).

THE PRIVILEGED ALLY

d;vine is a moving poem that **ricochets** between three realities:
'This,' 'That' and 'Neither-This-Nor-That'.
Two stories are happening simultaneously, and
'Neither-This-Nor-That' is the liminal glue that connects
'This' and 'That,' through choral refrains
representing a highly reflective **woke** state.

THE CRACKADEMIC

Following the graduation ceremony, I stopped by that open-plan office
to retrieve the last of my personal belongings.
I left a few traces of myself: A misunderstood poem I once wrote
in response to working conditions. I taped it underneath the desk;
a gift

for the sorry soul that will occupy that space after my departure.
On the chalkboard wall, cluttered with dates of meetings and acronyms,
I left a chalky message: *Stay Strong. Don't Drink the Kool-Aid.*

FIRE IN DA BELLY
In the weeks following my resignation, I dove into a surge of writing, drafting an adaptation of Aeschylus' *Prometheus* trilogy, the project **ignited** by Reichman

THE PRIVILEGED ALLY
d;vine will submerge the reader in an experience where one must dig deep in the memory bank of time to acknowledge that—

FIRE IN DA BELLY
A growing resistance to a culture steeped in corporate greed was embedded in my conscience, **fueling** this new telling of *Prometheus*, not to mention the recent Brexit vote and *the (ir)resistible rise of* Donald J. Trump towards the presidency.

THE PRIVILEGED ALLY
To acknowledge that: *Something is rotten in the state*[s]—
d;vine calls attention to a plague: a dis-ease that continues to manifest.
It will overwhelm purposely, to shake the amnesia,
compelling us to rip the tumor out, with our own bare hands.

THE HAIR
WHY are we resisting?! WHAT are we resisting?

Berg and Seeber (2016: 6) see 'individual practice as a site of resistance.' The mask that will become 'D.Spair' was gifted to me by Dr. Myer Taub, a friend and colleague from South Africa. Taub's masked character, 'JuJu the Pig,' has collaborated with my masked character, 'Dottore JoMiRo,' in *The S'Kool of Edumacation*, an ongoing series of performance interventions staged within classroom motifs. Taub had plans to visit London, and I suggested he bring JuJu. He did not bring JuJu, but instead brought a papier mâché mask resembling the distraught figure in Edvard Munch's *The Scream*, presented as a peculiar peace offering, or just another Taub-ian provocation (Fig. 11.1).

Fig. 11.1 'Dottore JoMiRo' and JuJu the Pig in *The S'kool of Edumacation* (July 2015)

THE HAIR
Why did Taub bring him this crude mask?
As he stares into the mask, I begin to imagine:
A character trapped in a Kafka-esque nightmare,
continuously encountering absurd situations, burdened with
bureaucracy and unthinking, uncritical, un-human peoples.
Rather than agonizing over this tragic state of affairs, the character will
be playful and childlike; an innocent disruptor of the System. Agency.

(pluck, cling, fade…)

Act 2

The (P)Artistic Researcher embarks on a 'Resignation Tour:' Stonehenge, Croatia, New York City, Providence (Rhode Island), the gorges of Ithaca in upstate New York, Toronto, Niagara, Sao Paulo and The Basque Country. His drive and hunger to create engaging, meaningful and socially conscious work burns in his belly. This is the beginning of his academic breakdown.

In a refusal to be 'serious about categories,' Haraway (Franklin 2017: 51) prefers to think in terms of 'companioning' and suggests that 'compost is a place of working, a place of making and unmak-ing … a place of failure, including, well, culpable failure. Compost can be a place of doing badly.' Haraway's compost(humanist) viewpoint brings the two triangles (playtext → reader → playwright and curriculum → learner → educator) in parallel where playtext and curriculum become palettes of possibilities unwritten, written and re-written; offering a vast landscape to absorb meaning framed by interpretations, stagings and readings, where participants (playwright/reader and educator/learner) are in companionship with one another, making and un-making.

FIRE IN DA BELLY
In my garden, I shift between drafting material for *Prometheus* and pulling weeds, mowing the lawn and planting flowers.
I sit in the **hot sun** for hours, scribbling ideas, consulting *Wikipedia* and conducting *Google* image searches, while re-arranging Aeschylus' fragments through trial and error. Writing was never been so freeing.

THE PRIVILEGED ALLY

i delve in: How do i come to terms with my own privilege?
This privileged position: to quit, to resign, to walk away.
To be afforded the opportunity *to be or not to be*. Even getting that job that i quit, was a privilege. Accruing a modest savings while working
was a privilege. Moving to the UK to pursue a doctoral degree funded
through US government loans was a privilege.
Maintaining resident status to remain in the UK, with an EU passport acquired through a somewhat ironic reversal of my great grandfather's
emigration to the US; To reclaim Italian citizenship through my
bloodline, was a privilege. To cross borders without too much hassle, with two passports, is a privilege.

THE HAIR

Taub's mask has its first public appearance at an anti-Brexit march in London. The character is undeveloped and yet to be named,
but the character wants to be at the march.
The march is also *his* return to activism. Ironic, since he has been teaching a political performance module for the past four years.
I am uplifted by the communal experience of the protest.
The unnamed character takes part in a re-staging of the iconic image of
the Battle of Iwo Jima, using the EU and Gay Pride flags.
The mask both detaches and connects him to the movement
in ways that I do not yet understand. (Fig. 11.2)

THE PRIVILEGED ALLY

i am not aiming to be a hero, or a savior, or a protagonist in writing
this work. i am trying to relinquish the position of the protagonist, while confronting a history and heritage of antagonism.
i am antagonizing my self, to pro-tagonize the rest (?)

11 Dramatizing an Articulation of the (P)Artistic Researcher's ...

Fig. 11.2 'D-Spair' participates in re-staging of 'Battle of Iwo Jima' (June 2016)

FIRE IN DA BELLY

I am back in New York. Reichman has organized his new group for a reading of the first draft of *(Promethe)üs*. Putting the play on its feet,
we slowly **burn** through this new material.

Through *d;vine*, I am waking up; becoming 'woke:' strengthening my social conscience and beginning to think more critically about my role within socially engaged work. Through *(Promethe)üs*, I am reclaiming my writerly rhythm. Through the mask, I become more acutely aware of how far away from my own practice I have become. I consciously turned the mirror inward, in order for my work to reach outward; to become accessible, and perhaps even, to have 'impact.'

THE CRACKADEMIC
I am applying to non-academic jobs, but my academically framed CV
feels weighted, heavy, over-intellectualized. How do I frame myself?
This new identity of form-filling triggers an endless cycle of
overly critical self-reflection.

THE HAIR
I am in hot and humid New York. Sticky.
It is his 35th birthday and he is chopping off his beard;
but keeping the moustache, which continues to get bigger, and more
ridiculous. Mad. Mad Dali.

FIRE IN DA BELLY
I am back in London, **cooking** up a revised draft of *(Promethe)üs*.

THE PRIVILEGED ALLY
i am trying to let go of the narrative. But, it feels like i'm just putting
another white male at the center of the narrative, and celebrating
his process of getting **woke**.

THE CRACKADEMIC
I am cut-and-pasting my life away. I frame, un-frame and re-frame
myself according to 'essential' and 'desirable' criteria, all redundant.

THE PRIVILEGED ALLY
i am gaining the courage to write this play, by tending to it each day.
My writer's muscle is being flexed. i am no longer waiting for the
ebb and flow of inspiration to determine productivity.

THE CRACKADEMIC
I am attempting to squeeze into my blue suit.
I have an interview for a Senior Lecturer post.

THE HAIR
I am lingering in a sea of text, lost in the words of others; the Union Square 'post-it' protest: *This is not the end.* Happy Christmas in New York. (Fig. 11.3)

Fig. 11.3 Union Square 'Post-It' Protest (December 2016)

THE CRACKADEMIC
I am notified that I am the 'Reserve Candidate' and will receive
follow-up once their first choice accepts or declines. I wait
several days. I build up the courage to send a follow up e-mail:
No reply. Weeks later, I write to the Head of Department: No reply.

THE PRIVILEGED ALLY
It is the first week of 2017: I am a passenger in a car that was just
pulled over by the Providence police, because of a burnt out light
bulb
above the license plate. We are coming from a workshop that D-K,
a close friend and long-time collaborator, organized in order to
read aloud and explore extracts from *d;vine* with a group of local
actors.
The officer plays a power game with the notoriously mouthy D-K,
who has no patience for authority. The officer calls for backup.
Things
get heated. All I can think is: if we were Black, one or both of us
would already be dead bodies on the street. Privilege.

THE CRACKADEMIC
Another Institution sends a body-less email, with just a header:
Unsuccessful Application. At least they responded.
I slip into reclusiveness.

FIRE IN DA BELLY
It is the first week of 2017. We are work-shopping the second draft of
(Promethe)üs. We tangle ourselves in discussions around language and
the undeniable parallels between Züs and Trump,
but we do not want this to become a Trump play—

(The fire goes out, unexpectedly. Fire In Da Belly disappears, unexplained:
Even through the ashes, growth can flourish.*)*

THE CRACKADEMIC
Another Human Resources e-mail from another academic institution:
'We are not ready to let you know
if your application has been successful.'
I never hear otherwise. I guess they're still trying to figure me out.
I can't blame them. I am too.

THE PRIVILEGED ALLY
It is the first week of 2017. On the subway platform for a
Flatbush-bound train, i notice two young ladies who look familiar.
They get off at the same stop and are heading in the same direction.
They keep looking back at me and one blurts out: *I swear I know you!*
They are former students from Brooklyn Theatre Arts, a high school
that i helped to form and develop several years back.
We have an explosive laugh on the street,
and they show me pictures of their babies.

Being out of the classroom for the first time in ten years, I have come to realize how much the act of teaching contributes to my research. The opportunity to dialogue with curious minds and test out rough ideas in the classroom, has been a privilege that I have overlooked, and one I deeply miss. In a classroom where trust has been nurtured, students become participants and collaborators in my body of work—but this 'entangled' state can no longer think in terms of my work/my body. 'To be entangled is not simply to be intertwined with another, as in the joining of separate entities, but to lack independent, self-contained existence. Existence is not an individual affair. Individuals do not preexist their interactions; rather, individuals emerge through and as part of their entangled intra-relating' (Barad 2007: ix). Who else would I engage with this work, if not my students? My colleagues at the Corporate University Complex were far too frazzled and bogged down to engage in an exchange of ideas. Oftentimes, we were teaching in vacuums, unaware of what theories or practitioners were being discussed in other modules, and doubling over each other's efforts rather than reinforcing them. Most of my colleagues had no comprehensive knowledge or understanding of the work I was engaged with, and I must admit, I had little time to be a participant in their research. The work we do as educators is continuously being documented in the minds of our students, and rarely do we ever get to see or understand how such knowledge is or isn't applied outside of the academic bubble. In the age of the corporate university, the rate of burnout for academics is far too high, and the emphasis on teaching and learning is far too low. In the UK, we are tongue-tied by talk of the Research Excellence Framework (REF) and Teaching Excellence Framework (TEF), exhaustingly long, un-poetic documents compiled into a set of guidelines that determine excellence based on the 'impact' of an 'output.' From the outside, I straddle the fence on whether or not it would be a healthy decision to re-enter Academia (if I ever left).

THE PRIVILEGED ALLY
d;vine is the story of a character who cannot let go of the narrative but desperately wants to. He wants to frame himself frameless…

THE CRACKADEMIC
At the suggestion of a concerned friend, I look into my eligibility for receiving 'benefits' to help make ends meet.
I enter the *JobCentre,* where I meet a new cast of characters…

THE PRIVILEGED ALLY
An idea crops up! What if *d;vine* is written alongside a social justice curriculum that helps to pull apart the aesthetic and poetic layers of the text, to stimulate intellectual curiosity, to encourage
critical thinking and self-reflection, to equip young people with truth-seeking and fact-checking skills, to develop the
imaginative muscle, and to celebrate the form of the play as a communal learning experience that also embraces the solitary confines of reading! Impact.

THE CRACKADEMIC
I need to pee. I rushed from that job interview to get to my compulsory
appointment at the JobCentre. I sign my name to the electronic pad to document my attendance. Before leaving, I ask:
Which way to the bathroom? My 'Job Coach' responds:
We don't have toilets for clients. People were doing things in them.
And we're not insured if something happens. I rubber band it.
Output.

In order to justify what it is that we are doing, just to keep doing the things that we are supposed to be doing, we bend, twist and turn our practicing selves; distracted, displaced and derailed from our unique research paths. This is no way to conduct research, or make theatre, or educate the next generation. As a result, educators and learners are being reduced to 'useful machines, rather than complete citizens who can think for themselves, criticize tradition, and understand the significance of another person's sufferings and achievements' (Nussbaum 2016: 2). For the (P)Artistic Researcher, the personal is unavoidable. One's personal narrative, by way of collaboration, inevitably becomes a multi-linear narrative.

THE CRACKADEMIC
I am heading back to that campus, for the first time since I left.
I was a**woke**n by a call from a former colleague, weeping:
Professor Poetry passed away.

THE PRIVILEGED ALLY
d;vine is in me. It lives in me. i can feel it—it's fighting to get out.
It is urgent, but i choose to take my time with it.

THE CRACKADEMIC
Professor Poetry had a magic about him: A great provocateur,
with an exceedingly high bar of expectations. He often joked about his

fascist approach to classroom management.
He had a wicked sense of humor: crude and raunchy.
His heart was full of high drama at its best; classy, yet bawdy.
I scroll up an old chat-screen on my phone, to re-read the last message
I had received from Professor Poetry:

*'There are cures around the world and at least I will travel to try them.
[INSERT NAME OF <u>THAT</u> INSTITUTION] literally 'killed' me with
two weeks of evil just before I first collapsed. But I have better things
to do than wasting time hating those pillocks. Miss you badly,'
(pluck, linger, burn)*

Epilogue

*The overall socio-political climate around the globe has distracted the
(P)Artistic Researcher. As his creative work refines his critical lens, he is
unraveled by his attempt to (re)frame himself; He discards the frame; too
many diffractions. This is his dénouement.*

                THE CRACKADEMIC
On a plane back from Sao Paulo. Delirious.
I have been offered a permanent post at a UK university
in a hauntingly familiar role:
Programme Leader for a BA Honours degree in Drama.
I am optimistic. Cautiously optimistic.

The 'entangled' nature of research and practice offers an 'approach to the world that is more *intra*-active, more mutually co-constitutive rather than one that is more *inter*-active, where ontologies separately encounter each other in space and time' (Bayley 2016: 48). In this work, I attempt to re-situate the discourse on (P)Artistic Research, through a blending of writing forms: academic and dramatic. Emerging from this playper's entanglement of research and practice, diffracted, I offer these 'six constituent elements' to being a (P)Artistic Researcher on a posthumanist pathway to a Slow professorship:

11 Dramatizing an Articulation of the (P)Artistic Researcher's ...

- Actively questioning
- Experimenting
- Taking risks
- Operating on hunches
- Drawing from past experiences
- Being vulnerable, humble and reflexive

The spine to these 'elements' is forged by collaboration and reflection. For Berg and Seeber, 'collaboration is about thinking together' where 'Slow Professors act with purpose, cultivating emotional and intellectual resilience to the effects of the corporatization of higher education' (2016: 90). The edges of the triad of triangles (human → animal → machine, playtext → reader → playwright and curriculum → learner → educator) become the tools that empower us to make 'agential cuts' carving a 'continuous present' where educators and learners can 'begin to *experience* the relationship between persons and other materialities more horizontally' (Bennett 2010: 10). I view my new post as an opportunity to forge theory and practice as a Slow professor with posthumanist underpinnings to ask students to engage 'with the "human" as problematic' (Snaza et al. 2014: 41) as I myself search for 'individual agency within the institutional context' (Berg and Seeber 2016: 4). Slowing down, here, becomes a political tool rather than coping mechanism. These elements, I believe, hold 'the potential to disrupt the corporate ethos of speed' (11).

To conclude, inconclusively, I return to Haraway's 'compost,' which 'includes living and dying… the questions of finitude and mortality are prominent, not in some kind of depressive or tragic way, but those who will return our flesh to the Earth are in the making of compost' (Franklin 2017: 51). Adopting a 'Slow' posthumanist outlook from within my research practice has stimulated a process of diffraction in both my playwrighting and pedagogical approaches, as well as navigating the circumstances given by the Corporate University Complex. My lesson plans have been re-imagined through the opportunity to design curriculum in my new role. An incomplete Act 3 to this playper was drafted with the residue of classroom sessions, teaching moments and failures from my first year in the (com)post. More poignantly, this research has diffracted and diffused my burning angst with/in the Corporate University Complex. The characters in this playper are traces, reminders, to shift perspective. The posthumanist landscape remains a vast and open field; composting conversations, curricula and creative production in companionship.

References

Aristotle. (1970). *Aristotle poetics* (G. F. Else, Trans.). Ann Arbor: The University of Michigan Press.

Barad, K. (2007). *Meeting the universe halfway: Quantum physics and the entanglement of matter and meaning*. Durham and London: Duke University Press.

Barad, K. (2014). Diffracting diffraction: Cutting together-apart. *Parallax, 20*(3), 168–187.

Bayley, A. (2016). Trans-forming higher education. *Performance Research, 21*(6), 44–49.

Bennett, J. (2004). The force of things: Steps towards an ecology of matter. *Political Theory, 32*(3), 347–372.

Bennett, J. (2010). *Vibrant matter: A political ecology of things*. Durham: Duke University Press.

Berg, M., & Seeber, B. (2016). *The slow professor: Challenging the culture of speed in the academy*. Toronto: University of Toronto Press.

Burkeman, O. (2018, November 18). Open-plan offices were devised by Satan in the deepest caverns of hell. *The Guardian*. Retrieved from https://www.theguardian.com/news/2013/nov/18/open-plan-offices-bad-harvard-business-review. Accessed 1 May 2018.

Franklin, S. (2017). Staying with the manifesto: An interview with Donna Haraway. *Theory, Culture & Society, 34*(4), 49–63.

Haraway, D. (1991). A cyborg manifesto: Science, technology, and socialist-feminism in the late twentieth century. In *Simians, cyborgs and women: The reinvention of nature*. London: Routledge.

Hill, M. L. (2017). *Nobody: Casualties of America's war on the vulnerable, from Ferguson to Flint and beyond*. New York: Atria Books.

Marranca, B. (1977). Introduction: Presence of mind. In C. V. Vechten (Ed.), *Last operas and plays by Gertrude Stein* (pp. vvii–xxviii). Baltimore: John Hopkins University Press.

Miller, R. S. (1949). *Gertrude Stein: Form and intelligibility*. New York: The Exposition Press.

Nussbaum, M. C. (2016). *Not for profit: Why democracy needs the humanities*. Princeton, NJ: Princeton University Press.

Pavis, P. (1992). *Theatre at the crossroads of culture* (L. Kruger, Trans.). London: Routledge.

Shakespeare, W. (2018). *Hamlet*. London: Bloomsbury Arden Shakespeare.

Snaza, N., Appelbaum, P., Bayne, S., Carlson, D., Morris, M., Rotas, N., et al. (2014). Toward a posthumanist education. *Journal of Curriculum Theorizing, 30*(2), 39–55.

Stein, G. (1935). Plays. In C. V. Vechten (Ed.), *Last operas and plays by Gertrude Stein* (pp. xxix–lii). Baltimore: John Hopkins University Press.

Willett, J. (Ed.). (1964). *Brecht on theatre: The development of an aesthetic*. New York: Hill and Wang.

12

A Posthuman Pedagogy for Childhood Studies (Viewpoint)

Amanda Hatton

This viewpoint focuses on some insights regarding the use of creative methods in a Childhood Studies course session, and explores how a posthumanist approach provided an opportunity for students to explore different aspects of the research process. The activity discussed was used to: (a) develop students' awareness of creative research methods through objects, space and materiality; and (b) to relate this awareness to how children may communicate their feelings, views and experiences. Such aims are not only important for educational research but relevant to the practice of developing higher education pedagogy in Childhood Studies. The activity discussed involved asking Childhood Studies students to experience and engage with a range of objects with different textures and smells and, from these, create their own assemblages.

A. Hatton (✉)
Sheffield Hallam University, Sheffield, UK
e-mail: a.hatton@shu.ac.uk

© The Author(s) 2019
C. A. Taylor and A. Bayley (eds.), *Posthumanism and Higher Education*,
https://doi.org/10.1007/978-3-030-14672-6_12

The Activity as Affective Assemblage

The purpose of this sensory activity was to enable students to explore and experience how different methods might be used to gather different types of data and information. Key to this was promoting students' awareness of how the process *felt* as a basis for appreciating how children may be aware of objects, space and environment. The objects included coloured paper, felt pens, crayons and chalk, play dough, buttons, keys, a supersoft piece of fabric, a soft blanket and cotton wool balls soaked in perfume and baby oil. I selected these objects in the hope that they would elicit a sensory response for students to experience the 'vital materiality that runs through and across bodies, both human and non-human' (Bennett 2010: 10). Students were asked to work in small groups, engage with the objects to create their own new assemblages and discuss what memories of childhood were evoked by touching, smelling and interacting with the objects. They were asked to consider the environment of the university teaching room they were in, the space which they recalled when discussing their memories, and to think about how the 'thing- power' of the objects provoked affects in them (Bennett 2010).

The immediate power of this sensory approach was evident in some students' choice of buttons as part of their assemblages—buttons provoked memories of their Grandmas; or of being at school and chewing the buttons on their clothes; or, more enigmatically, one student said that the buttons reminded them of false hope. Similarly the texture and smell of the play-dough recalled play with friends, siblings, parents and even tasting it. The soft texture of the cloths and blankets provoked memories of nurturing.

The Activity as Creative Research Methods Pedagogy

The multi-sensory engagement with materials and space was used as a device to develop students' awareness as researchers of how children may see and recall things from different perspectives than adults.

In this, it aimed to sensitise students to the point of view that as adults we cannot fully know what children see or think. More than that, as Burke's (2007) discussion of spaces, environments and affect indicates, an environment may be experienced differently by a child, and a child's entanglements with space, time and matter are emergent processes (Barad 2003). The activity encouraged students to consider learning as a connected and responsive condition of entanglement, and of children as multiple, fluid, interacting and becoming, rather than a singular, individual, and bounded. Such a view challenges the taken-for-granted aspects of the separation of environment, space and atmosphere.

Using this approach disrupted the usual, descriptive teaching of different research methods. It created a space for students to deepen their understanding of objects, materiality, space, and affect and enabled them to access a different (posthumanist) perspective which refused to prioritise human experience. Such a view of research also pushed at traditional notions of 'positionality' as students came to recognize how they as researchers impact upon the dynamics of the research process. Ironically, whilst students came to engage with multiplicity and emergence, they were then required to fix meaning and the fluid experience of research and record it in written comments and expression through assessment in their final research project.

The Activity as Uncomfortable Knowing

This sensory engagement with objects as something that is 'unexpressed' but felt (MacCannell 1985) problematises traditional research process by creating a complex and uncomfortable space in which new and uncomfortable modes of 'knowing' may emerge—this is knowing as feeling, as affect (Hickey-Moody 2013), as atmospheric assemblage (Anderson 2009). Dominant conceptualisations of pedagogies within Higher Education see the lecturer as narrator and the students as passive receptacles to receive information (Freire 1982; Beard and Wilson 2002). In contrast, and to counter this, the session used a posthumanist approach to develop students' insights of the research process itself as a 'doing' and experiencing. This is important for Childhood Studies pedagogy for, without this awareness, students may not appreciate the value of working with children in a participatory way (Cook and Hess 2007; Hatton 2014).

To Conclude

Law (2004: 10) notes that research can be 'a risky and troubling process, it will take time and effort to make realities and hold them steady for a moment against a background of flux and indeterminacy.' The activity I used aimed to complicate the process of asking research questions, to trouble the expectation of what data will be gained, and to push students' expectations beyond the usual. This moves methods from the descriptive and into the performative so that methods themselves open up spaces of meaning (Coleman and Ringrose 2013). My hope was that engaging students in posthuman research encounters would disrupt the usual way of doing things in Childhood Studies pedagogy and foreground research as a 'messy' (Law 2004) and entangled practice of embodiment, space, materiality, affect and atmosphere.

References

Anderson, B. (2009). Affective atmospheres. *Emotion, Space and Society, 2*, 77–81.

Barad, K. (2003). Posthumanist performativity: Towards an understanding of how matter comes to matter. *Signs: Journal of Women in Culture and Society, 28*(3), 801–831.

Beard, C., & Wilson, J. P. (2002). *The power of experiential learning: A handbook for trainers and educators.* London: Kogan Page.

Bennett, J. (2010). *Vibrant matter: A political ecology of things.* Durham: Duke University Press.

Burke, C. (2007). The view of the child: Releasing 'visual voices' in the design of learning environments. *Discourse: Studies in the Cultural Politics of Education, 28*(3), 359–372.

Coleman, R., & Ringrose, J. (2013). Introduction: Deleuze and research methodologies. In R. Coleman & J. Ringrose (Eds.), *Deleuze and research methodologies*. Croydon: Edinburgh University Press.

Cook, T., & Hess, E. (2007). What the camera sees and from whose perspective: Fun methodologies for engaging children in enlightening adults. *Childhood, 14*(1), 29–45.

Freire, P. (1982). *The pedagogy of the oppressed*. Harmondsworth: Penguin.

Hatton, A. J. (2014). Shallow democracy: In other peoples' shoes—Listening to the voices of children and young people. In J. Westwood, C. Larkins, D. Moxon, Y. Perry, & N. Thomas (Eds.), *Participation, citizenship and intergenerational relations in children and young people's lives* (pp. 43–53). Basingstoke: Palgrave Macmillan.

Hickey-Moody, A. (2013). Affect as method: Feelings, aesthetics and affective pedagogy. In R. Coleman & J. Ringrose (Eds.), *Deleuze and research methodologies*. Croydon: Edinburgh University Press.

Law, J. (2004). *After method, mess in social science research*. London: Routledge.

MacCannell, J. F. (1985). The temporality of textuality: Bakhtin and Derrida. *MLN, Comparative Literature, 100*(5), 968–988.

# 13

Disruptive Pedagogies for Teacher Education: The Power of *Potentia* in Posthuman Times

Kay Sidebottom

Introduction

The purpose of this chapter is to recount the experience of trainee teachers and their tutors, who, over the course of an academic year, viewed their post-14 teacher training curriculum through a post human lens in order to re-imagine the world of teaching and learning for the twenty-first century and beyond.

Although centred around a particular education setting (a Further Education college in the north of England), this 're-imagining' also involved a wider community of teachers, drawn in through the rhizomatic affordances of social media and my own nomadic working arrangements (at the time I worked for two additional adult learning organisations). The 'we' in this chapter therefore refers to the collective teacher-student assemblages that formed, reformed and emerged as wide 'constellations of practice' as we experimented with new ideas; disrupting and unsettling accepted pedagogical practices in a variety of affirmative ways.

K. Sidebottom (✉)
Leeds Beckett University, Leeds, UK

© The Author(s) 2019
C. A. Taylor and A. Bayley (eds.), *Posthumanism and Higher Education*,
https://doi.org/10.1007/978-3-030-14672-6_13

The ideas discussed in this chapter were drawn from the critical posthuman theory of Rosi Braidotti, in turn inspired by Deleuze and Spinoza. By entangling students-myself-colleagues with this at times dense, confusing and challenging theory, I sought to make the complex concepts approachable and understandable. In this my aim was to challenge the dominant humanistic philosophies of education and 'make nonlinear thinking accessible to mainstream audiences to interrupt the linear, status quo thinking undergirding a global educational neoliberal movement' (Strom 2017: 104).

Background

Life for teachers in the UK Further Education (FE) sector is becoming increasingly difficult: managerialist cultures, precarious working conditions, instrumental approaches to teaching, learning as 'exam factory' output (Coffield and Williamson 2011), and increasingly unmanageable workloads comprise just some of the challenges facing the profession today. Despite this shaping of knowledge according to dominant 'banking' system principles (Freire 1970: 45) many FE teachers seek to work creatively and imaginatively to enact change, grounded by a belief in the power of education to make a difference to students' lives. As a further education teacher-educator, I am motivated by the question: how can we, as educators, act in ways that resist these technocratic managerialist formations whilst maintaining hope and supporting an 'ethics of affirmation' (Braidotti 2008: 3)? My pedagogic efforts have long been grounded in critical education, aiming to embody Freire's (1970: 51) notion of praxis: 'Reflection and action upon the world in order to change it.' However, a chance visit to the University of Utrecht in 2015, rhizomatic itself in its own messy, informal and serendipitous path, led me to Rosi Braidotti's work, to nomadic thinking and critical posthuman theory. Through this came the realisation that myself and colleagues were undertaking work that may better be considered 'posthuman', in that we were trying to make 'an affirmative move towards new alternatives' (Braidotti 2016: 37), by including the non-human, working via technological mediation, and starting to take account of the agency of 'things' (Bennett 2010). My (self-appointed) task upon my return from Utrecht was to move my critical pedagogical approach through a posthuman ontological turn, in order to open up new spaces for thinking differently about education. Following discussion and exploration with my students, I introduced three pedagogic posthuman intra-ventions into the 'Reflective Practice' module which we then worked with together, over the course of one academic year:

1. Using art to reframe humanistic approaches to reflective practice
2. Taking account of 'liberating assemblages' and entanglements with non-human others
3. Examining and (re)introducing the 'missing slices of the past' (Ferrando 2012) which our teacher training curriculum was lacking.

These intra-ventions aimed to reshape and reconfigure our teacher education curriculum, drawing on posthumanist ideas, theory and practice. We aimed to disrupt 'pedagogy as usual' in order to move to a place of 'potentia'; this entailed a 'practice of the plunge' whereby we could 'activate modes of radical experimentation' (Taylor 2016: 20). At times this practice felt playful and clumsy as we struggled to interpret the concepts of 'high theory'; as teachers, not academics, we even wondered at times about our 'permission' to theorize in this way (Strom 2017). We discussed the changes and ideas together in online spaces, both privately and in public forums such as Facebook groups and Twitter chats, which allowed us to elicit the views of other teacher-educators across the Further Education sector. Proposals were also shared at the university consortium meetings during a year-long period of curriculum review. The imperative to work and think differently drove us to new approaches, as we used posthuman thinking not as another theory to add to the canon, but as a 'navigational tool through which to read the world' (Braidotti 2012). By moving from critical pedagogy to critical posthuman theory we were shifting the focus from emancipatory humanist teaching that aims to create (but of course never establishes) a 'world-for-us' (Jagodzinksi 2018: 84) and locating our embodied and embedded selves in the 'trouble' of the here and now (Haraway 2016).

Intra-vention 1: Using Art for Affirmative Action

> Becoming posthuman is regulated by an ethics of joy and affirmation that functions through the transformation of negative into positive passions. (Braidotti 2013: 194)

Frustrations and difficulties arising from the many institutional modes of 'academic capitalism' (Münch 2014) I outlined at the beginning of this chapter have recently been sharpened with the introduction of the TEF (Teaching Excellence Framework) across the Higher Education sector. Forstenzer (2016: 4) suggests that the TEF has shifted focus from the impact of academic study on social and personal outcomes and wider societal benefits towards the much narrower aim of serving the purposes of 'an imagined group of employers.' The TEF 'envisions higher education as a private good, as well as encouraging students and academics to be motivated by self-interest and self-advancement at the expense of public service and civic engagement' (Forstenzer 2016: 6). This new mode of 'territorialising' the HE system (Deleuze and Guattari 1987) seeks to reframe social justice in ways inimical to our aims. Our classes were often an outlet for the frustrations caused by teaching in a world of diminished autonomy, reductive methods and heightened individualism, but as Braidotti (2008: 8) suggests, we were in danger of 'promoting an ecology of belonging by upholding the collective memory of trauma or pain.' Prolonged reflection and discussion about our seemingly inescapable predicament as educators had the potential to bind us in shared negativity and hopelessness, so we needed a different approach.

Working in affirmative spirit, and inspired by the imperative 'Art as a thing that does' (Hlavajova 2015) I introduced artistic approaches into areas of the curriculum designed to develop trainees as 'reflective practitioners'. We began to problematize reflection as a reductive, retrospective and individual process. Typical cyclical models such as David Kolb's experiential model (Kolb 1984), which attempt to 'freeze-frame' moments for subsequent analysis and action, were proving inadequate for students who no longer accepted mind-body dualism or were comfortable with limited acknowledgement of affective responses.

Critical reflection was found not to be a linear or cyclical process, and not a purely cognitive one either, but messy, complex and often embodied, as emotions were revealed through corporeal postures and placings or physically manifested through tears or body trauma resulting from extreme fatigue and exhaustion. Reflective methods in teacher training curricula have traditionally taken the form of a written journal, as was the case on this course. However, the additional reflexive step of 'challenging your practice, values and beliefs' (University of Huddersfield 2016) permitted us to seize a moment of 'potentia' whereby students could seek out new and creative ways to engage with reflection on a deeper and potentially more critical level.

Inspired by Clover and Stalker's (2007: 3) suggestion that 'art-based adult education and learning provokes radical and creative visions of an alternative world; "as if" things could be otherwise,' the first part of the intra-vention was to visit a local art gallery and seek out objects that related in some way to our thoughts and feelings at that moment in time. This visit was a means of sparking the creative process and connecting the aesthetic to the reflective; for some students this also provided an important means of scaffolding, as art was at first viewed as something 'not for people like us.' We then moved on to creating our own art; which included photography, painting, modelling and collage. Being in such creative spaces allowed trainees to reject fixed notions of teacher identity and, over the period of an academic year as the creations were refined, remixed and co-created, we related the creative process to the notion of 'becoming' teacher, in a dynamic and emergent sense (Deleuze and Guattari 1987). This ontology of becoming, which rejects the notion of identity as stable, allowed us to work with notions of flux and plasticity, both in the physical process of creating artworks and in the dynamic exploration of identity. The art work produced by the students, and their reflections (shared here, with their permission) revealed that it was also not an individual process but dependent on the involvement of human and non-human agents, such as pets, physical location, or the actual tools employed for reflection itself (Fig. 13.1).

For one student the artistic escape from imposing a fixed teacher identity, and the permission to be uncertain and unsure was liberating:

Fig. 13.1 David Ball. Collective

> I painted myself as an empty shape, with empty shapes surrounding me. It got my feelings across quite well about feeling empty of thoughts, feelings, experiences and teaching experience.

For others, the creation of art pieces which experimented with different materials became a collective expression of the co-dependency of teacher and student. Some students explored their bodily relations to the art they were creating too, by experimenting with digital tools or even using tears mixed into paint to express the intensity of their experiences. As Braidotti states:

> By transposing us beyond the confines of bound identities, art becomes necessarily inhuman in the sense of non-human in that it connects to the animal, the vegetable, earthy and planetary forces that surround us. Art is also, moreover, cosmic in its resonance and hence posthuman by structure, as it carries us to the limits of what our embodied selves can do and endure. (Braidotti 2013: 107)

There were unanticipated outcomes. For some, the engagement with creative processes resulted in deeper, long-term changes. In the spirit of reflecting and working alongside students in this artistic assemblage I began to write poetry again myself, expressing the joy (and frustration) of undertaking lesson observations by writing a poem on official observation paperwork which I entitled 'Teaching Practice Form 2: Alternative Notes from a Teaching Observation' (Sidebottom 2017).

In a similar manner to the 'edu-crafts' instigated by Carol Taylor, our experiments felt new, disruptive and empowering; they were, in her words 'opening a way to think the unforeseen, temporary, unpredictable and contingent' (Taylor 2016: 20). As one student stated: 'I have found that doing creative things like poetry or writing a blog gives me confidence somehow, when things aren't going well. I think there is something about having control over what you create that gives comfort… it can't be "wrong" because it's yours.'

Collectively we decided to take the further step of exhibiting our artefacts, in a public exhibition which we entitled 'Becoming Teacher'. Our aim with this was to use the affective nature of art to share the painful, emergent and co-dependent process of teacher training (Fig. 13.2).

Fig. 13.2 Kay Sidebottom. Becoming teacher

13 Disruptive Pedagogies for Teacher Education: The Power ...

While our artistic acts were temporary moves to challenge stasis in the curriculum, we were nonetheless shuffling and disrupting the status quo. Once the results of trainee teachers becoming more reflexive and responsive were felt, (both on an individual level and by others intra-acting with their art) and as the students' teaching practice improved, other tutors on the programme began to consider creative approaches to reflective practice. The idea of expressing this approach more explicitly in curriculum materials was also discussed during curriculum review.

For those of us still writing and creating, the effects were transformative. In this way our practice became diffractive, rather than reflexive, as we moved away from the ego-centric notion of reflective practice to an acceptance of our entangled, enmeshed selves, and gained a heightened awareness of other forms of matter with which we were intra-acting. We were 'reading insights through one another' (Barad 2007: 71), not limiting our explorations to the immediate educational situations within which we found ourselves, but immersing ourselves in, and opening up to what differences could be perceived and made, thus '…responding to the details and specificities of relations of difference and how they matter' (ibid.: 71).

The affirmative nature of this approach was expressed by one trainee who said:

> I spent the summer creating an array of verse using rhythm and rhyme to my heart's content… Some reflected the plight of my students, others the dysfunction of society regarding issues such as prejudice, greed and ignorance… However, I did not use it as a coping mechanism, but rather as an opportunity to share my wonderful experience of teaching English to a fantastic group of people, who remain happy and positive in the face of adversity. I also wrote about the usual topics… Love and nature, using imagery for inspiration as well as my love for music, family and home.

As we push back against the time limited boundary of a programme of study and the linear nature of professional development, it is notable (and exciting) that the longer impact of this diffractive approach may not be known for some time.

Intra-vention 2: Noticing Affirmative Assemblages

> Nomadic thought rejects melancholia in favour of the politics of affirmation and mutual specification of self and other in sets of relations or assemblages. (Braidotti 2012: 55)

The Deleuzian concept of assemblage goes beyond the joining up of like-minded humans. In the words of Strom (2017: 7), an assemblage is 'an aggregate of elements, both human and non, that function collectively in a contextually unique manner to produce something (e.g. teaching practice, a situated identity).' In thinking about ways to work together and move forward we needed to consider more widely what constituted our assemblages and why.

For trainee teachers, the notions that animals have a role to play in their professional development seemed, at first, ridiculous. Yet (particularly as part-time, mature students) animals often infuse their learning spaces: sitting alongside them during their studies, acting as walking companions, impacting on, influencing, or at times derailing their thinking time.

Barad (2007) proposes that all things, human and non-human, are in a constant state of exchange, and that these exchanges are a result of things working inseparably. These exchanges, or 'intra-actions' entangle humans and their non-human companions, disrupting the usual human-centred activities of working and reflecting. By considering the impact of these entanglements, students were able to move beyond humanistic story-telling, creating 'multi-species narratives' (Nordstrom et al. 2018) that took account of the affective nature of the relationship and the multi-dimensional aspects of their teacher journeys (Fig. 13.3).

In order to explore the ideas of nonhuman-human relations pedagogically I introduced as a stimulus Donna Haraway's idea of animals as provocateurs: 'Jim's dog is a provocation to curiosity, which I regard as one of the first obligations and deepest pleasures of worldly companion species' (Haraway 2008: 7). Through a process of in-class activities and on-line discussions students were encouraged to share pictures

13 Disruptive Pedagogies for Teacher Education: The Power ...

Fig. 13.3 Kay Sidebottom. Study companion-rabbit

and stories of their non-human companions and to consider their role in their lives and learning journeys. To help students to reframe their learning 'communities' in this way, I shared the story of my own rabbit, Harriet, who had become an unanticipated writing companion when her outdoor hutch was overtaken by a nest of tree bumblebees. During her time as a house-rabbit she would sit next to me quietly as I read or typed, occasionally taking a nibble at a book or snuggling by the warmth of the laptop.

Trainee Hayley shared the experiences she was having at the time with her blind dog, Gromit, exploring the way in which the relationship helped her to understand the nature of 'permanent partiality' (Haraway 2006) and co-dependence in education:

> A Blind Dog's Sight/Trust
>
> Gromit (dog) is almost blind and can only hear high-pitched sounds. He's not walked this path before and neither had I. I followed as he led down

the path, trusting he would make all the deviations himself, which he did. Even when we cannot see the end result, we trust others to help us to see it.

In addition to animals, and inspired by Bennett (2010), we also started to explore the nature of the material agents surrounding us in our student lives which form important assemblages intra-acting with our learning. The cramped study spaces we carve out for ourselves in crowded living rooms; our children's work appearing on laptops; the background chatter in coffee shops where we sit in a draft near a plug socket; daily interruptions to make the tea. We explored together the fragmentary nature of learning as adults, and the need to grasp snatched moments of learning, where agents in the world around us not only impinge on us but integrate themselves deeply in our learning, creating affective responses to which we tried to become more alert.

Assemblages also came together rhizomatically, through connections made with other students and teachers via social media. Inspired by the work of Dave Cormier (2008), and the idea that 'the community is the curriculum', we began taking part in Twitter chats, and making better use of our internal online spaces to connect with each other. We instigated our own hashtag for a monthly on-line conversation which brought together participants from other colleges (locally, nationally and internationally), voices from other non-education related industries, and writers and theorists whose work we had read in class. Together this helped us co-construct new knowledge through a social, negotiated process and supported us to challenge our thinking by engaging with a diverse range of views and opinions:

> In the rhizomatic model of learning, curriculum is not driven by predefined inputs from experts; it is constructed and negotiated in real time by the contributions of those engaged in the learning process. This community acts as the curriculum, spontaneously shaping, constructing, and reconstructing itself and the subject of its learning in the same way that the rhizome responds to changing environmental conditions. (Cormier 2008)

The 'constellations of practice' emerging from our twitter and social media practices allowed us to discover new projects and work together beyond our organisational silos. Through our appreciation of the various entanglements described here—human and animal-companion; human and environment; human and digitally-mediated connections—we began to appreciate the need for 'response-ability' (Haraway 2016). This idea of reciprocal noticing and learning became a way to live out a 'praxis of care and response … in ongoing multispecies worlding on a wounded Terra' (Haraway 2016: 105). This new awareness has led to the instigation of a number of projects and collaborations, cross-organisational and inter-disciplinary, as we 'follow the flow of matter' (Deleuze and Guattari 1987: 345); and become an 'avant-garde without authority' (Jagodinzki 2018: 86), working creatively and across disciplines, outside formal hierarchies. Specific work has included time-limited 'pop-up' education spaces such as Twitter chats (comprising of students, colleagues, and a plethora of education contacts world-wide); an education 'unconference' (instigated after a chance online conversation), and shared diffractive reading and writing spaces which incorporate art, photography and poetry, often in natural settings.

Intra-vention 3: Composing Cartographic Genealogies

> The pursuit of collective projects aimed at the affirmation of hope, rooted in the ordinary micro-practices of everyday life, is a strategy to set up, sustain and map out sustainable transformations. (Braidotti 2012: 192)

The call to consider 'missing slices of the past' (Ferrando 2012) resonated with us as educators often 'othered' and overlooked by our own institutional systems and their histories. As trainee educators within the English adult learning sector, my students had a range of challenging roles: they were teaching assistants, prison educators, community workers, volunteers, English for Speakers of Other Languages (ESOL) teachers, and other educators in what is often described as the 'Cinderella' sector (Randle and Brady 1997). As a result, those working in FE often feel like bit-parts in an education curriculum dominated by schools, with a disproportionate focus on the young. This 'othering' gave us—as teachers and students—an impetus to embrace whole-heartedly Braidotti's call to knock the white, male, European, young, able-bodied, architecturally perfect Vitruvian Man human ideal from his pedestal and started to map our own histories as educators. In practical terms, this gave us the desire to produce cartographies of our teaching journeys, the moments of illumination, and the darker places where 'there be dragons', in line with Braidotti's (2013: 4) view of cartography as 'a theoretically based and politically informed reading of the process of power relations [assessing] the impact of material and discursive conditions upon our embodied and embedded subjectivities.' Viewing our teaching journeys through a cartographic lens encouraged us to take an activist view while also taking into account the wider range of influences, both human and non-human on our prior experiences and current work.

For this intra-vention we created our own maps, using large sheets of paper to both draw out and list influences, significant moments, events, locations and non-human agents who/which were entangled with our practice. These maps became three-dimensional as we introduced materials too: scraps of written work, pieces of cloth, even objects from the grounds of the stately home which formed our college and study space. As they unfolded, these cartographies revealed to us the gaps not just in the curriculum but in our personal stories as teachers—the barriers to learning where the system had let us down; the unheard voices who might have been familiar to our own had they been elevated to the education 'canon'; the potential that, if tapped, might have resulted in the drawing of very different educational maps in our later lives. In affirmative spirit we then worked to fill in those missing slices by 'investigating perspectives we usually leave aside' (Ferrando 2012)—that is, by including not only the human voices of those absent in our current teacher education syllabus, but also the non-human 'others' (animal companions, natural learning spaces, digital tools etc.) to whose significance we were becoming more attuned.

The National Union of Black Students' film 'Why is my curriculum white?' (2015) acted as a further catalyst for our thinking. We examined the biases present in the assigned university reading lists which supported our teacher education syllabus, and also in the systems that governed us, such as policies around extenuating circumstances, the buildings that we taught in, the teaching body, the names of the rooms we sat in. Myself and other tutors started work on projects such as 'Seeking Lost Women Educators' (2015) where we uncovered the stories of teachers such as Helen Parkhurst, Margaret McMillan, Dorothy Heathcote, and Maria Montessori, and examined their often overlooked influence on the education system. We took on the idea of referencing being a political act, as Ahmed (2017: 16) states: 'Citations can be feminist bricks: they are the materials through which, from which, we create our dwellings.' The question of who and what we referenced and why become a key imperative, materially shaping our reading and writing as we sought out new and different sources and used social media tools such as Twitter to surround ourselves with diverse voices and opinions. We considered this citational activity to be a form of posthuman activism, as we utilised non-human digital tools to magnify the work of marginalised writers and, thereby, made material shifts in the weight of increased citing and referencing. In these acts of 'feminicity' (Colman 2018: 154) we were reminded of Barad's point that theorising is a material activity, and we thus enacted 'a methodology that is attentive to, and responsive/responsible to, the specificity of material entanglements in their agential becoming' (Barad 2007: 91).

Conclusion

This chapter has attempted to explore why taking a 'posthuman turn' matters when training new teachers. It makes the case for critical posthuman pedagogic practices that:

1. Draw on 'potentia' as a productive form of power which has the potential to shift the politics of teaching and learning praxis into more affirmative mode;
2. Use creative methodologies to explore multiple ways of knowing and being;

3. Explore the way in which educators work with and are influenced by assemblages comprising both human and non-human others and agents;
4. Consider genealogical gaps and missing voices in order to reframe what it means to be 'human' in the world today.

The pedagogical approaches described above are suggestive of ways in which students and teachers may find 'spaces to dance' (Mycroft and Weatherby 2015). Such spaces are, as I noted, desperately needed in English Further Education. Palmer (1998: 94) refers to a model of 'hospitality' where we invite students and their insights into the teaching and learning conversations; working from the assumption that they have 'stories to tell'. Posthuman pedagogical practice takes this notion of hospitality further by welcoming non-human others into our spaces too, so that the ensuing assemblages became 're-creators of knowledge' and tutors also subjects, in creating a new, co-intentional reality.

Paradoxically, casual and fractional working practices, now rife in FE, offer the opportunity for teachers to act in ways that facilitate the enactment of this 'posthuman curriculum.' Looser attachments with organisations offer the potential for the forging of relationships which are rhizomatic and nomadic; digital mediation permits new assemblages and communities to form and 'deterritorialise' (Deleuze and Guattari 1987) academic practice and power structures, even if only for a short time. Strom (2017: 112) encourages educators to be alert to moments of possibility, where we can 'seize these "micro-transformations" [which] are the key to shifting the field of teacher education toward a more complex, multiplistic conceptualization of constructing and enacting teaching practice.'

This chapter has shown how enacting micro-transformations in pedagogy helps academics take an affirmative standpoint, so that 'potentia' becomes a productive form of power (Braidotti 2013) that overcomes 'places of pain' and seeks agency where it can be found. Braidotti's posthuman ethical approach incorporates the digital connectivity described here, alongside a reframing of what it means to be human in the world today. It offers a way in which to work within the constraints of the neo-liberal system in order to establish educational spaces as 'sites for prefigurative practice' (Suissa 2014: 25) through ethical practices which include:

> The principle of non-profit; emphasis on the collective; acceptance of relationality and of viral contaminations; concerted efforts at experimenting with and actualizing virtual options; and a new link between theory and practice, including a central role for creativity. (Braidotti 2016: 26)

Given the political imperatives to which staff and students within academia are currently subjected, it can be difficult to determine how to continue and sustain moves towards such 'disruptive pedagogies' (Reay 2012). Myself, and the students and colleagues making up our 'constellation of praxis' (Mycroft and Sidebottom 2018) will continue to reflect on the issues and work with the questions that first instigated this work and our hope is that this will lead to new questions and new lenses through which to view our practice. Despite the neoliberal, performative constraints on our abilities to realise socially-just academic organisations, this chapter has illuminated the need to pay more attention to our own agency and responsibility. In doing so, it is worth holding close Braidotti's call to affirmative action which may help keep us immanently situated in a spirit of hope and possibility:

> The only way we can act upon it [our world], in this difficult posthuman moment, is by composing multitudes of missing peoples, a 'we-are-in-this-together-but-are-not one-and-the-same' sort of people. They are the collective multiplicity, materially embedded but differential, that aspires to take its place, stumbling across the posthuman landscape, in this hyper-modern and proto-archaic world of ours, so that we can play out the potentials for affirmative transformations. In spite of our times, and out of love for our times. (Braidotti 2017: 50)

References

Ahmed, S. (2017). *Living a feminist life*. Durham: Duke University Press.
Barad, K. (2007). *Meeting the universe halfway: Quantum physics and the entanglement of matter and meaning*. Durham: Duke University Press.

Barad, K. (2009). Matter feels, converses, suffers, desires, yearns and remembers. In R. Dolphijn & I. van der Tuin, *New Materialism: Interviews & Cartographies*. Michigan: Open Humanities Press.

Bennett, J. (2010). *Vibrant matter: A political ecology of things*. London: Duke University Press.

Braidotti, R. (2008). Affirmation, pain and empowerment. *Asian Journal of Women's Studies, 14*(3), 7–36.

Braidotti, R. (2012). *Nomadic theory: The portable Rosi Braidotti*. New York: Columbia University Press.

Braidotti, R. (2013). *The posthuman*. Cambridge: Polity Press.

Braidotti, R. (2016). Posthuman critical theory. In *Critical posthumanism and planetary futures* (pp. 13–32). London: Springer.

Braidotti, R. (2017). *Posthuman, all too human: The memoirs and aspirations of a posthumanist* (The Tanner Lectures), Yale University.

Clover, D., & Stalker, J. (Eds.). (2007). *The arts and social justice*. Leicester: NIACE.

Coffield, F., & Williamson, B. (2011). *From exam factories to communities of discovery*. London: Institute of Education Press.

Colman, F. (2018). Feminicity. In R. Braidotti & M. Hlavajova (Eds.), *Posthuman glossary*. London: Bloomsbury.

Cormier, D. (2008). Rhizomatic education: Community as curriculum. http://davecormier.com/edblog/2008/06/03/rhizomatic-education-community-as-curriculum/. Accessed 14 December 2017.

Deleuze, G., & Guattari, F. (1987). *A thousand plateaus: Capitalism and schizophrenia*. London: Continuum.

Ferrando, F. (2012). Towards a posthumanist methodology. A statement. *Frame: Journal of Literary Studies*. Special Issue on *Narrating Posthumanism, 25*(1), 9–18.

Forstenzer, J. (2016). The teaching excellence framework: What's the purpose? The Sir Bernard Crick Centre. http://www.crickcentre.org/teaching-excellence-framework/. Accessed 25 October 2017.

Freire, P. (1970). *Pedagogy of the oppressed*. London: Penguin.

Haraway, D. (2006). A cyborg manifesto: Science, technology, and socialist-feminism in the late 20th century. In J. Weiss, J. Nolan, J. Hunsinger, & P. Trifonas (Eds.), *The international handbook of virtual learning environments*. Dordrecht: Springer.

Haraway, D. (2008). *When species meet*. Minneapolis: University of Minnesota Press.

Haraway, D. (2016). *Staying with the trouble: Making kin in the Chthulucene*. Durham: Duke University Press.

Hlavajova, M. (2015, August 26). *Critique-as-proposition: Thinking about, with, and through art in our time*. University of Utrecht.

Jagodzinksi, J. (2018). From the artist to the cosmic artisan: The educational task for art in anthropogenic times. In C. Naughton, G. Biesta, & D. Cole (Eds.), *Art, artists and pedagogy: Philosophy and the arts in education*. London: Routledge.

Kolb, D. (1984). *Experiential learning: Experience as the source of learning and development*. New York: Prentice Hall.

Münch, R. (2014). *Academic capitalism: Universities in the global struggle for excellence*. London, UK: Routledge.

Mycroft, L., & Sidebottom, K. (2018). Constellations of practice. In P. Bennett & R. Smith (Eds.), *Identity and resistance in further education*. London: Routledge.

Mycroft, L., & Weatherby, J. (2015). Spaces to dance: Community education. In M. Daley, K. Orr, & J. Petrie (Eds.), *Further education and the twelve dancing princesses*. London: Trentham Books.

Nordstrom, S., Nordstrom, A., & Nordstrom, C. (2018). Guilty of loving you: A multispecies narrative. *Qualitative Inquiry*, 1–8.

NUS Black Students. (2015). Why is my curriculum white? https://www.youtube.com/watch?v=Dscx4h2l-Pk. Accessed 14 January 2018.

Palmer, P. J. (1998). *The courage to teach: Exploring the inner landscape of a teacher's life*. San Francisco: Jossey-Bass.

Randle, K., & Brady, N. (1997). Managerialism and professionalism in the 'cinderella service'. *Journal of Vocational Education & Training, 49*(1), 121–139.

Reay, D. (2012). What would a socially just education system look like?: Saving the minnows from the pike. *Journal of Education Policy, 27*(5), 587–599.

Seeking Lost Women. (2015). *Lost women educators*. http://seekinglostwomen.blogspot.co.uk/. Accessed 21 January 2018.

Sidebottom, K. (2017). *Teaching form 2: Alternative notes from a teaching observation*. Belonging: Transformative Education in Challenging Times. https://teachdifferent2017.wordpress.com/magazine/. Accessed 28 August 2018.

Society for the Advancement of Philosophical Enquiry and Reflection in Education. (n.d.). *Community philosophy*. http://www.sapere.org.uk/Members,Schools,Partners/CommunityPhilosophy.aspx. Accessed 21 January 2018.

Strom, K. (2017). "That's not very Deleuzian": Thoughts on interrupting the exclusionary nature of "high theory". *Educational Philosophy and Theory, 50*(1), 104–113. http://www.tandfonline.com/doi/abs/10.1080/00131857.2017.1339340?journalCode=rept20. Accessed 12 January 2018.

Suissa, J. (2014). Towards an anarchist philosophy of education. *New perspectives in philosophy of education* (pp. 139–159). London: Bloomsbury Academic Press.

Taylor, C. A. (2016). Edu-crafting a cacophonous ecology: Posthuman research practice for education. In C. A. Taylor & C. Hughes (Eds.), *Posthuman research practices in education*. London: Palgrave.

University of Huddersfield. (2016). *In-service certificate in education (lifelong learning) module handbook*. Huddersfield, UK: Author.

14

Textual Practices as Already-Posthuman: Re-Imagining Text, Authorship and Meaning-Making in Higher Education

Lesley Gourlay

Introduction

Contemporary academic engagement, textual practices and the related notion of 'digital literacies' are theorized and imagined in a range of complex and contradictory ways in Higher Education research, policy and practice, leading to a situation where the day-to-day practices of reading and writing in digital contexts may be lost from view. Instead, there has been a tendency in mainstream policy development in particular to collapse into a generic 'skills and competencies' model, which underscores the notion of the neoliberal individual, imagined as context-free, as both repository and sole agential source of digital literacy practices. Alongside this, there is a somewhat contradictory 'brave new world' discourse associated with the digital in particular, which operates on a fairly abstract level, imagining the 'digitally literate' student or graduate as able to 'harness' what are portrayed as awe-inspiring

L. Gourlay (✉)
UCL Institute of Education (IOE), London, UK
e-mail: l.gourlay@ucl.ac.uk

potentials of the digital for learning and future employment. Although both of these framings may reflect some aspects of digital student engagement, the nature of embodied and emergent day-to-day practice is arguably 'tidied up' by both, resulting in a strongly humanist model which regards devices and artefacts of inscription as 'tools' at the command of the idealised 'user', who is stripped of markers of identity such as gender, race and social class. It also elides the specifics of social setting, temporality and spatiality, all of which are rendered as neutral backcloths to engagement.

In this chapter, I aim to explore these tensions, and draw out the effects that flow from these overly-abstract and ideologically-freighted humanist assumptions about the nature of texts, devices, the writer and the notion of authorship in the digital setting. I will trace what I characterize as a series of moves in the literature from a rejection of humanist abstraction towards a posthuman framing. In doing so I will review the contributions and ongoing diffractive potentials of New Literacy Studies (NLS), Actor-Network Theory (ANT), and theoretical challenges to the notion of spatiality and temporality as 'context' to digital literacy practices. Turning to the work of Karen Barad, I will consider the construct of the *apparatus* in particular, and the extent to which it may allow us to advance this theoretical move more coherently, towards a more nuanced recognition of the relationships between matter and meaning-making in the university.

Models of Digital Literacy in Higher Education

Due to the complexities surrounding the terminology associated with this area, in this chapter I will use the term 'digital literacy' in a relatively restricted way to refer to *all practices associated with the production of a digital academic text*, including literature searching, downloading, reading, notetaking, drafting, correction, response to feedback, discussion about the text and the use of all technologies of inscription, digital or analogue.

Student academic writing for assessment arguably tends to be focused on in mainstream Higher Education policy circles when there is a perception of deficit, specifically when it is felt that student writing needs to be developed or enhanced. This is useful as a starting point for this chapter, as these perceived deficits, and how they have been differentially accounted for and addressed, have led to what I propose are various related theorizations of student writing and a range of associated structures and staff roles in universities, aimed at addressing the issue of these perceived deficits. In the contemporary period, I would like to propose that in the UK and elsewhere, writing has come to be addressed in four parallel processes within the institution. (The model is somewhat different in the US with a greater prevalence of writing development within the mainstream academic undergraduate curriculum).

Firstly, 'home' students (in Anglophone contexts, broadly defined as students for whom English is a first language) are conventionally guided towards extra-curricular 'study skills' provision within the university. This is often provided by a specialist unit, and tends to focus on generic aspects of writing, often in a one-to-one, self-referral model of provision. Resources and the professional profile of the advisors generally mean that this advice is not specific to the academic discipline, although these are exceptions to this. As discussed above, this model is broadly based on a model of writing as a set of 'transferable skills', reflecting the powerful influence enjoyed by generic 'skills and competencies' models and their underlying ideology in Higher Education more broadly.

Secondly, in contrast, in the UK and beyond, 'international students' (specifically students for whom English is not the first language) are offered support typically by a Language Centre or English for Academic Purposes (EAP) unit. The format is again likely to take the form of extracurricular classes, although one-to-one consultations may be offered. EAP has its roots in English Language Teaching (ELT) and has been informed by the discipline of Applied Linguistics where ELT provides a focus on linguistic proficiency for academic writing, arguably taught in broadly generic terms. However, perhaps the main contribution of Applied Linguistics to EAP has been the concept of Genre (Swales 1990), which has been highly influential in the development of EAP pedagogy, in particular giving a recognition of the discipline-situated and differential conventions and textual features of academic meaning-making. Genre-based approaches have been critiqued for an over-emphasis on the surface text, and also for apparent assumptions of clearly delineated, uncontested and stable genres across the disciplines. However, despite these caveats, the insights provided by a focus on Genre might be seen as the first steps in the journey of embodying/materialising academic writing, in that it represents a move away from the generic towards the particular and the situated.

A separate and third model has emerged in recent years in the shape of 'Digital Literacy', a concept and strand of student development which has arisen from the field of 'Learning Technologies'. Although the term 'literacy' implies a focus on writing, arguably this is being used here more in the sense of 'know-how' or 'familiarity with', as with related terms such as 'media literacy'. However, given the centrality of textual practices to the university, student engagement with digital technology and writing are strongly interlinked, as students increasingly use digital resources for research and to produce texts. Arguably, the tendency to focus on student engagement with digital technologies at a more general level, and the associated failure of this concept and related frameworks of digital literacy to address academic writing directly, has contributed to the humanist assumptions discussed above.

The fourth model of writing is that which sits within specific academic curricula, where writing is seen through the lens of academic assessment. Here, the mainstream approach is for academics to set written assignments, which conventionally are submitted by students at the end of a module or unit of study. The point is often raised in writing development circles that academics tend not to focus on writing development or the practices of writing and independent study in their teaching and guidance to students, leading to a focus more on the completed text as evidence of learning, as opposed to the process of writing it. Although there are clearly exceptions, it would be fair to say that the emphasis here is on the finished text, the means by which it is produced receives comparatively little attention.

These four framings situate writing (and meaning-making in the digital context) in various ways as residing in the human, the cognitive, and in particular within the individual student. The first three—as extracurricular provision—perhaps inevitably view writing as standing somewhat apart from the disciplinary context, and arguably all four of them regard writing as sitting apart from the specific materiality and instantiation of texts, devices and practices. That is not to say that these models of writing are not useful to students—they provide invaluable support and development. However, I would propose that their strongly humanist theoretical underpinnings create a range of effects in epistemological and ontological terms, effects which may limit and distort how we see knowledge, texts, meaning-making and students themselves.

The tendency in the first model to draw on 'study skills' frameworks implies that elements of the meaning-making process can be clearly delineated and developed separately, and this emphasis serves to reinforce the notion of writing as primarily cognitive or skills-based, and residing in the mind of the individual. The (perhaps pragmatically necessary) stripping out of disciplinarity may make the focus of writing development more generic and straightforward, but it also serves to de-situate academic writing from its various and complex epistemological roots. The socially-situated, fluid and contested nature of these conventions is also lost in this approach, although this arguably may be a pragmatic necessity or 'price worth paying', and may also serve to close down more nuanced and advanced engagement with ideas and student awareness of the nature of writing as meaning-making itself. The agency of the (individual) human is placed centre-stage, and the materiality of writing is elided. The second model, EAP, focuses more on features of the text but allows for a more plural recognition of the range of textual conventions at play in the academy, and to some extent it recognises the contested and contingent nature of writing. However, like the 'study skills' approach, it tends to devote less attention to the material processes of writing, and does not generally engage with the profound changes to writing which have come about as a result of the permeation of digital mediation in the university, as students search for texts, read and write in predominantly digital formats. Again, the individual student is posited as the main agential site of writing. The third area, 'digital literacy' also recognises the interactions with digital devices and interfaces, but the discourse surrounding these entanglements tends to position the device as 'tool' and the texts to be read as 'resources'. The 'user' again tends to be imbued with all the agency, although this can be complicated by contrasting this with the—at times dystopian—technodeterminist discourses which arguably exaggerate the agency of the digital and its potential to 'take over' from the human. Some frameworks of digital literacy do focus on practices; however, these tend to be itemised into 'skills' and not discussed in terms of their material instantiation.

My intention is not to seek to overturn or reject the foregoing models, but instead to suggest how a posthuman framing and research agenda might alter how we approach writing, the digital and its development, by 're-materialising' practices and the messiness of how students entangle with texts, devices, spaces and temporality in a range of ways. As an example of this, Fig. 14.1 shows my desk while beginning to write this chapter. This everyday example serves as an illustration of the range of nonhuman agents I have been entangled with in the production of this text.

Fig. 14.1 Agents entangled in this text

Re-Embodying/Re-Materialising Writing in the Digital University

The previous section attempted to tease out the various strands of practice and provision in the UK sector and beyond, and in doing so it examined the assumptions and implicit humanist theoretical models of writing, texts, digital devices and authorship. This section will look at the various moves made in the educational literature which have begun a process of movement away from abstraction and emphasis on individual student cognition or 'transferable skills', towards an account of practice and distributed agency which takes in the embodied, the material, the nonhuman, the temporal and the spatial.

As highlighted above, Genre Analysis in Applied Linguistics as applied to EAP has provided an important set of insights into the specificity of academic writing in terms of disciplinary conventions of academic writing. This move has been fruitful in decentring the assumptions of the 'transferable skills' model, and in doing so it has highlighted the contingent, non-generic, and situated nature of meaning-making by writing, which is already recognised—perhaps implicitly—within disciplinary communities of scholars themselves. In an important move and seminal paper, Lea and Street (1998) challenged the assumptions of the 'study skills' model of academic writing, critiquing it on the basis of ground-breaking fieldwork in social anthropology (Street 1984; Bruce-Heath 1982) which had led to a questioning of the assumptions surrounding literacy as an either/or cognitive category. Street's critique of the cognitive model and proposed alternative social model re-drew the contours of how literacy could be understood: not as a cognitive binary residing in the individual, but as a set of situated and shared social practices. Lea and Street present a compelling critique of the skills model in an academic setting, proposing 'academic literacies' as an alternative construct. This account of writing recognised the disciplinary dimension, and also the co-constitutive nature of the relationship between writing, thinking and knowledge. This work formed part of the broader emergent subfield of NLS, which did important work in reinstating the centrality of social situatedness and writer subjectivities to the field. In this regard, this was a key move in the rejection of a view of writing in terms of free-floating skills, detached from historical, epistemological, geopolitical, social and individual circumstances. Scholars in this field also applied this framing to the digital, as it grew in importance and prevalence in the Higher Education sector. However, despite the powerful insights offered by this framing, it arguably falls short of granting us satisfactory theoretical purchase on contemporary writing practices in terms of how agency is understood in relation to material practices and devices.

The construct of Digital Literacy emerged from a Learning Technology skills and competencies base, and although it has perhaps absorbed some influence from NLS, as evidenced in the name, it has arguably retained many of the assumptions of its 'skills'-based theoretical underpinning. In fact, it might be argued that 'literacy' is used here as a proxy for 'know-how'—leading us back to a skills model through the back door, as can be evidenced in the increasing use of the increasingly prevalent portmanteau term 'digital literacy skills'. The field of research and development in Digital Literacy has gone on to expand beyond skills and towards a recognition of the social and interactive aspects of engagement with the digital (Gillen and Barton 2010), but in its mainstream application it is, in the main, still somewhat dominated by a desire to compartmentalize, categorize and accumulate elements of practice in an assumed 'journey' to a putative end state of 'literate' user. A further weakness in the construct is that it elides the centrality of textual practices in digitally-mediated meaning-making in the university and beyond.

(Mary Hamilton and Mary Lea) and I sought to extend the reach of NLS in terms of its account of agency and practice in digitally-mediated academic writing, by looking at it through the lens of ANT (Gourlay et al. 2013). The intention was to refract the insights of NLS through a further theoretical framing which explicitly recognises nonhuman agency. ANT allowed us to not only socially situate writing, but also materially situate it, in an account which moved beyond the notion of artefacts as 'tools'. I have also applied the posthuman conceptual framework offered by Hayles (1999) to academic writing, in particular her concept of 'embodied virtuality', in combination with Latour's (2005) distinction between *mediator* and *intermediary* (Gourlay 2015), where the *mediator* is used as a construct to account for the intra-active relationship between medium and message. This was another attempt to combine theoretical framings, in this case looking more specifically at the notion of virtuality and also the mediating roles of artefacts of inscription.

Martin Oliver and I (2016a) have also sought to undermine assumptions that space is a neutral backcloth to practices, drawing on the work of human geographer Doreen Massey (2005). In this paper, we argued that space should instead be seen as an active and agential element in digital writing practice, in direct interaction with human and nonhuman agencies. In another piece (Gourlay 2014), I attempted to critique the notion that temporality lies outside of digital writing practice, drawing on the work of Grosz (2004), Lemke (2000), and Horning et al. (1999) to explore the agentive aspects of temporality on digital writing. In all of the above, I feel some progress was made in a series of analytical moves which have had the overarching intention of accounting for writing in terms of the posthuman. However, they have been drawn from a range of associated theoretical developments which arguably do not cohere or 'talk to each other' directly. In the next section I will attempt to advance further these various moves, by putting to work Barad's notion of the *apparatus* as a potential account of academic writing which may allow for a more unified, and also perhaps more radically distributed, theorisation of agency and emergent practice.

Textual Practices as Apparatus

In her compelling and wide-ranging work *Meeting the Universe Halfway*, Barad mounts a challenge to the assumptions of social constructivism in general, and representationalism and mediation via language in particular which, she argues, evinces a 'distrust of matter' (Barad 2007: 132). Drawing on and extending Butler's (1990) notion of *performativity* as a means by which to reinstate a focus on materiality in our understandings of meaning-making practices, she argues that:

> A *performative* understanding of discursive practices challenges the representationalist belief in the power of words to represent pre-existing things. Unlike representationalism, which positions us above or outside the world we allegedly merely reflect on, a performative account insists on understanding thinking, observing, and theorising as practices of engagement with, as part of, the world in which we have our being. (Barad 2007: 132)

She proposes 'a posthumanist performative approach to understanding technoscientific and other naturalcultural practices that specifically acknowledges and takes account of matter's dynamism' (Barad 2007: 135) with a focus on 'matters of practices, doings and actions' (ibid.). In doing so, she rejects the assumption of independent objects as the primary ontological unit of analysis, instead proposing 'phenomena' as 'the ontological inseparability/entanglement of intra-acting "agencies"' (Barad 2007: 139). The concept of phenomena seems to encapsulate the ideas explored in the previous section, and as such I would propose that it can be usefully applied to textual practices, allowing us with one concept to take account of the various agencies described above. However, I would like to explore one of Barad's other key concepts—apparatus—in relation to writing as not only a set of intra-agential practices (as opposed to arising from singular human agency), but also as a technology of enquiry and meaning-making in itself. In what follows I will attempt to apply Barad's concept of 'apparatus' to textual practices in Higher Education as a posthuman assemblage/entanglement of meaning-making technologies and practices. Barad (2007: 146) provides a six-part definition of an *apparatus*, which I set out below, proposing this as a construct which offers a coherent theoretical framing of academic writing in terms of a posthuman conception of agency.

> Apparatuses are specific material-discursive practices.

Earlier in this chapter I alluded to the powerful lure of abstraction, and the tendency of the field of writing development and Digital Literacies to slide back into a 'skills and competencies' account of academic writing which can serve to elide both social situatedness and the materiality of practice as *always and only* emergent in specific instances. The latter point can be drawn out of ANT—Barad folds this into her first element of her definition of *apparatus*, which contains within it the notions of specificity, and also the notion that these practices are ontologically material-discursive, not prior to representation. This element of the definition seems to encapsulate the always-specific and emergent nature of writing which has been unaccounted for by the standard models critiqued above. An example can be seen below from the student data in the research project analysed in Gourlay and Oliver (2017), where a student illustrates his practices by a depiction of the emergent and contingent sociomaterial site of his entanglement with his device, in this case his bed (Fig. 14.2).

> Apparatuses produce differences that matter - they are boundary-making practices that are formative of matter and meaning, productive of, and part of, the phenomena produced.

Fig. 14.2 Student bed and devices

This second element of her definition echoes the point made by NLS, that writing practices and writing subjects are co-constitutive of each other. This element of the definition takes this notion further, by extending the scope of boundary-making to matter and meaning. It allows us to see writing as a *making* phenomenon, a set of practices which generates more texts, more practices, more knowledge, more material artefacts, and as such is also constitutive of human subjectivities, while making things happen in the world. In this regard, writing (despite being linguistic) should not be regarded as primarily representational. An example of this could be the complex 'making' work of inscription illustrated from the same project, as depicted by this detail from a student's representation of essay writing, showing an intensive, material and embodied engagement with the 'world' beyond the text (Fig. 14.3).

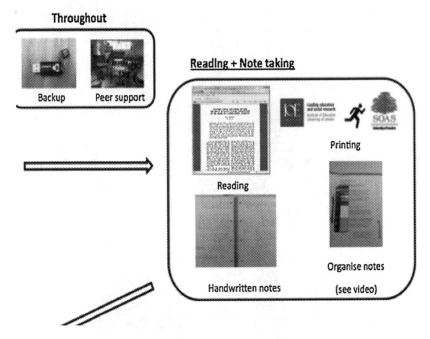

Fig. 14.3 Student representation of essay-writing practices

Apparatuses are material configurations/dynamic reconfigurations of the world.

While this somewhat gnomic third element of the definition could be interpreted at a number of levels, I put it to work here to account for the status of textual practices as simultaneously a material configuration (assemblage/entanglement) and a dynamic reconfiguration of the world through meaning-making. Related to the previous point, writing is itself a configuration which emerges, but it also configures and acts directly on the world. In the context of student writing, the effects may be for example the student 'becoming' a graduate, or at a more advanced level contributing directly to academic knowledge and/or scientific or professional practice. This further visual representation of student writing practices discussed in Gourlay and Oliver (2017) could be proposed as an example of this, where a student entangles with her iPad to 'dynamically reconstitute' an apparatus of inscription, and an ephemeral 'world' on a small temporal scale—in this case via the practice of doing academic reading on her iPad in the bath with a ziplock bag (Fig. 14.4).

Fig. 14.4 Student iPad, for academic reading in the bath

Fig. 14.5 Student papers and external hard drive

> Apparatuses are themselves phenomena (constituted and dynamically reconstituted as part of the ongoing intra-activity of the world).

This fourth element of the definition seems to offer us a means by which to view academic writing simultaneously as both a posthuman material/human/nonhuman assemblage in itself, but also a technology of enquiry and meaning-making, analogous to the scientific equipment she describes. Writing emerges as a *phenomenon*, but it is also an *apparatus* which asks questions, enquires, probes and explores beyond itself, via entanglements with other texts and the artefacts and voices which constitute research data. This aspect of the definition seems key, as it allows us to see writing as itself an *apparatus* of enquiry. This may be glimpsed in this student depiction from the same project, which shows an assemblage of print and digital literacy artefacts, which can be said to constitute a technology of enquiry and meaning-making analogous to the scientific equipment described by Barad (Fig. 14.5).

> Apparatuses have no intrinsic boundaries but are open ended practices.

The fifth element offers us a clear route away from skills-based, fragmented, taxonomic, cumulative, ultimately reductive frameworks as the dominant bases for accounts of digital writing practice. Instead, Barad provides a recognition of the emergent and constantly changing nature of this area of practice, which is particularly suited to theorisation of the digital. As we have found in fine-grained empirical work looking at student independent study practices and the digital (Gourlay and Oliver 2016b), these are highly contingent, constantly improvised, and characterised by a high degree of fluidity, as students entangle with various agencies in a range of ways which are in no way limited to prototypically 'traditional' approaches to writing in the university.

> Apparatuses are not located in the world but are material configurations or reconfigurings of the word that (re)configure spatiality and temporality as well as (the traditional notion of) dynamics (i.e. they do not exist as static structures, nor do they merely unfold or evolve in space and time).

The sixth and final element of her definition explicitly includes spatiality and temporality as co-constitutive and agentive elements of practice. In this regard, it extends the theoretical scope offered by the theoretical framings explored above, by bringing all of these aspects of agency together within the notion of the *apparatus*. This encapsulates the intra-agential role of space and also time in writing practices, in a way which seems to take us a significant step further on the journey away from a humanist set of abstractions and towards a posthuman account of writing, fully entangled in social, epistemological, material, spatial and temporal agencies, which crucially form part of practice, as opposed to context. This student depiction of his practices from Gourlay and Oliver (2017) illustrates this, as an example of the emergent, contingent, improvised, boundless and fluid nature of these practices (Fig. 14.6).

Conclusions: Already Posthuman?

In this chapter I have set out what I see as some of the limitations of mainstream models and conceptions of textual practices in the digital university, arguing that—however useful—they underscore a

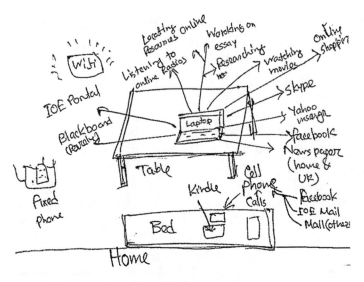

Fig. 14.6 Student depiction of his digital engagement

fundamentally humanist and abstract understanding of the nature of writing which posits the author as a free-floating subject, renders the artefacts and devices of inscription as 'tools', and space and time as inert backdrops. I went on to review work in the field which has moved us away from this perspective, and sought to 're-situate' writing in various ways. In doing this I also revisted my own attempts with collaborators to refract the insights of NLS through the additional theoretical lenses of ANT, posthumanism and theories of space and time, which recognise their agentive natures. Acknowledging that my own project has been somewhat partial and incoherent thus far, I turned to the work of Karen Barad and have attempted to argue that her concepts of both *phenomena* and *apparatus* are of utility in deepening this analysis of writing and posthuman agency, using examples from a research project into student writing practices. I would contend in conclusion, on the basis of this argument, that textual practices in Higher Education are 'already post-human' in terms of their epistemological and ontological status.

In terms of implications for research and practice, I would first suggest that this analysis calls for more emphasis in empirical work on what students and these agencies actually *do* together—how precisely they entangle. This necessitates a fine-grained, ethnographically-oriented approach, which aims to uncover the detail of practices which are often private, unobserved and therefore often occluded in policy and frameworks that seek to understand and develop student writing and the digital. I would also argue that this calls for a greater emphasis on an approach to developing writing which itself is entangled with specific disciplinary practices, already established as Writing Across the Curriculum (WAC), and also that as far as possible structures and groupings across the university such as the Study Skills advisors, EAP unit and the Information Literacies team in the library, work together to integrate their provision in a way that reflects—at least to some extent—the entangled nature of practice. A final potential link to practice is how such research and reframing might inform academic staff as to the somewhat hidden complexities of contemporary academic textual practices, and the nature of the challenges faced by students undertaking written assignments in independent study time. This could serve to reframe both writing and meaning-making as constitutive of the discipline and of knowledge, which would ultimately lead to more nuanced set of understandings of textual practices in the digital age.

References

Barad, K. (2007). *Meeting the universe halfway: Quantum physics and the entanglement of matter and meaning.* London: Duke University Press.
Bryce-Heath, S. (1982). What no bedtime story means: Narrative skills at home and school. *Language in Society, 11*(1), 49–76.
Butler, J. (1990). *Gender trouble: Feminism and the subversion of identity.* London: Routledge.
Gillen, J., & Barton, D. (2010). *Digital literacies: A research briefing by the technology enhanced learning phase of the teaching and learning research programme.* London: London Knowledge Lab, Institute of Education.
Gourlay, L. (2014). Creating time: Students, technologies and temporal practices in higher education. *Elearning and Digital Media, 11*(2), 141–153.
Gourlay, L. (2015). Posthuman texts: Nonhuman actors, mediators and the digital university. *Social Semiotics, 25*(4), 484–500.

Gourlay, L., & Oliver, M. (2016a). Students' digital and physical sites of study: Making, marking and breaking boundaries. In L. Carvahlo, P. Goodyear, & M. de Laat (Eds.), *Place-based spaces for networked learning* (pp. 73–86). New York: Routledge.

Gourlay, L., & Oliver, M. (2016b). It's not all about the learner: Reframing students' digital literacy and sociomaterial practice. In T. Ryberg, C. Sinclair, S. Bayne, & M. de Laat (Eds.), *Research, boundaries and policy in networked learning* (pp. 77–92). Cham, Switzerland: Springer.

Gourlay, L., & Oliver, M. (2017). *Student engagement in the digital university: Sociomaterial assemblages.* London: Routledge.

Gourlay, L., Hamilton, M., & Lea, M. (2013). Textual practices in the new media digital landscape: Messing with digital literacies. *Research in Learning Technology, 21,* 1–13.

Grosz, E. (2004). *The nick of time: Politics, evolution and the untimely.* London: Duke University Press.

Hayles, K. (1999). *How we became posthuman: Virtual bodies in cybernetics, literature and informatics.* London: University of Chicago Press.

Horning, K., Ahrens, D., & Gerard, A. (1999). Do technologies have time? New practices of time and transformation of communication technologies. *Time and Society, 8*(2), 293–308.

Latour, B. (2005). *Reassembling the social: An introduction to actor-network theory.* Oxford: Oxford University Press.

Lea, M., & Street, B. (1998). Student writing in higher education: An academic literacies approach. *Studies in Higher Education, 23*(2), 157–172.

Lemke, J. (2000). Across the scales of time: Artefacts, activities and meanings in ecosocial systems. *Mind, Culture and Activity, 7*(4), 273–290.

Massey, D. (2005). *For space.* London: Sage.

Street, B. (1984). *Literacy in theory and practice.* Cambridge: Cambridge University Press.

Swales, J. (1990). *Genre analysis: English in academic and research settings.* Cambridge: Cambridge University Press.

15

Body as Transformer: 'Teaching Without Teaching' in a Teacher Education Course

Karin Murris and Cara Borcherds

Difficulties in Decentering the Human in Teacher Education

Donna Haraway's (2016) passionate plea for a relationality between humanimals that 'render each other capable', and a 'thinking-with and 'becoming-with' that includes matter and nonhuman animals is inspiring, but achieving such a decentering ontoepistemic shift in teacher education is fraught with difficulties. Although a rapidly increasing number of books and articles are written about posthuman pedagogies in schooling (Olsson 2009; Lenz Taguchi 2010; Snaza and Weaver 2015; Taylor and Hughes 2016), practical pedagogical guidance for

---

K. Murris (✉) · C. Borcherds
School of Education, University of Cape Town, Cape Town, South Africa
e-mail: karin.murris@uct.ac.za

C. Borcherds
e-mail: cara@scubakavieng.com

preparing student teachers in higher education for such a dramatic ontoepistemic shift (see Murris 2016) is slow coming forward.

In this chapter, we explore some of these obstacles of decentering the human in teacher education with the help of Cara—a student on Karin's teacher education course. We show how including the philosophical course Childhood Studies into the *methods* part of teacher preparation can profoundly shift practice. Here we focus on one particular provocation—a bodymind map—and how the intra-vention can support a posthuman shift in thinking and practices by creating 'contexts' with open boundaries in which opportunities for in/determinate learning and an evolving rhizomatic open curriculum is made possible. The word 'bodymind' expresses the insight that humans are non-dualistic 'wholes' (from Lenz Taguchi [2010] drawing on Floyd Merrell).

We also describe how the on-going material-discursive work, formative assessment during the year and intra-active engagement with Cara's bodymind map (Fig. 15.2) brought about real tension intra-actively inbetween the two of us. In particular, we focus on one of Karin's pedagogical provocations, which she assumed was psychologically 'safe', because the activity was not intended to be humanist, representational or symbolic. The conflict turned out to be painful *and* affirmative, and we show how the Childhood Studies course, its' open evolving curriculum, creating classrooms as living, breathing ecosystems and, in particular, how Karin's 'teaching without teaching' worked productively to disrupt binaries and make an ontoepistemic shift possible for Cara. The philosophical shift is evidenced in her installation: an assemblage of her re-image(-ening)s months later and the final course assessment: a material-discursive work that needs to express shifting ideas about child and childhood.

The South African Teacher Education Programme

In 2012, Karin was employed at the University of Cape Town to design and lead a Post Graduate Certificate in Education (PGCE) Foundation Phase. To design an innovative de/colonising posthuman curriculum was challenging for various, entangled reasons: the hegemonic developmental orientation of childhood education in higher education institutions; student teachers' own expectations of what a good education is based on their own experiences of schooling; and thirdly, the government's solutions to the educational 'crisis' by introducing a new revised national curriculum. Since the implementation of the Curriculum Assessment Policy Statements (CAPS) in 2012, South African teachers have been under pressure to work with standardised national workbooks, including highly prescribed, specified, sequenced and paced guidance regarding the content that should be taught in schools with scripted lessons and worksheets.

Uniquely for teacher education, the course Childhood Studies as created by Karin is written into the programme as an intricate part of the *methods* courses and is afforded equal credits as the traditional methods courses: literacy, mathematics and life skills, thereby disrupting the theory (educational studies)/practice (methods, teaching practice) binary. Heavily informed by philosophies of education, the Childhood Studies course's 'natural' home would 'normally' be educational studies. Why is this course important as part of methods?

Student teachers have been socialised into hegemonic discourses about child and childhood(s) through their own experiences and memories of being child, sibling or sometimes a parent. Moreover, the posthuman pedagogical orientation taught and enacted in the childhood studies course does not resonate with the pedagogies students are taught elsewhere at university, neither in their prior undergraduate degrees (e.g., psychology, social work, the arts, health sciences), nor as part of their becoming a teacher in other courses in the PGCE. Moreover, during Teaching Practice (one-third of their degree), students often witness abusive child:adult relations, such as corporal punishment and verbal humiliation. Finally, students often voice their political concern about the highly abstract, densely written posthuman literature with no or little reference to age discrimination or practical guidance. Therefore, as part of the 'how' of teaching, students learn complex theories about decentering the human in teaching. So how does one, can one, educate posthuman(e)ly in foundation phase teacher education?

Cara and Karin kept in touch by email after Cara qualified as a teacher and in one email Cara wrote:

> At the start of the course, finding myself in unfamiliar territory applying my previous knowledge of learning, (having graduated in Fine Arts at the same institution in 1989) I struggled to not only fit into the learning community of a small class but to also understand the intention of your childhood studies course. Unsettled and out of my comfort zone, in attempt to gain control I pushed boundaries, challenged your authority and questioned activities you required us to do in the Childhood Studies course, with the only language I knew at the time.

Cara was not the only student who struggled. After the first reading of the textbook *The Posthuman Child* (2016), written especially by Karin for this and a Masters course, the students expressed their struggle with the complexity of the text (Fig. 15.1).

Fig. 15.1 Cara and other students' responses to the first Childhood Studies reading: *The Posthuman Child* (2016)

Reconfiguring Ontology and Epistemology

Karin's inspiration for a different, more ethical doing of education is the complex critical posthumanism developed by feminist philosophers Donna Haraway, Karen Barad and Rosi Braidotti. Although Haraway (2016: 101) prefers the term "compostist" to posthumanist, her writings have been and still are very influential in the development of critical posthumanism, especially Karen Barad's influential strand of posthumanism. Haraway (2016: 176 fn13) makes a useful distinction between seeing human animals as *autopoietic* systems and *sympoietic* systems. In the former, humans have 'self-produced binaries,' they are 'organizationally closed,' 'autonomous units,' centrally controlled (e.g., through a human will or intellect), orientated around growth and development with 'evolution between systems,' and are 'predictable.' In contrast, *sympoietic* systems lack boundaries, are 'complex amorphous entities,' have 'distributed control' with an 'evolution within systems' and are 'unpredictable.' Haraway (2016: 58) explains:

> Sympoiesis is a simple word; it means "making-with". Nothing makes itself; nothing is really autopoietic or self-organizing. In the words of the Inupiat computer "world game," earthlings are *never alone*. That is the radical implication of sympoiesis. *Sympoiesis* is a word proper to complex, dynamic, responsive, situated, historical systems. It is a word for worlding-with, in company.

Earthlings 'are never alone.' Theorizing subjectivity as an *existential* event is a paradigmatic shift from the discursive to the material-discursive and expresses a relational posthuman ontology salient for multispecies flourishing. The ontological fact that 'earthlings are never alone' means that teachers are always part of, and situated in (as Haraway points out), complex, dynamic, historical, and responsive systems that are both material and discursive at the very same time. Teaching and learning are, therefore, 'worlding-with' practices that disrupt power-producing Western humanist binaries, such as mind/body, culture/nature, cognition/emotion, theory/practice, adult/child, because categories that involve binaries are human-made and are all products of *relationships inbetween significant others* (Haraway 2003: 6–7). Similarly, Karen Barad's neologism *intra-action* at the heart of her agential realism, also emphasizes a de/colonising ontological shift in how humans and more-than-humans relate and influence each other (Barad 2007, 2014), further explained below.

Queering Child/Adult Relationality Through a Re-Turning to the Past

At any one time a plethora of assumptions about child: adult relationality manifest themselves in teaching and research practices, also in higher education. The *doing* of childhood is profoundly complex and contradictory, but structured efforts in disentangling some of these figurations and how they inform practice make it possible to start imagining other possible ways of doing child:adult relationality and pedagogy.

The work of Barad and Haraway is about the implosion of nature and culture—a plea to rethink relationality together *without* the Nature/Culture binary. The posthuman ontology of a sympoietic system disrupts the Nature/Culture binary on which modern schooling has been built and has profound implications for (child) subjectivity (Murris 2016). Posthumanism reconfigures subjectivity and with it radically changes what it means to teach and what it means to learn, because the Nature/Culture binary is central in what we have come to understand as real knowledge: asocial, apolitical and rational (in a disembodied manner). Binary logic, put in place by western metaphysics (and reinforced by capitalism and Christian theology), has rendered the body (Nature) inferior to the mind (Culture) in education (Murris 2018). The Nature/Culture dualism affirms the adult/child binary, but is ontologically redundant in posthumanism as a navigational tool.

Table 15.1 A map of figurations of child that presuppose the Nature/Culture dichotomy

Figurations of child	Theoretical influences	What child lacks by nature	What culture needs to provide child
Developing child	Aristotle, Darwin, Piaget, Vygotsky	Maturity	Maturation, guidance
Ignorant child	Plato, Aristotle, Locke	Rationality, experience	Instruction, training
Evil child	Christianity esp. Protestantism	Trustworthiness, natural goodness	Control, discipline, inculcation, drawing in
Innocent child	Romantics (Rousseau)	Responsibility	Protection, facilitation
Egocentric child	Piaget	Empathy, social norms and values,	Socialisation by elders, inculcation
Fragile child	Psycho-medical scientific model	Resilience	Protection, medication, diagnoses, remediation

The figurations of child and childhood presented in Table 15.1 are the apparatuses we tend to think and feel with and enact in our (educational) encounters with children and in programmes that prepare students for various professions that involve working with young children. However, the way in which the Nature/Culture binary works to in-form teaching expresses childism. We deliberately refer to 'child', and not *the* child' as the latter expresses individualised ontological identity, that is, 'a' determinate body bounded by a skin, rather than porous and brought into existence through her relations. As a hu/Man-made concept 'child' works to include and exclude. It is assumed that child needs to progress from Nature (wild, feral, animal child) to Culture (fully-human adult) through adult pedagogical interventions: guiding, facilitating, mediating, protecting, disciplining, diagnosing, etc.

These collective images shape our teaching and research practices, also in higher education across faculties and departments, and these historical, socio-cultural discourses and material practices affect human and nonhuman bodies. Hence the vital work of examining these entangled figures of child diffractively with student teachers, and tracing the marks these figurations have made (and continue to make) on our bodyminds. This work is always e/mergent and bound by the language and concepts of 'the past'. The new can only emerge with past, present and future diffractively threaded through one another (Barad 2007). *Re*-turning as a method slows down teaching: re-turning and re-turning again and again to the 'same' text, in this case students' 'own' childhoods as the text. As Barad points out: 'the mere mark of a hyphen [in re-turning], is an important reminder that reflection ('returning', not 're-turning') and diffraction are not opposites,' but overlapping optical intra-actions in practice (Barad 2014: 185 ftn2). In a relational ontology, we are 'neither inside, not outside,' and without fixed bodily boundaries, our 'story in its ongoing (re)patterning is (re)(con)figuring' us; we are '*of* the diffraction pattern' (Barad 2014: 181). It is in this sense that as subjects we are transindividual: 'always already multiply dispersed and diffracted throughout spacetime (mattering)…in its ongoing being-becoming' (Barad 2014: 181–182). What we can learn from Barad's diffractive reading of Quantum Field Theory (QFT) is that intra-actions and diffractions are in/determinate in both space and time, for both human and nonhuman. Barad (2014: 169) reminds us that in QFT each moment 'in' time is 'an infinite multiplicity … broken apart in different directions.' Barad's *agential realism* implies that the past is open for future re-workings, and yet, the traces of iterative materialisations are sedimented into the world (Barad 2018). So each re-turning to childhood leaves marks on the world, thickening the sedimentations of the world.

Using temporal diffraction means tracing human and nonhuman entanglements and moving beyond the anthropocentric focus on the discursive only and acknowledge the in/determinate agency of the relationality inbetween the material and the discursive. Barad's agential realism queers concepts that assume binary thinking, such as causality, agency, power and identity—concepts still at the heart of education. With 'queer' as a verb, Barad (2007) does not just mean 'strange' but disrupting the Nature/Culture binary and is therefore an 'undoing of identity'. The bodymind map is a materialdiscursive provocation to move from an ontology of identity to an ontology of difference.

Posthuman (Child) Subjectivity: A De/Colonising Move

During the Childhood Studies course in groups of three, students diffract in their collaborative journals on Google.docs and express new diffractive patterns of inclusion and exclusion, of 'othering' as they e/merge during the year. The work in class and the diffractive journaling are all part of their year-long formative assessment.

Of course, their shifting ideas and practices about childhood are forever 'under construction', forever becoming and *moving* (Dolphijn and van der Tuin 2012: 111), exposing increasingly fine nuances of difference in being, knowing and doing, culminating in their final installation at the end of the year. The main objective of this formative assessment is for students to think *and* be affected by how discriminatory and unjust early years practices are. The need to de/colonise education is a direct result of the power producing binary thinking that excludes the subhuman (child) through the different values adults attach to one side of each binary. The binaries that dominate modernity are structured by a relation of negations (e.g. immature, undeveloped, ignorant, savage and evil). New materialists Rick Dolphijn and Iris van der Tuin (2012: 126–127) explain how through 're-affirming these negations' it is possible to create new concepts as an ontoepistemological activity that is also ethical and political.

Colonialism has instilled a non-relational ontology and competitive individualised subjectivity in education that continues to regard people, land and knowledge as property. De/colonisation involves disrupting in particular the culture/nature binary that positions children in need of recapitulating the development of the species: like Indigenous people, children are regarded as simple, concrete, immature thinkers who need age-appropriate interventions in order to mature into autonomous fully-human beings. De/colonisation is written with a '/' to express the idea that de/colonising pedagogies trouble unilinear time and therefore progress(ion). De/colonisation is a particular relationship to knowledge—not predatory, hierarchical, or 'discovery', but *rhizomatic*: an exploration of difference, variation, relationality and fluidity.

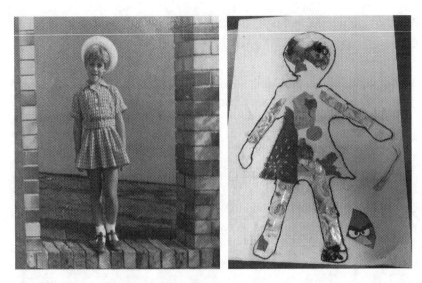

Fig. 15.2 In the left Cara's first school day. On the right her body mindmap as made in the university classroom

De/colonisation also expresses an in/determinate relationship towards truth: beyond predefined boundaries and assumed categories of difference. As a result the adult:child, teacher:learner relationality changes radically; as does the scope for transformative pedagogies and the creation of new subjectivities and concepts.

The concept 'posthuman child' expressed as 'iii' (Murris 2016) is such a new 'concept'. It expresses the *continuous process of individuation* that any subject *is* (including child and other earthlings) and therefore invites a different *doing* of subjectivity. The posthuman child *is* neither just a body (small and young), nor just a mind that would make a human body childlike, but a bodymind that at the same time is also linguistic, social, political, natural, material and cultural, therefore *transindividual*. Subjectivity is not bounded by a skin, but a transversal entangled becomings. Child is not a singular, fleshy being that is a bounded body *in* space and time, but always relational and *part* of the world: a sympoietic system Haraway (2016) would argue. This posthuman insight has profound implications for pedagogy (a process of 'worlding'), content ('rhizomatic') and the role of the ('diffractive') educator in schools and universities (Olsson 2009; Lenz-Taguchi 2010; Murris 2016, 2017). One of the intra-ventions Karin has designed to provoke a shift to posthuman subjectivity is the making of bodymind maps (see Fig. 15.2 for Cara's bodymind map). The photo of her first day in school is entangled in Cara's re-membering of her childhood, not as a representation of the event, but as an object that she has seen often and is agentic in the complex unbounded, always shifting and dynamic material-discursive entanglement that is the on-going process of 'her' childhood.

Bodymind Maps: Body as Transformer in a University Classroom

A posthumanist way of working with bodymind maps takes account of the complex interrelations between the 'inside' and the 'outside' of a subject, inbetween self and society and understands the subject as a sympoietic system: an entanglement of human and nonhuman materialities. The activity opens up possibilities for radically critiquing power and the humanist subject. Rosi Braidotti (2002: 20) argues that the embodied or enfleshed subject is no longer the Cartesian '*cogito ergo sum*', but a '*desidero ergo sum*'—a subject whose thinking is 'enlarged to encompass a number of faculties of which affectivity, desire and the imagination are prime movers.'

The creation of bodymind maps intra-acts with the genealogy of six well-known configurations in Table 15.1 (Murris 2016, 2018). Rather than situating one-self outside one's own history as it were—a going back in time, as if time were linear like beads on a string (Barad 2007)—intra-action or diffraction is a re-turning. An ongoing (re)patterning (re)(con)figuring of self. The diffractive political reading of Table 15.1 helps to 'fracture' and 'open up the past' in order to 'bring forth the new' (Rotas 2015: 98)—an 'affirmative approach that undoes binary logic by thinking and doing simultaneously' (Rotas 2015: 101). The students do their own further research provoked by the table and bring their findings to class. They then work in their small diffractive journal groups (randomly chosen groups of three students) on the internet (each group has their own document in Google drive), sometimes on their own as was the case with the bodymind map activity, or, at other times, discussing discourses that position child materially, socio-culturally and historically within the western system of binaries, such as 'savage/domesticated', 'good/evil', 'dangerous/safe', 'male/female', 'egocentric/selfless', 'sexual/innocent', 'mature/immature', 'developing/developed', 'fragile/resilient'.

Materials for the transmodal construction of new ideas are always available in the room: different kinds of fabric, wool, play dough, clay; natural materials such as stones, twigs and leaves; waste and recycled materials (e.g. bottles, egg boxes and toilet roll holders); art materials (e.g. paint, glue, pencils, thick felt tip pens and old newspaper). In Cara's case, students had been asked to collect their own materials and bring them to class on Monday morning 16 March 2015. Re-turning, Cara wonders how this particular collection randomly placed on the floor that Monday morning *es-sense-tially* intra-acted with her and others while constructing their bodymind maps. The blue wool she chose to use (or chose her) for her bodymind map outline/boundary, the floral patterned cloth, biscuit, chocolate and breakfast cereal box with the angry birds motif, newspaper, cotton wool and even the paper—how they all intra-acted and came to matter.

Cara, overwhelmed and unsettled had already expressed her discomfort in her diffractive journal and questioned her own intentions considering how to proceed and even not to join in at all.

On the morning of Karin's bodymind map provocation Cara re-calls questioning silently: 'Is this an art activity to experience child/childhood?', 'Why isn't Karin providing insight into the previous weeks required reading?', 'It is Monday – art and play based activities are normally assigned to Friday afternoons?', 'Is this really learning?', 'Why haven't we been told what we are learning, what we need to know and why?'. After initial resistance and with Karin's subtle prompting, Cara chose to work on a piece of discarded flip chart paper rather than the small A4 paper others were using. She resisted drawing an outline of child with pencil or marker as was suggested, finding this too bounded

15 Body as Transformer: 'Teaching Without Teaching' ...

and framing, describing it at the time in her diffractive journal as 'humanist.' She chose rather to use a piece of blue wool to construct her child boundary/outline. To do this she had to dip the wool into paper glue and proceeded with forming this fluid outline starting from just above the right hand slowly working around the arm, head, neck and dress to the legs feet, hands pasting the wool down using her fingers and hands to construct the outline. Some in the PGCE class thought of this as messy but familiar territory for Cara, who excelled in visual arts as a child but recalls often being reprimanded for 'wearing her art and *mess-ing* her uniform.' At this point Cara recalls being totally immersed in this activity, making marks on the nonhuman body (paper) with and without intention and not being able to articulate it in words. Re-working 'hidden' memories of a troubled childhood; lost/denied, ill health and abuse. Cara chose to work on her own, asking Karin probing questions and offering further ideas to diffract with whilst documenting with her iPad. Cara put a photo of her bodymind map in her diffractive journal and wrote:

> My recall regards this exercise isn't clear, i recall cutting up an empty cereal box to create an orange/red, triangle/diamond and a blue circle - why did i make this and only photo at the end of the class? not sure if I intended to use the 'angry bird' icon or twig, the photo was made at this time and place and even if it wasn't with intention can this be considered to give agency to my bodymind map. What you 'see' is not what is apparent.

At the end of the session, Karin commented on Cara's choice of colours and called the map 'beautiful'. Her bodymind map may have been aesthetically pleasing for others, but for Cara this was not art or craft made to adorn someone's wall! For her, it was anything and everything but beautiful. Angered she recalls wanting to lash out at Karin and ask: 'How dare you play with us with our/mine emotions for research/learning?' Leaving her bodymind map on the desk to dry, hands and clothes full of glue, she recalls 'stomping off' to an Educational Studies lecture. This was the comfortable familiar territory she knew: Read this, learn these slides, you will be tested on Friday with a multiple choice quiz.

Later that afternoon Cara fetched her now almost dry bodymind map folded it up in anger and when she got home discarded it in a corner in her room. She re-calls how a few weeks later her mother and father (using her room when visiting) noticed the paper folded up and asked whether the bodymind map was Vicki's, Cara's then 5 year old daughter. Cara answered 'yes' so as not to have to explain.

The bodymind map activity evolves around the theorypractice that the body can be a 'transformer'. So Karin had instructed the class in an email to explicitly engage with the Nature/Culture dichotomy and the child configurations in Table 15.1—as it applied to their bodymind maps—and to discuss this in their diffractive groups on Google.docs. The students' diffractions show not only how difficult, but also how impossible it was for them not to slip into symbolic ways of thinking and to use the much more familiar psychological discourses, especially for some of our students who are psychology graduates. Karin then invited the students to hang their bodymind maps up on a 'washing line' to diffract with when next in class (Fig. 15.3).

Cara's Affirmative Resistance

Cara was profoundly uncomfortable with Karin's suggestion to display her bodymind map on the washing line (Fig. 15.3) or to discuss the marks she had made in connection with the Nature/Culture dichotomies. She resisted discussing it, either in the plenary, or in her diffractive journal group. At the time, Cara expressed her concern to Karin, verbally and in writing. She argued that this activity may be one of introspection, self-examination and or therapeutic regression and therefore not appropriate to be conducted in this open classroom context. She strongly objected to what she called the 'regressive' nature of the bodymind map provocation as it was conducted in 'an uncontained environment'. Karin offered to discuss these concerns privately at several occasions and proposed to Cara an alternative assessment: providing readings and setting a written exam. It was also suggested that Cara seek guidance and support of a therapist to work through the triggered disturbances. Deeply affected by Cara's resistance, Karin started

15 Body as Transformer: 'Teaching Without Teaching' ...

Fig. 15.3 Bodymind maps hung up on a washing line in our university classroom

to experience uncertainty and doubt about the appropriateness of the provocation, but did not show it to Cara. It was her first year of teaching the course using posthumanism explicitly as a navigational tool, and her desire to make it work was strong. Although Karin has a certificate in Rogerian counselling, she got worried about the depth of the challenge and Cara's insistence that she needed a strong therapeutic background in order for such activities to be safe. Karin wondered whether unwittingly she was also holding onto the Nature/Culture binary? How posthuman was her teaching really?

With a strong urge to ensure the provocation was not humanist, representational and symbolic, and therefore (she presumed) psychologically 'safe', Karin started the next session by inviting the students to re-turn to their bodymind maps and diffract further in their collaborative journals with a few paragraphs from Braidotti's *Metamorphosis*:

> I take the body as the complex interplay of highly constructed social and symbolic forces: it is not an essence, let alone a biological structure, but a play of…social and affective forces…This is a clear move away from the

psychoanalytic idea of the body as a map of semiotic inscriptions and culturally enforced codes. I see it instead as a transformer and a relay point for the flow of energies: a surface of intensities... [Inhabiting different time zones the body refers to] simultaneously incorporating and transcending the very variables – class, race, sex, nationality, culture, etc. – which structure it...The body remains a bundle of contradictions: it is a zoological entity, a genetic data-bank, while it also remains a bio-social entity, that is to say a slab of codified, personalized memories. (Braidotti 2002: 20–21)

'Transformer' could be taken to mean an appliance that changes the voltage in an electric circuit, or the Hollywood creation of robots who can take humanoid form, or transform themselves into vehicles (and vice versa). Either way, the idea of a transformer expresses the desire, vitality and high-voltage energy generated by re-configuring child and childhood. Karin's responsibility as a lecturer was her ability to respond, and to 'listen for the response of the other and an obligation to be responsive to the other, who is not entirely separate from what we call self' (Barad in interview with Dolphijn and Van der Tuin 2012: 69). However, Karin asked 'herself': By selecting texts, and asking probing questions, was I 'mediating' their learning? Was it a case of Culture (the more knowledgeable lecturer) facilitating Nature (the less knowledgeable student)?

'Growing Down': Cara's Childhood Studies Installation

Regular rhizomatic and entangled intra-ventions during the rest of the year in Childhood Studies in-formed Cara's installation at the end of the year (Figs. 15.4). The disruption of subject/object dualisms, in particular in the way in which it was provoked by various experiential workshops, some reported on elsewhere (Murris and Muller 2018), brought into existence Cara's undoing of child subjectivity, from immature, ignorant, developing, unfinished, fragile, incapable, becoming adult, growing up, emerging, innocent, unpracticed, not in control, naïve, unsophisticated … (Fig. 15.4 left image), to mature, skilled, competent, feeling, knowing, thinking, capable, resilient, adept, unique, e/merging, diverse … (Fig. 15.4 right image).

Furthermore, even more radically, ontologically re-moving the boundary of the subject (which can be accessed in the QR code in Fig. 15.5), queers the separation inbetween human and subhuman (child) and between human and nonhuman and creates the posthuman subject. Another way of putting this, is that this shift is the shift in subjectivity from human animals as *autopoietic* systems to *sympoietic* systems: a complex amorphous entity with distributed agency (Haraway 2016: 58).

The bodymind map provocation as Cara now understands it, is intended to bring about a re-turning or diffracting through past-present-future entangled knowledges of childhood, and an awareness of the discriminatory nature/culture dichotomies of humanism, rather than as an exercise of introspection, self-examination and/or therapeutic regression (psychologising, that which has come to dominate our way of being and thinking, also in higher education).

Choosing to use the blue wool as what may appear as the obvious, symbolic representation of boy and then removing this outline in the installation intended not to show a divide between boy and girl but rather to show that, which is within, and not separate, girl-boy-girl-boy. Cara re-calls and writes in her essay:

> From an early age I can recall multiplicitous feelings and sense-ability, intense curiosity, 'e-motions', relations and attachment. I struggle to find any images of myself before I went to crèche or kindergarten where I am not engaging and don't have something I am gazing at. I recall not having the 'language' and still struggle to find expression to articulate my experience, thinking, feelings and 'es-sense' to others. Having been allowed this opportunity to access this knowing is paramount to my changing view, 'new beginning', of the unique diverse child (me).

Cara continues by explaining that she now sees the bodymind map activity through direct engagement. Not adult as separated from child but recognising that the child she still *is* comes existentially 'into

Fig. 15.4 The humanist child subject (left image) and the posthuman (child) subject (right image)

presence' (Biesta 2014). She re-calls previously referring to this process as *growing down*, momentarily, to access childhood. The making, creating of her bodymind map and its 'deconstruction', that is, the re-moval of the girl-child-boy outline in the installation is intended to express this journey of becoming and express-ing connections. Cara's changing view of child and the role of teacher involves a re-moval of the human from the centre in teaching and learning. Teaching is neither teacher-centred, nor child-centred, but about creating the transindividual conditions for learning to occur (Murris 2017). This of course, does not mean that the subject does not matter, but she is re-configured as a sympoietic system that is agentic and always relational and entangled with the material and the discursive. Cara notes that she now understands that this journey cannot be done alone and in isolation. By 'deconstructing' the boundary, the outline, of girl-child-boy/object and removing the 'skin' of the body she is becoming part of and not separate from the world. She writes in her journal:

15 Body as Transformer: 'Teaching Without Teaching' ... 273

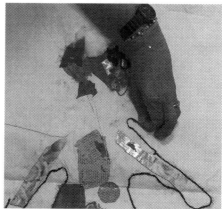

Fig. 15.5 Ontologically re-moving the boundary of the human subject

My bodymind map reveals the marks .. the marks you see is not the way it appears .. all is a thought, energy .. i came from nowhere, a thought, I am now-here and every action even every thought impacts .. we all do collectively.

(i *have been* an i - in an egotistical state of lower consciousness.. struggling with myself. The purpose of this exercise as i now understand is to step away from the i and learn to adopt a different lens of outward inquiry /diffraction?... *The learning, opportunity presented has been intense and stimulating, but also so disjointed at times, it can be very conflicting and challenging. Especially for those of us, old school taught, who are not accustomed to learning or acquiring knowledge in this manner. I have been overwhelmed, it is so unfamiliar and at times out of control* - conflict of head - heart - heart - head. like a pyramid balancing on its apex…

Cara now understands knowing as a direct material engagement without a separation of subject and object, but rather an entanglement, which is expressed in her installation, letting that which is not external but within, showing transformation and difference.

Re-Image(-Ening)s

Nikki Rotas (2015: 93) explains how teaching posthumanly 'disrupts the repetition of reason' and provokes a shift from asking questions that are problem-solving based to those that are curiosity-generating and divergent, 'questions that foster a transdisciplinary praxis that is effected by the past but not determined by it.' Such events have 'an intensive quality of experience that fosters an emergent praxis that bears material implications' (Rotas 2015: 97), and an experience that 'desires crisis … if students are to become affected' in spaces that are 'chaotic and disruptive' (Rotas 2015: 94). Therefore, students' resistance to being affected is to be expected and lecturers need to accommodate exploration of these disturbances as part of their teaching. The most typical form of student resistance is to ignore the posthuman and use already acquired knowledge about child development as the truth or last word about children. Another form of resistance encountered is students' refusal to participate in the task, because the exercise can generate painful memories. This was the case for Cara and affected Karin deeply.

Cara writes in her final essay how much the course meant to her:

> Having always been told what is of value knowing, Karin in her posthuman education/pedagogy with her intra-vention created an environment of self-directed learning and collaboration in which I discovered the most valuable lesson of knowing, teaching and learning as an active process of becoming, change, growth and making connections. With considerable insight she created this ontoepistemic shift. Most importantly, Karin didn't stand above but rather alongside and with us in this journey of knowing. We will continue to learn as Karin has provided us with the tools to continue this Journey.

In other words, Cara's resistance is not so much a case of that something has gone 'wrong' requiring 'intervention' by the lecturer in order 'to repair the damage', but as Rotas observes, the classroom has its own 'ecological capacity'—alive and breathing—'to un/learn through its own int-e(r)vent-ion' (Rotas 2015: 95). The 'wrong' as it of course seemed at the time was always already entangled in our knowing/doing and was affirmative as we experienced these experiences again and again—the never-ending past-present-futures. The idea of classrooms as living, breathing ecosystems resonates with both of us in all phases of education as it is a 'teaching without teaching' and positions a more ethical, egalitarian lecturer:student relationality. This posthuman way of teaching creates conditions whereby student teachers learn without being taught and thereby unlearn what teaching and learning is. It therefore, will influence how student teachers themselves will be/come teachers.

Unlearning How to Teach

The purpose of the activity was to disrupt humanist subjectivity. The student teachers were invited to do this by re-configuring child subjectivity and relationality inbetween child, adult and also the more-than-human, including, for example, the atmosphere in the room, the diffractive journals on Google drive and materials used for the bodymind activity. The learning that took place includes the idea that subjects as *sympoietic* systems lack boundaries, and as Haraway (2016: 176 fn13) put it, are "complex amorphous entities", have "distributed control" with an "evolution within systems" and are "unpredictable". This is very different from the psychological approach that involves inner reflection on the mental life of the subject (including children) as *autopoietic* systems. Critically, the way the concept childhood is used in teaching, research, policy-making and curriculum design presupposes the nature-culture dichotomy, with child associated with Nature and adult with Culture (Murris 2016). Child is either positioned as good or as bad (e.g., immature) by Nature, and therefore, adults needs to protect child, or adults need to be protected *from* child from building 'real common world relationships' and the real world gets lost … 'worlds full of entangled and uneven historical and geographical relations, political tensions, ethical dilemmas and unending possibilities' where crucially nature and culture come back together again (Taylor 2013: 62). These figurations in Table 15.1 have made, and continue to make, (always fluid, *emergent*, never 'finished') material-discursive marks on educators' bodyminds: child as 'innocent', 'evil', 'ignorant', 'developing', 'egocentric' and 'fragile'. The Nature/Culture dichotomy each presupposes positions child as *deficit*. As Carla Rinaldi (2006: 123) puts it: we are always living with certain images of child and the child of psychoanalysis and 'various branches of psychology and sociology' identify child as deterministic, as 'a weak subject, a person with needs rather than rights.' For transformation it is therefore imperative to explore these figurations at length with student teachers, teachers and teacher educators.

Acknowledgements This writing is based on research supported by the National Research Foundation of South Africa [Grant Number 98992].

References

Barad, K. (2007). *Meeting the universe halfway: Quantum physics and the entanglement of matter and meaning*. Durham: Duke University Press.

Barad, K. (2014). Diffracting diffraction: Cutting together-apart. *Parallax, 20*(3), 168–187.

Barad, K. (2018). Troubling time/s and ecologies of nothingness: Re-turning, re-membering, and facing the incalculable. In M. Fritsch, P. Lynes, & D. Wood (Eds.), *Eco-deconstruction: Derrida and environmental philosophy* (pp. 206–248). New York: Fordham U Press.

Biesta, G. (2014). *The beautiful risk of education*. Boulder, CO: Paradigm Publishers.

Braidotti, R. (2002). *Metamorphoses: Towards a materialist theory of becoming*. Oxford: Blackwell.

Dolphijn, R., & van der Tuin, I. (2012). *New materialism: Interviews & cartographies*. Open Humanities Press. http://openhumanitiespress.org/new-materialism.html. Accessed 12 March 2015.

Haraway, D. (2003). *The companion species manifesto: Dogs, people, and other significant otherness*. Chicago: Prickly Paradigm Press.

Haraway, D. (2016). *Staying with the trouble: Making kin in the Chthulucene*. Durham and London: Duke University Press.

Lenz Taguchi, H. (2010). *Going beyond the theory/practice divide in early childhood education*. London: Routledge Contesting Early Childhood Series.

Murris, K. (2016). *The posthuman child: Educational transformation through philosophy with picturebooks* (G. Dahlberg & P. Moss, Eds.). Contesting Early Childhood Series. London: Routledge.

Murris, K. (2017). Reconfiguring educational relationality in education: The educator as pregnant stingray. *Journal of Education, 69,* 117–138.

Murris, K. (2018). Posthuman child and the diffractive teacher: Decolonizing the nature/culture binary. In A. Cutter-Mackenzie, K. Malone, & E. Barratt Hacking (Eds.), *Research handbook on childhoodnature: Assemblages of childhood and nature research* (pp. 1–25). Dordrecht: Springer International Handbooks of Education.

Murris, K., & Muller, K. (2018). Finding child beyond 'child': A posthuman orientation to foundation phase teacher education in South Africa. In V. Bozalek, R. Braidotti, M. Zembylas, & T. Shefer (Eds.), *Socially just pedagogies: Posthumanist, feminist and materialist perspectives in higher education* (pp. 151–171). London: Palgrave Macmillan.

Olsson, L. M. (2009). *Movement and experimentation in young children's learning: Deleuze and Guattari in early childhood education.* London: Routledge.

Rinaldi, C. (2006). *In dialogue with Reggio Emilia: Listening, researching and learning.* London: Routledge Contesting Early Childhood Series.

Rotas, N. (2015). Ecologies of practice: Teaching and learning against the obvious. In N. Snaza & J. Weaver (Eds.), *Posthumanism and educational research* (pp. 91–104). New York: Routledge.

Snaza, N., & Weaver, J. A. (Eds.). (2015). *Posthumanism and educational research.* New York and London: Routledge.

Taylor, A. (2013). *Reconfiguring the natures of childhood.* London: Routledge Contesting Early Childhood Series.

Taylor, C. A., & Hughes, C. (Eds.). (2016). *Posthuman research practices in education.* Basingstoke, UK: Palgrave Macmillan.

Part III
Experimental Research Engagements

280   Part III: Experimental Research Engagements

Never the same October 2016. Photo: Carol A. Taylor

16

Playful Pedagogy: Autoethnography in the Anthropocene

Clare Hammoor

Introduction

This inquiry-driven, autoethnographic essay is a theoretical project rooted in its author's higher education pedagogy which collaborates with a multiplicity of objects and ontologies. By playfully reveling in the decentralization of the anthro- within the auto- of autoethnography, this performative essay vibrates with Barad's challenge that 'language has been granted too much power' (2003) through a diffractive exploration of a surprising, materialist intervention in the philosophy classroom. It is simultaneously troubled by the potentialities of contaminating agencies with language and the sharing of a performative, posthuman praxis that thrives in the fantastic now.

C. Hammoor (✉)
Independent Scholar, Denver, CO, USA
e-mail: sch399@nyu.edu

© The Author(s) 2019
C. A. Taylor and A. Bayley (eds.), *Posthumanism and Higher Education*,
https://doi.org/10.1007/978-3-030-14672-6_16

The Pedagogic Event

Twenty-three students stood in a pensive a circle around three rigid classroom chairs and a large, capped, plastic bottle of water. Each student could silently move one of these objects at a time wherever and in whatever position they liked, as long as it stayed in the circle. The goal for the whole group was to create a single, physical image of objects that featured the water bottle in a position of ultimate power. The final image would need everyone's approval and each person could make as many individual moves as they felt necessary. In other classes, these rules often inspired dozens of images before a group could settle on one clear picture that featured the water bottle as the most powerful object in the circle. I had been looking forward to this physical discussion and debate as we began our first class investigating power. This variation on Augusto Boal's theatre exercise 'Great game of power' (2010: 163) animated the first ten minutes of our new semester studying philosophy together. We were beginning an undergraduate 'Introduction to Philosophy' course during which we would investigate basic philosophical concepts through physical provocations and theatrical improvisations.

As the provocation picked up energy, so did the students and the objects. Faces scrunched while students tried to consider new possibilities. Chairs glided through the air to hold new positions on top of each other. Feet anxiously tapped the floor as twenty-three people pushed for their turn to move the next object—a few ordinary classroom elements had become excitable things to collaborate with. I invited the students to rotate their standing circle continuously in order to constantly evaluate each image from a number of viewpoints.

After a number of potential images of power, one student placed the bottle back in the center of the circle and others thoughtfully rested the three chairs in bowing positions, the tops of their backs on the floor facing the water bottle. Nods of approval from the circle signaled the beginning of a consensus among the students. This could be our image of ultimate power. A moment later, another student stepped into the circle of bowing chairs, picked up the bottle and froze with it inverted triumphantly above his head. He was bending the rules by bringing himself into and becoming a part of the image but his peers broke out in chuckles, claps and snaps signifying their approval of this

16 Playful Pedagogy: Autoethnography in the Anthropocene

final image of ultimate power. And then the water bottle lost its cap. Splashhhhhhhhh came a stream of water onto the student's head, covering his face and the front of his shirt and pants. The water's intra-vention within the provocation elicited loud cheers from the class and the student dropped the bottle onto the ground, furthering the water's reach as it sloshed into a puddle on the floor, covering the backs of the prostrated chairs and pooling a few feet from the other students' shoes. With soaking wet clothes and an enormous grin, the student excused himself from the room to dry off as the rest of us continued to rotate around the image left behind. The bottle, half empty and on its side, appeared abandoned by the three precisely placed chairs as the remaining water glistened in the fluorescent lights. Moments later, the water had pulled off some of the grime from the linoleum tiles rendering it a dispassionate brown.

I had used this provocation dozens of times before that introductory class and watched as chairs toppled when perched precariously on each other—I even saw a bottle break when crushed by an excited student's foot. I also witnessed beautifully complex images that came from collaborative precision and poise. But this water's leap into the moment, out of its pre-packaged bottle, offered me a new insight to the provocation's potentialities. It demonstrated, for me, an image of the collision between contemporary, interdisciplinary pedagogy practices in higher education and the catastrophes the Anthropocene continues to produce and threaten. Through a playful discourse open to everyone in the room, one student and a particular configuration of water were brought physically into relationship with each other through their own dynamic agencies. This inter-agential relationship lies beyond the human-centered notion of intentionality in favor of a much more magical and equitable concept that Jane Bennett describes as 'distributive agency' (2009: 32).

Contaminating Pedagogy: Reworking Collaboration

It is important for me to bring Bennett's thinking into this autoethnographic project because when her now ubiquitous *Vibrant Matter: A Political Ecology of Things* was published in 2009, I was smitten. I was enamored by the magical possibilities this text brought into being for me. I found it described the uncanny world and language of things that I had lived with since a childhood full of religious rituals, theatre and drama, and wild imagination. Encountering Bennett's text for the first time, years later as an adult, I found my pedagogy animated by her writing and the materiality of *Vibrant Matter* became a critical addition to my teaching practice—it has appeared on a number of my seemingly unrelated syllabi as an accessible provocation for undergraduates and a multimodal challenge for graduate students. Of course Bennett is not the first or the most recent object-oriented provocateur, many other things, names, and ideas are featured in this chapter but Bennett's notion of 'distributive agency' is critical to my project because it 'does not deny the existence of that thrust called intentionality, but it does see it as less definitive of outcomes. It loosens the connections between efficacy and the moral subject, bringing efficacy closer to the idea of the power to make a difference that calls for a response' (2009: 32).

The formulation of power Bennett brings awareness to offered an entryway into a discussion of poststructuralism and postmodernism (and a few weeks later, posthumanism). As such, a foundational formulation in my class's philosophical exercise came into being with three chairs and a bottle of water. By challenging students to work collaboratively with things and each other through the constantly shifting prism of their own vision as they circled the inter- and intra-actions in pursuit of an abstract goal, we were able to have a rich dialogue about the work of power at play in imagery and aesthetics but more importantly, in our political and cultural realities during the exercise through our interactions and after its messy finish through a whole class discussion. The water's rupture, which ended one phase of our exploration, was undoubtedly an interjection of 'the power to make a difference that calls for a response' (Bennett 2009: 32).

While the presence of a particular response (or lack thereof) is commonly seen as a testament to the efficacy of an interjection, I am particularly interested in the first part of Bennett's equation which zooms in on the 'power to make a difference'. For pedagogy to become *post-human*, it must eschew the capitalist machinations that drive much of today's product-oriented and quantifiable pedagogy in ways that have already been initiated by critical performative pedagogy (CPP) (Giroux 2001; Pineau 2005; Weltsek and Medina 2007). 'While all pedagogy is made up of performative utterances, performative pedagogy locates the pedagogue and their own subject position and performativity as central to the critical, epistemological project. It is especially useful for this research because it goes beyond the epistemological consequences of pedagogy and into the ontological possibilities of performativity for people and things' (Hammoor 2018). Such a critical practice of pedagogy relies on a Harawayan diffractive practice of knowing and being in a multiplicity of ways for both the pedagogue and students within provocations. This provocation model for enacting pedagogy is an intravention into contemporary higher education practices that demands new ways of organizing temporality and classroom structures.

The power of a provocation sits squarely within potential and potentiality and as such aligns an analogy alongside the essential role of inquiry within pedagogy. Inquiry holds the potential for any number of discoveries without the impediments of presupposition because presuppositions can only work to limit the potentialities of an interjection; if a pedagogic event need only corroborate a particular idea, its potential is foreclosed by such a corroboration. Instead of a linear form of pedagogy that corroborates ideas, I am interested in a messy process that works in collaboration.

Within an inquiry-driven, performative pedagogy paradigm, all actors work in collaboration through cross-cultural communications in order to be in a particular series of moments. Such moments hold posthumanist potentiality because they eschew futurity in favor of collaborative presence in all beings. It is important here to underscore the collaborative nature of this type of pedagogy which is most vibrant within intersecting forms of cross-cultural communication. Such forms of dialogue do not directly refer to verbal communication across different human cultures (although this is an important element in developing contemporary pedagogy). Instead, I am interested in pursuing cross-cultural communication through understandings that de-centre human ways of experiencing, knowing and being in the world by demanding a dialogic relationship with non-human sensations, interactions, and, ultimately, ontologies. Such a collaboration between a variety of non-humans, and humans as well, is brought into focus by Anna Tsing's excitable exploration of Matsutake mushrooms and her notion of collaboration 'which means working across difference, which leads to contamination. Without collaborations, we all die' (2015: 28).

Tsing's (2015) determination that collaboration is essential to our continued survival 'in capitalist ruins' can be used to underscore the importance of developing a pedagogic paradigm that places all-being collaboration at its center because such a paradigm literally involves the process of 'worlding worlds' as Donna Haraway (2016) imagines such a task. The worlds produced by provocations indicate new ways of being within and beyond higher education and are the focus of this chapter's autoethnographic object-oriented pedagogy. The application of posthumanism is beneficial beyond its clear interjections into philosophy, ecology and politics. I have found it to be an abundantly fruitful framework in my education and theatre classrooms, where I challenge all collaborators to have an effervescent understanding of Karen Barad's (2003) challenge that 'language has been granted too much power.' Physical interventions, artistic responses, polyvocal dialogues, multimedia performances, and spiraling collaborations are critical elements of a playful, diffractive practice of pedagogy I am advocating in the face of static seminars and pedagogue-determined outcomes. I find a delightful irony in framing this written, reflective exercise with Barad's challenge and hope you will be willing to play with such contradictions as potential sites for discovery.

Contaminating Autoethnography

I am sure that my own writing and its dissemination acts as a contaminant in the ecosystem of collaborative pedagogy and the material-driven practice I am so devoted to. Yet, the dissemination of this work across any means is exciting to me and I hope my own voice intertwines with the intervention it outlines as a way of being in the fantastic now which cannot escape the totality of the Anthropocene. In this way, I hope the language of this viewpoint is merely in support of its messy provocation which collides and collaborates with/in our current epoch.

In examining this pedagogy's diffractive iterations, it is important to hold my own words and thoughts accountable to the things I narrate and their ways of beings. Surely, my own positioning within an autoethnographic structure as a means of reflection and dissemination contaminates the pedagogy and knowledge production that arose in my philosophy class. I do not mean this as if there could somehow be an objective view of that water's intravention into our class—surely there is no such thing. I do mean this as a way of opening myself up for criticism as the human writing about the collaborative knowledge production in that classroom. Surely the water bottle and students would have their own account well worth investigating. However, understanding is deeper for me than a tousle with my subject position as teacher and facilitator in the classroom. It is a challenge for me to inhabit my own voice, much like my own ontology in a multiplicity of ontologies, as potential. Potentially harmful and generative, simultaneously. Such a potential is a responsibility, even an ethical obligation, that tugs at my heart and my own epistemology.

My responsibility to all of the beings in that room does not give me the rights or the tools to translate their experiences into written discourse and my writing is only one possible account of a series of events that will replay in my mind for years to come; while I can only write from my own experience, even that is a fleeting and fickle memory forced into words. Words that certainly do something but are also, in many ways, done. Yet, this account is the one I have chosen to share within this one context because I have witnessed the power of personal narrative and its value in creating meaning. That is why I kept the plastic bottle with the remaining water in the classroom for the rest of the semester.

Inviting Play Through Provocation

I kept the chairs, too, but they somehow became absorbed back into the regularity of the space. After I put the water bottle on top of a file cabinet near the board, it remained in its position for the rest of the semester. This was quite remarkable given the hundreds of other people who must have cycled through that classroom throughout those months. The maintenance staff didn't bother to throw it away and other faculty decided that it belonged just where I placed it after that first class. With the cap re-secured, the remaining centimeters of water were secure atop the cabinet. Such a security is fascinating to me because of the collaboration of beings that actively chose to support its placement after our class' encounter with it. Stasis here emanates the potentiality of an individual temporality—a challenge for pedagogues to invite more things into our rooms.

A continual interlocutor within our class and others, the bottle and water were surely not, as Barad (2014: 17) challenges, 'in need of some supplement to put it in motion, to enliven it, to give it agency.' Instead, these materials became a critical presence within our classroom experience. They were more than mementos and reminders because they were active participants in our philosophical work. The conversation we had with them in our first class was foundational and interwoven into our projects; the presence of the bottle and water became a form of simultaneous dramaturgy.

In creating arts-driven provocations, a relationship with what other practitioners think and write about their own work as theory, case study and autoethnography, is critical. Augusto Boal, whose game became my class' initial provocation, defines simultaneous dramaturgy as the 'first invitation made to the spectator to intervene without necessitating his (or her, or its) physical presence on the "stage"' (Boal 2000: 13). For Boal, such interventions are often made through verbal discourse that influences the action of a particular scene. For me, the simultaneity of the bottle and water within the inquiry of the philosophy classroom demands a dramaturgic understanding that does not necessitate physical interventions by the materials themselves. I posit this not because the objects had previously created such a dramatic interjection into our work together, they surely did, but because the agentic presence of objects themselves is a challenge to create a collaborative, discursive practice across forms of being. Such a practice is undoubtedly messy in its implementation, but for me, it is an exciting potentiality especially when it reconnects with my own diffractive practice.

The messiness I am fascinated with has brought clarity to the aesthetics of my teaching practices; I am working toward a pedagogy that invests heavily in the day-to-day imagery of the classroom (three chairs and a bottle of water) because tomorrow does not necessitate a futurity for my students, for me, or for the ecology of beings that we are all deeply intertwined within. The erasure of a secure future demands a playful instability today that does not necessarily act as a preparation for our current students, but as a cross-culturally responsive understanding of the fantastic now in which we recognize our being.

My aesthetic understanding of teaching is indebted to educational philosopher Maxine Greene's (1977) notions of aesthetic education and its production of 'wide awakefulness.' For Greene, aesthetics are produced by interactions between people and artforms. For me, aesthetics are produced by intra-actions between all beings with an eye toward a multiplicity of ontologies. The propulsion of water from a seemingly sealed bottle onto a student's head is both an aesthetic event and an intervention into a way of being. It surely resulted in a new type of awakefulness for all of us in that circle while simultaneously creating a dramaturgical, physical, and pedagogic mess for us to wade through. It was a surprise that invited inquiry; an unplanned event that challenged our expectations of stability. An openness to surprising events in education calls for a supportive commitment to their presence in the classroom.

Surprising events need invitations, they need to be able to fall into place not only because student-collaborators decide a topic or idea is engaging (student-driven learning) but also because a pastiche of human and non-human possibilities have arrived in a particular moment. Such a framework for knowledge production runs parallel to the pedagogic paradigms that inform its practice. Pedagogy and practice here form an intimate relationship of chaotic collision and collaboration which both mirrors and responds to the possibilities of higher education in the Anthropocene. I want to invite this messy and surprising form of collaborative pedagogy into my teaching practice.

When I returned to teach in that room the next semester, the water bottle had disappeared. So had the students. So had I. Yet, the matter(s) of that space-time continued to matter (Barad 2003). I wondered if I would be disconcerted by the ephemerality of the space and my own understanding of self. Some sort of stable self is often understood as elemental to the work of autoethnography; the experiences of my own pedagogy and thinking need to be interpreted by a stagnant me. Instead, I found myself and my teaching practice animated not just by disappearances but by the disjointedness Barad (2014: 18) invites us into as she articulates 'the nature of "dis" and "jointedness," of discontinuity and continuity of separation and entanglement, and their im/possible intra-relationships.' These impossible relationships are exactly the ones I want to discover and construct in my higher education pedagogy.

They are aesthetic and dramaturgical relationships with things, students, and my own presence in the classroom. They are relationships that rely on unpredictability and disjointedness which I am not solely responsible for crafting. I am not advocating for a pre-planned practice that is somehow surprising to my students at the moments I think will have the most impact. Instead, I am challenging myself and my own comfort as a pedagogue, practitioner, and autoethnographer to relinquish anthropocentrism in favor of a practice that does not center my voice, or even the human voice—in favor of an equality of being(s) in the classroom. It is a scary prospect in a life or death higher education environment overridden with corporatized academic structures, reviews, and overinflated diplomas. But if this practice has taught me anything, it is the indelible promise of a playful relationship with life and non-life that can only come from my willingness to leap into (im)possibility with things because they hold 'the power to make a difference that calls for a response' (Bennett 2009: 32). That response is the knowledge production in relationship with things and people that leaves me feeling wide awake. I hope it is a power that invites you to experience the joy of potentiality and the playfulness of a posthuman pedagogy.

References

Barad, K. (2003). Posthumanist performativity: Toward an understanding of how matter comes to matter. *Signs: Journal of Women in Culture and Society*, 28(3), 801–831. https://doi.org/10.1086/345321.

Barad, K. (2014). *How matter matters: Objects, artifacts, and materiality in organization studies* (P. R. Carlile, Ed.). Oxford: Oxford University Press.

Bennett, J. (2009). *Vibrant matter: A political ecology of things.* Durham, NC: Duke University Press.

Boal, A. (2000). *Theatre of the oppressed.* London: Pluto Press.

Boal, A. (2010). *Games for actors and non-actors.* London: Routledge.

Giroux, H. (2001). Cultural studies as performative politics. *Cultural Studies-Critical Methodologies, 1*(1), 5–23.

Greene, M. (1977). Toward wide-awakeness: An argument for the arts and humanities in education. *Issues in Focus, 79*(1), 119–125.

Hammoor, C. (2018). *Theatre of children; absurd agencies in the anthropocene* (Dissertation).

Haraway, D. J. (2016). *Staying with the trouble: Making kin in the Chthulucene.* Durham: Duke University Press.

Pineau, E. L. (2005). Teaching is performance: Reconceptualizing a problematic metaphor. In B. K. Alexander, G. L. Anderson, & B. P. Gallegos (Eds.), *Performance theories in education* (pp. 15–39). Mahwah, NJ: Lawrence Erlbaum.

Tsing, A. L. (2015). *The mushroom at the end of the world on the possibility of life in capitalist ruins.* Princeton, NJ: Princeton University Press.

Weltsek, G., & Medina, C. (2007). In search of the glocal through process drama. In ed. M. V. Blackburn and C. Clark (Eds.), *Literary research for political action and social change* (pp. 255–275). New York: Peter Lang.

17

Refiguring Presences in Kichwa-Lamista Territories: Natural-Cultural (Re)Storying with Indigenous Place

Marc Higgins and Brooke Madden

Introduction

The land is ontologically alive: it is breathing, breeding, dreaming, kicking, sweating, cursing, morphing, laughing, crying, dancing, drumming, singing, eating, burping, farting, shitting, decaying, dying, and being born again. It does not fit notions of linear ticking rushing time. It is cognitively incomprehensible and metaphysically mysterious, but sensually accessible as an extension of our bodies, except when we are contained in a box of ontological concrete. (Ahenakew 2017: 81)

M. Higgins (✉)
Department of Secondary Education,
University of Alberta, Edmonton, AB, Canada
e-mail: marc1@ualberta.ca

B. Madden
Department of Educational Policy Studies,
University of Alberta, Edmonton, AB, Canada
e-mail: bmadden@ualberta.ca

© The Author(s) 2019
C. A. Taylor and A. Bayley (eds.), *Posthumanism and Higher Education*,
https://doi.org/10.1007/978-3-030-14672-6_17

Underscoring the significance of Anhenakew's (2017) construction of land, Nxumalo and Cedillo (2017: 102–103) state that:

> If place is intrinsic to settler colonialism as an ongoing structure…, it matters how place is conceptualized and enacted in place-based and environmental education in settler colonial contexts … place stories can potentially interrupt absent presences in pedagogical encounters with 'nature' on stolen Indigenous lands.

Madden (2015) positions Indigenous and place-based education as a pedagogical pathway that brings educators in relation with situated Indigenous knowledges, as well as Indigenous–non-Indigenous histories and contemporary realities that emerge from interconnected relationships formed in and through place. We suggest how place is conceptualized and enacted in Indigenous and place-based education matters. Notably, constructions of place matter if we are to account for, and be accountable to, the ways in which land is simultaneously conceived of as the heart of Indigenous resurgence—'regeneration of Indigenous knowledges and ways of being in the world, as well as their necessary contestation with settler colonial power' (Wildcat et al. 2014: iv)—and as settler property (Apffel-Marglin 2011; Simpson 2014). Significantly, attending to the latter—the absent presence of the foundational assumption of *terra nullius* that secures and privileges land as property and economic resource—troubles the oft received message of neutrality that places of learning (e.g. schools, universities) operationalize through a pedagogy of placelenessness. It also illuminates a competing (in relation to the illusion of placelessness) settler-colonial curriculum hidden in plain sight (Battiste et al. 2005; Higgins and Madden 2017).

Part of resisting and refusing such place-based relations steeped in (neo-)colonial logics requires, as Plains Cree scholar Cash Ahenakew (2017) poetically states above, working towards recognizing the ways in which land is alive, agentic, and relating through a plurality of 'voices' so different from our own. This recognition is always already fraught and not-fully-intelligible within the ways-of-knowing-in-being that we inherit within the academy (Ahenakew 2016; Bang and Marin 2015; Kuokkanen 2010; Watts 2013). For example, a significant mode through which the disciplines discipline is the continued reproduction of Nature as a mute and passive backdrop against which cultural meanings are made (i.e. as 'nature') and projected.

Further, resisting and refusing (neo-)colonial practices of and in place also entails attuning to the humanities *othered* by Western humanism, such as Indigenous ways-of-living-with-Nature (see Battiste et al. 2005; Watts 2013). We see this as taking seriously the notion that posthumanist theories call for a double(d) decentering of *both* the human *and* Western humanism. This entails problematizing the positioning of the 'ontological turn'—where post-humanisms are situated—as but a recent turn within the academy. Above and beyond challenging claims of "newness", we contend that this positioning risks subsuming or suturing over the ways in which Indigenous ways-of-knowing-in-being have been thinking and practicing co-constitutive relations to other-than- and more-than-human worlds since time immemorial, and thus differentially (re)producing (neo-)colonial relations (see Bang and Marin 2015; Todd 2016; Watts 2013). As Todd (2016) states explicitly, 'ontology' might come to be 'just another word for colonialism' if these dynamics go unmarked and unchallenged. Herein, one of the ways we attend to this erasure is through the politics of citation. We aim to privilege and think with Indigenous thought-practices that have been working within, against, and beyond Western humanism since the beginnings of colonization.

In this chapter, we engage with the (never innocent) task of acknowledging, accounting for, and being ethically accountable to Indigenous place (as more than 'nature'). Specifically, we are guided by a central question posed by Ahenakew (2017: 81): 'how can we (re)learn to listen to and be taught by the land, in the context of ongoing efforts to objectify, to commodify, to silence, or to speak for the land?' We begin by turning to Nxumalo's (2016) 'refiguring presences'—'a decolonial ethics of unsettling presences and absences' (Nxumalo and Cedillo 2017: 104)—to orient our work of attending to and troubling the ways in which absent presences (e.g. curriculum of Land as settler property and economic resource) and present absences (e.g. Indigenous resurgence) come to create, complicate, differ, and defer *response-able* (Kuokkanen 2007, 2010) possibilities of engaging with place. From this orientation, we consider (a) troubling the Western modernist nature/culture binary and (b) Indigenous forms of storying place to generate new analytic questions, types of findings, and possibilities for representing knowledge claims. Next, we provide glances at our place stories of (re)learning to listen to and be taught by human, natural, and spirit worlds in relation in the context of Indigenous education in higher education in Lamas, Peru. Lastly, we discuss how Indigenous relational ontologies—with deep roots in living places and spiritual practices—enhanced our understanding of their role in reimagining pedagogy, practice and research in higher education.

Methods and Data Sources

Our approach to inquiry in this chapter is largely philosophical. However, to demonstrate the practical applications of theory building, select data productions are presented. As a means to refigure the nature/culture binary and Indigenous forms of storying place we re-present our stories of participating with/in a month-long graduate-level summer institute offered through a Canadian faculty of education. The summer institute focused on the traditional technologies of the Kichwa-Lamista Indigenous peoples and took place in Lamas, Peru. The data includes our journals, pictures, and videos to open up space to (re)consider absent presences and present absences, other-than and more-than human agency, a metaphysics of becoming and ever shifting norms of bodily production, and regeneration of relational knowledge in higher education.

Theoretical and Methodological Framing

Refiguring Presences

While not new to attending to inconsistencies, snags, and ruptures in the (neo-)colonial fabric of educational research, we are inspired by and turn to Nxumalo's (2016: 642) 'refiguring presences', which is designed to orient work within, against, and beyond 'spectres of settler colonialism in everyday place encounters.' Nxumalo (2016: 641, emphasis in original) frames her use of and motivation for refiguring presences:

> I draw inspiration from Anishinaabe scholar Leanne Simpson's… call for *presencing* as anti-colonial acts that resist the erasures of Indigenous presences from settler colonial places and politicize engagements with place. I use the concept *refiguring* to emphasize orientations to research that re-animate, re-think and relate differently to absent presences in everyday place encounters, and that resist the normative practices and taken-for-granted understandings therein.

In addition to emphasizing how settler colonialism makes both Indigeneity and Nature its abject Other, refiguring presences reveals and creates space to non-innocently reconfigure the ways in which the three (i.e. settler colonialism, Indigeneity, and Nature) are always already related in micro-political everyday moments. It does so by simultaneously:

(a) 'engag[ing] with Indigenous relationalities to counter (neo)colonial erasures in connection with knowledge production in the academy' (Nxumalo 2016: 647).
(b) 'shifting attention from the child as the subject of research and practice to [learners'] entanglements within multiple human and more-than-human relations' (Nxumalo 2016: 645).

This orientation continuously reminds us of the de/colonizing character of Indigenous education generally, and Indigenous and place-based education in this exploration. Like others (e.g. Rhee and Subreenduth 2006) we utilize the term de/colonizing to signal the ways in which decolonizing initiatives enfold (neo-)colonial logics and ways of being in relation. As we explain elsewhere (Higgins and Madden 2017: 35):

> De/colonizing underscores the complexity of the material-discursive structures, commitments, and practices of educational institutions and the Indigenizing initiatives they pursue. It suggests that decolonization need not be (and conceivably cannot be) constructed in neat opposition to colonization, and calls for consistent examination of colonial logics and productions that seep into hybrid colonizing and decolonizing contexts

Nxumalo (2016) creatively and critically draws from multiple theoretical approaches in developing refiguring presences as a theoretical orientation. This weaving can be viewed as simultaneously resisting and refusing the (neo-)colonial desire for theoretical purity based on the recognition that no singular theory could ever account for or be ethically accountable to the complex and contingent relations that are at play in everyday placed encounters on stolen land.

Tewa scholar Gregory Cajete (2000: 27, emphasis ours) states that 'science in every form [or every account of and with Nature's other-than and more-than-humans] … is *a story* of the world'. As such, the ways in which we account for and are accountable to place becomes a significant site of reconfiguring absences and presences. However, Nxumalo (2016: 648) emphasizes that 'importantly, refiguring presences is not simply about making present that which is absent – for example, Indigenous relationalities are always 'already there', even as they remain as absent presences due to the erasures manifested through colonial worldings'. Furthermore, it is not possible to make 'fully' present that which is absent within the current logics of the academy. The attempt to fit Indigenous ways-of-knowing-in-being into Western modernist frameworks cannot be disassociated from the (neo-)colonial desires and discursive structures that require they 'fit in' in order to be considered valid or even valuable (see Ahenakew 2016; Higgins and Kim 2018). In other words, intelligibility largely shapes the Western academy's (and higher education's) response-ability. Yet, what is intelligible is also shaped by the academy's multiple vectors of power (Kuokkanen 2010). In turn, it is important to work towards writing 'in a way that makes what is invisible noticeably absent so that it can be remembered and missed' Ahenakew (2016: 333).

Refiguring Analysis: Thinking Theory Within and Against the Nature/Culture Binary

Guided by a desire to explore how reconfiguring presences can heighten perception of absent presences (e.g. erasures of Indigenous presences from settler colonial places) and present absences (e.g. spectres of settler colonialism in everyday place encounters) (see Table 17.1), we focus first on a particularly troublesome (neo-)colonial complexity and complicity in Indigenous and place-based education: the nature/culture binary. In short, the nature/culture binary is a Western modernist ontological configuration (i.e. a configuration of *what is*) through which Nature and Culture are conceptualized and enacted as wholly separate and separable, marked by a relation of dichotomous exclusivity (i.e. Nature is what Culture is not, and vice versa).

This dichotomy matters when Culture is continuously (re)defined as that of Western modernity. Simultaneously, its abject alterity—Nature and those 'closer to Nature'—is consistently positioned in opposition and associated with characteristic such as un-agentic, un-cultured, irrational, and wild. Further, (neo-)colonial logics position and continually reaffirm the nature/culture binary not as *an* ontology, but rather *the* (only) ontological configuration. Some knowledge systems, such as Western modern science, are established as 'real' and universal, while others like Indigenous ways-of-knowing-in-being are constructed as cultural beliefs and assumptions. This dichotomy relegates Indigenous relational ontologies to the realm of absent presence and (re)presents them as a less valid or invalid epistemological framework from which to know Nature (see Ahenakew 2016; Higgins and Kim 2018). Such often entails equating Indigenous place-thought with the Eurocentric concept of animism, and makes other negative forms of separation and separability possible. For example, the past and present are often constructed in mutually exclusive ways that place settlers in the present and Indigenous peoples in the past.

Displacing the nature/culture binary is of particular significance in conceptualizing (and to some extent (re)presenting) Indigenous

Table 17.1 Reconfiguring presences + nature/culture and Indigenous storywork

Theorist/theory or orientation	Schematic cue (Jackson and Mazzei 2012)	Analytic questions/frames produced through thinking with theory (Jackson and Mazzei 2012)	From this orientation, consideration of the Western modernist nature/culture binary (to generate new analytic questions, types of findings, and possibilities for representing knowledge claims)	From this orientation consideration of Indigenous storywork (to generate new analytic questions, types of findings, and possibilities for representing knowledge claims)
Nxumalo/ refiguring presences (2016)	Unsettling presence/absence	• How does reconfiguring presences heighten perception of absent presences (e.g. erasures of Indigenous presences from settler colonial places) and present absences (e.g. spectres of settler colonialism in everyday place encounters)? • How might it offer opportunities to challenge how these (seeming) invisibilities shape response-able possibilities of engaging with place? • How does refiguring presences offer frames to reveal the ways in which settler colonialism, Indigeneity, and Nature are always already entangled in micro-political everyday moments?	• How are the landscapes in which we learn anthropogenic? • Where do we see evidence of Indigenous peoples sustaining and sustained by their ecologies since time immemorial? • How are more-than-human agents contributing to the regeneration of the world's ongoing becoming? • What are the ritualized actions and ceremony that confirm relationship with and enact reciprocity among spirit, human, and natural worlds?	• If, through storywork, the whole (i.e. the ecology of relationships) is enfolded in the part (i.e. the story), (how) do relations of power gives shape to the ecology of relationships presented? What modes of representation might shine light on these never innocent interactions? • How is the listener (or reader) engaged in relational meaning-making as a de/colonizing subject through this reconfigured storywork? What components of human interiority (i.e. mind, body, heart, and spirit) are brought into relation and nurtured? What components are not? How are particular components disciplined (e.g. through writing, norms of a particular field) to remain as absent presences? What strategies might work against these omissions? • How do colonial structures and strategies act as barriers to bringing a human interiority in proximal relation with other-than-and-more-than-human exteriority? • How might a reconfigured storywork work against cultivating a notion of response-ability to one's local ecology of relationships that is over-coded by lovely knowledge?

and place-based education to shine light on its de/colonizing character. Unperturbed, this binary acts as a form 'colonial containment—whether arrogant or benevolent' (Kuokkanen 2010: 70). 'Nature' is either arrogantly (re)produced as a site of knowledge (i.e. science), extraction, and/or ownership (i.e. settler colonialism) or benevolently as a romanticized site to be protected and conserved. While the latter can work against the ever growing environmental precarity of our contemporary moment, both rely on the construction of 'nature' as separated from and opposed to culture (e.g. wilderness) described above. Reconfiguring nature/culture towards (re)learning from and being accountable to natural-cultural presences in storying our participation in Indigenous education on the traditional territory of the Kichwa-Lamistas might involve revealing the ways in which *all* landscapes are anthropogenic (i.e. shaped in part through human agency). We attempt to trouble the notion of wild place (and by extension wild peoples and wild resources) that not only denies the agency of place, but obscures how Indigenous peoples have been sustaining and sustained by their ecologies since time immemorial. Further, if we are to take Indigenous thought seriously, our storying must recognize that there are also *more-than-human* (i.e. spiritual) agents and actors contributing to the regeneration of the world's ongoing becoming (see Apffel-Marglin 2011; Cajete 1994, 2000). The spirit world, along with the ritualized actions and ceremonies that confirm and enact its reciprocal relationship with human and natural worlds, is often conspicuously absent in discussion of education. We suggest that these approaches to reconfiguring (see Table 17.1) work against the logics that make possible and palatable the individualistic and economic practices that result in ecological devastation of the places in which Indigenous knowledge sits (Bang and Marin 2015; Watts 2013).

Refiguring (Re)Presentation: Thinking Theory with Indigenous Storywork

Refiguring presences invites us not only to attend to *whose* knowledge is with/in the interplay of absence and presence but also *through* whose knowledge this comes to be produced. Thinking Indigenous storywork through this orientation provided us with locations to labour in (re)presenting our engagement anew. Here, we highlight how Indigenous storywork continues to be used as an ongoing tradition, as well as how thinking this approach alongside refiguring presences helps us imagine (re)storying our non-innocent engagements anew in de/colonizing contexts.

Indigenous storywork, since time immemorial, is conceptualized and enacted as a multi-relational performative act in which the whole (i.e. the ecology of relationships) is enfolded in the part (i.e. the story). These relations are epistemological, ontological, and ethical. First, it works to create a relationship between humans. Sto:lo scholar Jo-Ann Archibald (2008) states that Indigenous storywork does not prescriptively teach. Rather, it operates as a differential pedagogy in which the listener (or reader) is required to engage in relational meaning-making practice (Archibald 2008: 112):

> A synergistic action happens between the storyteller and story, but it is the storyteller who ultimately gives breath, or life, to the story. From listening to and reading what storytellers say about making meaning from story, I have learned that the traditional ways favour no or very little direct guidance from the storyteller.

It brings what is sometimes represented as human interiority into relation. As Archibald (2008: 143) states, 'Indigenous storywork is not an easy process but it is essential to educating the heart, mind, body, and spirit.' Secondly, storywork brings into proximal relation an other-than-, and more-than-human exteriority. Storywork always already operates as a rich source of knowledge *about* the natural world yet its differential strength is that it is conceived of and enacted as a way of knowing *with* Nature (Barnhardt and Kawagley 2008; Cajete 1994, 2000). Lastly, knowing *with* and *through* story entails response-ability: 'the communal principle of storytelling implies that a listener is or becomes a member of the community' (Archibald 2008: 26). In other words, storywork is at once the gift of an invitation, as well as a responsibility that precedes *being* in the form of (re)telling and a living with *a* story (Archibald 2008: 126):

Practicing respect and responsibility in relationships with people and toward storywork led to a traditional concept of reciprocity. Within many Indigenous cultures, one is taught to pass on what she/he has learned to those who are interested. This passing on of knowledge is a way of perpetuating it.

In short, Indigenous storywork can be said to be a differential enactment and ontological articulation of an ecology of relationships—it is perhaps for this reason that Cherokee author Thomas King (2003: 2) states 'the truth about stories is that that's all we are'. *Place, story,* and *ethics* in Indigenous paradigms are often co-constitutive by design. Place-stories not only express a sacred geography of place, but also outline what it means to *be* of that place and the responsibilities towards nurturing those places (Cajete 1994, 2000).

Yet, to think refiguring presences alongside Indigenous storywork invites an 'intentional experimentation with how to notice the material-discursive boundaries and hierarchical orderings that come to matter in encounters with particular settler colonial places' (Nxumalo 2016: 644). It is to resist taking up Indigenous ways-of-knowing as strictly lovely knowledge. It is a commitment to also take up the difficult knowledge of (neo-)colonial relations of power that often 'materialize place stories in diverse ways' (Nxumalo 2016: 644). These de/colonizing relations are not only enfolded within part of the story, but also the communicative moment of storying. What might it mean to consider a de/colonizing subject as the recipient? Further, how do the disciplines come to discipline this scene of address? What can(not) be said and what can(not) be heard as a function of longstanding forms of Indigenous erasure?

Place Stories and Storying Place

In this section, we draw inspiration from the analytic questions produced through thinking Nxumalo's (2016) reconfiguring presences alongside reworkings of nature/culture and Indigenous storywork to revisit and represent our stories of engaging research (Marc) and coursework (Brooke) with/in a month-long graduate-level summer institute in Lamas, Peru.

Marc: From Interview to Intra-view

As I began my first interview with Frédérique Apffel-Marglin, I stuck *very* closely to the script via the interview questions I had written. I was *being* and *becoming* rigid. Perhaps I was embodying the simple wooden chair in the outdoor classroom that I had been sitting on for weeks. Perhaps it was embodying me. Or more specifically, the me shaped by the multiple forms of methodological *rigor* (*mortis*) that I had inherited in my learning journey up-to-that point; their assumptions, beliefs, and practices coalescing in a research methodology that was (not) my own. I was curious and confused as the interview was going in a direction that was drastically different than what I had envisioned.

Yet, excess happens. I assumed that Frédérique's voice in the interview would echo the one produced through my reading of her 2011 book, *Subversive Spiritualities: How Rituals Enact the World*. Linking Indigeneity and new materialisms, this work centres the pedagogical potentiality of ritual, while also reversing the gaze back onto Western modern ways-of-knowing-in-being. I wanted to learn more about what this pairing might allow in terms of rupturing the Western modern metaphysics that defer possibilities of Indigenous justice-to-come. However, I hadn't considered how the differential flows and intensities of space, time, matter, and meaning between encounters would produce voice beyond the ways in which such a metaphysics enacts (fore)closure and containment. I would need to 'tune-up' my apparatus and work towards being attuned.

Emerging through interference patterns is the entanglement of the personal, the political, knowing, and being. From the get-go, I (re)produce frames that separate theory from everyday practice through designing and asking interview questions that assumed and obscured Frederique's theoretical and methodological inclinations. Despite the cuts I made, Frederique responds with a narrative that is deeply personal and tied to her life story within, beyond, before, and after her time in the academy.

Frédérique states that if her interdisciplinary theory-practice is as rich as I suggest, it isn't necessarily due to an explicit engagement with methodology. Rather, it may be a production of a tangle of material/discursive/spiritual life experiences by which she was had. For example, debates with her ex-husband—an economist—required interdisciplinary and cross paradigmatic tinkering to access a spectrum of tools in order to stay in 'the game'. Even if everyday theorizing was never fully hers, the intent was always deeply strategic. Perhaps entirely appropriate to someone who works with/in post-Cartesian and Indigenous frameworks towards regenerating Kichwa-Lamista knowledges, theory and methodology are emerging as neither static or chosen, but rather enacted and lived. Furthermore, they are not something that you choose, but in some ways, they choose you.

> *woof   thump thump thump*
> *bark   thump thump thump*
> *grrr…owl bark woof woof bark woof bark bark*
> *Fussing over a fence, the dogs remind us of the fervour, futility, and, oddly enough, the fun that goes with fencing (in/out natural-cultural bodies).*

Place calls: *Hello?* The dogs, ensuring their 'voices' are heard, make their first (interview) visit amongst many. The holes in the fence configure the ways in which they see and greet one another, making it impossible for us to forget about the other-than-humans around while talking about other-than-humans. As the neighbouring dogs on the *other side* of the fence bark, the Sachamama dogs—who had been chaperoning student runs each morning—continue to take their ongoing roles and responsibilities seriously by re-joining the chorus. They remind us of the importance of porosity, of having a hole in one's soul (or methodology!). While this might evoke images of one's guts or essence leaking out, or socio-natural toxicity seeping in (or out if you are ill, or ill-intentioned), it is this porosity that allows for the ongoing re(con)figuration of relations through the differential production of bodily boundaries.

As Frédérique continues discussing ritualized enactments, I begin to make connections with *elsewheres* and *elsewhens* that are enfolded into the *here-now*. The feasting-body in Shukshuyaku, the community we've just returned from after a multi-day stay, comes to mind-body-heart-spirit (the physicality of the graduate coursework was forever juxtaposed to the university's motto: 'a place of mind'). The feasting-body's phases, processes, flows, and intensities blur Cartesian bodies that compose this assemblage: human bodies preparing and consuming the feast, other-than-human bodies being prepared and consuming alongside, as well as the more-than-human bodies receive our offerings in seemingly imperceptible ways (although I am also learning to attune to more-than-humans as well).

The elsewheres and elsewhens of the feast come to bear on the entanglement of meaning-matter-spirit: the spirit of the vegetables grown through labouring the community gardens using the revitalized knowledges and techniques of the ancestors; the recipes they inspired and the grinding, pounding, kneading, stirring they required; the fired clay on which they were served; and their service in the form of offerings to the spirits come into focus. Not to mention the conquistadors who laid claim to the land hundreds of years ago and those who continue to do so in the name of economics; this ceremony is done despite them. The feasting-body is an infinite and differential regression and progression with a built-in consciousness.

Brooke: Sachamama Becomings

scratch hisscrackle
phewwwww
crackle
phewwwww

Sachamama hums the constant sound of a low hanging electrical wire whose insulation is worn from sharp toes and beaks. White noise overlaid with a winged symphony, punctuated by a promiscuous parrot catcalling *indiscriminately*—whoot whooooo.

I inhale the harsh mapacho and silently introduce myself to the rainforest, before asking permission to enter. As I exhale, I attempt to direct the smoke towards the path that lies ahead. However, it binds with the offerings of my classmates, forming a thick cloud that hangs in the heavy noon air. At the protection ritual that initiated our arrival to

Kichwa-Lamista traditional territory, we learned mapacho also purifies. I wonder, 'How am I going to cleanse the top of my head and the back of my neck like Don Abillio did?' I contort my lips and blow upwards unsuccessfully, laughing at a vision of myself as a displaced and visibly uncomfortable Elvis impersonator.

I look left and right hoping to recruit a puffing partner when I glimpse Rylee, my classmate Roxane's 11 year-old son. I question whether the community Elder has allotted a ceremonial cigarette for Rylee? How will Roxane feel? For at least the second significant time today, I note the de/colonizing logics in which I am marinating (Battiste 2005). In this instance they play out in my inability to momentarily disentangle sacred medicines and their uses by many Nations since time immemorial from Big Tobacco's targeted advertising and smoking rates among Indigenous youth that are three times higher than their non-Indigenous counterparts (Canadian Paediatric Society 2017)

The first instance—the morning's complicated curiosity—comes into focus. A motley crew of mostly student visitors line the interior perimeter of the tambo that has been temporarily erected for our short-term stay in Shukshuyaku. We're here from Vancouver, BC to learn about pre-Columbian Amazonian processes of producing *terra preta de indio* (Indian black earth; yana allpa in Quechua). Regeneration effort arc largely being facilitated by Frédérique Apffel-Marglin's *Sachamama Center for Biocultural Regeneration* (2018) and piloted through partnerships with several surrounding Indigenous communities. The technologies are literally yielding fruit in the form of bountiful and diverse harvests, nutrient rich soil, revitalization of ritualized actions that regenerate life ways, and a modest inflow of eco-tourists and educators for social and environmental justice like ourselves. Perhaps in an attempt to build relationship, Frederique gestures towards our instructors and several others in the class and says to community members in Spanish, then English 'They're also Indigenous. They're Indigenous like you.' In response to little perceivable reaction, our interpreter tries again in Quechua. Our hosts don't seem to see themselves reflected in the Indigenous/non-Indigenous binary being constructed. I question whether the spectrum of Indigeneity is just too vast in this instance to resonate. Our group is obviously not of this place—pink, swollen, and stuffed into head to toe Lululemon outfits we've begun referring to as bug suits that we don in a futile attempt to 'protect' ourselves from particular members of their community.

As we being to move with the forest, I take a cue from the tools I've honed as a science major; from getting ready with girlfriends on Saturday nights; from smudging with smoke from sage. Wafting and walking through the puff I've exhaled, I purify my head, chest, neck, hands, and take extra care with my feet as the shaman did. This is different from the Anishinaabe, Mi'kmaq, and Cree rituals I've participated in that concentrate on the openings that connect the internal body and the body in the world. I wonder why? Karlee told me earlier that, to her, the offerings signal her presence and intentions to the microorganisms we are about to harvest. I'm still struggling to really feel this, so I whisper a prayer of thanks for the many lives they will sustain and placate their impending eviction with promises of getting them drunk on sugar once it's all over. My prayers still come out creepy, calling to mind a warning like, 'I'm coming for youuuuu…..'

The knowledge holders navigate the terrain with precision as we follow like the snaking lines of ants that often join our outdoor classroom. Much to our delight, they use a thick stick to expose a sweet spot on the forest floor that appears to be blanketed with translucent cotton candy. We all gather around, genuinely ogling at the mass, seeing mould in a brand new light. I pull Rylee close and exclaim, 'See, it doesn't just grow on cheese!'

Now aware of what we're hunting, a new cohort of urban chacareros disperses. We're not exactly prepared, armed with 2 sacs, 2 gloves, and the vertically challenged sticks that Marc has pulled from a felled tree. What at first might have seemed like a limitation soon becomes a body that synchronizes. Marc gets us ready, doling out the pokers, sunblock, and water. Roxane balances Micah in a baby sling as she applies bugspray to our unit that is temporarily suffering from flesh sacrifices abound to the midges, mosquitos, and mites of Lamas. Rylee and I comb the brush and when he locates a patch of microorganisms, he runs over with a big smile to whisper, 'There's some over here.' Similarly, I want to learn with him, to see this place through the lens of youth. I cover up what I've just exposed before calling him over so that he can discover the monstrous bugs and twigs suspended by gossamer as I look on. We call to a classmate, a self-proclaimed city slicker, to loan us his gloved left hand for a moment. He is followed closely by a small group of women alternating turns of carrying the grain sack that is steadily filling.

As we head back to our community home, the knowledge holders finger plants, point to the canopy, and meticulously wield their machetes to liberate a trickle of brown liquid from a tree trunk. They share how Sachamama is at once a residence, place of worship, pharmacy, supermarket, and hardware store. They are not separate from this place—traces of their presence "all the way back and all the way forward" (Wolfe 2016) are becoming more apparent as we are guided to blur and reveal nature-culture. The spirit of the plants lives in us all as we ingest the garden's bounty that is fed by the *terra preta* we're learning to co-produce. The wild tobacco that lingers on my tongue acts as a mnemonic that reminds me to walk in a good way.

Conclusion

As Nxumalo and Cedillo (2017: 102) suggest, 'relational place stories hold potential to challenge modernist, anthropocentric settler colonial place relations while attending to [learner's] differential situatedness within specific places'. While Indigenous place stories hold rich representations of nature—stated otherwise, knowledge *about* nature when read with/in Cartesian representationalism—their potential lies in honouring a knowing-in-being *with* the plants, the water beings, the winged beings, the four-leggeds, the many-leggeds, and a wide range of other-than-human bodies that are teachers with/in the ecologies of relationships particular to place (Barnhardt and Kawagley 2008). As a pedagogy through which Indigenous peoples 'come to perceive themselves as living in a sea of relationships' (Cajete 2000: 178) in which humans are not the centre, reconfigured natural-cultural presences and storywork is a way to witness already existing complex relations and foster the possibility of new ones.

Yet, 'if it is literally the ground beneath our feet, why is it so difficult to acknowledge it?' (Kuokkanen 2010: 67). In acknowledging, as well as accounting for and being ethically accountable to, Indigenous place, we recognized the need to engage de/colonizing processes that come to resist, refuse, and resignify the ways in which (neo-)colonialism grounds, erases, and makes absent presences of places and peoples who have been involved in reciprocal nurturance since time immemorial. Nxumalo's (2016) 'refiguring presences' provided frames to imagine new possibilities for response-able engagement with and representation of place. This orientation, as our two place stories show, contests the Western modernist nature/culture binary and thinks with Indigenous storywork to generate new analytic questions, types of findings, and possibilities for representing knowledge claims. By providing glances at our place stories, we demonstrate our efforts of (re)learning to listen to and be taught by human, natural, and spirit worlds in relation in the context of Indigenous education in Lamas, Peru.

Our argument in this chapter is that shaping and being shaped by Indigenous place-stories allows us to non-innocently consider material-discursive bodily porosity and assemblages, alongside ways-of-knowing-in-being that might not only generate the world, but also (re)generate it. We finish with an invitation to differentially take up forms of responsibility that precede being and knowing in higher education: to work towards the (re)opening of responsiveness and response-ability towards Indigenous relational ontologies, and to attend to the ways in which they are always already inflecting becomings. As Thomas King (2003: 116) states, 'don't say in the years to come that you would have lived your life differently if only you had heard this story. You've heard it now'.

References

Ahenakew, C. (2016). Grafting Indigenous ways of knowing onto non-Indigenous ways of being. *International Review of Qualitative Research, 9*(3), 323–340.

Ahenakew, C. (2017). Mapping and complicating conversations about Indigenous education. *Diaspora, Indigenous, and Minority Education, 11*(2), 80–91.

Apffel-Marglin, F. (2011). *Subversive spiritualities: How rituals enact the world.* Oxford, UK: Oxford University Press.

Archibald, J. (2008). *Indigenous storywork: Educating the heart, mind, body, and spirit.* Vancouver, BC: UBC Press.

Bang, M., & Marin, A. (2015). Nature–culture constructs in science learning: Human/non-human agency and intentionality. *Journal of Research in Science Teaching, 52*(4), 530–544.

Barnhardt, R., & Kawagley, A. O. (2008). Chapter 16: Indigenous knowledge systems and education. *Yearbook of the National Society for the Study of Education, 107*(1), 223–241.

Battiste, M. (2005). You can't be the global doctor if you're the colonial disease. In P. Tripp & L. Muzzin (Eds.), *Teaching as activism: Equity meets environmentalism* (pp. 121–133). Montreal, QC: McGill-Queen's University Press.

Battiste, M., Bell, L., Findlay, I. M., Findlay, L., & Henderson, J. S. Y. (2005). Thinking place: Animating the Indigenous humanities in education. *The Australian Journal of Indigenous Education, 34,* 7–19.

Cajete, G. (1994). *Look to the mountain: An ecology of Indigenous education.* Skyland, NC: Kivaki Press.

Cajete, G. (2000). *Native science: Natural laws of interdependence.* Sante Fe, NM: Clear Light Publishers.

Canadian Paediatric Society. (2017). *Tobacco use and misuse among Indigenous children and youth in Canada.* Retrieved from https://www.cps.ca/en/documents/position/tobacco-aboriginal-people.

Higgins, M., & Kim, E. J. (2018). De/colonizing methodologies in science education: Rebraiding research theory-practice-ethics with Indigenous theories and theorists. *Cultural Studies of Science Education.* Advance online publication. https://doi.org/10.1007/s11422-018-9862-4.

Higgins, M., & Madden, B. (2017). (Not So) Monumental agents: De/Colonizing places of learning. *Canadian Social Studies, 49*(1), 34–38.

Jackson, A. Y., & Mazzei, L. (2012). *Thinking with theory in qualitative research: Viewing data across multiple perspectives.* New York, NY: Routledge.

King, T. (2003). *The truth about stories: A native narrative.* Toronto, ON: House of Anansi Press.

Kuokkanen, R. (2007). *Reshaping the university: Responsibility, Indigenous epistemes, and the logic of the gift.* Vancouver, BC: UBC Press.

Kuokkanen, R. (2010). The responsibility of the academy: A call for doing homework. *Journal of Curriculum Theorizing, 26*(3), 61–74.

Madden, B. (2015). Pedagogical pathways for Indigenous education with/in teacher education. *Teaching and Teacher Education, 51,* 1–15.

Marin, A., & Bang, M. (2015). Designing pedagogies for Indigenous science education: Finding our way to storywork. *Journal of American Indian Education, 54*(2), 29–51.

Nxumalo, F. (2016). Towards 'refiguring presences' as an anti-colonial orientation to research in early childhood studies. *International Journal of Qualitative Studies in Education, 29*(5), 640–654.

Nxumalo, F., & Cedillo, S. (2017). Decolonizing place in early childhood studies: Thinking with Indigenous onto-epistemologies and Black feminist geographies. *Global Studies of Childhood, 7*(2), 99–112.

Rhee, J., & Subreenduth, S. (2006). De/colonizing education: Examining transnational localities. *International Journal of Qualitative Studies in Education, 19*(5), 545–548.

Sachamama Center for Biocultural Regeneration. (2018). *Sachamama Center for Biocultural Regeneration: Protecting soil, regenerating culture in the Peruvian Amazon.* Retrieved from http://sachamamacenter.org/.

Simpson, L. B. (2014). Land as pedagogy: Nishnaabeg intelligence and rebellious transformation. *Decolonization: Indigeneity, Education & Society, 3*(3), 1–25.

Todd, Z. (2016). An Indigenous feminist's take on the ontological turn: 'Ontology' is just another word for colonialism. *Journal of Historical Sociology, 29*(1), 4–22.

Watts, V. (2013). Indigenous place-thought and agency amongst humans and non humans (First Woman and Sky Woman go on a European world tour!). *Decolonization: Indigeneity, Education & Society, 2*(1), 20–34.

Wildcat, M., McDonald, M., Irlbacher-Fox, S., & Coulthard, G. (2014). Learning from the land: Indigenous land based pedagogy and decolonization. *Decolonization: Indigeneity, Education & Society, 3*(3), 1–15.

Wolfe, A. (2016). *All the way back and all the way forward: Unpacking and understanding the legacy of the Indian residential school system* (Unpublished capping project). Edmonton, AB: University of Alberta.

18

Indigenous Education in Higher Education in Canada: Settler Re-Education Through New Materialist Theory

Jeannie Kerr

Introduction

In this viewpoint, I consider the contributions of new materialist theorizing to the field of Indigenous educational initiatives in Canadian universities in the context of Settler colonialism. My own experience in Indigenous education has been engaging teacher candidates of predominantly Settler and newer immigrant backgrounds with Indigenous knowledges, pedagogies and perspectives to inform their developing K-12 classroom praxis. Indigenous pedagogical priorities have been widely prioritized in higher education in Canada in recognition of the arduous work and revelations of the Truth and Reconciliation Commission of Canada (TRC 2015a), and their 'Calls to Action' (TRC 2015b). The TRC spent years collecting testimony of survivors of 'Indian Residential Schools' (IRS) that were dominant across Canada from the 1870s to the 1990s, and documented the colonial violences and abuses that were targeted towards Indigenous children. The TRC

J. Kerr (✉)
University of Winnipeg, Winnipeg, MB, Canada

© The Author(s) 2019
C. A. Taylor and A. Bayley (eds.), *Posthumanism and Higher Education*,
https://doi.org/10.1007/978-3-030-14672-6_18

positions the IRS System as part of a 'paternalistic and racist' system of exclusion for Indigenous peoples in Canada with ongoing societal legacies (TRC 2015a: VI). The national 'truth telling' (Regan 2010) and 'Calls to Action' (TRC 2015b) emerging from the TRC work have set the priorities in higher education of working to support educational experiences for Indigenous students, but also working to ensure that non-Indigenous people in Canada have a greater understanding of Indigenous perspectives and knowledges through their university experience (Cote-Meek 2017). In my institution at the University of Winnipeg, since the Fall of 2016 all students are required to complete an Indigenous Course Requirement for graduation. In this piece, I will first provide greater understanding of the material and discursive context of Settler colonialism in Canadian society, and my perspective on the related work of what I term Settler re-education in higher education. I will follow with a discussion of how new materialisms and Barad's theorization of agential realism provide theoretical grounding and pedagogical possibilities in Settler re-education. I will conclude with examples of pedagogical possibilities in higher education.

Settler Colonialism in Canada and the Need for Settler Re-Education

Settler re-education involves revealing the discursive productions and narratives that are entangled with the material experiences of Settler colonial society. Indigenous peoples continue to materially experience stark inequality and violences in Settler colonial society, yet the distinct role of Settler colonial policies are often masked and seemingly invisible within Settler society (Kerr and Parent, in press). Settler-Indigenous encounters, whether in the courts, child and family services, hospitals and educational institutions are still marked by subtle and overt colonial violences. These violences are directly related to colonial practices and assumptions about the nature of land ownership (Mackey 2016; Marker 2006), the superiority and benevolence of Settler systems and actors (Battiste and Henderson 2009; Thobani 2012); the universalizing of Euro-Western knowledges (Battiste and Henderson 2009;

Kuokkanen 2003); and colonial legislation that provides Settler governments with authority to act on Indigenous territory (Palmater 2015). The term Settler in Settler colonial theorizing is not used in the way of validating land claims of Euro-descendant peoples in Canada, but to acknowledge the context of dispossession and displacement of Indigenous peoples in relation to their territories that is performed through bodies enacting Settler sovereign capacities. Veracini (2010) critically points out that white Settlers manifest a sovereign capacity achieved through colonial systems of authority. Whereas he terms 'exogenous others' as those who settle but do not manifest a sovereign capacity through being racialized within colonial dynamics. I identify as a white Settler to acknowledge my, and my ancestors', participation in problematic and ongoing colonial relations and as an imperative to recognize and enact ethical relations with Indigenous peoples in the territories in which I live.

A key feature of the higher educational context are the Canadian meta-narratives that most non-Indigenous students bring with them into the higher education classroom. The eighteenth to nineteenth century migration of European peoples to Indigenous territories is retold through a meta-narrative of the 'courageous pioneers and adventurers' bringing European 'civilization' to wild and dangerous places in the forging of a new nation (Donald 2012: 95). This meta-narrative is told in slightly different ways, in different places, but is generally taught through places of public pedagogy such as monuments and art galleries, national holiday events, and public gatherings, and is reinforced in Canadian public education (Anderson 2017; Mackey 2002). Donald (2012: 95) refers to these nationalistic performances as 'truth-myths'—'idealized versions of history that are made simple and coherent' in their reference to true experiences for dominant group members that 'morph into hegemonic expression of existing value structures and worldviews of the dominant groups.' In the latter half of the twentieth century this Settler nationalist mythology slowly eroded and became background to a newer meta-narrative of multiculturalism. This narrative is no less mythic in touting Canada's inclusionary stance where non-European immigrants and cultural difference are welcome and foundational to Canadian identity

(Anderson 2017; Mackey 2002; St. Denis 2011). Similarly troublesome in its ultimate exclusionary expression, this multicultural national mythology represents white Euro-descendant Canadians as innocent and beneficent in welcoming the cultural *other* and thus continues to hide and perpetuate the violences of Settler colonialism and the dominance of white Euro-descendant peoples in Settler society (Kerr and Andreotti 2017; Mackey 2002; Marker 2006; St. Denis 2011; Thobani 2012). Donald (2012) argues that these truth-myths embody colonial logics that 'serve to naturalize assumed divides' (p. 92) and thus support a problematic 'denial of relationality' between Settlers and Indigenous peoples (p. 102). In my view, it is this denial of relationality that needs to be a key target of Settler re-education, and the most generative place for new materialist theorizing.

Another important feature of the higher education context is Settler students' misrecognition of Indigenous knowledge and perspectives which results in their dismissals of and/or paternalistic engagements with Indigenous knowledges. The Eurocentric nature of curriculum in the Canadian education context is recognized as being related to the cognitive imperialism of Settler colonialism (Battiste 2005; Battiste and Henderson 2009). Examples of Eurocentricity in curriculum are: the nature of dividing curricular areas into specific disciplines that are foundational to Euro-Western ways of understanding the world; assuming that written forms of knowledge are unrelated to place but are codifications of the highest forms of understanding and applicable universally; assuming that ethics is something that might be applied to areas of investigation instead of constitutive of it; and centring Euro-Western people as the exemplars of those who have developed the highest forms of knowledge. This Eurocentricity emerges from the practices of universalizing epistemic assumptions and commitments of Euro-Western traditions of thought and practice within the grammars and logics of modernity that (re)configure these systems in educational contexts across the globe (Ahenakew et al. 2014; Mignolo 2011).

I see these Eurocentric epistemic assumptions performed in the classroom. The students generally have been taught through years of participation in society and educational systems that valid knowledge is written, abstract and universal, without recognizing the Euro-cultural context and history that informs these problematic epistemic *certainties*. Indigenous knowledges are not antithetical to Euro-Western knowledges, but overlap and differ due to ontological distinctions. Indigenous knowledges are unique to diverse territories and Indigenous cultures, and emerge from specific places—based on thousands of years of engaging as relatives with the spiritual and material beings in these places through ceremony and study. Within this view there is a pluriversal perspective that knowledge is not possibly universal, but emerges in a multiplicity through diverse ways of the body participating in different places with different beings. When Settler students engage with Indigenous knowledge that emerges in oral, located and pluriversal ways, there is at times a rejection or refusal (Kerr 2014), and other times a colonial fascination that engages Indigenous knowledge and peoples as exotic cultural artifacts (Dion 2007). I can recognize these dynamics, as I have participated in these dynamics as a Settler.

New Materialist Theorizations—Pedagogical Possibilities in Settler Re-Education

In my view, non-Indigenous students need to engage in what Barad (2014) terms a *re-turning* to disrupt specific problematic certainties that preclude an ethical relationship with Indigenous peoples, knowledges and territories. By re-turning Barad (2014: 168) refers to a multiplicity of processes that involves turning something 'over and over again.' While I discuss re-turning later in this piece, for now I would highlight that the need for re-turning emerges from non-Indigenous students' often:

- unexamined immersion in Canadian nationalist narratives;
- unquestioned acceptance of colonial stereotypes, constructed divides and government sanctioned violence to Indigenous peoples;
- embodied experience of white privilege;
- and long-term participation in Eurocentric education.

I too have gone through experiences of re-turning as a second-generation Settler in Canada—and continue to do so. Some of these experiences have been intentional and some emerge without my conscious intentionality. An example of this was in my work in garden-based education in teacher education where I completely disregarded a Mayan-based garden as it was not constituted by the familiar colonial rows and separations to which I am familiar. I then passed this disregard on to teacher candidates through my position of authority in the institution. It was through re-turning to this experience that I was able to understand the particularity of my own forms of colonial dominance and complicity within my institutional work of which I had been unaware. I would argue that there is a period of *getting ready to listen* to Indigenous scholars and community members in Settler re-education and that new materialist thinking can provide some transitional supports for engaging in non-dominant ways of being and knowing. In what follows, I suggest four ways in which new materialist theorizing has significant potential in this task.

Deconstructions of the Material-Discursive Within Colonial Intra-Activity

New materialist theorizing directly addresses binaries emerging from modernity, as do post-structural and critical thought, but offers something more in recognizing the significance of materiality as entangled with meaning. Alaimo and Hekman (2008) acknowledge that the linguistic/discursive turn arising from post-structuralist theory allows for deconstructions of dichotomies in modern thought regarding culture/nature, mind/body, object/subject, and rationality/emotionality. Although these scholars point out that a post-structuralist orientation continues to operate within the language/reality dichotomy, due to post-structural scepticism of modernity's claim of access to the real and material, the effect is that the focus on representation, ideology and discourse excludes or evades the 'lived experience and corporeal practice and biological substance' of knowing (Alaimo and Hekman 2008: 4).

In Euro-Western thought, there has been a shifting focus on 'the lived body, the specular body, and the discursive body' (Palermo 2002: 170). In my view, new materialist theorizations maintain attentiveness to the discursive forces on a body without evading the material experience of that body intra-acting in an indeterminate and related world. In examinations of Settler colonial encounters that are marked by real cuts on real bodies, to the human and more-than-human, the materiality of colonial encounter cannot be evaded through an exclusionary focus on discursive performances.

As a key new materialist theorization, Karen Barad's agential realism provides generative theoretical space wherein Settler colonial logics and practices of material-discursive divides can be deconstructed. In Barad's agential realist elaboration, phenomena are the *intra-acting* movements of things that are always already in entangled relations. Barad (2007: 30) coins the term intra-relational to highlight the point that no thing can exist outside of relations: 'reality is not composed of things-in-themselves or things-behind-phenomena but things in phenomena.' In her theorization, boundaries are constituted by material and discursive agent*s* enacting an agential cut as the 'local condition of exteriority' within phenomena (p. 30). Barad states that these cuts are specific agential practices/intra-actions/performances that cause dynamic (re)configurations of the world and leave real marks on real bodies. The cuts by both material and discursive practices bring the world into its ongoing and differentiated becoming (p. 30). The enactment of 'exteriority-within-phenomena' (Barad 2014: 177) is a material practice that is agential regardless of conscious intention. In Barad's theorization, agency is not an attribute of a subject or an object, but is the 'condition of intra-acting' (Barad 2008: 144). In this view, beings within phenomena are never passive, but actively being and doing in the material and discursive conditions within which they are in relation—whether such agency is consciously intentional or not. These theorizations guide my work as I draw students to contemplate the phenomenon of Settler colonialism and the discursive constructions that problematically frame their lives as distinctly separate from Indigenous peoples. Through looking at their own immersion in Settler colonial society through the perspectives of Indigenous scholars and community members, they have the possibility to understand the distinct inequality experienced by Indigenous peoples in their own society and their own agency within their inescapable entanglement in this phenomenon.

Recognizing the Ethical Demands of Colonial Entanglement

Barad's theorization contains the resources to deconstruct Settler performativity of Canadian national narratives, and the colonial logics that support them, through theorizing non-intentional agency. First, the colonial logics of separation and the assumed material divide can be shown to be a discursive construction. Indigenous and non-Indigenous peoples are located on the same land and are materially intra-acting in colonial phenomena that have been (re)configuring over (at least) five hundred years. Yet the discursive productions of assumed divides create different material realities in Canadian society for Indigenous and non-Indigenous human bodies in terms of: experience of material comforts; freedom from Governmental restrictions (incarceration, child apprehension, land sovereignty, heightened policing); degree of access to potable water; well-being of more-than-human relatives; access to education; etc. Second, the discursive productions and material practices by Settlers and Settler governments enact agential cuts as active agents—as a condition of intra-acting. In this way there is a cutting together/apart (Barad 2014: 177) that (re)produces and further entangles a violent colonial entanglement.

The belief of non-Indigenous students in their own lack of relation and agency in colonial encounters, also known as 'settler moves to innocence' (Tuck and Yang 2012), is a common performance in the classroom. I have had many students who materially continue to benefit from colonialism, and who explain through meta-narratives that colonial violences are the result of actions in the past, and they do not recognize any relational responsibility for the material conditions of Indigenous peoples where they live. Using Barad's theorization helps reveal Settler performances that emerge with and through Canadian meta-narratives as part of colonial intra-actions—and that they are agential. Thus, providing the potential for bringing Settlers who see themselves as unrelated to the well-being of Indigenous peoples and more-than-human beings into the possibility of recognition of their agency in ongoing colonial entanglements.

Barad posits that these material and discursive *entanglements* of beings in relation are constituted by ethicality. This theorization offers a decidedly different way of understanding ethical responsibility in contrast to ancient and modern Euro-Western ethical traditions focused on moral rules or phronetic judgment (Kerr 2013: 77–78). Barad states that the entanglements are not an intertwining of separate entities, but rather irreducible relations of responsibility. As there is no inherent separateness, the localized cuts that both cut and entangle, create an otherness and thus entails an obligation or indebtedness to the other who is 'materially bound to, threaded through, the self' (Barad 2010: 265). In this sense, an entanglement is not meant to refer to the interconnectedness of all things, but to the specific material relations that bring about the ongoing differentiation in the world, and the ethical responsibility of being entangled. Barad clearly states that this is not the superimposition of human values onto the ontology of the world, but that the nature of matter entails an exposure to the *other* that requires ethicality. As Barad (2010: 265) states: 'Responsibility is not an obligation that the subject chooses but rather an incarnate relation that precedes the intentionality of consciousness.' This sense of ethical responsibility offers a way for Settlers to understand that their participation in Canadian Settler colonial society requires an ethical relation to Indigenous peoples that for many is currently unrecognized and often actively denied. Pedagogically, this requires that Settler students are brought to: recognize the narratives that are informing their sense of separation from Indigenous peoples and more-than-human relatives; understand the ways these narratives have manifested in their own material experiences; and provide them with the material opportunity to enact relations in the places they live with a sense of ethical responsibility. These recognitions are encouraged through getting out of the classroom and materially engaging with Indigenous peoples in community-based settings.

Recognizing Colonial Patterns Through Diffractions of Space-Time-Mattering

Barad elaborates within agential realism the important concepts of diffraction and space-time mattering, which I believe can help illuminate colonial patterns of encounter, as well as ethical responsibility that emerges through colonial intra-actions. As Barad (2014: 168) argues: 'Diffraction is not a set pattern, but rather an iterative (re)configuring of patterns of differentiating-entangling.' Barad's diffractive methodology of understanding phenomena through the multiplicity of traces of agential cuts is generative for engaging students in Settler re-education through examining colonial phenomenon in different places and across time. Through diffraction, it is possible to see the patterns of colonial encounters in varied places as iterative material-discursive (re)configurations of colonial entanglements. Through discussing quantum entanglements, Barad (2010) points out that space and time are phenomenal and do not exist as universals outside of phenomena. As diffractions are not constituted by time, agential cuts are not something that can be left in the past or erased. Barad (2012: 13) argues that 'diffraction is a matter of inheritance and indebtedness to the past as well as the future.' Conceptions of space-time mattering and diffraction reveal the current and ongoing indebtedness of Settlers through the inheritance of responsibility that is not only 'there-then' but 'here-now' (Barad 2010: 168).

Theorization of diffraction and space-time mattering is important pedagogically, as it moves from the focus of the individual in terms of colonial relations, to looking more specifically for patterns of colonial entanglement. Students can be encouraged to see how patterns manifest not only in the local context, but also the Canadian context, as well as globally. Patrick Wolfe (2006) considers the dynamics of racialization and genocidal tendencies in Settler colonial encounters to highlight that it is not that Settler colonial violence is only about where a person is, but how they are racialized in that context. Wolfe (2006: 388) draws attention to the racialization of African descendant and Indigenous peoples who become racialized as 'slave' and 'Indian' within different forms of violence and erasure—explaining that the racializations are 'made in the targeting.'

In this case, legal frameworks of Settler colonial governments in North America and beyond work to support the elimination and removal of Indigenous peoples to gain their land, while simultaneously expanding identification and control of African descendants to ensure their labour on that land. Tracing these movements through current and historical events, literature and art as told through the peoples that experience colonial violence, again provides a larger connection and understanding for students in examining their participation and ethical responsibilities.

Revealing Eurocentric Engagements with Indigenous Knowledges

The term *onto-epistem-ological* is coined by Barad to express the idea that our epistemological assumptions and commitments, and our ontological understandings, are mutually constitutive. Barad (2008) asserts a metaphysical position that knowing is inseparable from being, and both emerge from our material discursive experience of the world. In some contexts, Barad uses the word ethico-epistem-on-tological to acknowledge the fundamental ethical nature of all knowing and being (Barad 2012: 15). These theorizations are able to disrupt Eurocentric assumptions that knowledge is universal and objective, and that Euro-Western knowledges are somehow *culture-free*. Students often carry a view that Euro-Western peoples have knowledge, and Indigenous peoples have culture. Barad's theorization helps non-Indigenous students to appreciate that all knowing happens through the material-discursive experiences in which we participate within our socio-cultural context. Thus, their ways of engaging in knowing in the world have emerged from their culturally informed ideas of what is real and knowable— their ontological cultural assumptions. Further, that these ontological commitments are inseparable from how they will go about knowing—their culturally informed epistemic assumptions and relation to ethics. Self-understanding that students' ways of knowing in the world are not universal, but culturally emergent, helps to disrupt the preoccupation with Indigenous knowledge as a cultural artifact. These realizations can also disrupt beliefs in the superiority of their own ways of knowing and being in the world as they encounter Indigenous ethico-onto-epistemologies—hopefully avoiding problematic responses of dismissal and paternalism. In my teaching practice, I have students trace through their own experiences to identify their formative assumptions of knowing through their experiences as young children through to higher education. I help them to relate these foundational epistemic assumptions and commitments to their own cultural backgrounds to appreciate the cultural locatedness of their knowing. I then introduce Indigenous knowledge holders that engage similarly in relating cultural experience to knowledge as they foreground how they are taught and what they know through their culture.

Related Practices in Higher Education

My related practices in higher education classrooms attempt to engage students in a methodology of re-turning (Barad 2014) as a mode of intra-acting with diffraction where we are not merely reflecting on something, but turning it over and over again. In this sense, re-turning is paying attention to the diffracted patterns that emerge through material-discursive entanglements and related agential cuts. I feel that the grammars that Barad introduces can be somewhat overwhelming for under-graduate students in Settler re-education, and do not forefront her terminology and full theory in the practices I discuss here. In classrooms with non-Indigenous students engaging with Indigenous education there is already a degree of complexity that is being negotiated. Within the activities described here, I introduce Barad's terminology over time and gauge the level of theorization needed with each class. Throughout my classes, I engage students in an examination of their relations in located phenomena that they are invited to document through material experiences. Over the course of the semester, I ask students to document their experiences of relation to the entangled places where they teach, learn and live, through photographs, government documents, music, poetry and other mediums they feel are meaningful. I ask them to document their relations in the places that they live and move through. I also introduce them to a succession of

Indigenous scholars and community members, texts and art that offer critical counter-perspectives to Canadian meta-narratives and contrast to Euro-Western onto-epistemologies. Their related assignments rely on material/discursive re-turnings of the students' lived experience of meta-narratives, which is encouraged through engaging with Indigenous perspectives. The desire is for the students to:

- understand their ongoing entanglement and relational responsibility with Indigenous peoples in their Settler colonial context;
- recognize the material and discursive cuts in which they have been involved in both a material and embodied sense;
- illuminate the diffracted patterns being (re)constituted in space-time mattering in local and global contexts; and
- appreciate the ethical imperative that exists that has preceded the intentionality of consciousness.

Conclusion

This viewpoint has articulated the complex material and discursive context in which the work of Indigenous Education in Canada takes place. In the Settler colonial context of Canada, and the nature of the TRC Calls to Action, I have argued that there is a need for Settler re-education to engage non-Indigenous Canadians with Indigenous Education in higher education. And I have identified disrupting the logics, grammars and meta-narratives of colonial intra-actions as a priority. I have suggested that new materialist thinking can be an effective disruptive force, and have considered how Barad's agential realism might work to help non-Indigenous students recognize and trace their colonial intra-actions and related ethical responsibilities through a methodology of re-turning. It is my hope that engaging these theorizations with higher education students will help them *get ready to listen* to Indigenous scholars and scholarship in their coursework in Indigenous education, and have outlined four ways in which the work of re-turning may be enacted in higher education pedagogies. I share these ideas not in the sense of offering *solutions* within a teleological ethos of betterment and progress. I recognize the complicity of working in institutions and a society that is configured by modernity's grammars, and that seeks to solve problems and move on. By recognizing my own complicities within higher education, and the impossibility of ignoring the systemic inheritance in Settler colonial society, my aim is to work to support (re)configurations that are at once indeterminate but which aspire to ethical relation with Indigenous peoples in Canada. I am grateful to continue my work on the traditional territories of the Anishnabeg, Nêhiyawak, Oji-Cree, Dakota and Dene peoples and homeland of the Métis nation.

References

Ahenakew, C., Andreotti, V., Cooper, G., & Hireme, H. (2014). Beyond epistemic provincialism: De-provincializing Indigenous resistance. *AlterNative: An International Journal of Indigenous Peoples, 10*(3), 216–231.

Alaimo, S., & Hekman, S. (2008). *Material feminisms*. Bloomington: Indiana University Press.

Anderson, S. (2017). The stories nations tell: Sites of pedagogy, historical consciousness and national narratives. *Canadian Journal of Education, 40*(1), 1–38.

Barad, K. (2007). *Meeting the universe halfway: Quantum physics and the entanglement of matter and meaning*. Durham: Duke University Press.

Barad, K. (2008). Posthumanist performativity: Toward an understanding of how matter comes to matter. In S. Alaimo & S. Hekman (Eds.), *Material feminisms* (pp. 120–154). Bloomington: Indiana University Press.

Barad, K. (2010). Quantum entanglements and hauntological relations of inheritance: Dis/continuities, spacetime enfoldings, and justice-to-come. *Derrida Today, 3*(3), 240–268.

Barad, K. (2012). Intra-active entanglements—An interview with Karen Barad by M. Juelskjaer and Nete Schwennesen. *Women, Gender and Research, 1*(2), 10–24.

Barad, K. (2014). Diffracting diffraction: Cutting together-apart. *Parallax, 20*(3), 168–187. https://doi.org/10.1080/13534645.2014.927623.

Battiste, M. (2005). You can't be the global doctor if you're the colonial disease. In P. Tripp & L. Muzzins (Eds.), *Teaching as activism: Equity meets environmentalism* (pp. 121–133). Montreal and Kingston: McGill-Queen's University Press.

Battiste, M., & Henderson, J. S. Y. (2009). Naturalizing Indigenous knowledge in Eurocentric education. *Canadian Journal of Native Education, 32*(1), 5–18.

Cote-Meek, S. (2017). *Post-secondary education and reconciliation.* Retrieved from https://www.univcan.ca/media-room/media-releases/postsecondary-education-reconciliation/.

Dion, S. (2007). Disrupting molded images: Identities, responsibilities and relationships—Teachers and Indigenous subject material. *Teaching Education, 18*(4), 329–342.

Donald, D. (2012). Forts, colonial frontier logics, and Aboriginal-Canadian relations: Imagining decolonizing educational philosophies in Canadian contexts. In A. A. Abdi (Ed.), *Decolonizing philosophies of education* (pp. 91–111). Rotterdam: Sense Publishers.

Kerr, J. (2013). *Pedagogical thoughts on knowing bodies: The teacher educator encounters the Phronimos and the Elder* (Doctoral dissertation). Retrieved from cIRcle database at https://open.library.ubc.ca/cIRcle/collections/ubctheses/24/items/1.0165675.

Kerr, J. (2014). Western epistemic dominance and colonial structures: Considerations for thought and practice in programs of teacher education. *Decolonization: Indigeneity, Education & Society, 3*(2), 83–104.

Kerr, J., & Andreotti, V. (2017). Crossing borders in initial teacher education: Mapping dispositions to diversity and inequity. *Race Ethnicity and Education.* https://doi.org/10.1080/13613324.2017.1395326.

Kerr, J., & Parent, A. (in press). Contemporary colonialism and (im)possibilities in higher education: An anti-colonial response to reconciliation. In A. Kemp & S. Styres (Eds.), *Troubling trickster: Reconciliation and decolonization as colonial discourses.* Edmonton: University of Alberta Press.

Kuokkanen, R. (2003). Toward a new relation of hospitality in the academy. *American Indian Quarterly, 27*(1/2), 267–295.

Mackey, E. (2002). *In the house of difference: Cultural politics and national identity in Canada.* Toronto: University of Toronto Press.

Mackey, E. (2016). *Unsettled expectations: Uncertainty, land and settler expectations.* Winnipeg, BC: Fernwood Publishing.

Marker, M. (2006). After the Makah whale hunt: Indigenous knowledge and limits to multicultural discourse. *Urban Education, 41*(5), 482–505.

Mignolo, W. D. (2011). *The darker side of Western modernity: Global futures, decolonial options*. Durham: Duke University Press.

Palermo, J. (2002). *Poststructuralist readings of the pedagogical encounter*. New York: Peter Lang.

Palmater, Pam. (2015). *Indigenous nationhood: Empowering grassroots citizens*. Winnipeg: Fernwood Publishing.

Regan, P. (2010). *Unsettling the settler within: Indian residential schools, truth telling, and reconciliation in Canada*. Vancouver: UBC Press.

St. Denis, V. (2011). Silencing Aboriginal curricular content and perspectives through multiculturalism: 'There are other children here'. *Review of Education, Pedagogy, and Cultural Studies, 33*(4), 306–317.

Thobani, S. (2012). Empire, bare life and the constitution of whiteness: Sovereignty in the age of terror. *Borderlands E-Journal, 11*(1), 1–30.

Truth and Reconciliation Commission of Canada. (2015a). *Truth and Reconciliation Commission of Canada: Summary of the final report of the Truth and Reconciliation Commission of Canada*. Winnipeg: Truth and Reconciliation Commission of Canada. Retrieved from http://www.trc.ca/websites/trcinstitution/File/2015/Honouring_the_Truth_Reconciling_for_the_Future_July_23_2015.pdf.

Truth and Reconciliation Commission of Canada. (2015b). *Truth and Reconciliation Commission of Canada: Calls to action*. Winnipeg: Truth and Reconciliation Commission of Canada. Retrieved from http://www.trc.ca/websites/trcinstitution/File/2015/Findings/Calls_to_Action_English2.pdf.

Tuck, E., & Yang, K. W. (2012). Decolonization is not a metaphor. *Decolonization: Indigeneity, Education & Society, 1*(1), 1–40.

Veracini, L. (2010). *Settler colonialism: A theoretical overview*. London: Palgrave Macmillan.

Wolfe, Patrick. (2006). Settler colonialism and the elimination of the native. *Journal of Genocide Research, 8*(4), 387–409.

19

Posthuman Methodology and Pedagogy: Uneasy Assemblages and Affective Choreographies

Jennifer Charteris and Adele Nye

Introduction

Across the Australian Education sector, the rise of posthumanism (Braidotti 2016) has prompted new and fresh ways of theorising material relationalities. A plethora of research has centred the notions of vital materialism and affect: in early childhood research (Taylor and Pacinini-Ketchabaw 2015); studies of kindergarten through to year 12 schooling (Mayes 2017; Wolf 2017); and higher education (Charteris et al. 2016). These moves offer scope to destabilise existing hierarchies of knowledge production and perceptions of pedagogical practice through recognising the vitality of matter (Bennett 2010), the importance of the non-human, and the role of affective practices.

J. Charteris (✉) · A. Nye
University of New England, Armidale, NSW, Australia
e-mail: jcharte5@une.edu.au

A. Nye
e-mail: anye@une.edu.au

As researchers in an Australian regional university, we welcome opportunities to up-end our own taken-for-granted assumptions about how we locate our embodied human selves in our research practice, the assemblages we are enfolded in, and the entanglements we encounter. Assemblages or *agencements* are combinations of various elements (Deleuze and Guattari 1987) and, as such, are 'troublesome'—mixed up and 'overflowing with both pain and joy' (Haraway 2016: 1). In this chapter, we write of an affective choreography (Youdell and Armstrong 2011) undertaken at a national education research conference, which involved first curating affective data into an 'uneasy assemblage' (Bone and Blaise 2015: 18). An affective choreography is embodied movement that co-constructs entities (human and non-human) and is 'productive of both reduction or affirmation' (Wolf 2017: 65). Our provocation is that posthuman pedagogy in higher education can evoke affective choreographies which are immersed in affective relations that influence the body's capacity to act.

We draw on pedagogic work in conference spaces as a context for posthuman practice. The particular research presentation leveraged a posthuman pedagogic (uneasy) assemblage, constituting an affective choreography with a multiplicity of speeds and slownesses that exceeded its form in the materiality of the conference space and place. Affective choreographies are multiplicities that remove the focus from the individual subject and body to a 'concern with bodies as amalgam and an analysis that foregrounds collectivities and the event and so is anti-subjectivation' (Youdell and Armstrong 2011: 144).

We like the fluidity and postidentitarian nature of choreography. As Manning (2013: 101) points out, 'choreography becomes a field for movement expression when the body becomes an intensive participant with the evolving milieu rather than simply the instigator of the action'. In the choreographies of the neoliberal university, where bodies and their products are quantified, women are often positioned as 'lacking' (Honan et al. 2015: 47), and there can be a perverse sense of 'feeling managed, compared, stressed, demoralised, distracted and fragmented by the constant and frantic pace, work overload and relentless demands for increased product and productivity in jobs with no boundaries'

(Black et al. 2017: 139). Through taking up posthuman pedagogies and research practices, we argue that it is possible to practice otherwise, to mobilise feminist arguments, safely navigate and trouble boundaries of academicity (Charteris et al. 2016) and engage with the interplay of human and non-human multiplicities of the workplace.

This chapter commences with an outline of a data curation process as an uneasy assemblage (Bone and Blaise 2015), as a means for reimagining, rethinking and reworking pedagogy, practice and research in higher education. We illustrate posthumanist performative methodology and pedagogy through the manifestation of an affective choreography. We use poetry in this chapter to articulate the mobilisations of affect that enfolded us as we presented the uneasy assemblage at The Australian Research in Education Conference in Canberra in 2017. Although there has been recent work on the importance of affective methodology in higher education (Charteris et al. 2016; Gale 2016), this is still an emergent field. Likewise, the curation of uneasy assemblages (Bone and Blaise 2015) and their dissemination through affective choreographies (Mulcahy 2012; Youdell and Armstrong 2011) is an emerging approach to be applied to research and pedagogy in higher education contexts. Thus we consider how affective practices that have emerged from the corpus of Deleuzian philosophy can enable us to imagine higher education otherwise.

An Uneasy Assemblage

Affect theory offers a means for thinking about intensities that are barely (in)visible (and often overwhelmingly present), circulating through human and non-human bodies. Non-human bodies include the material objects and animals around us, and human and non-human bodies operate in relations that are mutually affective. Affective flows inhabit the fleeting, unconscious and temporal territories of the spaces and encounters we find ourselves in. These spaces can be online or physical embodied experiences. In the wake of the affective turn (Clough 2008), scholars have described 'a magnification of affect'

(Shaviro 2010: 4), with recognition that our social theory is 'characterized by a surfeit of [affect]' (Massumi 1995: 88). In the last five years with 'fast paced technological advances', the politics of othering linked with 'economic globalization', the 'war on terror and [associated] global security issues' (Braidotti 2016: 13), we are seeing bodies, technologies, discourses, and associated images colliding in intensities of affect. Intensities can be seen in mobilisations of affect where there are shifts to the qualities of the objects, bodies, and concepts in a milieu and there are changes involving different and sometimes elusive 'points of connection and cluster' (Bissell 2009: 911).

Initially we noted provocative intensities circulating with a website that profiled sexually explicit non-consensual images of young women. The site was publicised widely in the Australian print and online media. In August 2016, the incident was described as a crisis of youth pornography. Reportedly profiling explicit images of thousands of schoolgirls online from over seventy schools, a moral panic was triggered that engaged affective intensities. Many of these young women had their names attached to the images so that the male community of social media participants could 'rate' them. Social media technologies were inherent in the establishment and ongoing relations of this misogynist online community, whereby young women could be predatorily targeted so that their sexualised images could be sourced and uploaded.

We initially gathered 30 newspaper articles, published online in Australia, that detailed the unfolding controversy. The media articles included images of women for illustration, accounts of reporters, quotations from the illicit website, and interview comments from police, parents, women and girls. Our meetings were held in a boardroom, overseen by a dour painting of a senior male academic. There we used a data projector to flash articles up on a big screen so that we could discuss them.

Of particular interest to us was the networked public (Boyd 2014) formed around the objectification of women through a 'homosocial code of brotherhood' (Ford 2016, August 18: para. 7). Interestingly, during the initial research process, we noticed that 'school-girls' were fetishised in many of these media articles that reported the incident.

The Australian authorities struggled to shut down the website that targeted an international audience because it was hosted off shore. Over the month that the story was prominent in print media, it appeared that there was little that the young women or the authorities could do to remove the online images or close the website.

The incident was an interface between human and non-human factors that caused an affective irruption in cyberspace and across schools and homes. Cyberspace intra-acted with human and non-human technological bodies as agential matter. 'Agential matter' (Bolt 2013: 3), in the form of digital technologies and applications, not only record form and content, they pass affective flows between bodies. These flows produce a range of affects that spill over from the media into homes and offices. In our assemblage we drew together material that proliferate intra-personal affect. Affective intensities associated with lust, shame and anger are evoked when sexualised online images and media stories go viral. They constitute incorporeal transformations and objectify individuals in a networked gaze.

This media firestorm mobilised a range of bodily responses, sparking off a process of curation for us as researchers. The uneasy assemblage emerged through a process of musing that was both diffractive (Taylor 2016) and came in fits and spurts of speeds and slownesses. Taylor (2016: 204) defines 'musing as theory' which involves 'meditative contemplation; thoughtful abstraction; critique as intellectual food; gustatory thinking'. It is musing that 'partakes of the slow movement's commitment to deceleration, consumption reduction, ethical environmentalism, and the nurturing of non-commercial forms of well-being' (Taylor 2016: 204). The affective choreography exceeded the moment, stretching into further events like ongoing conversations, the conference we presented at back on our university campus with the writing of this chapter, and the scholarship we proceed with as we navigate the next stages of our work.

We held meetings and collected articles with their associated comments and images. Both intrigued by the affect produced, and incensed by the salient threads of misogyny inherent in many of the comments, we curated these online media articles. In doing so, we were captured by these imbrications of affect. Acknowledging the tenuousness of feminist anger and the affect of the killjoy (Ahmed 2010) we engaged research practice as an uneasy assemblage (Bone and Blaise 2015)—assembling articles as news continued to break, revealing what we identified as gendered violence. The concept of gendered violence, here defined as an expression of power and control over individuals or groups because of gender (University of New South Wales Gendered Violence Research Network 2017) provides a central focus for our curation practice.

Line of Flight

We were both moved and affected in the process of our curation. Taking a line of flight from the curation of media images pertaining to the cyberstalking of schoolgirls, we extended our curation to data that glowed (MacLure 2013). These were articles that expressed nuanced gendered violence that illustrated shifting sensitivities to what could be condoned and normalised. Normalisation is where inequity is left unproblematised, and in its extreme, corresponds with 'rape culture' (Phipps et al. 2017) where women are portrayed passively as victims of sexual crimes (Easteal et al. 2015). In this expanded assemblage we included articles about the damaging social fallout from the Australian Same Sex Marriage Vote (Tilly and Hoad 2017), the #MeToo campaign (Zillman 2017), rape culture and allusions to women as meat (Tran 2006), the alleged sexual assault perpetrated by President Trump, and a plethora of articles surfacing the pervasive culture of misconduct in Hollywood and across high profile media organisations, where high profile celebrities allegedly used their power and status to sexually harass and assault women and to manipulate their silence (Peters and Besley 2018). The texts and images were curated materials in a presentation that, when juxtaposed and shared through technology, constituted vibrant matter (Bennett 2010). The use of affect and gendered violence as concepts enabled us to 'gather together an already existing set of things' and 'allow for movements and connection' (Colebrook 2010: 1).

We used the following questions to interrogate our uneasy assemblage:

- *What affective flows are in evidence in media produced accounts of gendered violence?*
- *What does our media assemblage indicate about affect and emergent conditions of possibility in collective assemblages of enunciation?*

Figures 19.1 and 19.2 are examples where we drew from an online news article (https://www.smh.com.au/lifestyle/the-epidemic-of-rape-culture-in-schools-can-no-longer-be-ignored-20160817-gquv53.html) written by a prominent feminist reporter (Ford 2016) who railed against the website that profiled sexually explicit non-consensual images of young women, in which numerous schools were named in this scandal that sustained media attention in Australia for weeks.

As we conveyed to the audience at the time, the affect emanating from the term creates 'outrage' for Adrian that it may reduce capacity to act. It is ironic that he is emotive in his rejection of rape culture

> **Florence**
> I am just so incensed by the actions of these boys and men who think that this is acceptable, but so appalled (at myself as much as anything) about our apparent inability to counter it. The damage being done is just inconceivable - and it's to their friends and sisters and cousins, and ultimately themselves. *(Affective Response-ability)*
>
> **Adrian**
> To use words like "rape" and "violence" when discussing photos being shared is to rob the words of their meaning.
> The article is pure outrage without sensible discussion and very unhelpful and will make many people ignore the seriousness of the topic as people will lump it it with the rest of the outrage culture garbage out there. Be less emotive so that the problem can be taken seriously.
> *(Affective incorporeal transformation- discrediting emotive journalist and capacity to comment)*

Fig. 19.1 Powerpoint slide: Responses to the article from the public (Our researcher notes are in italics)

> **Tone it down**
>
> I wish commentators would stop using the phrase "rape culture". It's not. It's objectification of women. Yes, it promotes misogyny and it's unhealthy. We can agree on that. But to link it directly to rape is ridiculous.
> Say I have a beer. It's a drug. Of the millions of people that have beers, some might also do a bit of ecstasy. And a very small few of those might try heroin and go on to be a junkie. Do people go around calling beer-drinking, "junkie culture"?
> *(Affect producing denial and resistance through a form of discursive repositioning.)*

Fig. 19.2 Powerpoint slide: A further response to the article (Our researcher notes are in italics)

as an emotive term. We highlighted that like 'Adrian'. 'Tone it down' (Fig. 19.2) rejects the affectivity of rape culture and the spectrum of gendered violence that legitimises powerlessness in women.

These slides are an illustration of one of the range of topics we curated in the assemblage. After the conference presentation, we

Fig. 19.3 Remaking the space

storied the affective choreography, initially drawing from oral recordings of our musings after the presentation and our field notes. We wrote prose and then poetry—a medium we see replete with affect. The individually authored stories were shared, and then collaboratively sliced up and reassembled to create a further postidentitarian data assemblage (Charteris et al. 2018), as in the poem which follows. Like McKnight (2016), we juxtapose poetry with educational theory and philosophy to provide an anti-anthropocentric account of an affective choreography.

The Affective Choreography

> The politics of space suggest that the posthuman
> Special interest group operates at the conference margins.
> The impossible lift; going nowhere until provided
> With the temporal gift of a plastic access key
> On the approval of a hotel usher.
>
> The chairs in the presentation room are tightly arranged,
> Butted up in neat rows against each other. Uncomfortable.
> The presentation room on this executive floor of hotel
> Far from the big ballrooms
> Where elite presentations rotate.
>
> The bathroom, bedroom and small kitchen
> Are a regular hotel room.
> Pushing the chairs aside, arranging the space, piling cushions
> From the bedroom into the middle of the floor.
> We try to remake the space. (see Fig. 19.3)
>
> Opening the doors and pushing back the curtains we let light in.
> Urban Canberra's towering apartments are visible.
> The conference buzz is distant
> We claim the space as our own, taking photos, feeling bold
> If just for a few moments.

Fig. 19.4 Cornered by the technology

Our symposium colleagues arrive and we are greeted with warmth.
Joy carries the computer. Hope appears on it in a skype call.
We greet her and her new baby.
The small room fills up.
Colleagues from our university, gender theorists, scholars.

The room is full of bodies.
Jammed beside the computer in the corner
Locked in by the technology we stand – our papers in hand. (see Fig. 19.4)

We stand on country of the Ngunnawal peoples *
The tyranny of colonization is named –too easily.

Slides evoke affect that is palpable in the room.
Shame and fear.
Looking out at faces witness to the uneasy assemblage
Is the scholarly work rigorous enough?
There is shame associated with reporting pain stories.

These humiliation stories
Are most compelling in social science research**
Are we gratuitously reporting painful subject matter?
Is this uneasy assemblage really
An analytical research practice of refusal?

The pedagogic act of presenting it evokes pedagogic affect.
The response comments refer to women as 'potato peelers',
Gorilla male silverbacks in power positions of privilege
Evoking a natural biology argument and references
To women as pieces of meat.

The assemblage evokes and circulates affect.
Does the anger in the room mobilise
further affect to sustain action?
Does the anger communicate
A shared solidarity?

After the presentation, there is talk about intersectionality
The range of women variously located within feminist assemblages
According to affective flows of power.
Who does the media storm privilege?
Who does not receive media coverage?

Is there an undue amount of media airtime spent
Canvassing white male indignation and crimes
Perpetrated on the bodies of powerful white women?
Feminist outrage is surfaced and shared through critique.
In so doing, affective solidarity and response-ability is evoked**

Pedagogic affect is mobilised
In the hope
That critiques flow
On and percolate
And take lines of flight.

*A welcome to country is seen as appropriate practice in Australia where the first custodians of the land on which the meeting is held are acknowledged.
**Tuck and Yang (2014) critique the trope of reporting on that pain with detailed qualitative data in order to yield political resources.

As the poem highlights the affective choreography presented promoted shame and anger and possibly other emotions in the participants in the hotel room, and provides insight into practicing otherwise at a higher education research conference where feminist arguments can be mobilised along with an interplay of human and non-human multiplicities. We now interrogate how the curation of uneasy assemblages as a research practice can construct new knowledges and provide pedagogic opportunities for juxtaposing concepts, images, discourses, theories, human and non-human bodies in ways that jar and unsettle assumed ways of being in the world.

Reimagining Higher Education Research Practice

Affect circulates through the vitality of matter and alerts us to politics. According to Mulcahy (2012: 9), 'registering bodily as intensity, affect effects change in pedagogical relationships, impelling acknowledgement of its substantive nature and its political import'. Using affect as a vehicle for pedagogic work is evocative, yet risky. It is a potentially powerful approach to higher education research and pedagogic practice. Probyn (2004) tells us that affective responses are extremely complex and are embedded in embodied histories to which and with which bodies react. Therefore it is vital that we 'acknowledge and work with' affective reactions, taking into careful consideration that affective responses can be profoundly disturbing and 'safety structures' [are required] for all those who may be affectively 'triggered' (Probyn 2004: 29–30). Mindful that we were alluding to rape culture and violence against women, we signaled this to our audience at the conference from the outset of our affective choreography. We knew that that there may be audience members with adverse personal experiences and content shared could potentially trigger pain and shame.

Hemmings (2005: 552) sums up Deleuzian affect as 'describing the passage from one state to another, as an *intensity* characterized by an increase or decrease in power'. Affect is a 'contagion… a set of flows moving through the bodies of humans and other beings' ceaselessly circulating messages (Thrift 2008: 235–236). Affective intensities cast multiple threads for weaving and thinking, yet they offer no tangible or credible certainties. We identify and interpret affect through uncertain glimpses as we seek to both problematise and make sense of our research work.

Shame was a salient risk inherent in presenting to this uncertain crowd, jammed high in the almost inaccessible room. It was raw—talking about women as meat. We wondered if we, in our discursive appellations, called this ugly discourse into being, and in doing so, were contributing towards its ongoing construction.

Tuck and Yang (2014: 812) critique 'serving up pain stories on a silver platter for the… academy, which hungers so ravenously for them'. Instead of speaking about gendered violence with academic detachment that was sanitised through a filter of conventional research methods, we imbued our presentation with a sense of anger, using fire as a starting image. Nevertheless, we worried that the assemblage of media stories and images created an affective intensity that was too emotive, burning too brightly, implying that our work was unsophisticated and unconvincingly theorised.

How Might Posthuman Pedagogic Research Practice 'Travel'?

There is risk: in venturing into dangerous spaces; in speaking out of turn; in being misheard; or even worse, in perpetuating pain. The risk of offering an uneasy assemblage, was its floating time (Deleuze and Parnet 2007), written with the speeds and slownesses of that time—simultaneously collapsing and expanding data in the curation process, and transposing it into the materiality of the conference space, performing the affective choreography with all of the bodies there.

There is danger in working with uneasy assemblages that, rather than being evocative, can stabilise, become static, solidified into an arborescent structure (Deleuze and Guatarri 1987). The data becomes overly positioned, with too much emotion, so that it becomes motionless and reduced to stasis. When wondering how the notions of uneasy assemblages and affective choreographies may be taken up, we are struck by the humanist arrogance of assuming that others should necessarily feel a particular way. Affect is a bodily response and it is uncertain whether a knowable and identifiable indignation and outrage could be evoked through a curated assemblage. The assemblage is beyond the hand of the human to produce. Affect as it circulates through and between bodies both human and non-human is too evasive in its ongoing mobilisations to be stable and predictable.

We know politicians mobilise affect for their own political purposes (Thrift 2004). Unstable and unpredictable, affect can be explored by researchers as the intra-activity of pedagogic actions. We offer the following questions for consideration in regard to how affective choreographies as a posthuman pedagogic practice might 'travel' and be taken up by others in the academy.

- To what degree do our own uneasy pasts contour and mark the assemblage, how do they bend and interrupt our fragile choreography?
- To what extent are our academic positions safer if we avoid evoking affect?
- What spatialities of affect are there in the academy?
- What legacies come with these affects that are interconnected with the historicity of place and the nodes and knots of the assemblage?

Thus posthuman practice in the academy is less concerned with finding out internal truths in the epistemological knowledge systems of research contexts, but rather about undertaking research that unravels material discursive practice. Such practice enables lines of flight and new embodied ways of entangling the material with thought to produce critique. This critique is produced through intensities that flow in the spaces between bodies. These are 'fleshy moments' that convey 'particular, local and situated truths' (Davies and Gannon 2006: 5).

Conclusion

Ingold depicts the competitive marketised academy as a 'grubby scramble' (2011: xiii). He writes

> The prostitution of scholarship before the twin idols of innovation and competitiveness has reduced once fine traditions of learning to market brands, the pursuit of excellence to a grubby scramble for funding and prestige, and books such as this to outputs whose value is measured by rating and impact rather that by what they might have to contribute to human understanding. (Ingold 2011: xiii)

Although we often play the game, scrumming down into the 'grubby scramble' that inevitably narrows our academic work for the purposes of a marketised system, we also seek and locate points for refusal and re-imagination. This chapter aims to push back against this grubby narrowness by seeking new ways, via our affective choreography, to produce research as desire, to collaborate richly and, in Springgay's (2014: 86) words, to use posthumanist research procedures which 'make felt the unknowability within the unknown'. In this, our work partakes of Deleuzian-inspired, materialist and new empiricist (St. Pierre 2016b) approaches which seize the possibility of contemplating how concepts can be used for different purposes and different intellectual tasks (Dovey 2010). Our poems are, therefore, intensely political and evocative, and the processes of their creation can generate collective spaces for slow musings in the academy. Our work aims to celebrate feminist work and the emerging field of posthumanist education philosophy in materialist entanglements that are situated, simultaneously partial and replete, and overflowing with affective politics.

References

Ahmed, S. (2010). *Feminist killjoys (and other wilful subjects)*. http://sfonline.barnard.edu/polyphonic/print_ahmed.htm. Accessed 10 December 2016.

Bennett, J. (2010). *Vibrant matter: A political ecology of things*. Durham, NC: Duke University Press.

Bissell, D. (2009). Obdurate pains, transient intensities: Affect and the chronically pained body. *Environment and Planning A, 4*(41), 911–928.

Black, A., Crimmins, G., & Henderson, L. (2017). Reducing the drag: Creating V formations through slow scholarship and story. In S. Riddle, M. K. Harmes, & P. A. Danaher (Eds.), *Producing pleasure in the contemporary university*. Rotterdam: Sense Publishers.

Bolt, B. (2013). Introduction: Toward a 'new materialism' through the arts. In E. Barrett & B. Bolt (Eds.), *Carnal knowledge: Towards a 'new materialism' through the arts*. London: I.B. Tauris.

Bone, B., & Blaise, M. (2015). An uneasy assemblage: Prisoners, animals, asylum-seeking children and posthuman packaging. *Contemporary Issues in Early Childhood, 16*(1), 18–31.

Boyd, D. (2014). *It's complicated: The social lives of networked teens*. New Haven: Yale University Press.

Braidotti, R. (2016). Posthuman critical theory. In D. Banerji & M. Paranjape (Eds.), *Critical posthumanism and planetary futures*. New Delhi: Springer.

Charteris, J., Gannon, S., Mayes, E., Nye, A., & Stephenson, L. (2016). The emotional knots of academicity: A collective biography of academic subjectivities and spaces. *Higher Education Research & Development, 35*(1), 31–44.

Charteris, J., Nye, A., & Jones, M. (2018). Feasible Utopias and affective flows in the academy: A mobilisation of hope and optimism. In A. L. Black & S. Garvis (Eds.), *Women activating agency in academia: Metaphors, manifestos and memoir*. London: Routledge.

Clough, P. (2008). The affective turn: Political economy, biomedia and bodies. *Theory, Culture & Society, 5*, 1–22.

Colebrook, C. (2010). Introduction. In A. Parr (Ed.), *The Deleuze dictionary*. Edinburgh: Edinburgh University Press.

Davies, B., & Gannon, S. (2006). *Doing collective biography: Investigating the production of subjectivity*. New York, NY: Open University Press.

Deleuze, G., & Guattari, F. (1987). *A thousand Plateaus: Capitalism and Schizophrenia* (B. Massumi, Trans.). Minneapolis, MN: University of Minnesota Press.

Deleuze, G., & Parnet, C. (2007). *Dialogues II* (H. Tomlinson & B. Habberjam, Trans.). New York, NY: Columbia University Press.

Dovey, K. (2010). *Becoming places: Urbanism/architecture/identity/power*. New York, NY: Routledge.

Easteal, P., Holland, K., & Judd, K. (2015). Enduring themes and silences in media portrayals of violence against women. *Women's Studies International Forum, 48,* 103–113.

Ford, C. (2016, August 18) The epidemic of rape culture in schools can no longer be ignored. *Sydney Morning Herald*. http://www.smh.com.au/lifestyle/news-and-views/opinion/the-epidemic-of-rape-culture-in-schools-can-no-longer-be-ignored-20160817-gquv53.html. Accessed 18 August 2016.

Gale, K. (2016). Theorizing as practice: Engaging the posthuman as method of inquiry and pedagogic practice within contemporary higher education. In C. A. Taylor & C. Hughes (Eds.), *Posthuman research practices in education*. London: Palgrave Macmillan.

Haraway, D. (2016). *Staying with the trouble*. London: Duke University Press.

Hemmings, C. (2005). Invoking affect: Cultural theory and the ontological turn. *Cultural Studies, 19*(5), 548–567.

Honan, E., Henderson, L., & Loch, S. (2015). Producing moments of pleasure within the confines of an academic quantified self. *Creative Approaches to Research, 8*(3), 44–62.

Ingold, T. (2011). *Being alive: Essays on movement, knowledge and description*. New York, NY: Routledge.

MacLure, M. (2013). Researching without representation? Language and materiality in post-qualitative methodology. *International Journal of Qualitative Studies in Education, 26*(6), 658–667.

Manning, E. (2013). *Always more than one: Individuation's dance*. Durham, NC: Duke University Press.

Massumi, B. (1995). The autonomy of affect. *Cultural Critique, 31,* 83–109.

Mayes, E. (2017). Reconceptualizing the presence of students on school governance councils: The a/effects of spatial positioning. *Policy Futures in Education,* 1–17. https://doi.org/10.1177/1478210317739468.

McKnight, L. (2016). *The deep end: Pedagogy, poetry and the public pool*. www.publicpedagogies.org/wp-content/uploads/2015/08/McKnightL.pdf. Accessed 8 May 2018.

Mulcahy, D. (2012). Affective assemblages: Body matters in the pedagogic practices of contemporary school classrooms. *Pedagogy, Culture & Society, 20*(1), 9–27.

Peters, M. A., & Besley, T. (2018). Weinstein, sexual predation, and 'rape culture': Public pedagogies and hashtag internet activism. *Education Philosophy and Theory*, 1–8. https://doi.org/10.1080/00131857.2018.1427850.

Phipps, A., Ringrose, J., Renold, E., & Jackson, C. (2017). Rape culture, lad culture and everyday sexism: Researching, conceptualizing and politicizing new mediations of gender and sexual violence. *Journal of Gender Studies*, 1–8. http://dx.doi.org/10.1080/09589236.2016.1266792.

Probyn, E. (2004). Teaching bodies: Affects in the classroom. *Body & Society*, *10*(4), 21–43.

Shaviro, S. (2010). *Post-cinematic affect*. Washington, DC: Zero Books.

Springgay, S. (2014). Approximate-rigorous-abstractions: Propositions for posthumanist activation in educational research. In N. Snaza & J. A. Weaver (Eds.), *Posthumanism and educational research*. New York, NY: Routledge.

St. Pierre, E. (2016a). Deleuze and Guattari's language for new empirical inquiry. *Educational Philosophy and Theory*, *49*(11), 1080–1089.

St. Pierre, E. (2016b). Rethinking the empirical in the Posthuman. In C. Taylor & C. Hughes (Eds.), *Posthuman research practices in education*. London: Palgrave Macmillan.

Taylor, C. A. (2016). Close encounters of a critical kind: A diffractive musing in/between new material feminism and object-oriented ontology. *Cultural Studies-Critical Methodologies*, *16*(2), 201–212.

Taylor, A., & Pacini-Ketchabaw, V. (2015). Learning with children, ants, and worms in the anthropocene: Towards a common world pedagogy of multispecies vulnerability. *Pedagogy, Culture & Society*, *23*(4), 507–529.

Thrift, N. (2004). Intensities of feeling: Towards a spatial politics of affect. Special Issue: The political challenge of relational space. *Geografiska Annaler. Series B, Human Geography*, *86*(1), 57–78.

Thrift, N. (2008). *Non-representational theory: Space, politics, affect*. London: Routledge.

Tilly, C., & Hoad, N. (2017). *Interactive digital storytelling team*. Australian Broadcasting Commission (ABC). http://www.abc.net.au/news/2017-10-11/ssm-same-sex-marriage-respectful-debate-ugly-side/8996500. Accessed 26 October 2017.

Tran, M. (2006, October 26). Australian Muslim leader compares women to uncovered meat. *The Guardian*. https://www.theguardian.com/world/2006/oct/26/australia.marktran. Accessed 20 September 2017.

Tuck, E., & Yang, K. (2014). Unbecoming claims: Pedagogies of refusal in qualitative research. *Qualitative Inquiry*, *20*(6), 811–818.

University of New South Wales Gendered Violence Research Network. (2017). *Gendered violence & work. What is gendered violence.* https://www.arts.unsw.edu.au/research/gendered-violence-research-network/gendered-violence-work/. Accessed 10 September 2017.

Wolf, M. (2017). Affective schoolgirl assemblages making school spaces of non/belonging: Emotion. *Space and Society, 25,* 63–70.

Youdell, D., & Armstrong, F. (2011). A politics beyond subjects: The affective choreographies and smooth spaces of schooling. *Emotion, Space and Society, 4*(3), 144–150.

Zillman, C. (2017, October 16). 'Me too': How Alyssa Milano's two-word protest against sexual harassment went viral. *Fortune.* http://fortune.com/2017/10/16/me-too-facebook-alyssa-milano/. Accessed 18 October 2017.

20

Response-Able (Peer) Reviewing Matters in Higher Education: A Manifesto

Vivienne Bozalek, Michalinos Zembylas and Tamara Shefer

Introduction

How might academic reviewing be reconfigured as a more affirmative process that is directed at the larger social good rather than individual competitive imperatives? This manifesto considers how reviewing might become more responsive to writers through a response-able and diffractive methodology. Such a methodology could form a dual function—that of doing justice to the text of the writer, whilst at the same time

---

V. Bozalek (✉) · T. Shefer
University of the Western Cape, Cape Town, South Africa

T. Shefer
e-mail: tshefer@icon.co.za

M. Zembylas
Open University of Cyprus, Nicosia, Cyprus
e-mail: m.zembylas@ouc.ac.cy

Nelson Mandela University, Port Elizabeth, South Africa

making it possible for the work of reviewing to be acknowledged and to be publicised, and given an ISBN number so that it could be cited. Reviewing is time consuming and unpaid academic labour, so this would be one way of giving back to the reviewer.

The Problem with Peer-Reviewing

Peer-reviewing is an academic practice which has important implications for higher education and how it is configured. It is powerfully shaped by Eurocentric normative practices in knowledge production, which assume an authoritative expert and rely on critique within a framework of individualistic competition. Such practices are exacerbated by the corporatisation of universities resulting from the contemporary neoliberal conditions under which higher education operates. These conditions have led to increasing competitiveness in academic scholarship and put pressure on academics to publish quickly and prolifically, with emphasis on quantity rather than quality. In this context, academics are under considerable pressure to publish in what are considered to be high status 'gold standard' peer-reviewed books or journals, and their academic careers are built on the number of citations and publications they have managed to accumulate in such journals. This means that they are dependent on peer reviewing of their work in order to gain access to publishing their work. This necessitates not only submitting their work for scrutiny to their peers, but being obligated to continuously subject themselves to *blind* peer-review processes.

Reviewers (and journal editors who act as gatekeepers) wield a great deal of power in proposing whether manuscripts are accepted or rejected, frequently deploying aggressive critique, as encouraged or even expected within the dominant canon. This is exacerbated through practices of anonymity in peer-reviewing, where reviewers do not have to reveal their identities to the authors. Tronto's (1990) notion of 'privileged irresponsibility' is useful in explaining these processes as a means by which the group-in-power fails to acknowledge the exercise of their power, thus maintaining their taken-for-granted positions of privilege.

In peer reviewing, this may give reviewers freedom to push their own ideas or theoretical approaches, rather than attending to the ideas the author is putting forward. Anonymised peer reviewing further distances the reader from the author, allowing for possible 'epistemological damage' a notion used by Barad to describe the harm that is done by critique which essentialises, objectifies and often moralises when a phenomenon is being investigated, as she puts it, not picking up a work and dismissing it or slamming before its given its due, before it is even understood (Barad 2017; Juelskjær and Schwennesen 2012). Such practices of exteriority and superiority of the reviewer as outside expert, knowing better and feeling entitled to scrutinise and interrogate the work of another from a distance, assume that these insights are not available to the writer him or herself. These reviewing practices often undermine the confidence of inexperienced and early-career authors, in particular, but may even unnerve experienced writers, whose rejected and critiqued contributions may never see the light of day as a consequence. Indeed, authors frequently experience reviews as an attack on their scholarship, as pathologising and shaming. However, the possibility of doing epistemological damage to the ideas of the author/s of the paper is never publicly acknowledged, but silenced in or beyond academia. This lack of transparency means reviewers tend not to pay attention to the ethical implications of reviewing. Nor do they work within a framework acknowledging the interconnectedness of scholars and the dialogical nature of scholarly endeavours, which might well lead to productive engagements between reviewers and authors of texts, and the academic communities who read the texts. How, then, can peer reviewing be shaped to encourage the academic writer and support scholarly development of their arguments?

Peer Review: New Possibilities—A Manifesto for Change

What we are calling for is *response-able reviewing*—an affirmative process where texts are read, responded to and written in a dialogical way, opening spaces for new imaginings and creative engagements with ideas.

We suggest that response-able reviewing can be done through a *diffractive methodology* of reading, an approach that is based on the work of Donna Haraway (1992, 1997) and Karen Barad (2007), who are both regarded as posthumanist and new feminist materialist scholars. Diffraction is a concept in quantum physics which refers to the behavior of waves—light, sound or water waves which can overlap and form patterns of difference. A diffractive methodology focuses on reading one text *through* another rather than juxtaposing one text/oeuvre/theory/set of ideas *against* another. It is an affirmative reading of texts which can produce new insights and new patterns of thought that matter, acknowledging the entanglements of reviewer/author/text and the ideas which are produced from the processes of reading and writing.

We propose a diffractive methodology as having the potential to change the way that reviews are currently enacted, through an attentive and generous intra-action (Barad 2007) with the manuscript under review. Such a diffractive way of reviewing involves respectful perusing of the text under review. In this way, the reviewing process focuses on how to enable maximum potential for reconfiguring the text in a productive manner. This would mean that instead of distancing oneself from the text, the reviewer would pay close and care-full attention, connecting to fine details of what the writer of the text is trying to convey. Of course, it is also important for the reviewee to be open and receptive when encountering the reviewer's comments.

Rather than seeing reviewing as a one way, burdensome process, a diffractive reviewing methodology could be seen to lead to a change in capacity of the reviewer, the reviewee, and the text. Thinking text as material and something that matters in how academics are constructed as subjects in the academy, the ideal situation would be that reviewer, reviewee and the text would be rendered capable (Despret 2016) or become-with one another (Haraway 2016) through the process of intra-acting with one another's ideas. The text could, then, be viewed as an actor instead of a product, especially since the eventual reader of the text will be quite literally thinking-with the material text. What if the text is viewed as the ultimate non-human other that is always in the process of becoming given the unknown and unexpected readers who will take it up? For example, we are indebted to the reviewers who intra-acted materially with our chapter and pushed us to raise this question.

Rendering the other capable would change conventional normative reviewing practices from an attack on the scholarship of the other, judging texts to be right or wrong, to practices involving an ethic of care and justice, premised on a relational ontology rather than bounded individualism and competitiveness. If authors, texts, reviewers, editors, research sites, and participants were thought of as being entangled in intra-action and relational ontology through which they are constituted, then viewing re-viewing as a separate process of critique that goes *against* the other actors hardly makes any sense. Posthumanist and feminist new materialist scholars whose work is predicated on a relational ontology, such as Despret, Haraway and Barad, all offer opportunities for doing peer review differently through response-able practices of becoming-with and rendering the other capable.

Open Reviewing—One Example of Response-Able Reviewing

There are a range of open-reviewing models, using various levels of collaboration between the author and reviewer and, in some cases, opening participation to the broader public to comment and respond to texts too. Some journals, such as *OpenPhysio Journal* (https://www.openphysiojournal.com/) have started to experiment with processes of peer review where the reviewers are no longer anonymous, and the peer reviews are published along with the articles, and receive their own ISBNs. Importantly, the review process followed includes a discussion between the authors and reviewers to collaboratively negotiate changes to be made. In this way, normative power relations in which the author is responsive and submissive to the reviewer are destabilized, and the reviewer is positioned not as expert judge but as critical friend to the author.

There are many other practices which open-reviewing makes possible. Ross-Hellauer (2017) lists the following possibilities:

- *Open identities*: Authors and reviewers are aware of each other's identity.
- *Open reports*: Review reports are published alongside the relevant article.
- *Open participation*: The wider community to able to contribute to the review process.
- *Open interaction*: Direct reciprocal discussion between author(s) and reviewers, and/or between reviewers, is allowed and encouraged.
- *Open pre-review manuscripts*: Manuscripts are made immediately available (e.g., via pre-print servers like ArXiv) in advance of any formal peer review procedures.
- *Open final-version commenting*: Review or commenting on final "version of record" publications.
- *Open platforms*: Review is de-coupled from publishing in that it is facilitated by a different organizational entity than the venue of publication.

The openness of reviews is, however, only part of making the reviewing process a more response-able one in that it is more transparent, accountable and inclusive. The other important parts are the quality of the review and how it capacitates or incapacitates the participants and moves the writing processes through new imaginings and insights.

How Might Response-Able Peer-Reviewing Be Taken Up by Others?

Response-able reviewing could change the way in which reviews of academic manuscripts for peer-reviewed journals are conducted and also have an impact on giving feedback on postgraduate theses, as well as how examination reports are written. In this section we outline strategies that can be used to engage in response-able reviewing. These

20 Response-Able (Peer) Reviewing Matters in Higher Education: …

strategies, which are both individual and collective, facilitate ethical, caring and relational ways of reviewing others' work in academia.

1. Part of the neoliberal conditions of the university is the notion that academics should publish more rather than take the time to support the process of writing and reviewing. We urge academics, especially those in senior positions, to pay close attention to the fine details of the ideas expressed, engage these ideas with other colleagues, and support the process of providing feedback to our students and early career academics. We encourage care-full attention and ethical responsiveness to others' writing as a way to change the academic culture of 'publish or perish'. Changing this culture would require first of all to change the practices through which this culture is sustained.
2. Diffractive reviewing is part of the larger project of re-thinking and re-making response-able knowledge in the academy. Therefore, a response-able methodology for reviewing is not a once off reading, but an ongoing and ever-changing entanglement of experimentation with the ideas of the text in ongoing dialogue of knowledge making. Creating spaces for new modes of reviewing helps us move beyond the neoliberal conditions of the university. It may open up new possibilities for collective scholarship which acknowledges dialogue as key to knowledge production, thus disrupting individualised and combative practices that dominate in current contexts.
3. We can resist the polemic frame of peer-reviewing by making reviews 'count' in publishing, hiring, tenure and promotion. Care-full attentiveness and quality in reviewing should be acknowledged and rewarded. Also mentorship, collaboration, and community building should be recognised as important aspects of peer-reviewing. One way of making peer-reviewing count would be by publishing peer-reviews as scholarly contributions which will ensure their recognition as both an important scholarly labour as well as ensure more transparent and ethical practices in reviewing.
4. Diffractive reviewing assumes difference without negation (difference within)—an affirmative stance to difference in the interests of scholarship that matters; it resists oppositional habits and the violences of

current orthodoxies of scholarship and critique that is endemic to this. An ethics of care and attentiveness towards others through diffractive reviewing raises new questions of what counts and for whom and expands the community of caring in academia. These questions can be, for example: How can I provide feedback that recognizes the possibilities of improvement while affirming the contributions of the piece? How can I write a review report without humiliating the author? How can I see the peer-review as a process that that is framed by an ethics of care and community? How can I acknowledge my own becoming-with and capacity as an academic through engaging with ideas encountered in the process of reviewing?
5. Anonymity is the basis for reduced accountability and the promotion of irresponsibility and malice, yet it is legitimized in current everyday practices in higher education. Bitter and abusive reviews are morally inappropriate, insofar as they disregard the dignity of the author those work is under review. Open review-process avoid anonymity and reminds us that peer-reviewing is above everything an ethical and relational conversation.

Conclusion

Response-able reviewing is a critical part of the larger project of challenging current conditions and practices in higher education. Although academic publishing is standardized worldwide, local university requirements and expectations for publishing affect different scholars differently and, therefore, there is a lot to learn from one another about how to acknowledge more effectively the contributions of all involved actors. Paying care-full attention to how we review the contributions of others is but one occasion in the greater challenge of re-imagining socially just pedagogical and scholarly practices. Alternative practices of reviewing both rely on larger changes in the conditions of the university, but will also inspire new ways of being and doing in our everyday engagements in research and pedagogical practice. Response-able reviewing makes for not only more socially just practice but for arguably better scholarship achieved through collaborative and dialogical scholarship.

References

Barad, K. (2007). *Meeting the universe halfway: Quantum physics and the entanglement of matter and meaning.* Durham and London: Duke University Press.

Barad, K. (2017). What flashes up: Theological-political-scientific fragments. In C. Keller & M-J. Rubenstein (Eds.), *Entangled worlds: Religion, science and new materialisms.* New York: Fordham University Press.

Despret, V. (2016). *What would animals say if we asked the right questions.* Minneapolis: University of Minnesota Press.

Haraway, D. (1992). The promises of monsters: A regenerative politics for inapproporiate/d others. In L. Grossberg, C. Nelson, & P. A. Treichler (Eds.), *Cultural studies* (pp. 295–337). New York: Routledge.

Haraway, D. (1997). *Modest_witness@second_millenium: FemaleMan©meets_oncoMouse™: Feminism and technoscience.* New York: Routledge.

Haraway, D. (2016). *Staying with the trouble: Making kin in the Chthulucene.* Durham and London: Duke University Press.

Juelskjær, M., & Schwennesen, N. (2012). Intra-active entanglements: An interview with Karen Barad. *Kvinder, Koen og Forskning, 21*(1–2), 10–23.

Ross-Hellauer, T. (2017). *OpenAIRE2020.* https://blogs.openaire.eu/?p=1465.

Tronto, J. (1990). *Chilly racists.* Paper presented to the Annual Meeting of the American Political Science Association.

21

How Did 'We' Become Human in the First Place? Entanglements of Posthumanism and Critical Pedagogy for the Twenty-First Century

Annouchka Bayley

Posthumanism is perhaps an odd term. Odd in that it is inscribed, like so many *posts-*, with a history and legacy of that which it strains with. Here, the legacy is perhaps the very Enlightenment itself, famous (amongst so many of its achievements) for the Vitruvian Man and *his* drive to conquer not only land but mind, to square the circle, to exist *as is his right* at the centre of the known universe. He is European, white, at the peak of health and 'able-bodied'. And as such he becomes the *measure* of all things.

As an academic working in the UK, I experience the constant remit of achieving educational *excellence*. Excellence in research, excellence in teaching, excellence in knowledge exchange and so on … In pursuit of excellence have 'we' (that is, 'we' included ones) in the academy become Vitruvian slaves, lamenting our respective lackings, aiming to hold our heads up high and proclaim: I have squared this circle, I am emulating Vitruvius, echoing *his* language, culture, body and

A. Bayley (✉)
Royal College of Art, London, UK
e-mail: annouchka.bayley@rca.ac.uk

performativities, *and I am right!* And where does this fit with the legacies of critical pedagogies? Who and what are we critical of, for if we labour, for example, for equality and inclusion *for all*, what foundational discourses are we giving our *buy-in* to (a phrase I have heard in echoing in every corridor and at every meeting until it has almost tattooed itself onto my neural pathways) and how can we critically engage with these? As we strive to participate in the creation of landscapes of teaching and learning, does it serve or not serve to be critical not only of the terrain (in this metaphor) of higher education, but of the very atomic structures of this landscape itself? These fibrous, electrifying and vital *matters* are arguably at the heart of a posthuman thinking that often considers ontology and epistemology as entangled together, generating together, co-constituting together. *Matters* of concern are thus engaged, to speak with Barad, right the way down, even to the level of atoms. The stories we tell—even the 'good' ones—come to *matter* in both senses of the word. What stories are we making?

Returning to the legacy of humanism, contextually speaking posthumanism is entangled with and often foregrounded by the work of alternative modes of 'storymaking' (Haraway 2016: 40). This work can be beautiful and painful, challenging, uplifting and grotesque. But I argue that it is also vital. Indeed, it plays an integral part of critical pedagogic thinking for the twenty-first century as, like many investigations prior and to come, posthumanisms of all kinds fundamentally question who or what gets to *matter*—even at an atomic level (Barad 2007)—and if not, why not? Who or what is understood to have agency? This kind of questioning is deeply important to a twenty-first century dogged with complexities of ecological disaster, population explosion (and exploitation), and technological change the sheer rate of which has never before been experienced in human history. As Gottesman (2016: 4) states of academics working in critical pedagogy, 'If the name of the game is to publish, we are fine, but if the name of the game is radical social change, we are in trouble.'

Thus, *post*humanism enters into the critical fray with vital force. It brings a vibrant dimension to matters of critical pedagogy in a so-called 'post-truth' era. It also profoundly entangles with issues of decoloniality. When critical discussions on who gets to participate, who or what gets to stand and be counted and what truths get to be proclaimed in a Western cultural moment when 'truths' have become almost entirely suspect, scholars engaging with posthumanism (I am thinking particularly of Barad and Haraway, but also include Kirby, Bennett and Braidotti in this imagining) investigate *how* differences are made, and furthermore how they are made (in)to matter.

Entangled with such thoughts on matter and meaning, comes Haraway's urge to show the processes of difference differing (Haraway 2008: 27–35). Perhaps if 'we' can creatively and critically consider the *how*—right down to the level of atoms and how bodies become marked in their material-discursive specificity (Barad 2007)—we might be able to participate more fully in the present and future of *what* comes now. If we suspect that who or what gets to *matter* in the frame of critical pedagogic projects is a form, in one guise or another, of the Vitruvian man (be he and his project made mimetic in any number of cultural, gendered and even racialised ways) then an investigation of how this process might occur at the deepest and most material of levels (or as Barad might have it, at the level of 'marks on bodies') is at worst worthwhile and at best, perhaps nothing short of necessary in order to engage with twenty-first century challenges *response-ably* (Barad 2007).

In the introduction to his edited book, *Posthumanism and Educational Research*, Nathan Snaza states:

> Delinking education from the structures of *humanizing* education, detaching it from the anthropological machine, requires radical educators to connect the dehumanizations enabled by state-administered compulsory educational institutions (segregated in so many, many, many ways) to the ways in which 'we' humans pass over in silence the extraordinary violence 'humans' do to animals, to ecosystems, to whole species, and, of course, to each other. These violences are inextricably linked. (Snaza and Weaver 2015: 21)

Further to, and perhaps in entangled communion with this, can be read Mignolo's decolonial position on the Vitruvian Man and how *he* has acted as a significant structuring agent in the historical development of discourses on becoming-human.

> By uncoupling Man (the Vitruvian Man) as a model of Humanity, the point is not to find the true and objective definition of 'what is Human', but to show that such projects are filled with an imperial bend, a will to objectivity and truth – a truth that as Maturana explains, bolsters the belief system that supports such an epistemology. (Mignolo, cited in McKittrick 2015: 110)

Thus, the humanist preoccupation 'what does it mean to be human' is usefully transformed in a posthuman context into 'how did "we" become human in the first place?' This is no longer an abstract question of philosophy to be debated from one's comfortably included armchair. Rather, it becomes a question of matter and meaning fused at the level of 'marks on bodies', of processes of mattering and making matter meaningful in immensely powerful and consequential ways. In the scope of extending debates on critical pedagogy into twenty-first century complexities and preoccupations, this is nothing short of vital work.

Turbulence has always been a problem on Earth. Fault-lines rumble and tremble, empires rise and fall, markets shift and are always-already hungry for growth opportunities, populations human and nonhuman surge and die out (or are murdered, absorbed and/or re-formed), technologies hum and buzz and reshape and re-member events into kaleidoscopic iterations of human and nonhuman entanglements. We are all entangled with narratives of living and dying together in ways that vitally matter, that vitally mark our bodies, scoring us in and out of being in multiple ways (some far more violent than others). In short, we are always living and dying 'with each other in a thick present' (Haraway 2016: 1). How then can education and pedagogy learn to change, adapt and work with such complex times? Thinking with Haraway, 'we' are perhaps required to:

> Passionately understand the need to change the story, to learn somehow how to narrate – to think – outside the prick tale of Humans in History, when the knowledge of how to murder each other – and along with each other, uncountable multitudes of the living earth – is not scarce. Think we must; we must think. That means, simply, we *must* change the story; the story *must* change. (Haraway 2016: 40)

So, what would changing the story look like in terms of developing new critical ways of reimagining pedagogy for urgent times? How might stakeholders in and of twenty-first century teaching and learning imagine new, vital forms of pedagogy that *matter*, especially when, as Gottesman states, "[t]here are very real divisions in the critical community and I do not believe our differences of thought and experience should be 'rationally' deliberated away. These differences matter" (Gottesman 2016: 3).

bell hooks (1994: 11) suggests that 'teaching is a performative act' and that

> [I]t is this aspect of our work that offers the space for change, invention, spontaneous shifts that can serve as a catalyst drawing out the unique elements in each classroom. To embrace the performative aspect of teaching, we are compelled to engage 'audiences,' to consider issues of reciprocity. Teachers are not performers in the traditional sense of the word in that our work is not meant to be a spectacle. Yet it is meant to serve as a catalyst that calls everyone to become more and more engaged, to become active participants in learning.

Performativity, here, suggests that teaching and learning is not simply a static thing, or that knowledge and knowledge-making is about describing separate and separable units that constitute a stable universe, a stable *body of knowledge* that lies waiting outside 'us' to be discovered. Such monopolies on truth and on who gets to access it no longer hold the same centrifugal position in this accounting. Rather, performativity in a posthuman understanding, points to a far, far broader view of agentic capacities. Matter and meaning merge and are entangled. Cuts across entanglements are made, ontologies emerge and articulate in new and complex ways and with them the *potential* for active participation in the world becomes something far greater and more powerful than merely expanding on remits of widening participation in education policymaking.

Who participates in our myths and stories of education—of thinking about thinking and learning to learn? Changing who participates means critically thinking about who and what gets to matter *and how our stories shape these ontologies*. This can operate at the level of critically considering stories of inclusion in policy and practice, but further, it can also operate right down to the fundamental level of who (or what) might be considered a teacher, a learner or a subject of knowledge-making. Such changes are perhaps the very tip of the iceberg—the first shuffle towards a new storymaking for urgent times. What I am proposing is not *just* to elevate some actants to the 'level' of more privileged actants and thus, perversely, reinstate the dominance of Vitruvian humanisms simply with broader parameters this time. Rather, I am suggesting that posthumanism can offer a dimension to pedagogic thinking that labours to deterritorialise the powerful imaginary associated with the legacy of Vitruvian Man. Such a posthuman re-storymaking might go on to help refashion the entire framework in ways that are more rhizomatic (Deleuze and Guattari 1987) and entangled (Barad 2007) and that offer alternative options for thinking about what twenty-first century participation might look like in the face of new complexities and multiplicities.

Reimagining pedagogy away from Vitruvianisms (whilst understanding that his is a powerful ghost and the hauntings are likely to remain deep and uncanny) is no small task. It is daunting, it resists salvific futurizing and postulates 'myriad unfinished configurations of places, times, matters and meanings' (Haraway 2016: 1). Rather than balk at the enormity of such a critical task, I argue that this work might all start with the consideration of a seemingly prosaic question: how did 'we' become human in the first place. How did we become 'we'—and not just in terms of power and promise between 'humans', but across species, as powerful actants across earthly terrains? This kind of work invites new imaginings of alternative agencies—agencies that are non-human, multispecies, algorithmic, that lie deep in the earth, or newly formed in a technician's lab. These imaginings cannot and should never be creatively exhaustive. They can lend themselves to critically investigating how 'we' have cut the world into pieces. How 'we' have become human, dehumanised ourselves and others according to racial, gendered and local lines and invented forms of plunder and destruction that have intensified living and dying to alarming rates.

I have written elsewhere on practices, methods and modes of teaching and learning that might start to speak to and with posthuman thinking for twenty-first century educational contexts (Bayley 2018). As part of the host of scholars contributing to this edited book and to the field at large, I urge that we pedagogues continue to work across innumerable contexts, that we must all continue to roll up our sleeves and engage passionately, playfully and critically with the work of re-imagining education for urgent times. Thus, it remains in the context of this short call-to-arms, as it were, to hope that posthumanism and higher education shall continue to become entangled and diffracted across many borders, reimagined in ever critical, radical and inventive ways, and speaking with and to multiple, polyphonic and cacophonous voices from across (and within) the earth.

References

Barad, K. (2007). *Meeting the universe halfway: Quantum physics and the entanglement of matter and meaning*. Durham: Duke University Press.
Bayley, A. (2018). *Posthuman pedagogies in practice: Arts based approaches to developing participatory futures*. Basingstoke: Palgrave Macmillan.
Deleuze, G. & Guattari, F. (1987). *A thousand plateaus*. Minneapolis: Minnesota Press.
Gottesman, I. (2016). *The critical turn in education: From Marxist critique to poststructuralist feminism to critical theories of race*. London: Routledge.
Haraway, D. (2008). *When species meet*. Minneapolis: University of Minnesota Press.
Haraway, D. (2016). *Staying with the trouble: Making kin in the Chthuluscene*. Durham: Duke University Press.
hooks, b. (1994). *Teaching to transgress: Education as the practice of freedom*. London: Routledge.
McKittrick, K. (2015). *Sylvia Wynter: On being human as praxis*. Durham: Duke University Press.
Snaza, N., & Weaver, J. A. (2015). *Posthumanism and educational research*. London: Routledge.

Index

Academic Reading Groups 146
Academic writing 21, 189, 238–241, 243–247, 250
Accountability 2, 5, 8, 104, 109, 111, 128, 356
Actor-Network Theory (ANT) 238, 244, 247, 252
Affect 9, 44, 89, 111, 130, 135, 170, 182, 213, 214, 261, 329, 331–335, 337–342, 356
Affective choreography 330, 331, 333, 337, 340, 342, 343
Affirmation 7, 220, 226, 229, 330
  affirmative ethics 7
Agency 5, 14, 15, 67, 111, 112, 159, 168, 177, 207, 219, 232, 233, 241, 244–246, 251, 252, 262, 267, 288, 296, 301, 319–321, 360
  distributive 283, 284

Agential realism 14, 260, 262, 314, 319, 322, 325
American feminist-philosophical classroom 123
Animal pedagogy 117
Animals 14, 56, 66, 226, 228, 255, 259, 271, 331, 361
Aotearoa New Zealand 20, 86, 88–90, 96
A-personal energies 33, 35, 38, 39, 50
Apparatus 20, 60, 136, 171, 173, 176, 189, 238, 245–247, 249–252, 261, 304
Art(s) 7, 63, 65, 73–76, 79, 81, 92, 135, 168–170, 188, 189, 191, 203, 219–221, 223, 225, 229, 257, 266, 267, 315, 323, 325
Arts-based approaches 76
Assemblage 13, 21, 41, 69, 104, 106, 111, 113, 118, 133, 211–213,

© The Editor(s) (if applicable) and The Author(s) 2019
C. A. Taylor and A. Bayley (eds.), *Posthumanism and Higher Education*,
https://doi.org/10.1007/978-3-030-14672-6

217, 219, 223, 226, 228, 232, 246, 249, 250, 256, 306, 310, 330, 331, 333, 334, 336, 337, 341, 342
assemblage theory 105
Attentionality 172
Attentiveness 183, 193, 319, 355, 356
Autoethnography 55, 281, 288, 289
Autopoietic systems 259, 271, 275

B

Barad, Karen 7, 8, 17, 18, 20, 46, 55, 59–61, 69, 73, 75, 76, 81, 99, 124, 125, 127, 128, 131–133, 143, 147, 170–173, 176, 177, 181, 183, 189, 194, 203, 213, 225, 226, 231, 238, 245–247, 250–252, 259, 260, 262, 265, 270, 281, 286, 288–290, 314, 317, 319–325, 351–353, 360, 361, 364
Bennett, Jane 58, 65, 67, 75, 111, 193, 207, 212, 219, 228, 283, 284, 290, 329, 334, 361
Bilodeau, Chantal 58
Bodies 3, 6, 17, 20, 33, 35, 44, 46, 48, 61–65, 67–69, 95, 105, 128, 129, 135, 145, 173, 212, 261, 306, 309, 315, 319, 320, 330, 332, 333, 338–343, 361, 362
Body as transformer 265
Bodymind maps 18, 256, 262, 265–269, 271, 273
Borderline times 124, 127

Braidotti, Rosi 7, 11, 43, 51, 75, 85–88, 90, 91, 95, 96, 98, 99, 104–106, 111–113, 117, 118, 124, 126, 127, 177, 218–220, 223, 226, 229, 230, 232, 233, 259, 265, 269, 270, 329, 332, 361
Butler, Judith 220, 245

C

Care-full 9, 11, 20, 352, 355, 356
Cartography 230
Child 11, 18, 32, 33, 35, 41, 46, 48, 58, 146, 213, 256, 257, 260, 261, 263, 264, 266–268, 270–272, 274–276, 297, 314, 320
    Posthuman child 264
Childhood Studies 18, 23, 32, 211, 214, 256–258, 263, 270
Climate 7, 45, 55–59, 61, 62, 65, 67–69, 106, 128, 129, 206
Collaboration/collaborative 3, 7, 9, 16, 19, 40, 69, 105, 129, 130, 132, 136, 179, 189, 196, 203, 205, 207, 229, 252, 263, 269, 274, 281–289, 337, 353, 356
Colonial logics 294, 297–299, 316, 319, 320
Complexity 3, 87, 88, 92, 112, 188, 258, 298, 299, 324
Compost(ist) 150, 158, 197, 207, 208, 259
Contamination 189, 233, 286
Cowhig, Frances Ya Chu 58, 61, 62
Creations 23, 35, 39, 43, 118, 127, 221, 223, 264, 265, 270, 343, 360

Creative research methods 211
Critical animal studies 107
Critical pedagogy 109, 126, 219, 360, 362
Critical posthumanism 105, 106, 118, 218, 259
Critical posthuman pedagogy 105, 107, 231
Curriculum 12, 16, 32, 33, 50, 55, 81, 89, 167, 188, 190, 197, 204, 207, 217, 219, 220, 225, 228–230, 232, 239, 256, 257, 275, 294, 295, 316

D

Daredevil thoughts 23, 33, 35, 39, 50
Decoloniality 360
Decolonization 12–14, 16, 298
Deleuze, Gilles 1, 2, 21, 33, 35, 38–41, 45, 48, 50, 73–75, 81, 104–106, 111, 117, 135, 142, 145, 147, 150, 161, 218, 220, 221, 229, 232, 330, 341, 342, 364
Deterritorialisation 232, 364
Dialogical 128, 129, 135, 172, 351, 356
Diffraction 21, 60, 69, 127, 128, 131, 132, 135–137, 143, 170–172, 189, 190, 206, 207, 262, 265, 268, 273, 322, 324, 352
Diffractive autoethnography 22, 59
Diffractive journals 263, 265–268, 275
Diffractive methodology 322, 349, 352

Diffractive pedagogies 19, 127, 130, 131, 133, 135
Diffractive reading 57, 142, 143, 229, 262, 352
Diffractive writing 142, 143, 229, 352
Digital literacy(ies) 237, 238, 240, 241, 244, 246, 250
Digital mediation 232, 241
Distributed agency 243, 271
Drama 22, 56, 57, 64, 67, 189, 284

E

Early childhood teacher education 86–88, 91, 96, 98, 100
Ecocritical pedagogy 107
Ecodramaturgy 59
EdD programmes 109–111
Educational leadership 105, 106
Edu-crafting 223
Embodied practice 60, 175, 176, 214, 238, 243, 330, 340, 342
Embodiment 86, 98
Enelow, Shonni 58, 65, 66
Entanglement 5, 44, 59, 60, 88, 90, 127, 132, 135, 173, 189, 206, 213, 219, 226, 229, 231, 241, 246, 247, 249, 250, 262, 265, 273, 290, 297, 304, 306, 320–322, 324, 325, 330, 343, 352, 355, 362, 363
Epistemic ignorance 263
Epistemology 32, 50, 76, 170, 177, 287, 360, 362
Ethical relations 15, 17, 315, 317
Ethico-onto-epistemology 7–9

Ethics 7, 16, 96, 118, 161, 162, 295, 303, 316, 323, 356
affirmative ethics 7
Eurocentric/eurocentricity 13, 14, 107, 115, 128, 299, 316, 317, 323, 350
Eventicising 32, 50
Experimentation 33, 46, 113, 125, 219, 303, 355

F

Feedback 19, 112, 116, 238, 354–356
Feminicity 231
Feminist new materialisms 14, 18, 99, 125, 131, 135
Feminist new materialist pedagogy 126
Feminist pedagogy 126
Flashes of understanding 33, 38, 39, 43, 44, 50
Flashtag 23, 35, 39, 41, 43, 45, 46, 48, 50
Further Education (FE) 217–219, 232

G

Ghelani, Sheila 56
Google Documents 132
Guattari, Felix 21, 33, 40, 48, 73–75, 81, 104–106, 111, 118, 135, 145, 147, 150, 161, 221, 229, 232, 330, 364

H

Haraway, Donna 9, 10, 14, 15, 19–21, 55, 57, 58, 68, 69, 76, 80, 81, 87, 88, 90, 99, 104, 112, 118, 124, 125, 127, 132, 142–146, 150, 157–159, 162, 163, 165–169, 173, 177, 179, 182, 189, 197, 207, 219, 226, 227, 229, 255, 259, 260, 264, 271, 275, 286, 330, 352, 353, 360–362, 364
Hickson, Ella 58
Higher education 2, 4–8, 10, 12, 13, 16, 19–23, 32, 33, 38, 50, 57, 69, 75, 79, 85–89, 96, 99, 105, 118, 123–126, 128, 136, 183, 188, 207, 211, 213, 220, 237–239, 244, 246, 252, 256, 257, 260, 261, 271, 281, 283, 285, 286, 289, 290, 296, 298, 310, 313–316, 324–326, 329, 331, 340, 350, 356, 360, 365
  measurement 2, 21, 22
  performativity 69, 179, 245, 285, 320, 363
Human and non-human bodies 331, 340
Human supremacy 107, 114, 116

I

Immanence 50, 74
Indigenous education 296, 297, 301, 310, 313, 324, 325
Indigenous knowledges 16, 131, 294, 301, 313, 316, 317
Indigenous storywork 300–303, 310
Intensities 136, 150, 270, 304, 306, 331–333, 341, 343
Intentionality 283, 284, 318, 321, 325
Intra-action/intra-activity 7, 8, 18, 61, 62, 76, 125, 128, 132,

133, 143, 144, 172, 182, 194, 226, 260, 262, 265, 289, 319, 321, 322, 325, 342, 352, 353
Intra-vention 57, 130, 219, 221, 226, 229, 230, 256, 265, 270, 274, 283

K

Killjoy 334
Kirkwood, Lucy 58
Knowledge/knowledge-ing 4, 6, 10, 13–15, 17, 21, 32, 33, 39, 48, 50, 65, 86, 89, 90, 97, 104, 105, 107, 109, 111, 112, 114–116, 129, 131, 132, 137, 155, 156, 166–171, 177, 178, 180, 183, 188, 194, 204, 218, 228, 232, 241, 243, 248, 249, 253, 258, 260, 262, 263, 271, 273, 274, 287, 289, 290, 296, 297, 299–303, 306, 308–310, 314, 316, 317, 323, 324, 329, 340, 342, 350, 355, 359, 363, 364
Kristeva, Julia 20, 86, 87, 90–99

L

Lines of flight 147, 339, 342
Listening 48, 116, 171–175, 178–182, 302

M

Manifesto 7, 9, 11, 73–75, 81, 156, 157, 160, 189, 349
Material-discursive 76, 112, 132, 246, 247, 256, 259, 265, 275, 298, 303, 310, 319, 322–324, 361

Materiality 56, 57, 62, 64, 65, 95, 125, 179, 211–214, 241, 245, 247, 284, 318, 319, 330, 342
Memes 133, 135
Metaphors 3, 12, 16, 69, 127, 128, 143, 168–170, 360
Metaphysics 85, 90, 99, 167, 260, 293, 296, 304, 323
Methodology/methodologies 15, 17, 76, 125, 128, 136, 171, 172, 188, 231, 304, 305, 324, 325, 331, 352, 355
Minor thought 161, 162
Modernity 157, 263, 299, 316, 318, 326
More-than-human agency 300
More-than-human subject 86
More-than-human teachers 114–117
Multiplicity(ies) 42, 85, 106, 111, 213, 233, 262, 281, 285, 287, 289, 317, 322, 330
Music 3, 165, 167, 169–183, 225, 324

N

Narratives 6, 9, 10, 48, 60, 62, 79, 107, 108, 110, 111, 176, 189, 226, 287, 304, 314, 315, 317, 320, 321, 362
Nature 11, 14, 16, 18, 20, 33, 62, 97, 125, 136, 155–157, 159, 161–163, 166, 168–170, 173, 179, 182, 188, 189, 192, 206, 223, 225–228, 238, 241, 243, 247, 251–253, 260, 261, 268, 270, 275, 285, 290, 294, 295, 297–303, 309, 314, 321, 323, 325, 330, 340, 351

Nature/culture 90, 91, 99, 260, 271, 276, 301
Nature/culture binary 260–262, 269, 296, 299, 310
Neoliberalization (of higher education) 5–7, 33, 124, 125, 130
Neoliberal reason 124, 128, 129, 136
Networked public 332
New literacy studies (NLS) 238, 243, 244, 248, 252
New materialism 14, 18, 99, 113, 125, 131, 304, 314
New materialist pedagogy 126
New ontologies in education 16, 281, 296, 310
Nomad/nomadic 87, 90, 96–99, 105, 106, 169, 177, 217, 218, 232

O

Observing 60, 172, 246
Ontological shifts 105, 260
Ontological turn 155, 156, 158, 219, 295
Ontology 2, 13–15, 32, 43, 50, 60, 76, 106, 107, 113, 168, 221, 259, 260, 262, 263, 287, 295, 299, 321, 353, 360
Ontology of immanence 143
Open-reviewing 353, 354

P

Palmer, Sue 56, 232
Passionate powers 23, 33, 35, 39, 50
Pedagogy 3, 4, 6, 7, 10, 16, 17, 22, 23, 32, 57, 60, 68, 69, 73–76, 81, 105, 126, 128–130, 161, 188, 211, 214, 219, 232, 239, 260, 264, 274, 281, 283–290, 294, 296, 302, 309, 315, 331, 362–364
Peer reviewing 350, 351
Performance 5, 40, 55–57, 59, 60, 62, 63, 65, 67, 69, 99, 188, 192, 193, 196, 286, 315, 319, 320
Performative pedagogies 3, 33, 285
Performativity 69, 285, 320, 363
Phenomena 55, 59, 108, 113, 130, 132, 168, 171, 246, 252, 319, 320, 322, 324
Philosophy 7, 15, 38, 73–75, 80, 107, 113, 118, 129, 131–133, 135, 168, 281, 282, 286–288, 331, 337, 343, 362
Place 8, 11, 12, 15, 16, 39, 42, 59, 78, 80, 86–88, 94, 95, 106, 126, 150, 160, 169, 176, 177, 189, 197, 219, 230, 232, 233, 260, 267, 275, 286, 289, 294–301, 303, 305–310, 315–317, 321, 322, 324, 325, 330, 342, 362, 364
Place-based education 299, 301
Playwriting 188–190, 193, 194, 197, 207
Poetry 38, 40, 43, 50, 223, 229, 324, 331, 337
Politics of location 104, 112, 113
Posthuman argument 86
Posthuman child 258, 264
Posthumanism 2, 10, 14, 15, 18, 20, 57, 59, 68, 86, 113, 118, 183, 187, 252, 260, 269, 284, 286, 359–361, 364, 365

Posthuman pedagogies 9, 22, 55, 59, 69, 86, 88, 255, 290, 330, 331, 342
Postidentitarian 330, 337
Power 10, 11, 13, 35, 38, 43, 46, 67, 74, 75, 80, 81, 111, 113, 117, 118, 123, 128, 130, 135, 136, 157–159, 161, 175, 183, 212, 218, 230–232, 246, 259, 262, 263, 265, 282–287, 290, 294, 298, 303, 334, 341, 350, 353, 364
Practice-led Research 188
Productivity 89, 145, 330
Provocation(s) 2, 18, 67, 69, 86, 183, 226, 256, 262, 266, 268, 269, 271, 282–286, 288, 330

Q
Qualitative inquiry (QI) 7, 73–81
Quantum Field Theory (QFT) 262

R
Rape culture 334–336, 340
Reflective practice 219, 225
Relationality 9, 18, 85, 94, 177, 180, 183, 233, 255, 260, 262, 263, 275, 316
Relational ontologies 16, 296, 299, 310, 353
Rendering capable 353
Response-able/response-ability 9, 15, 23, 81, 147, 166, 169, 177, 179, 180, 182, 183, 229, 295, 298, 300, 302, 310, 339, 349, 351–356

Re-turning 17, 262, 265, 266, 271, 317, 318, 324, 325
re-turning as method 262, 324, 325
Reviewing 9, 349–356
Re-vitalization 125
Rhizomatic learning 228
Rhizomatics 105, 217, 218, 228, 232, 256, 263, 264, 270
Rhizome 21
Rupture 22, 23, 33, 44, 147, 162, 284, 296

S
Scholarly practices 356
Science 3, 10, 11, 66, 73–75, 78, 79, 81, 106, 113, 127, 129, 131, 132, 156–163, 167, 169–171, 176, 179, 180, 257, 298, 299, 301, 308
Science education 11, 156, 157, 161–163, 175–178, 181
Senses/sensations 33, 86, 94, 169, 170, 173, 285, 360
Sensorium 169
Sensory learning 3
Settler 12, 13, 15–17, 89, 294, 295, 297, 299, 301, 303, 309, 313–324
settler colonialism 13, 15, 294, 297, 299–301, 303, 309, 313–316, 319, 322, 323, 325, 326
Shearing, David 56
Signification 93, 95
Slow/slowness 9, 39, 136, 157, 160, 188, 206, 207, 256, 262, 330, 333, 341, 343

Slow movement 333
Slow science 156, 160
Smooth space 105, 118
Socially just pedagogy 108, 356
Socio-material 170, 179
Sovereign 13, 16, 315, 320
Space/place 4, 6, 7, 10, 13, 22, 23, 50, 55, 60, 63, 65, 68, 74–76, 78–80, 86–88, 91, 93–95, 98, 118, 125, 130, 132, 143–145, 147, 150, 155, 169, 173, 179–183, 188, 190, 206, 211–214, 219, 221, 226, 228–230, 232, 242, 245, 251, 252, 262, 264, 274, 287, 289, 296, 297, 304, 319, 322, 325, 330, 331, 341–343, 351, 355, 363
Speculative propositions 33, 35
Speeds 330, 333, 341
Spinoza, Baruch 20, 21, 33, 35, 38, 43, 50, 106, 218
Stengers, Isabelle 23, 156, 158, 160
Student engagement 21, 238, 240
Stuttering 50
Subjectivity 20, 92, 95, 106, 259, 260, 263–265, 270, 271, 275
Subjects in process 91, 92
Syllabus, jointly-designed 130, 131
Sympoiesis 259

T

Tables 22, 66, 144–147
Teacher education 3, 16, 85–88, 90–92, 97, 99, 105, 156, 166, 167, 170, 182, 219, 230–232, 255–257, 318
Teaching Excellence Framework (TEF) 204, 220
Tempo/temporal 40, 67
Temporal diffraction 262
Tentacular 10, 144
Textual practices 20, 237, 240, 244, 246, 249, 251–253
Theatre 55–58, 60, 63, 65, 67–69, 188–190, 194, 205, 284, 286
Thing-power 193
Transindividual 20, 262, 264, 272
Trouble 3, 10, 50, 57, 58, 68, 69, 74, 76, 87, 88, 92, 157, 160, 162, 163, 166, 167, 172, 173, 183, 214, 219, 263, 281, 294, 301, 331, 360
Truth and Reconciliation Commission (TRC) 17, 313, 314, 325
Truth-myths 315, 316
Tsing, Anna 129, 162, 286
21st century teaching and learning 190, 363

U

Uneasy assemblage 330, 331, 333–335, 340–342
Unfolding/enfolding/folding 1, 2, 10, 44, 332

V

Vital materialism 329

W

Walking 62, 172, 226, 308
Weather/weathering 22, 56, 61, 62, 64, 66–69
Worlding-with 259

Writing 20–22, 55, 58–60, 69, 73, 74, 80, 115, 116, 126, 132, 133, 143, 144, 150, 206, 223, 225, 227, 231, 237, 239–253, 268, 276, 284, 286, 287, 298, 333, 354, 355

Z

Zoe 118
Zoe-philia 8

Printed in the United States
By Bookmasters